# Living Stones

## Your Journey into Habitation with the Living God

MARIE FOWLER

LIVING STONES

FIRST EDITION

Maon Publishing
503 E Polk Avenue
Lake Wales, Florida 33853

ISBN-10:0-692-86765-1
ISBN-13:978-0-692-86765-5

Unless otherwise marked, Scripture quotations are taken from the NEW AMERICAN STANDARD BIBLE®, Copyright © 1960, 1962, 1963, 1968, 1971, 1972, 1973, 1975, 1977, 1995 by The Lockman Foundation. Used by permission.

Scripture quotations marked "KJV" are taken from the Holy Bible, King James Version (Public Domain).

Scripture quotations marked "AMP" are taken from the Amplified® Bible, Copyright © 1954, 1958, 1962, 1964, 1965, 1987 by The Lockman Foundation. Used by permission.

Scripture quotations marked "CEV" are from the Contemporary English Version Copyright © 1991, 1992, 1995 by American Bible Society, Used by Permission.

Scripture quotations marked "NIV" are taken from The Holy Bible, New International Version® NIV® Copyright © 1973, 197? 1984 by International Bible Society® Used by permission.

Scripture quotations marked "NLT" Holy Bible. New Living Translation copyright Â© 1996 by Tyndale Charitable Trust. Use by permission of Tyndale House Publishers.

Scripture quotations marked "ERV" are taken from the HOLY BIBLE: EASY-TO-READ VERSION © 2001 by Bible Lea International. Used by permission.

Floral logo created by Alex Tanya/Shuttershock.com permission under standard license, "New Jerusalem" by Spencer Wi' www.jesuspaintings.com used by artist permission, additional cover design and interior format by Marie Fowler. Author photograph by Jennifer Miskov.

Author website: www.allgloriouswithin.com

This book is dedicated to Yeshua, my heavenly Bridegroom, the Chief Cornerstone, and to the true Bride of Christ, His precious living stones.

*And I saw the holy city, new Jerusalem, coming down out of heaven from God, made ready as a bride adorned for her husband.*
Revelation 21:2

# CONTENTS

# ACKNOWLEDGMENTS

I would like to offer my sincerest love and gratitude to the following spiritual midwives who helped to birth *Living Stones*:

Michael and Sherry Major: *Living Stones* would not exist (and frankly neither would I) without your counsel and encouragement. You had the innate ability to foresee the glorious resting place of the Lord within the tribes of Israel and my calling to pen this love letter. The house of Israel is indebted to you for its revealing and restoration. Michael, thank you for painstakingly editing my first draft. You and Sherry both are two of the most exquisite gems on this earth whom I have the extreme privilege of calling my spiritual parents!

Jennifer Westbrook: What an enormous gift you are! You saw the good soil in me and *Living Stones* and toiled sacrificially with such love and care. Your excellence, wisdom, expertise, grace, and humor while editing this book has been invaluable to me! *Todah Rabah!*

Christy Cravey: Mother of Israel, nations, and fellow Levite, your countless hours of intercession and encouragement for me and this project not only birthed me into my destiny but many sons and daughters into the kingdom. What glory shall be revealed from such a beautiful laid-down lover of Yeshua!

Jen Miskov and Destiny House: My dear fellow revolutionary and Levite Jen, what an immense treasure you are to me and the Body, always calling the gold out of others and never letting us settle for silver. When I think of you I like to coin the Hebrew term *lev zahav*, heart of gold! Thank you for creating a sacred space that served as the birthing room for *Living Stones*. To Destiny House, my Levitical family of radical laid-down lovers who know the secret of the Maaleh Ashan (Psalm 27:4), thank you for birthing me into my destiny. You are the exuberant cheerleaders with golden pom-poms whose encouragement proved to be the catalyst for this movement. This message of habitation could not have been birthed outside of the glorious context of family you provided.

# ENDORSEMENTS

*Living Stones* is an incredible labor of love. The many years of research, prayers, and time spent in God's presence to release this gem are invaluable. Living Stones will help you recognize your true spiritual DNA and help you align you with your tribe. This book is a must for communities and others who want to partner together to release God's Kingdom. The Destiny House family has been marked by the insights Marie has discovered in this book. *Living Stones* holds keys to destiny that are waiting to be discovered. As your true inheritance is unveiled, may you experience the fullness of God's love like never before. I highly recommend this book to all who are hungry to display the glory of God in increasing measures throughout their lives.

-Jennifer A. Miskov, PhD, Author, Speaker, and Founding Director of Destiny House

*Living Stones* is an expansive and tender journey into the Father's heart for His children. The greatest spiritual crisis faced by Jesus' church is identity—heart-level knowledge of who we are as sons and daughters. In Ms. Fowler's exploration of the God-given identity of the tribes of Israel, you will experience undiscovered facets of God's heart for you and within you, and discover keys to living out your identity, purpose, and destiny. The story of Israel is the story of humankind and God's desire for a people set apart for His purposes—and this is available to all in Yeshua. Nourish your soul with the words in this book and enter into the New Jerusalem life Yeshua came to give you.

—Dennis Ricci, Author, Speaker, and Director of Conejo Valley Healing Rooms.

Marie Fowler is a very gifted artist and writer. Her medium for art is painting large prophetic scenes on fabric. The glorious scenes that are either described or mentioned in the Bible, captivate the viewers and draw them into greater depths of truth and understanding. With the same artistic style and skill, Marie has labored many years praying, researching, and studying the Scriptures to produce her exciting and exhaustive exposition about the Twelve Tribes of Israel in her book, *Living Stones*. The content of this book has been thoroughly researched, prayed through and, professionally written. It offers excellent insight into the manifestation of the awesome coming kingdom of our Redeemer and King Jesus, Yeshua Messiah. The glorious prophesied millennial kingdom reign is seldom expounded upon and brought into realistic terms. Marie has written a profound description that explains each tribe's name, representative stone and symbol, attributes, weaknesses and destinies. With prayer and the guiding of Almighty Yah's Holy Spirit, this very important information enables the reader to connect to the tribe they are destined to be a part of for the kingdom work to be engaged in now, and in the coming millennial kingdom when Yeshua returns in glory. In this complex work, Marie has woven together a beautiful tapestry of our Abba Yahweh's master plan for His remnant people Israel (Jew and Gentile) to become the "One New Man" in Him as recorded in the Scriptures.

I encourage you to read this book and pray for Abba Yah to bless you to embrace the wonderful truths and revelation in *Living Stones* that can help you reach your full potential in ministry now, and prepare for the difficult days ahead. I recommend this book for every person desiring a deeper relationship with our Heavenly Father and His Son our savior, great high priest, healer, provider, king and judge.

—Perry Ennis, Menorah Books, Author and Publisher of the free e-book, "Prepare for the Coming of Messiah" www.thejewishmessiahiscoming.com

# INTRODUCTION

*And they shall be mine, saith the Lord, in that day when I make up my jewels; and I will*
*spare them, as a man spareth his own son that serveth him* (Malachi 3:17 KJV).

The Father and His Son gazed in awe at the mountain in front of them. This mountain was unlike any other mountain. It possessed a celestial beauty and majesty. Within the mountain's recesses and caves could be found millions upon millions of living stones. These stones far surpassed the beauty of the rocks from neighboring mountains. Each stone was unique, a jewel of great price, and set apart for a specific purpose.

The two had come with one purpose: to redeem it. It had originally belonged to them but had fallen into the hands of their archenemy, Hasatan, the Hebrew name of Satan, meaning "the enemy." He was the ruler of the kingdom of darkness. The enemy had continually tried to steal these stones from the mountain. Although the Father and His Son had rightful claim to this mountain, Hasatan was allowed access to it by way of the valley of sin. The only way a stone could fall into captivity to the enemy was through his or her own self-doubt of sonship.

They knew the task ahead would be hard, but its reward far outweighed the cost.

"My Son, there is only one way to redeem our mountain," spoke the Father with such compassionate grief that only a father could possess.

"Father, I know the cost is great, but I am willing to pay," said the Son with great longing in His heart.

"So you are willing to lay down your life?" asked the Father.

The Son replied, "With joy, Abba, with joy."

Who is the Father and what is His name? His name is YHVH[1] (pronounced Yah-vey). His Son is rightfully named Yeshua, meaning "salvation." What was the name of this mountain and why was it so special to them? The mountain was the Bride of Yeshua, her name, *Yerushalyim* (Jerusalem). Yeshua loved His bride so much that it was clear to Him what He must do to restore broken fellowship with her. No cost was too great to win back His Beloved. Alone, separated from His Father, in anguish and torment, He died. That is what the law required, a lamb without defect, pure, to be sacrificed to make atonement. He was the only one who could meet the requirements. With joyful expectation of the restoration of His Bride, He bore her shame of harlotry caused by sin, He took upon himself her diseases and all of her pain in the hope that she would be redeemed to Himself and His Father's kingdom of love.

*And I saw the holy city, new Jerusalem, coming down out of heaven from God, made ready as a*
*bride adorned for her husband* (Revelation 21:2).

In the beginning God created us for one purpose: *maon*, (maw-ohn), [1] which in Hebrew means "a dwelling or habitation." The Hebrew root word for maon is *ownah* (oh-naw), meaning "to dwell together," as in the consummation of marriage, indicating a oneness, which is also expressed by the Hebrew word *echad* (oneness). Yeshua and the Father are echad as He spoke of in John 17.

---

[1] Author's note: Hebrew names and words are intentionally used to afford the reader with the rich revelation God's nature and identity as the God of Israel and the original Hebraic design of His Word. Hebrew names and terminology are not meant as religious dogma or doctrine but rather a historical biblical context that leads the reader into an intimate revelation of God.

*The glory which You have given Me I have given to them, that they may be one, just as We are one;*
*I in them and You in Me, that they may be perfected in unity, so that the world may know that*
*You sent Me, and loved them, even as You have loved Me* (John 17:22-23).

Question: "What consummated the marriage between God and man?".

This has one simple answer: the Cross! Through the sacrifice of His son, Yeshua, Abba Father consummated our sonship. Since the fall of man in the Garden, God has been wooing His creation back to Himself for the sole purpose of maon. More specifically, His desire is to have *maon kadosh* (*kadosh* is the Hebrew word for holy) meaning "holy habitation." True maon lies in the finished work of the Cross and will be fully realized at the second coming of Messiah when the Bride enters into the fullness of the Marriage Supper of the Lamb (final consummation). Until this glorious day, we yearn for our heavenly habitation and to come into its fullness. This being said, it does not mean we cannot partake of habitation in the here and now.

Creation has been groaning for its true identity, dominion, and ultimately restored intimacy and communion with the Father. If we are in Christ, we are a new creation. We are made in His image. But what does it mean to be made in His image? Who am I as a new creation? What is my destiny? These are questions I spent years pondering, as I was searching to know Abba Father, who I was, and my destiny in Him. I've always walked with God, even from a young age, but I never knew who I was. I never fit into the cookie-cutter image that man says we must be molded to. I didn't even fit into the traditional church role. What I discovered through this study is that I was never meant to conform to any man-made pre-conceived idea of what it means to be a Christian. I am set apart unto God for His purposes, and so are you.

When I began this journey, I was alone, searching to discover who I was. No man taught me; it was just me, my Bible, and the Holy Spirit, my teacher. Not only did I discover who I am but who the Bride truly is. God gave me a deeper passion to know Him through this revelation. I began to search the Scriptures, and God revealed to me that I was a Levite. My gifts, calling, struggles, and failures in life came to light. I discovered my destiny in the heart of God. He showed His destiny for me through the tribe of Levi. He called me to repentance, delivered me from bondage to anger and unforgiveness, stripped me of filthy old rags of religiosity, and healed me of my wounded past. This revelation came because I was desperate to know Him and to know who I am in Him.

Many of you are searching as well. If you will take time and dig into the Word of God using this study, the Holy Spirit will reveal who you are. Not only will you discover your destiny in God's divine order, you will discover the Bride's destiny. When I found who I was created to be in my Father's image, I began to experience great freedom. I had finally found my place in the kingdom of God! I also began to see my brothers and sister in Christ. This further liberated me to know them after the Spirit and not after the flesh (as Scripture commands us to do!).

*From now on, therefore, we regard no one according to the flesh. Even though we once regarded*
*Christ according to the flesh, we regard him thus no longer* (II Corinthians 5:16).

Seeing ourselves through the Father's eyes will bring us into the fullness of identity, destiny, and dominion. The tribes teach us this. To see through the Father's eyes is to awaken to the glory of God inside us. More importantly, it is an awakening to love. To see one another through the Father's eyes (thus being jointly fit as a Body in unity) is the emergence of the true mature Church, the Bride ready for her Groom, without spot or wrinkle!

Communion is what the Father seeks. The Holy Spirit is wooing the Bride of Christ as never before. His return is soon. Our destiny in the Beloved is revealed in so many pictures throughout His Word. God wants to reveal who He truly is. The Church has so many misconceptions of who God is. To know God, to know the Bridegroom, you must dive deep into the mysteries of intimacy and divine revelation. They are like treasures found by a deep-sea diver. Deep calls to deep—can you feel it, Beloved? There are deep mysteries or truths that lie waiting for all who are willing to search the depths of the heart of God. The meaning of the tribes of Israel is one of the many deep mysteries I believe the Father is releasing to His children.

## OUR JEWISH ROOTS
## RETURNING TO THE ANCIENT PATHS

God is restoring us back to our foundation, to the rock from which we were hewn, our Hebraic roots. Scripture foretells that in the end days that God will restore us back to His ancient paths.

> *Thus says the Lord, "Stand by the ways and see and ask for the ancient paths, Where the good way is, and walk in it; an you will find rest for your souls. But they said, 'We will not walk in it'"* (Jeremiah 6:16).

Now some of you may question why we need our Jewish roots and what use they may be for us today. You, like many, may say, "We're not under the law." It is true we are not under the law of sin and death, but we are commanded to live under the law of God's love. God, rich in love, mercy, and wisdom, gave us the law to show how to live a holy, set apart life, distinguished from the world. Yeshua did not come to abolish the law but to fulfill it. Paul himself said the law is holy.

> *So, the Law is holy, and the commandment is holy, righteous and good* (Romans 7:12).

God's law, being the Spirit of the law, not the letter of the law, which brings death, is an ancient road map by which we may find Him and the treasures of His kingdom. It is the core of those who are being built up into His house of Living Stones. Yeshua is the fulfillment of the law (the payment of sin) and in Him we celebrate the feasts, which are God's feasts: God's plan of redemption and restoration and the appointed times He chooses to meet with us (Lev. 23). The tribes reveal who we are in Abba's image and our destiny He designed. We have been grafted into the commonwealth of Israel.

Read Ephesians 2:10-15. As the workmanship of the Father, we display His nature through His DNA. Each tribe has DNA markers of His character woven into the fiber of our identity and discovered through intimacy with Him. The DNA of each tribe carries out the "good works" through partnering with the Holy Spirit, thereby building the kingdom of God. Ephesians 4:1 says for us to "walk in a manner worthy of our calling," also referring to the gifts and callings. It is important to note that gifts and callings—though vital—are not who we are, but rather how God invites us to build His kingdom with Him. This will be thoroughly discussed in the following chapters of the tribes. Each tribe's gifts and callings reveal how, as a Body, we can joint-to-joint supply one another in Messiah's glorious Body, the Church!

> *…you also, as living stones, are being built up as a spiritual house for a holy priesthood, to offer up spiritual sacrifices acceptable to God through Jesus Christ* (I Peter 2:5).

The One New Man (verse 15) is a picture of the house of Israel restored.

## THE END-TIME MOVE OF GOD

God is restoring the whole house of Israel through these ancient paths. This restoration is pivotal to Messiah's return, restoring the Church and the Jewish people (together in unity, no separation) into fullness and the widespread end-time move of God. It is the whole house of Israel coming into the fullness of the Third Day, the emerging of the One New Man—it is the final outpouring! The One New Man movement will be comprised of a company of sons and daughters who have awakened to the glory of God, taking place in Abba's *maon kadosh*, the tribes of Israel.
This must happen before the consummation of the ages.

Read Ezekiel 37: 1-23. The Jewish people and the Church need an awakening, a resurrection from the dead. Both are stuck in traditions, faulty theology, and lack of empathy. Most importantly, they each hold keys of destiny they provide one another. When Solomon turned away from God, the Southern Kingdom (Judah) and the Northern Kingdom (Ephraim) split the House of Israel in two. Since then the House of Israel has been divided. The disunion of the tribes of Israel caused a shift that birthed dissension, confusion, and mistaken identity. Ezekiel 37 foretells of the restoration of the house of Israel and the end-time move of God (the One New Man, Ephesians 2:15). It prophesies that one king shall be ruler over the once divided Southern and Northern kingdoms. Who is that one king (vs. 22)? YESHUA!

> He says, "Is it too small a thing that You should be My Servant to raise up the tribes of Jacob, and to restore the preserved ones of Israel I will also make you a light to the nations so that My salvation may reach to the end of the earth" (Isaiah 49:6).

"My Servant" is capitalized because it refers to a deity, Yeshua. Israel is called to be a light to the nations. The term salvation in Hebrew is Yeshua (Jesus). Through His sacrifice the whole house of Israel—Jew and Gentile—is restored to sonship.

> There is neither Jew or Greek, there is neither slave nor free man, there is neither male nor female; for you are all one in Christ Jesus. And if you belong to Christ Jesus, then you are Abraham's offspring, heirs according to the promise (Galatians 3:28-29).

## GOD'S WORD: A TREASURE CHEST OF TYPES AND SHADOWS

> In Him all the treasures of [divine] wisdom [comprehensive insight into the ways and purposes of God] and [all the riches of Christ Jesus] knowledge and enlightenment are stored up and lie hidden (Colossians 2:3 AMP).

For those who will dive into the depths of revelation, a wealth of liberating wisdom in Yeshua will be found. Treasures can be found in the Word through types and shadows He left for us. This study holds vital truths for God's end-time army on how to overcome our weaknesses and know our place in God's holy habitation. There are three ways God paints us a picture of His habitation in Scripture: The Breastplate is a picture of intercession. The Tabernacle is the wilderness order in which the tribes camped around the tabernacle, also known as their marching order (expressly for times of war). The Temple: The New Jerusalem, the Bride of Yeshua, each tribe's place in praise (the government), worship (the atmosphere), the inheritance (the city), and our ultimate destiny revealed in the heart of God. We'll discuss the temple/New Jerusalem at the end of this book.

## THE BREASTPLATE

Yeshua, our great High Priest, carries each one of us on His heart. We are the living stones in the breastplate of our High Priest, Yeshua the Messiah. The breastplate is a symbol of intimacy, a union of the heart.

> …but He, on the other hand, because He abides forever, holds His priesthood permanently. Hence, also, He is able to save forever those who draw near to God through Him, since He always lives to make intercession for them (Hebrews 7:24-25).

> And coming to Him as to a living stone, rejected by men, but choice and precious in the sight of God, you also as living stones, are being built up as a spiritual house for a holy priesthood, to offer up sacrifices acceptable to God through Jesus Christ (I Peter 2:4-5).

## MARCHING ORDER

The breastplate was more of a symbol of intimacy and intercession with our Heavenly Father. The marching order in which the tribes camped is a threatening picture to our enemy, Satan. The Word mentions this order in Numbers Chapter 2. Levi is not numbered, and we will discuss later why God chose not to number them.

> *Now Lord spake Moses and Aaron, saying, "The sons of Israel shall camp, each by his own standard, with banners of their father's households; they shall camp around the tent of meeting at a distance* (Numbers 2:1-2).

Each camp joined under the banner of a captain tribe; Judah the lion, Reuben the man, Ephraim the ox, and Dan the eagle. Upon the front side of each captain tribes' banners were the corresponding symbols (plus a secondary one in addition to the tribe symbol which will be mentioned later), and on the back side of their banners were the corresponding constellations depicting these tribes. The other tribes had banners as well, with their constellations upon the back of their banners also.

Creation groans to reveal the sons and daughters of God. When Abraham was given the promise that he would be a father of many nations (the whole house of Israel), the Lord told Abraham that his seed would be like the grains of the sand and the stars in the sky. Beloved the gospel (or the good news) is written in the stars! Man has profaned this beautiful truth with the zodiac and pagan astrology. I feel that when the Lord made this promise to Abraham he used creation to tell him not just about the tribes (his descendants, the whole house of Israel, Jew and Gentile alike), but His plan for creation from start to finish! The heavens declare the glory of God! Amen! Through the tribes of Israel God is revealing who His family is. As living stones we are being built as a family unit to reveal our Father's kingdom on earth! This is what was revealed to Abraham.

> *By faith Abraham, when he was called, obeyed by going out to a place which he was to receive for an inheritance; and he went out, not knowing where he was going. By faith he lived as an alien in the land of promise, as in a foreign land, dwelling in tents with Isaac and Jacob, fellow heirs of the same promise; for he was looking for the city which has foundations, whose architect and builder is God* (Hebrews 11:8-10 KJV).

These tribal ensigns were not only a way to identify each tribe, but a declaration of identity and a warning to hell itself: HERE COMES THE BRIDE! Each fit in glorious battle array, the tribes around the tabernacle with their banners were a deafening cry against Satan and the darkness.

> *Thou art beautiful, O my love, as Tirzah, comely as Jerusalem, terrible as an army with banners* (Song of Songs 6:4 KJV).

Take note of these four captain tribe symbols. What are the four living creatures: the lion, the man, the ox, and the eagle. In Revelation 4:7, where are they? Before the very throne of God! Now isn't it awesome that God would show His Divine Order in His throne room, our place of worship? Amen! When you look at these positions around the tabernacle, what do you see? The shape of the Cross! Brethren, we live and move in the power of the Cross.

Abraham was given a promise of how God would both reveal and establish his family. Through intimacy with Father God, Abraham discovered his destiny as a father of many nations. Abraham's destiny was to reveal a kingdom of sons and daughters, both Jew and Gentile. The habitation of sonship (being the tribes of Israel and our place in them) is inheritance.

Romans 11:1-2 says: "For I too am an Israelite, a descendant of Abraham, of the tribe of Benjamin." Remember: God is in the details! Paul is identifying himself to the Gentiles as part of God's divine order. He goes on in verse 2: "God has not rejected His people whom He foreknew." Romans 8:28-30 speaks of this foreknowledge, which is referring to the gifts and callings and God's character within His people. In verses 11: 7-15 we see God's heart for restoration for the Jewish people. God loves His people. The Church has not *replaced* Israel but is *grafted into* the commonwealth of Israel. Our true identity is revealed in the whole house of Israel. We are all in His family.

The tribes are pivotal to God's plan of restoration to His holy habitation. Each of the tribes is symbolic of God's overcoming army and the identity of the Bride of Christ. The tribes of Israel hold the keys of authority for believers in Christ today. I believe the tribes reveal who we are, our gifts and callings, strengths and weaknesses. More importantly, the tribes reveal who we are as worshippers and the children of God. This teaching can be a wonderful tool for pastors and counselors when they need wisdom. When you know what tribe someone is, you'll know how to minister to them because you'll know their strengths and weaknesses. You'll gain understanding how to pray for them, instruct them, and encourage them. It's also great insight for husbands and wives.

We all have weaknesses that we are constantly surrendering to God. Each one of the tribes struggled with its own particular weakness, which hindered each destiny as well. The Bible is full of their trials and triumphs. This insight is rich, and if you'll dig into this deep mystery, I know you will find freedom. These examples were provided to us as a guide. The lessons learned from the tribes provide such a wealth of knowledge for the Bride of Christ. We perish for a lack of knowledge.

The tribes are the history of the family of God. There is so much dissension and jealousy within the Church today. It is my sincere belief that if we know we are in Yeshua and who our brothers and sisters are, all of this needless garbage would end. God's heart is for unity. A house or army divided against itself will not stand!

> *Behold, how good and how pleasant it is for brothers to dwell together in unity!* (Psalm 133:1).

The key is walking in the Spirit. How do we do this? God's *maon kadosh*, the tribes of Israel, teach us how to live in unity as we build with our heavenly Father. Some of you have battled for so long to know where you fit in. You may have thought yourself insignificant or strange, maybe even unworthy, but God says:

> *But ye are a elect race, a royal priesthood, a holy nation, a people for God's own possession, that ye may show forth the excellencies of him who called you out of darkness into his marvelous light* (I Peter 2:9).

The Father does have a place for you as you seek Him with your whole heart. His glory is waiting to be awakened in you so that you may be built up in Messiah Yeshua as His glorious resting place. May God shine His marvelous light on you, His priceless Living Stones. Amen.

---

[1] Spiros Zodhiates, Th.D. , *The Hebrew-Greek Key Word Study Bible New American Standard Bible Revised Edition* (Chattanooga, TN: AMG Publishers, ©1984, 1990, 2008), Page 1933 Strong's 4583. Unless otherwise noted all Hebrew-Greek words are taken from this source.

# CHAPTER 1
# YOUR JOURNEY INTO HABITATION

In life we are all on a journey. As believers, we are each on a journey of returning to the Father. We are making *aliyah* (Hebrew for "returning or ascending") to the New Jerusalem. This journey is one of transformation, where we are delivered from the dominion of darkness to the kingdom of God to become His holy habitation.

Most believers suffer with an identity crisis. If we don't know who we are, as soldiers of the Cross, how can we defeat our foe? The reason believers today live in defeat and confusion is simple: We have not taken hold of our God-given authority in Christ. We can take hold of our authority by knowing who we are in God's image. In his book, *Breaking Intimidation*,[1] John Bevere shares a powerful prophetic word he was given: Walk in your God-given authority, or someone will take it and use it against you.

This is so true. "And the evil spirit answered and said unto them, Yeshua I know, and Paul I know, but who are you?" (Acts 19:15). The demons know who we are. The only time the enemy has a foothold with us is when we are not walking in our God-given authority. We must recognize that we are the treasured possession of the Father. We are accepted in the Beloved.

One of the biggest strongholds in most believers today is the orphan spirit. The orphan spirit will hold us like prisoners from our true calling—sonship—whereby we radiate the nature of the Father Himself, which is revealed and accessed in Christ. This stronghold will deceive men to have thoughts like: *Has God forgotten me? I don't fit in. I am not important.* These are lies that keep us from our rightful inheritance. The Father's greatest joy is to have communion with us. It is why we were created.

Every gift given to us is from the Father. These gifts express a piece of who God is. The word *charisma*, meaning "gift," stems from the Greek root word *charis*, meaning "grace" (our spiritual gifts are often referred to as spiritual "graces"). God's grace is freely given to us. His grace is our glory. The Greek word *charakter* sounds like the word *character*. He fashioned His character within us before the beginning of time to become His sons and daughters in His image. If we allow rejection to hold us back from being the priests of the Lord, then the enemy has won. Satan is not after you because you are a nice person. Satan is after the glory that the Father has given to you as His great treasured possession.

> *For you are a holy people to God; the Lord your God has chosen you to be a people for His own possession out of all the peoples who are on the face of the earth*
> (Deuteronomy 7:6).

When we walk in condemnation of old sins and the wounds from the past, we never rise above the Egypt mentality to which we are enslaved. Egypt is a type and shadow of sin, the past, and the wounding of others, whereas Canaan represents our inheritance in Christ, who mirrors the Father. If we abide in Christ, we abide in the Father's image that He created us to be. Our destiny is found in the very character and heart of God. Each tribe was positioned around the Tabernacle—God's picture of worship.

> *And I heard a great voice out of heaven saying, "Behold, the tabernacle of God is with men, and he will dwell with them, and they shall be his people, and God himself shall be with them, and be their God"* (Revelation 21:3 KJV).

The Israelites held the keys to victory through this picture. They wandered aimlessly for forty years in the desert, clueless of their gifts and callings and the power they possessed as God's overcoming army. The Israelites lived in fear and dread of their enemies, when in fact their enemies were shaking in their boots, having heard of how God miraculously delivered the Israelites out of Egypt and destroyed their enemies. We are held back by fear, but in reality Satan and his cohorts are in fear and trembling of our gifts and callings—the very character of God that you and I possess. The Body of Christ will advance as we come into who we are individually and as we see one another for who we are and where God has placed us around His tabernacle.

There were specific callings and gifts for the tribes, a picture of the character of God within each one. The history of the tribes demonstrates their strengths as well as the carnal nature they warred with daily. It is my earnest prayer that each one of you will come into the fullness that God has for you. For when we truly know who we are and know each other in the Spirit, we can then come into our God-given authority and take our place around His heavenly dwelling place. Take time to pray, search the Scriptures concerning the tribes, and ask God to reveal who you are and your rightful place in the Body. I am excited about the journey of self-discovery you are about to embark on. He will change you from glory to glory as you seek Him. Be led by the Spirit, and He will reveal who you are as a son or daughter of God.

*And He answered and said to them, "To you it has been granted to know the mysteries of heaven, but to them it has not been granted"* (Matthew 13:11).

## DOMINION:
## RELEASING THE KINGDOM OF HEAVEN FROM WITHIN YOU

*But seek first His kingdom and His righteousness; and all these things will be added to you* (Matthew 6:33).

While serving at Succat Hallel, a 24/7 house of prayer in Jerusalem, the cry of Romans 8:19 began to resound from within and through me and others as well. During the watches I would pray continually that the sons and daughters of glory would be revealed. I sensed the Father's deep longing for His children not only to know Him intimately but to be known as His glorious creation. It is His deepest desire to have intimacy with us. Why must we be revealed? When we are revealed, He is revealed, for we are a mirror of Him!

Creation as a whole, and even more expressly, the Bride of Christ, has been like Queen Esther: hidden to be revealed. Satan is our Haman, and he will stop at nothing in order to abort the revealing of God's sons and daughters. Now the Father knows who we truly are and in many respects our enemy, Satan, knows, but most of us (speaking not only of believers, but mankind in general), sadly, do not know who we are and the purpose for which we have "come into the kingdom." Many "see through a glass darkly" (I Cor. 13:12) and have been led by the Spirit of the Lord on a journey of identity, clueless yet desperately seeking. Everywhere I look, I see that mankind is pregnant with a longing for identity and purpose. The entertainment industry is full of lures of identity. Even the lost are desperately seeking to find who they are. What, or *who*, we are really seeking is love: Yeshua the Messiah, the embodiment of love. As believers, we know we can find true love in Messiah alone. This is one reason I feel the Lord has called me to write about this revelation of the tribes. The tribes are not a total picture but rather a type and shadow, a revelation or perception from the Father's heart that unveils hidden mysteries of sonship in His glorious kingdom of love.

*For the anxious longing of creation waits eagerly for the revealing of the sons of God* (Romans 8: 19).

I believe we are approaching the greatest hour for all of mankind. I feel that this is the revealing of the sons and daughters of God, which is the most important aspect of the knowledge of His glory covering the earth, just as Scripture promises:

> *For the earth will be filled with the knowledge of the glory of the Lord, as the waters cover the sea* (Habakkuk 2:14).

Beloved, the earth is pregnant with our revealing! Do you not hear the groaning; can you not perceive that an emergence of the true image of God is longing to be released into the earth? The finest hour of the earth is upon us. Does your heart rejoice? Does your spirit leap within you? This is good news, brethren! The Father's desire has always been about sonship. His chief desire toward us is communion.

> *Now I say, as long as the heir is a child, he does not differ at all from a slave although he is owner of everything, but he is under guardians and managers until the date set by the father. So also we, while we were children, were held in bondage under the elemental things of the world. But when the fullness of the time came, God sent forth His Son, born of a woman, born under the Law, so that He might redeem those who were under the Law, that we might receive the adoption as sons. Because you are sons, God has sent forth the Spirit of His Son into our hearts, crying, "Abba! Father!" Therefore you are no longer a slave, but a son; and if a son, then an heir through God* (Galatians 4:1-7).

Beloved, as we are heirs through Christ, we possess the most glorious inheritance: eternal redemption and sonship. We are no longer slaves, so we need to live like we are free because communion coupled with truth is how we can live in kingdom reality! The lie is slavery and the orphan spirit! The enemy's objective is to keep us from fellowship from the Father by robbing us of identity and communion through facades.

What is a façade? A façade is a false perception, lie, or appearance opposing the heart of God. Façades have been around since the fall of Adam and Eve, where the first façade befell creation. Adam and Eve forsook dominion through sin in the Garden of Eden.

> *Now the serpent was more crafty than any beast of the field which the Lord GOD had made. And he said to the woman, "Indeed, has God said, 'You shall not eat from any tree of the Garden'?" And the women said to the serpent, "From the fruit of the trees of the Garden we may eat; but from the fruit of the tree which is in the middle of the Garden, the Lord has said, 'You shall not eat from it or touch it, lest you die.'" And the serpent said to the woman, "You surely shall not die! For God knows that in the day you eat from it with your eyes opened, and you will be like God, knowing good and evil"* (Genesis 3:1-5).

Satan offered Adam and Eve a counterfeit dominion when he said, you will be like God. The lie that the enemy perpetuates to us is that we have to strive to be like God. The truth is we already are. Are we not fashioned in the very image of the Father? So the truth is that we have dominion available to us. It is unlocked by pursuing intimacy and repentance. Dominion is restored when façades are torn down. Each one of the tribes struggled with façades that kept them from dominion. Façades can either be a sin that one engages in or a false perception either of yourself, of others, or that others may have of you. It is vital that as a Body in Christ we live without façades of ourselves or each other. Think about seeing yourself as you were truly created. More importantly, see others without façades. Imagine ministering to the lost as you see them through the Father's eyes—free of façades! Yeshua spoke of this when He said:

*Or how can you say to your brother, "Let me take the speck out of your eye," and behold, the log is in your own eye? You hypocrite, first take the log out of your own eye, and then you will see clearly to take the speck out of your brother's eye* (Matthew 7:4-5).

The spirit of accusation will keep us out of unity as the Bride of Christ, but more importantly, it will keep us from our Father's greatest desire of communion with Him and living in kingdom reality. The tribes warred with façades that kept each one from living in full kingdom reality. Through Christ alone we possess kingdom reality, for He is the Way to kingdom reality—Abba Father Himself!

## ENGAGING IN FAÇADES

*For since the creation of the world His invisible attributes, His eternal power and divine nature, have been clearly seen, being understood through what has been made, so that they are without excuse. For even though they knew God, they did not honor Him as God or give thanks, but they became futile in their speculations, and their foolish heart was darkened. Professing to be wise, they became fools, and exchanged the glory of the incorruptible God for an image in the form of corruptible man and of birds and four-footed animals and crawling creatures. Therefore God gave them over in the lusts of their hearts to impurity, so that their bodies would be dishonored among them. For they exchanged the truth of God for a lie, and worshiped and served the creature rather than the Creator, who is blessed forever* (Romans 1:20-25).

We engage in façades when we buy into their lies, either in our behavior or by believing in our minds the lies of Satan or the speculations of men. Truth cannot live where a lie remains. If we engage in a sin, then it is our hearts that must be turned (repentance). When we become tempted and give into the stronghold of sin through disobedience, we are believing a façade. If the facade is nothing more than a lie held within the thought life, we must cast down all vain imaginations that exalt themselves against the knowledge of Christ and command them to come into the obedience of Him (II Cor. 10:5).

Take, for instance, someone who may have grown up in an abusive home and been told that they are worthless. This lie seeps in over the years, and this person begins to believe it. Sometimes a façade can be generational: "Well, your mother is that way so that explains why you are the way you are," etc. Other times it can come through speculation. The enemy can deceive through false opinions you might have of yourself, or others can have a false opinion that they believe as truth (gossip, misunderstanding, and dissension come in here). Sadly, some believers can call this discernment, when in reality it is nothing more than a façade of accusation. All sin and old hurts are façades, stemming from the father of lies, Satan himself. He and his façades must be cast down in the name of Yeshua by the power of His blood!

## FAÇADE BUSTING THROUGH TRANSFORMATION GLORY

Yeshua is the façade buster. It's like turning on a light switch. When you go into a dark room, what do you do? You turn the light on! When you believe in façades, you are stuck inside a dark room…until the Truth, being the person of Yeshua, turns the light on! Yeshua is the illumination (light) and exact representation of the Father.

*For we do not preach ourselves but Christ Jesus as the Lord, and ourselves as your bond-servants for Jesus' sake. For God, who said, "Light shall shine out of darkness," is the One who has shone in our hearts to give the Light of the knowledge of the glory of God in the face of Christ. But we have this treasure in earthen vessels, so that the surpassing greatness of the power will be of God and not from ourselves* (II Corinthians 4:5-7).

We were once veiled, but now through the blood and the flesh of our Lord, that veil, that façade, has come down. Embrace the Cross—the façade buster!

> *But their minds were hardened; for until this very day at their reading of the old covenant the same veil remains unlifted, because it is removed in Christ. But to this day whenever Moses is read, a veil lies over their heart; but whenever a person turns to the Lord, the veil is taken away. Now the Lord is the Spirit, and where the Spirit of the Lord is, there is liberty. But we all, with unveiled face, beholding as in a mirror the glory of the Lord, are being transformed into the same image from glory to glory, just as from the Lord, the Spirit* (II Corinthians 3:14-18).

Our true keys to authority and dominion lie within us. The Father is calling to us to awaken from our slumber. Each chapter in this book holds a prayer of repentance and keys to freedom from façades for each tribe. The tribes are a picture or aid to help us to come out of façades and into the glorious light of sonship!

> *For this reason it says, "Awake, sleeper, and rise from the dead. And Christ will shine upon you"* (Ephesians 5:14).

The call is simple: LOVE. Façades are anti-Christ, therefore anti-love. Façades will keep us from possessing and keeping our God-given identities. It is only through Divine Love Himself that we, His glorious living stones, can possess our true identities and fulfill the work of the Father's kingdom. Love is the first and most vital command to us. The Father is calling us to awake to His love! Hear His heartbeat for you. He is calling, "Arise, O sleeper, let the light of My glory transform you and awaken you to true love." It is through love that God restores us to our rightful place of dominion and inheritance.

## PRAYER OF DESTINY

Abba! Father! Your creation is crying out to You to reveal Yourself to us. We yearn, even travail, to come into the revelation knowledge of who we are as Your sons and daughters. Your kingdom of love brings us freedom! Father, we leave Egypt (sin, the old man, the past, and old wounds) behind. We thank You for raising up our deliverer, Yeshua, Your Son, to help us cross over into the promised land! Thank you, Abba, that every foe is buried at the bottom of the Red Sea, the blood of Yeshua. With righteous zeal we vow to pursue our glorious inheritance. Forgive us, oh Father, for wandering aimlessly around in the desert. Help us come into the fullness of who You are and who You have predestined us to be. Call us to repentance from the idols that have restrained our destiny. Break us, mold us, as only You can, for we are only clay. Beloved Father, may we return to our glorious inheritance in You, which we forfeited since the Fall. Restore our dominion and place of rest in You. Transform us, dear Father, into the Bride for whom Your Son so desperately longs. Reveal to us the mysteries of Your heart as we study Your *maon kadosh*, the tribes of Israel. Prepare Your Bride. In Yeshua's name, Amen.

---

[1] John Bevere, *Breaking Intimidation* (Lake Mary, FL, Charisma House, 1995) page 2.

# CHAPTER 2
# REUBEN: THE PASSIONATE LOVER

Abba is love. How appropriate that the first son of the twelve tribes is called specifically to love. Love is the foundation upon which the Father builds His Kingdom. Reuben is a lover. If you find yourself within the tribe of Reuben, your main calling is to be a lover of God and mankind. Younger siblings always look up to the oldest for guidance and wisdom. God begins his family and divine order with the eldest, Reuben, the epitome of love. We can learn much about God's love from our elder brother, Reuben.

> *If I speak with the tongues of men and angels, but do not have love, I have become a noisy gong or a clanging cymbal. And if I have the gift of prophecy, and know all mysteries and all knowledge; and if I have all faith so as to remove mountains, but do not have love, I am nothing. And if I give all my possessions to feed the poor, and if I deliver my body to be burned, but do not have love, it profits me nothing. Love is patient, love is kind, and is not jealous; love does not brag and is not arrogant, does not act unbecomingly; it does not seek its own, is not provoked, does not take into account a wrong suffered, does not rejoice in unrighteousness; but rejoices with the truth; bears all things, believes all things, hopes all things, endures all things* (I Corinthians 13:1-7).

Dear Reuben, brother or sister, we so desperately need you. You are a foundational stone of love; God is using you to build His holy habitation. When the body of Christ begins to truly live a lifestyle of love, with no hidden self-made agendas, then and only then will there be unity and an unadulterated gospel preached. The world is waiting to see the true Yeshua within us. If you want to see unconditional love exemplified, look no further than a Reubenite; for without your Christ-like example of selfless love, where would we be?

Reuben's story begins with love. His father Jacob was promised Rachel as his betrothed and worked for seven years of hard labor to Laban. Laban deceived Jacob by giving him his eldest daughter Leah.

Read Genesis 29:21-26. Jacob was well acquainted with deception, for he himself was a deceiver. His very name means "deceiver, supplanter." Remember, he had deceived his father Jacob to receive Esau's birthright. What irony that he would also be deceived by Laban, who invoked the firstborn rights of his daughter, Leah, and disguised her as Rachel, the one whom Jacob favored and loved. Rejected and unloved by her husband, Leah cried out to God. The Lord saw Leah's hurting heart and blessed her with Reuben. Reuben was God's gift of love, and so are all others from this tribe.

> *Now God saw that Leah was unloved, and He opened her womb, but Rachel was barren. And Leah conceived and bore a son and named him Reuben, for she said, "Because God has seen my affliction; surely now my husband will love me"* (Genesis 29:31-32).

## THE MEANING OF THE NAME

> *"Because the Lord has **seen** my affliction; surely now my husband will love me."*
> (Genesis 29:32).

Reuben means "See a son! A dawning of a new day!" It comes from two Hebrew root words: *raah* and *ben*.

**Raah**(raw-aw): "To see, consider, look, make, enjoy, have, experience, perceive, present, provide."

What does love do? Love causes us to see and be seen. The birth of Reuben caused Leah to see God's love for her and gain her husband Jacob's affections. Love has the ability to change perceptions, focus, and ultimately identity.

**Ben**: "A son." The theologian R.W.F. Wilhelm Gesenius believed that the Hebrew word *ben* stems from the Hebrew root word *bana*. [1] Bana means "to build or rebuild." Literally the word *ben* denotes a building block. Abba's holy habitation is built through His sons and daughters. Without the foundational stone of love (Reuben), it would not stand. The masculine plural for *ben* is the Hebrew word *benim*. The feminine plural for *benim* is *benut*. What a powerful confirmation for women in ministry, and more importantly, for our identity as Abba's daughters!

> *Many waters cannot quench love, nor will rivers overflow it; If a man were to give all the riches of his house for love, It would be utterly despised* (Song of Songs 8:7).

Love is the fiercest force. God's love defines who He is as Father and who we are as sons and daughters. Some biblical scholars have concluded that the Hebrew word *eben* (stone) is related to the word *bana* and therefore related to the Hebrew word *ben*. The Kingdom of God is revealed through Abba's holy habitation of living stones. He is both intentional in how He carefully crafted each one of us and where we are placed.

> "*...you will be sons of the Most High*" (Luke 6:35).

> *You also, as living stones, are being built up as a spiritual house for a holy priesthood, to offer up spiritual sacrifices acceptable to God through Jesus Christ* (I Peter 2:5).

The tribes of Reuben (oldest) and Benjamin (youngest) are the only tribes where *ben*, meaning "son," comprises part of their names. The beautiful revelation here is that from the beginning (Reuben) to the end (Benjamin), God calls us His sons and daughters. The Father is identifying Himself to His children even down to the smallest detail of the names of these two tribes. What a beautiful confirmation to know that we have truly received the spirit of adoption. What love the Father has lavished upon us through the revelation of His word. Amen!

## THE GEMSTONE OF REUBEN

The gemstone of Reuben is the sardius or, more commonly, the ruby. It is a gemstone of red blood color. God sees us through the blood of Yeshua. What a glorious testimony of sonship you have dear Reubenite: the blood!

> *In whom we have redemption through his blood, the forgiveness of sins, according to the riches of his grace* (Ephesians 1:7).

> *But now in Christ Jesus you who sometimes were far off are made nigh by the blood of Christ* (Ephesians 2:13).

How appropriate that the first stone in the breastplate is the ruby, symbolizing the precious blood of Yeshua. When we first came to Yeshua, we came to know His forgiveness because of His shed blood. Reubenites' passionate natures make them sensitive to sin. For this reason they can easily be snared by condemnation. Their sensitivity makes them uneasy and usually quicker to repent than some. Freedom lies in knowing who you are as a son or daughter and that Yeshua's blood paid for everything. Dear Reuben, your victory lies in the blood. Hold onto this truth. It will bring great freedom. What a promise of hope for every Reubenite and for us as well!

 Another revelation concerning the tribe of Reuben and his stone is found in Revelation 4:3:

*Benjamin* *Reubens*

*And He who was sitting was like a jasper stone and a sardius in appearance; and there was a rainbow around the throne, like an emerald in appearance.*

Benjamin's stone is the jasper, and Reuben's, the sardius. This Scripture is referring to Yeshua. It says that his appearance was like that of jasper and sardius. Interestingly, Benjamin, the youngest of the twelve, is mentioned first and the firstborn, Reuben, last.

*"But many who are first will be last; and the last, first"* (Matthew 19:30).

We are the expressed image of Yeshua. Our identity is found in Him. Reuben is the passionate lover, and Benjamin is the beloved. That's how we come to him: as His passionate lover and His Beloved.

## THE SYMBOLS

There are so many beautiful pictures of hope, deliverance, and destiny for Reuben revealed to us in God's Word. Reuben has three symbols: the rising sun, the mandrake plant, and the man. The symbol of the man, Reuben's captain tribe symbol, will be discussed at the latter portion of this chapter.

## RISING SUN

*Thus let all your enemies perish oh Lord, but let those who love Him be like the rising of the sun in its might* (Judges 5:31).

A rising sun speaks of a new beginning, a new day, or hope. Reuben must look to the Lord to be the sun on his horizon.

*The Mighty one, God the Lord, has spoken, and summoned the earth from the rising of the sun to its setting. Out of Zion, the perfection of beauty, God has shone forth* (Psalm 50:1-2).

God is shining the perfection of His beauty forth through Reuben. Reuben's name even speaks of this, meaning "See, a son, a new beginning." Reuben, you must see yourself as a new creation in Christ. Do not allow the old man and condemnation to steal your hope. You're a new man because you are crucified with Christ. A new day is dawning for you, a day of deliverance!

## THE NEW DAY: BREAKER ANOINTING

*The Lord says to my Lord: "Sit at My right hand until I make Your enemies a footstool for Your feet." The Lord will stretch forth Your strong scepter from Zion, saying, "Rule in the midst of Your enemies." Your people will volunteer freely in the day of Your power; In holy array, from the womb of the dawn, Your youth are to You as the dew* (Psalm 110:1-3).

In the womb of the dawn a new day is arising. The mercies of God are new every morning, and breakthrough is on the horizon. The rising sun speaks of the breaker anointing and message of hope within the spiritual DNA of every Reubenite. Love is a powerful force; I believe it's *the* most powerful force. Love mends the brokenhearted, restores ancient ruins, brings new life, and breaks bondages of sin and death. Love Divine Himself came to cover (through His shed blood) a multitude of sins so you and I would have a new day!

Just before dawn, the night is full of wrestling and warfare. Yeshua Himself wrestled until morning in the Garden of Gethsemane. It was during the third watch when He wrestled, but it was at dawn when victory came. You see, Christ had already travailed for our freedom in the dark night of the soul, where He drank the cup of the Father's will. He consummated the victory at night, but at dawn it was revealed that redemption would come to His beloved, fallen creation. Joy came in the morning! Many victories in Scripture came at dawn: the walls of Jericho fell at dawn, and the conquest at Ai was won at dawn.

> *After two days Jehovah will revive us, on the third day He will raise us up, and we shall live before Him and we shall know, and we shall follow on to know Jehovah; His going forth is as the dawn* (Hosea 6:2-3).

The womb of the morning can be seen crowning as the darkest part of night gives way before dawn where the victory is laid. It is the travail against the enemy's kingdom and the intercession of the hope of a new day about to dawn. Prophetically, dawn is the separation of darkness and light in the spiritual atmosphere. The works of darkness cease, and the dawning of the new day (God's promise) arises! The third day is the new day, a day of resurrection! Reuben, God is calling you to live in the third day!

> *The God of Israel said, The Rock of Israel spoke to me, "He who rules over men righteously, who rules in the fear of the Lord, is as the light of the morning when the sun rises, A morning without clouds, when the tender grass springs out of the earth, through sunshine after rain"* (II Samuel 23:3-4).

Reubenites carry the dawn in order to have and bring breakthrough with the delivering power of God's love. They are carriers of hope and restoration, for this is the reconciliation of God back to man through the earth's most powerful force: Love Divine! When ruling and reigning in the fear of the Lord with Christ (the Rock of Israel), Reubenites bring breakthrough!

> *Awake, my glory! Awake, harp and lyre! I will awaken the dawn* (Psalm 57:8).

Reuben, the glory of God is waiting to awaken within you. He is awakening you to His love and nature. You, in turn, are called to "awaken the dawn," meaning you are called to bring a breakthrough in the new day. So arise and shine, Reuben, and let the light of the Son arise upon your soul, making whole the deepest parts of your being and calling you to carry the dawn wherever you go.

> *Jehovah in the midst of her is righteous, He will not do perversity; in the morning, in the morning will He give judgment for light* (Zephaniah 3:5).

The King's judgments are sealed until morning, but at dawn the decree of breakthrough is sent!

> *Then your light will break out like the dawn, and your recovery will speedily spring forth, and your righteousness will go before you; The glory of the Lord will be your rear guard* (Isaiah 58:8).

Who is the glory of the Lord? Yeshua! He is arising with healing in His wings on your new day, Reuben, so rejoice!

> *But for you who fear My name, the sun of righteousness will rise with healing in its wings* (Malachi 4:2a).

The Son of righteousness is calling you to dwell in His light. The express image of the Father that you are called to carry to a fallen earth is the revelation of Him as the Sun (and Son) that creation may break forth out of darkness!

> *The heavens are telling of the glory of God; and their expanse is declaring the work of His hands. Day to day pours forth speech and night to night reveals knowledge. There is no speech, nor are there words; their voice is not heard. Their line has gone out through all the earth, and their utterances to the end of the world. In them He has placed a tent for the sun, Which is as a bridegroom coming out of his chamber; It rejoices as a strong man to run his course. Its rising is from one end of the heavens, and its circuit to the other end of them; and there is nothing hidden from its heat* (Psalm 19:1-7).

This is a revelation of Yeshua, our Bridegroom Himself, bidding us into the Father's glory (John 15 says they are one) from the *chuppah* of Heaven (Jewish wedding tent). This is the betrothal promise of every Reuben of breakthrough! It is a calling of intimacy and victory through Yeshua Messiah Himself, the Son of righteousness! In like manner, you carry this bidding from the throne to breakthrough for mankind. Dear Reuben, your victory is consummated in the dawning of every new day! Look for it, wait expectantly for it, for Love Divine Himself will reveal a new day to you. Yeshua is the new day, the new and living way!

## THE MANDRAKE

Mandrakes: Hebrew, *dudraim* or *duwday*, meaning "love apple." The *Atropa mandragora* mandrake is closely allied to the well-known deadly nightshade, *Atropa belladonna*, as well as the tomato, and belongs to the order *Solanaceae*, or potato family. It grows in Palestine and Mesopotamia. [2] It grows low, like lettuce, which its leaves somewhat resemble, except that they are of a dark green. The flowers are purple, and the root is usually forked. Its fruit, when ripe (early in May), is about the size of a small apple, 24 inches in diameter, ruddy or yellow, and of a most agreeable odor and an equally agreeable taste. The Arabs call it "devil's apple," from its power to excite voluptuousness. In his "Lectures on Alcohol" in 1881, Dr. Richardson described his experiments with wine made of the root of mandrake and found it had a narcotic effect, causing sleep, so that the ancients used it as an anesthetic. Used in small quantities like opium, it excites the nerves and is a stimulant. [3]

The mandrake is an aphrodisiac. The mandrake speaks of Reuben's passionate love, both as his strength and his weakness.

> *Now in the days of wheat harvest Reuben went and found mandrakes in the field, and brought them to his mother Leah. Then Rachel said to Leah, "Please give me some more of your son's mandrakes." But she said to her, "Is it a small matter for you have to take my husband? And would take my son's mandrakes also? So Rachel said, "Therefore he may lie with you tonight in return for your son's mandrakes." When Jacob came in from the field in the evening, then Leah went out to meet him and said, "You must come into me, for I have surely hired you with my son's mandrakes." So he lay with her that night. And the Lord gave heed to Leah, and she conceived and bore Jacob a fifth son* (Genesis 30:14-17).

Reuben is a giver. He saw his mother's heartache and was moved with compassion. Reuben was hoping that the mandrake would help his parents' marriage. He could have taken them for himself; he was a young man with passionate urges. He was not selfish. It broke his heart to see his mother lonely and unloved by his father. This is a true heart of a Reuben. Reuben is a lover and not a willing fighter. Reubenites avoid confrontation at all costs. Sometimes this can develop into compromise if they are not led by the Spirit in their relationships. Often they have the motivational gifts of mercy, giving, and the gift of helps. Reubenites often give to be accepted or to give acceptance. They are encouragers who need to be encouraged, they are soul winners or evangelists. Actually, the camps of Reuben, Simeon, and Gad are called to evangelism, but in different ways. A Reubenite would literally give you the shirt off his back.

The mandrake is also a picture of intimacy:

> *The mandrakes have given forth fragrance; and over our doors are all choice fruits, Both new and old, Which I have saved up for you my beloved* (Song of Songs 7:13).

We captivate our beloved, Yeshua, with our worship. What a beautiful promise for Reuben! This is a call to worship for every Reubenite: Reuben, be head over heels in love for your Bridegroom. Feel His comforting embrace under the apple tree. Get lovesick for Him and Him alone. He's calling you to His apple tree!

## JACOB'S PROPHECY

> *"Reuben, you are my first-born; My might and the beginning of my strength, Preeminent in dignity and preeminent in power. Uncontrolled as water, you shall not have preeminence, because you went up to your father's bed; Then you defiled it—he went up to my couch"* (Genesis 49: 3-4).

### "REUBEN, YOU ARE MY FIRST-BORN"

Most first-born children in a family are expected to carry on the family name and uphold its honor. Reuben is the firstborn of the family of God, and he carries the honor or renown of Christ. What is the renown of Christ? The renown of Christ is that His name is love, His name has power, and His name is healing. His name causes kingdoms of darkness to tremble and angels to fall prostrate before Him. This charge is given to every Reubenite; bear it well, with purity and righteous fervor.

### "MY MIGHT AND THE BEGINNING OF MY STRENGTH"

Jacob was saying, "Reuben, you are the finest part of me. I've put all my heart and soul into you." God has placed His power and might within every spirit of Reuben. He has given you the power to overcome your enemy. When you are weak, He is strong. God's Word has promises for you, dear Reuben. When you can no longer stand in your own strength, hold on to these promises, and you will overcome.

> *And I was with you in weakness and in fear and in much trembling* (I Corinthians 2:3).
> *...it is sown in dishonor, it is raised in glory; it is sown in weakness, it is raised in power; it is sown a natural body, it is raised a spiritual body. If there is a natural body, there is also a spiritual body* (I Corinthians 15:43-44).

*And He said to me, "My grace is sufficient for you, for power is perfected in weakness"* (II Corinthians 12:9).

## "PREEMINENT IN DIGNITY AND PREEMINENT IN POWER"

The King James Version says: *The excellency of dignity, the excellency of power.* God has endowed the tribe of Reuben with His excellence. The Father has called us all to live a life of excellence. Excellence calls to a higher level of maturity and integrity. The pinnacle of excellence in believers' lives is when we no longer live, but Christ lives within us. It requires we put away the profane, to be doers of the Word, to seek out the good of another above our own, to hear the cry of the poor, and to come out of childish elementary things. Excellence also calls out of striving into the deeper things of God. Excellence is the way of wisdom, the very counsel of the Lord. There can be good counsel or a way that may seem good, but God's counsels and ways far exceed any temporality of this life for His way is excellent. True excellence is born of the holiness of God. Seeking first the kingdom will always lead into excellence, dear Reuben.

> *And the peace of God, which surpasses all comprehension, shall guard your hearts and your minds in Christ. Finally, brethren, whatever is true, whatever is honorable, whatever is right whatever is of a good repute, if there is any* **excellence** *and anything worthy of praise let your mind dwell on these things. The things you have learned and received and heard and seen in me practice these things: and there God of peace will be with you* (Philippians 4:7-9).

Read Proverbs 16:25 and Philippians 1:10. God has also given us His power.

> *Behold, I have given authority to tread upon serpents and scorpions, and over all the power of the enemy, and nothing shall injure you* (Luke 10:19).

God's power is His grace and the empowerment of the Holy Spirit. Grace enables us to live a holy, set apart life unto the Lord. The Spirit gives us power to be His witnesses. Power to be His witnesses is vital to kingdom living. Without it our lives would be some mundane chore of religiosity. We are empowered to be history makers, co-laborers with the Father, and ultimately the Bride of Christ.

## "UNCONTROLLED AS WATER"

When Jacob prophesied this over Reuben, he was referring to his unstable nature. One trait consistent with the facade of Reuben is that he is a person of great extremes and self-contradiction. He battles with the old man and instability to the point of bondage and idolatry. Reuben is a chameleon. He changes to the surroundings, which can sometimes be detrimental. Water conforms to whatever form you place it in. If you put it in an ice tray, it will take its shape, but if you pour it out, it's a mess. Reuben must constantly seek God to be his stability. He must not allow idolatrous influences into his life. If he does, they will easily lead him into sin. If you are a Reubenite, strive to surround yourself with godly people and influences. A mature Levite or Judah are good sources of counsel and encouragement.

## "YOU SHALL NOT HAVE PREEMINENCE, BECAUSE YOU WENT UP TO YOUR FATHER'S BED; THEN YOU DEFILED IT—HE WENT UP TO MY COUCH."

Whenever sin rules our hearts, Yeshua cannot. Idols (sin), whether they are lust, pride, religion, judgment, etc., "muddy" our wedding attire. The stronghold(s) Reuben must keep nailed to his cross are his lust and his unstable nature. At the time Jacob prophesied over his sons, Reuben's sin was fresh in his mind. He had intimate relations with his father's concubine, Bilhah, and shamed his father and family name.

*And it came about while Israel was dwelling in that land, that Reuben went and lay with Bilhah his father's concubine; and Israel heard of it (Genesis 35:22).*

The tribe of Reuben's lifelong quest is to love and be loved. Many who suffer from rejection go looking for love in all the wrong places. This is true of a Reubenite. A heart can easily be led astray because of rejection. If you are a Reuben, you have been searching for love all your life. You have a great passion for God and compassion for your fellow man. However, this love can become misguided and become lust. Although not all who struggle with lust are Reubenites, it is the major facade for this tribe. God is love; His desire for us is always freedom. Yeshua came so that we might be free from the bondage of sin.

## THE FAÇADES OF LUST AND ADULTERY

*Thou shalt not commit adultery (Exodus 20:14 KJV).*

*For all that is in the world, the lust of the flesh, and the lust of the eyes, and the pride of life, is not of the Father, but is of the world (I John 2:16 KJV).*

The façades of lust and adultery are the age-old slippery slopes that cause many to go astray. God is holy, and when He gave His holy law at Mount Sinai, He was leaving instructions that would serve as a foundation of His holy nature. To lust and commit adultery is to sell love cheaply, to hold no value to love. For a Reubenite, to lose sight of the purity of love causes him to lose his spiritual sight, for love is his place of dominion! When Reubenites (or any of us) sell themselves for cheap thrills and wanton pleasures, they forego their calling of true intimacy.

The natural is a picture of the spiritual. Scripture is clear that the gift of sexual intimacy is holy unto God and meant to be between one man and one woman within the bond of marriage only. Allowing strange bedfellows, whether that be naturally or spiritually, is sin. God made the marriage bed to be undefiled to demonstrate a picture of a pure and holy covenant. God is a passionate God, but His passions are holy and not to be prostituted.

*But at the beginning of creation, God MADE THEM MALE AND FEMALE. FOR THIS REASON A MAN SHALL LEAVE HIS FATHER AND MOTHER, AND THE TWO SHALL BECOME ONE FLESH; so they are no longer two, but one flesh (Mark 10:6-8).*

When one falls prey to the lust of the eyes and flesh, a sincere heartfelt repentance, accountability, deliverance, and healing is required. Not the slightest bit of leaven of this beguiling sin can be tolerated. We live in a world that has many glamorously enticing traps. Do not be deceived by them! It is easy to allow the spirit of the world to come and desensitize us so that we ignore God's calling of purity and holiness. Yeshua was very clear about how to deal with this façade.

Read Matthew 5:27-32. Do not forego your inheritance because of wanton pleasures. Lust is a fleeting pleasure whose seductive devices will lead you on the broad path of destruction. Narrow is the gate, and few are those who find it. Much of the Church is deceived by the spirit of the world. It is sometimes hard to tell the difference between a worldly person and an idolatrous pew warmer. A form of godliness that denies the power of the Cross (the beckoning of repentance) gives license to the sins of lust and adultery. We can have no tolerance of this lie if we are to walk in a manner worthy of the Cross of Yeshua. Lust leads to adultery, and adultery not repented of can cause you to forego inheriting the kingdom.

> *Know ye not that the unrighteous shall not inherit the kingdom of God? Be not deceived: neither fornicators, nor idolaters, nor adulterers, nor effeminate, nor abusers of themselves with mankind, nor thieves, nor covetous, nor drunkards, nor revilers, nor extortioners, shall inherit the kingdom of God* (I Corinthians 6:9-10 KJV).

I have good news for you, dear Reubenite: Embrace the Cross, repent, and live! Repentance brings freedom. I believe Reuben did repent of his sin. Yeshua shed his blood for your freedom, brother and sister Reubenite. Come to Him and surrender all your failings. He is faithful and just to forgive and cleanse you of all unrighteousness. Cry out to Him in sincerity and lowliness of heart, and He will deliver you!

> *The Lord knoweth how to deliver the godly out of temptations…* (II Peter 2:9 KJV).

## MOSES'S PROPHECY

> *"May Reuben live and not die, nor his men be few"* (Deuteronomy 33:6).

Moses's word to the tribe of Reuben may have been short, but it speaks volumes. Moses, a mature Levite, sees Reuben the way God saw him. He sees Reuben not in his current unstable-as-water state, but as that rising sun and passionate lover of God. We all need to see one another in this light.

A short time before this prophecy, Reuben had made a few detours on his road to destiny. We all take those, don't we? Numbers 16 records a story where several members from the Reuben clan lost their lives in one day for one reason: Reuben was easily swayed because of idolatry in his heart. What was that idol? Self. The idol of self will take up residence within those who choose to do it their way and not the Lord's. What happened to Lucifer? He desired his own glory, his own praise, just like Korah and the sons of Reuben. Satan fell from glory, and the earth swallowed up Korah and the sons of Reuben. Rebellion kills. Sometimes our rebellion not only leads us into spiritual death, but others as well. What is so beautiful is that Moses in his prophecy speaks with great compassion to Reuben. I'm sure that the tribe of Reuben went through some serious repentance after this incident. So God speaks to them in mercy, as He always does when we turn and repent, that He would multiply Reuben. "Let Reuben live and not die, nor his men be few." How beautiful! God is again showing His love and hope to Reuben. If you draw near to the Lord with all of your heart, you will find Him.

## REUBEN COMPROMISES HIS INHERITANCE

Read Numbers 32:1-15. Settling for less than you were created for is truly a grievous thing to the Father. The tribe of Reuben, the half tribe of Manasseh, and Gad saw Gilead and Jazer as land that would be profitable for them. They did not take into consideration what the Lord thought. When you settle for less than what you were created for, you rob God of giving you His very best. A spirit of gluttony took over Reuben, Manasseh, and Gad. They saw something that was good in their own eyes and lusted after it greedily. Moses was probably thinking: "These tribes have some nerve. Did their forefather's disobedience and misfortune mean nothing?" A whole generation passed away and never fulfilled their destiny due to their own murmuring and complaining, spiritual disillusionment, self-ambition, and idolatry. That inherited seed of rebellion was still living inside Reuben and Gad some forty years later. Personally, I feel Gad was the instigator in this situation. A trait you will learn of Gad later on is that he is always looking for greener pastures. He is never content where God places him until He surrenders his own strong self-will. I believe Reuben allowed himself to be swayed by Gad (whom, by the way, he is to be a mentor to) by his own lust.

Lust does not always come in the form of sexual promiscuity. Lust can be for material things, power, etc. Once it takes root, it can choke the very life out of us. If Reuben had stood in his rightful God-given authority, he would have been discerning of Gad's rebelliousness, greed, and gluttony, and he would have rebuked Gad in love. In this scripture, you can see the spiritual laziness of these tribes. Spiritual laziness brings death to the destiny of God resident within us. They were also reluctant to fight. Verse 6: "But Moses said to the sons of Gad and to the sons of Reuben, 'Shall your brothers go to war while you yourselves sit here?'" Reuben is a reluctant fighter and leader. There are several reasons for this. One reason is that he doesn't think himself worthy enough to fight. He also constantly struggles with the guilt of his sin nature. He's lazy. He'd rather compromise for fear of receiving someone's rejection of love and/or fear of displeasing someone.

If you are a Reubenite, please, I beg of you, do not settle for less than you've been created for. God will hand us over to our own desires and dreams, but they won't be His desires, they won't be His destiny for us. Reuben, half of Manasseh, and Gad forfeited their freedom. They died never knowing the miraculous sovereignty of God's provision. How sad. What is tragic is that believers today do the very same thing. They never come into the fullness of their destiny in Christ.

> *So Moses commanded the sons of Israel, saying "this land that you are to apportion by the lot among you as a possession,* **which the Lord has commanded** *to give to the nine and half tribes. For the tribe or the sons of Reuben have received theirs according to their fathers households, and the tribe of the sons of Gad according to their fathers' households, and the half-tribe of Manasseh have received their possession. The two and a half tribes have received their possession across the Jordan opposite Jericho, eastward toward the sun rising"* (Numbers 34:13-15).

Notice that the other tribes received what the *Lord commanded.* The two-and-a-half tribes, it says, received *their possession.* It wasn't what God commanded, it's what they desired, what they lusted after. If you are in a place that God has not planned for you to be (spiritually or physically), your destiny will be hindered.

God does redeem these tribes, but not until some heartache and sincere repentance takes place. Sometimes we go through all kinds of unnecessary hurts and warfare simply because we are not in the will of God. Later on, God restores them by bringing His healing balm to Gilead.

## REUBEN'S ULTIMATE DESTINY

Before the beginning of time we were fashioned by our heavenly Father with His heart and purposes in mind. Our destinies were formed from His own character. In Him lies all the hidden treasures of revelation for His creation. He does not want our destiny to be hidden from us. However, He cannot entrust us with our divine nature unless we relinquish our old Adam nature. He reveals this nature to us through His Holy Word. If we look into the mirror of God's Word and see what needs to be changed, He will be faithful to transform us into our destiny. The destiny of Reuben is so beautifully depicted in Scripture. The first point is found in Genesis, as Reuben the elder brother.

## REUBEN: THE SELFLESS OLDER BROTHER

*When they saw him from a distance and before he came close to them, they plotted against him to put him to death. And they said to one another, "Here comes the dreamer! Now then, come and let us kill him and throw him into one of the pits; and we will say, 'A wild beast devoured him.' Then let us see what will become of his dreams!" But Reuben heard this and rescued him out of their hands and said, "Let us not take his life." Reuben further said to them, "Shed no blood. Throw him into this pit that is in the wilderness, but do not lay hands on him"—that he might rescue him out of their hands, to restore him to his father* (Genesis 37:18-22).

Reuben displays his true God given wisdom and selfless love in this story. He knew his angry brothers were too strong to fight off himself. So he says to them: "Let us not take his life." Reuben further said to them, "Shed no blood. Throw him into this pit that is in the wilderness, but do not lay hands on him." He had every intention of returning and rescuing Joseph, as the latter portion states. Reuben was very brave. His brothers could have killed him as well. But Reuben did not care. His unconditional love far outweighed his brothers' hate: *that he might rescue him out of their hands, to restore him to his father.* Reuben is called to the ministry of winning souls, healing, and mercy. The burden of restoration is the burden of every true Reubenite because that is the burden of true love. Love covers a multitude of sins.

*And it is he who will go as a forerunner before Him in the Spirit and power of Elijah, to turn the hearts of the fathers back to the children and the disobedient to the attitude of the righteous; so as to make ready a people prepared for God* (Luke 1:17).

God's ultimate desire is to bring restoration unto Himself. He longs to restore families, churches, communities, and nations. Yeshua is our elder brother, who has restored us to the Father. If you are a Reubenite, you are called to be a source of healing and hope to the destitute. In Genesis 37:29, when Reuben returned to the pit and Joseph wasn't there, he tore his clothes. Any lost soul will always break the heart of a Reuben. He will not rest until he can come up with a way to save him. This is the evangelistic gifting within Reuben. His heartbeat is always beating, *souls, souls, souls.*

## REUBEN'S SYMBOL OF THE MAN

Reuben, as mentioned previously, is a captain tribe. His symbol is the man. If any one of the tribes needs to identify that Yeshua sympathized with the human plight, it's Reuben. What a comfort to Reuben, that Yeshua bore your shame, guilt, sin, and hopelessness. He paid it all, so just surrender to His love, dear Reuben. He came as a man, lowly, a rejected elder brother to restore us to our Father God. Reuben demonstrates his regal sonship through his greatest act of selfless love.

*And their father Jacob said to them, "You have bereaved me of my children: Joseph is no more, and Simeon is no more, and you would take Benjamin: all these things are against me." Then Reuben spoke to his father, saying, "You may put my two sons to death if I do not bring him back to you"* (Genesis 42:36-37).

*"He who loves father or mother more than Me is not worthy of Me; and he who loves son or daughter more than Me is not worthy of Me"* (Matthew 10:37-38).

Reuben proved through this selfless act of love that he was worthy. Through his love he wins many souls to Yeshua by his own example of purity, perseverance through adversity, and passion for the presence of God. The song of Deborah in Judges 5:15-16 says: "Among the divisions of Reuben there were great resolves of heart…and there were great searchings of the heart." A mature Reubenite has the discernment to see heart motives. His own heart is strong because he has been transformed into a selfless lover of God and humanity.

## REUBEN RESTORED TO AUTHORITY

*As for the Hebronites, Jerijah the chief (these Hebronites were investigated according to their genealogies and fathers' households, in the fortieth year of David's reign, and men of outstanding capability among them were found at Jazer of Gilead). And his relatives, capable men, were 2,700 in number, heads of fathers' households. And King David made them overseers of the Reubenites, the Gadites, and the half-tribe of Manassites concerning all the affairs of God and of the king* (I Chronicles 26:31-32).

King David restored these two-and-a-half tribes. God had seen their sincere repentance and restored to them their God-given authority. The "men" in verse 31 refers to men who were from Gilead, some of whom were Reubenites called to leadership. God restored the destiny that Reuben had forfeited.

## DOMINION RESTORED THROUGH PASSIONATE LOVE

I implore you, Reuben, to fall madly in love with your Bridegroom King. Your God-given key to the kingdom and dominion is your passionate love. What the enemy has meant to ensnare you with, God chooses to use to redeem and restore you. Your passionate love of the Savior is the catalyst for the Body of Christ to be drawn into intimacy.

*May he kiss me with the kisses of his mouth! For your love is better than wine. Your oils have a pleasing fragrance, Your name is like purified oil; Therefore the maidens love you. Draw me after you and let us run together! The king has brought me into his chambers. We will rejoice and be glad; we will extol your love more than wine. Rightly do they love you* (Song of Solomon 1:2-4).

In Hebrew thought, a kiss is a revelation word from God. We often hear it referred to as a *rhema* word. God has instilled within every Reubenite a kiss for the Body. Reuben himself is a kiss to the Body. He is a living revelation and representation of God's love. Love is his very realm of authority and dominion. He is ever ready with a fresh word of love from the throne. *Draw me after you and let us run together.* Love is contagious. It has a trickle-down effect. Reuben starts running after the Beloved in great passion and many begin to follow. I encourage you to feed that holy passion within you. The deep mysteries of God's love are stored up in you and longing to be released upon the earth. Take time and come away with the Beloved. He is calling you to His banqueting table.

*He has brought me to his banquet hall, and his banner over me is love* (Song of Solomon 2:4).

Come into the banqueting house, O Reuben. The Father and the Beloved are waiting for you with arms outstretched. Come into the depths of the chambers of His heart. Reuben, He is the sun on your horizon. Look for His mercies with each new day. He has called you as a passionate lover to minister to Him and Him alone. Rejoice in this, for His banner over you is LOVE!

## PRAYER OF REPENTANCE AND DESTINY
## FOR THE TRIBE OF REUBEN

Thank You, Abba, for Your love for me. In Your great love and purpose for me You sent your firstborn son, Yeshua, to die for my sin. Through His death and resurrection I have obtained absolute victory over all my weaknesses. I not only have a hope of glory in You, my Beloved Yeshua, but in my destiny as well. By Your infinite mercy and boundless grace I seek Your face so that I may be transformed into the passionate and faithful lover I truly am. Release the seed of destiny within me planted by You, before I was in my mother's womb. Holy Spirit, water and nurture this seed. When weeds of apathy, lust, and idolatry begin to grow, lovingly uproot them. Your kindness leads me to repentance, so I repent of my self-seeking ways, lust, instability, and compromise. Through Your blood I am washed whiter than snow.

I have a new name and my mind is renewed. Fill the void within me. I have sought for love in all the wrong places. Fill me, God, with the knowledge of Your love, which knows no bounds for me. Show me who I am as the Father's priceless and treasured possession. I am a ruby of great price. I am the head and not the tail. You have made my life to be excellent and praiseworthy to carry Your renown. I look to You and see the sun on my horizon. It is a new day for me. With all my heart and soul I pray that You change me into a selfless servant to You and my fellow man. Draw me, and I will run after you as a faithful and surrendered lover. I love you my Savior, my God, and beloved Bridegroom. Prepare me for destiny. Transform me in Your glory and infinite wisdom. In Yeshua's name, Amen

---

[1] Arie Uittenbogaard, "Abarim Publications Biblical Name Vault,"

*Abarim Publications,* April 30, 2015. http://www.abarimpublications.com/Meaning/Reuben.html#.VZzo6_lVikq

[2] William Smith, *Smith's Bible Dictionary* (London, England; 1863), Public Domain.

[3] Benjamin W. Richardson M.A., M.D., F.R.S., *Ten Lectures On Alcohol* (New York, NY: National Temperance Society and Publication House, 1881) Public Domain, page 32.

# CHAPTER 3
## SIMEON: THE ZEALOUS HEARER

*He that hath an ear, let him hear what the Spirit saith unto the churches* (Revelation 2:7).

It is pivotal in the hour we are in for the Church to hear what the Spirit is saying. Hearing what the Father is saying aligns us with His Word and His kingdom. Hearing is both a tool for intimacy and warfare strategies. For if we will be still and hear the end-time plan of God, it will be revealed to us. We become positioned and transformed through what we hear. Hearing, therefore, is a catalyst for the Bride to prepare for Her Bridegroom.

## THE SH'MA

*Sh'ma Israel, Adonai Elohaynu, Adonai Echad! Barukh sheim K'vod malkhuto l'olam va'ed. V'ahav'ta eit Adonai Elohekha b'khol l'vav'kha uv'khol naf'sh'kha uv'khol m'odekha. V'hayu had'varim ha'eileh asher anokhi m'tzav'kha hayom al l'vavekha V'shinan'tam l'vanekha v'dibar'ta bam, b'shiv't'kh) a b'veitekha uv'lekh't'kha vaderekh uv'shakh'b'kha uv'kumekha, Uk'shar'tam l'ot al yadekha v'hayu l'totafot bein einekha. Ukh'tav'tam al m'zuzot beitekha uvish'arekha.*

The Sh'ma is the declaration the Jewish people recite to affirm their identity, calling, and, most of all, their marriage vow to the God of Israel. Translated from Hebrew it is taken from the following scripture:

*Hear, O Israel! The Lord is our God, the Lord is one! And you shall love the Lord your God with all your heart and with all your soul and with all your might* (Deuteronomy 6:4-5).

Yeshua also reiterates this commandment in Scripture:

*And one of the scribes came and heard them arguing, and recognizing that He answered them well, asked Him, "What commandment is the foremost of all?" Jesus answered, "The foremost is, 'HEAR, O ISRAEL! THE LORD OUR GOD IS ONE LORD; AND YOU SHALL LOVE THE LORD YOUR GOD WITH ALL YOUR HEART, AND WITH ALL YOUR SOUL, AND WITH ALL YOUR MIND, AND WITH ALL YOUR STRENGTH.' The second is this, 'YOU SHALL LOVE YOUR NEIGHBOR AS YOURSELF.' There is no other commandment greater than these"* (Mark 12:28-31).

Yeshua says in this verse that to love God is the foremost commandment. It is my sincere belief that if we kept this commandment, we would be able to keep all the other commandments. When God gave the law to Moses on Mount Sinai, He made the distinction of who He was, that He was the one true God, and that He was to be feared and reverenced as a holy God full of zealous love.

In Exodus 19:1-25 the nation of Israel had a profound encounter with God at Mount Sinai. Why did God single this precious people out from all other nations? He wanted to display His nature in and through a people. God is a zealous God. At the time of the Israelites' exodus from Egypt, there were many pagan gods in the earth. The Israelites themselves lived among the Egyptians, whose pagan practices and gods were more abominable than any other. The Father took His people Israel and delivered them from the oppression of their enemies and the influence of pagan gods. In Israel (the Jewish people and the land) He desired to hallow His name and reveal Himself as a zealous God. The Sh'ma was not just given to the Jewish people, it was given to all who would hear and thereby come to know the Holy One of Israel.

The sense of hearing was given to us to know God's voice and obey Him. Time and time again Israel would fall prey to harlotry because they neglected to hear and obey. The zealous love of God repeatedly chastised them to return to the holy marriage vow they made with Him upon Mount Sinai. The call to be a holy, set apart nation is no different for you and me today. Idols are like bedfellows. When we neglect to remain chaste, the zealous heart of God burns and is grieved because we neglect covenant. This is spiritual adultery, and repentance must be made. We must allow Him to shake off the golden calves of idolatry.

The gift of hearing and the zealous nature of God are intertwined. We can see this revealed to us through the tribe of Simeon. Simeon is a valuable part of the Body of Christ. Simeonites are the "ears" of the body. In the tribe of Simeon, God calls us to see His nature as zealous God, to hear Him and obey Him. Simeon's calling is to hear, discern, and provide wisdom through this gifting to the Body. His very name means "to hear."

## THE NAMING OF SIMEON

*Then she conceived again and bore a son and said, "Because the Lord has **heard** that I am unloved, He has therefore given me this son also." So she named him Simeon* (Genesis 29:33).

The bible mentions the words *hear* and *hearing* 550 times. If you did a word study on this subject, it would be an exhaustive one. If God mentions hearing so many times in His Word, it must be important to Him. Hearing God is all about intimacy. Hearing and wisdom are vital to us as believers. When we neglect to take time and hear the voice of God, we often find ourselves lonely, confused, despairing, and lost. If you want to be intimate with someone, you must first be a hearer. When one is idly prattling on, never taking time to listen, do you think they'd gain respect or be ignored? Yet how many times in our relationship with God do we come to him with our self-centered wish lists as if He's our Santa Claus? How many times do we truly come just to adore Him, be still, and hang on His every word? The Father longs for selfless passionate hearers. We can find this within every heart of a mature Simeonite.

The ear is a sensitive instrument of the body. This member is vital for our wellbeing. Through it comes truth or lies. Simeon's calling to hear can serve both as his strength and his facade. The gift of hearing takes time, patience, and persistence, but most importantly, it takes a teachable spirit to be developed. When we were children, it took time for us to learn not only to speak the language but to comprehend its meaning. When we first came to God, did we automatically understand the oracles of God? No, it takes a lifetime of learning to become still and know the voice of God.

One thing you learn of Simeon is that being still is contrary to his self-nature. Every Simeonite goes through the school of hard knocks. He learns through suffering. Sometimes suffering is brought on by disobedience. Other times suffering comes by the hands of those who try to break our spirit and wound us. If you are a Simeon, you know God has molded and always will mold you through His fire. Simeon is like a wild stallion that God has to break and tame. A Simeonite's spirit is very fiery, independent, and strong-willed. God's desire is to mold every Simeon into a peaceful and zealous hearer. Simeon has no trouble being passionate or zealous. This passionate, zealous nature can easily be turned into a jealous, critical, and even cruel nature. The quiet nature of Simeon is fashioned through much fire, suffering, and breaking.

## BECOMING A BONDSERVANT:
## HOW TO DEVELOP THE GIFT OF HEARING

Read Deuteronomy 15:12-17. There is a vast difference between a slave and a bondservant. A slave is connected to duty only. After serving his or her six years, the slave was released in the seventh year. Drastically different, the bondservant gives the faithful devotion to serve his whole life. The bondservant's ear is nailed to the door. Hearing God begins with a crucifixion of our wills. When we surrender our will, we then joyously obey upon hearing the Lord's voice. A true Simeon must nail his ears to the Cross.

> *And Mary said, 'Behold, the bondslave of the Lord; be it done to me according to Your word.' And the angel departed from her* (Luke 1:38).

Mary's heart was that of a bondservant. Her heart was willing to conform to the will of the Father. Her life was poured out before the Lord in sincere, pure worship because of her obedience to the word of the Lord. Our lives must also be poured out in obedient worship to the Father. Mary knew that the principle of hearing was tied to intimacy. Because of her childlike faith to hear, she obeyed. One bondservant's simple obedience wrought the SAVIOR OF THE WORLD!

Becoming a bondservant of the Lord is a process of dying to self, coupled with an unrelenting faith. Bondservants don't doubt their Master. They lay down their lives to serve and obey out of love. A true bondservant is truly a laid-down lover of God who, in the relinquishment of his or her own will and upon hearing, obeys the Lord. This is pivotal to the fear of the Lord. If we don't hear and obey the Lord, then we don't truly fear Him. We are either building our own kingdom, living in fear, or being persuaded by another voice. For the tribe of Simeon to come into dominion, they must be transformed. A Simeonite in immaturity can be like one who may obey out of an unyielded, disgruntled slave mindset, wishing to do things his own way. The Lord does not accept insincere obedience born out of appeasement. A bondservant is one who joyfully lays down his or her own life for their master. A true bond slave relinquishes all rights. He has no control. When you give up your "control," you in essence are vulnerable and willing, laying your life before the throne. With this surrender you must let go of your own agenda, ideals, your right to be right, and judgments.

> *And the Lord's bondservant must not be quarrelsome, but be kind to all, able to teach, patient when wronged, with gentleness correcting those in opposition, if perhaps God might grant them repentance leading to the knowledge of the truth, and they may come into their senses and escape the snare of the devil, having been held captive by him to do his will* (II Timothy 2:24-26).

A contentious and quarrelsome spirit is not only contrary to being a bondslave, it fights against the Spirit of God. Take heed, dear Simeonite, that you are not fighting against the Spirit of God. A yielded and contrite spirit the Lord will not despise. Simeon, a most valuable place of authority lies in your ability to be the bondslave of Christ, surrendered, hearing, and obedient. For in your surrender, you possess the ability to hear the sound waves of Heaven. You will pick up on frequencies most are unable to discern. Your true authority lies in your surrender; the greater your surrender, the greater your ability to hear and be transformed into a bondslave for the Master's use.

To be reluctant to hear and obey the voice of God is to be a slave—a slave to sin. A zealous lover of God will immediately, upon hearing the voice of God, obey and do the will of God. For Simeon, this is the key to identity and intimacy. An impetuous slave is foolishly defiant. He is like a child who is told to sit down, but when he does, in his heart he is standing up. The mark of maturity for every Simeonite is when he transforms from reluctant hearer, drenched in his strong-willed nature, into a zealous lover, quick to hear and ready to lay down his life for Christ.

> *Act as free men, and do not use your freedom as a covering for evil but use it as*
> *bondslaves of God* (I Peter 2:16).

## THE VALUE OF BEING STILL

The value of being still is essential to every believer, but it is paramount for the tribe of Simeon. The Lord speaks into stillness. Where there is chaos, a multitude of opinions, or a clamor of spirits, His voice is either dull or drowned completely out. To entertain any of these, or even the busyness of life, will cause you, dear brother, to forego dominion. In the stillness God speaks fathoms of wisdom, revelation, prophecy, direction, and strategies.

> *Stand in awe, and sin not: commune with your own heart upon your bed, and be still.*
> *Selah* (Psalm 4:4 KJV).

### "STAND IN AWE"

Abba is calling you, Simeon, to stand in awe of Him. He wants to reveal Himself to you. An appointment with the Lord awaits those who take time to worship, to fathom His endless mercies and loving-kindness, and to see His glory.

### "SIN NOT"

Sin leads us out of the secret place. A rebellious spirit is not still, for it strives to do its own will. Refrain from sin and allow yourself to come into the wealth of a still, sacred place with the Lord.

### "COMMUNE WITH YOUR OWN HEART UPON YOUR BED, AND BE STILL"

The greatest place of authority comes from a place of rest. Yeshua knew this well, as he would often steal away to meet with the Father and replenish his soul. Yeshua is the Sabbath rest. As you commune with Him and become still, He will reveal His glory. The children of Israel neglected to come into the rest of the Lord. Take their plight as a word of warning. You must know Yeshua as the Lord of the Sabbath in order to come into true dominion. From a still, secret place, you will hear your Father's heart.

Read Hebrews 3:7-19 and Hebrews 4:1-11. Not entering into the rest of the Lord is disobedience. Before the fall, Adam and Eve lived in the rest of the Lord. The rest of the Lord is meant to be our portion. It is the fallen human nature that is contrary—even rebellious—to the call of rest. It is human nature to strive and wrestle. It is God's nature to rest, hear, and obey.

> *Be still, and know that I am God: I will be exalted among the heathen, I will be exalted*
> *in the earth* (Psalm 46:10).

Being still before God is a primary prerequisite to the glory of God. The Lord has endowed the tribe of Simeon to cry out for knowledge. They do this by becoming still and taming fleshly desires. Truly exalting Yeshua begins with our decision to die to self. As we embrace the Cross, we embrace the still small voice of God where He thunders.

## THE GEMSTONE OF SIMEON

The gemstone of Simeon is the topaz or chrysolite. The topaz ranges from a deep golden color, almost like amber, to a blue color. Simeon's stone in particular is the yellow topaz. It is known for its hardness. Simeon's character can also be very hard, and he is very stubborn, strong-willed in a way that can lead to rebellion. He must rely on the Holy Spirit to deal with this nature and soften him. His nature is also very critical if not tamed by the Spirit. When a Simeonite relies on his hearing, his God-given tool of intimacy, he surrenders his harsh, rebellious nature in sincere repentance. The color of the stone, golden yellow, speaks of wisdom, light, and truth, all which are necessary for truly hearing God. Wisdom requires not only hearing but also obedience.

> *The wise in heart will accept and obey commandments, but the foolishness of lips will fall headlong* (Proverbs 10:8).

It is wisdom to hear and obey the Word of God, for from the Word we receive knowledge of how to live a holy life. Direction is afforded to all who heed wisdom. Engaging in foolishness, especially in our speech, is a snowball which will turn into a devastating avalanche. Take heed, Simeon, not to sow words of foolishness but to sow words of wisdom that are aligned with the Word of God.

> *Whoever loves instruction and correction loves knowledge, but he who hates reproof is like a brute beast, stupid, and indiscriminating* (Proverbs 12:1).

The way of wisdom enlightens our path. Not to heed wisdom, to oppose it, will bring deep depravity of soul and spirit. Wisdom is one of your greatest weapons, Simeon. Do not despise the chastening of the Lord and become like a brute beast. Kicking against the goads will just keep you enslaved to a life of rebellion. Satan's scheme is to keep you disconnected from the voice of the Lord, either by you entertaining your own voice drenched in self-will or by you listening to the enemy's voice. Heed wisdom and live. Every answer you need is found in His Word. Quiet your inner man. Let it become disciplined by the Spirit and heed where He might lead you. Blessing, favor, and destiny await all those who heed wisdom.

> *The topaz of Ethiopia cannot equal it, Nor can it be valued in pure gold. Where then does wisdom come from? And where is the place of understanding?* (Job 28:19).

You are a beautiful topaz, whose worth and beauty cannot be equaled. In your gemstone we see the spirit of wisdom, understanding, and knowledge. It is important for you, brother and sister Simeonite, to be schooled by the Holy Spirit, the voice of wisdom. He is your best friend. The Spirit will bring refinement as you heed the wisdom afforded to you. As you walk in the way of wisdom, your true life's calling and destiny will unfold for you.

If you are from this tribe, allow God's love to melt away that hardness in your heart. Hardness can come through suffering, either by the wrongs of others or by our own sin. God wants to restore the fullness of sonship, and He does it through your surrender and by your heeding wisdom. Be a pliable topaz in the hand of God. Submit to His refinement and reproof, for it is life. You carry one of the most valuable tools to the Body—wisdom. The Body needs your wisdom, for without it we perish. You are an important tool that fashions God's perfection in others.

## THE SYMBOLS

Simeon has three symbols: the earthen pitcher, the sword, and the city gates.

### THE EARTHEN PITCHER

*But we have this treasure in earthen vessels, that the surpassing greatness of power may be of God and not of ourselves* (II Corinthians 4:7).

God has called His people to be vessels of honor. He is prophetically speaking many things with this symbol. A pitcher is a vessel or container which holds a substance. What substance do we hold within us? The Holy Spirit lives and dwells in each of us. For the tribe of Simeon, this has a special meaning. They are vessels filled with the anointing of God. They are especially called to revival; in fact, they are carriers of revival. Simeon's zealous passion is a torch by which revival fires ignite. They fan the flames of cold and distant love in the lost and in lukewarm believers. You can never accuse a mature Simeon's love of being cold. He is red hot and burning with the Spirit of God. Simeonites are workers of miracles, soul-winners, and prophetic voices in times of revival. They "hear" what the Father is doing and gladly join Him.

The pitcher also speaks of Simeon's human nature. God wanted to remind Simeon that he came from dust, that he is only clay. God must always be your potter, Simeon. Stay on His wheel until He's done with you. Don't jump off and follow every wild tangent your will desires. If you allow Him to perfect you, His glory will surely fill you. He will then take you and pour you out into lives that have been broken like you. Though you may go through the fire, you will always come forth as pure gold.

### THE SWORD

*…and ye shall chase your enemies, and they shall fall before you by the sword* (Leviticus 26:7 KJV).

Simeon is a warrior, a born fighter who lives to devour his enemy. He is quick to draw his sword and run to the battle. He does not weigh the cost or the immensity of the battle. Simeon is propelled by his warlike nature.

*Happy art thou, O Israel: who is like unto thee, O people saved by the Lord, the shield of thy help, and who is the sword of thy excellency and thine enemies shall be found liars unto thee; and thou shalt tread upon their high places* (Deuteronomy 33:29 KJV).

God is calling the tribe of Simeon to the war council room of Heaven. Upon the table are laid intricate plans of battle. Those who sit at this table have surrendered their lives even unto death. With their mighty swords they destroy facades and tear down strongholds in high places. The Lord has assured victory to the tribe of Simeon as they wage war against darkness.

He has gifted you with a sword of excellence. What does having a sword of excellence mean? It means to fight as the Spirit would lead you. We can only engage in war where God's Word and wisdom lead us. To engage in our own strength or by our carnal means can reap great havoc in the kingdom of God. Simeon must become a disciple first in order to fight with the sword of excellence. His over-eager character can lead to trouble when He neglects the inner voice of God. The sword is both his folly and his strength.

*For my sword shall be bathed in heaven: behold, it shall come down upon Idumea, and upon the people of my curse, to judgment* (Isaiah 34:5 KJV).

Simeon, when your sword is bathed in Heaven, you are unstoppable. This verse is particularly deep in meaning. Idumea and the people under a curse refers to Edom; the descendants of Esau. Esau sold his birthright, cursing him and descendants to a life of striving against God and carnality. Esau (and his descendants) forfeited the most valuable thing we could possess—sonship.

> *…as it is written, Jacob have I loved, but Esau have I hated* (Romans 9:13 KJV)

> *…lest there be any fornicator, or profane person, as Esau, who for one morsel of meat sold his birthright* (Hebrews 12:16 KJV).

Take care, dear Simeon, which sword you pick up: the sword of the Lord, bathed in heavenly glory, or the sword of the flesh, dipped in the works of flesh.

> *For we wrestle not against flesh and blood, but against principalities, against powers, against the rulers of the darkness of this world, against spiritual wickedness in high places* (Ephesians 6:12).

The sword also symbolizes Simeon's need to rightly divide the Word of truth. When Simeon relies on the Word of God, he can discern between both flesh and Spirit in his life as well as others.

> *…and take the helmet of salvation, and the sword of the Spirit, which is the word of God* (Ephesians 6:17).

> *…for the word of God is quick, and powerful, and sharper than any two-edged sword, piercing even to the dividing asunder of soul and spirit, and of the joints and marrow, and is a discerner of the thoughts and intents of the heart* (Hebrew 4:12).

## THE SWORD OF THE LORD: A WEAPON OF END-TIME JUDGMENT

> *For by fire and by his sword will the Lord plead with all flesh: and the slain of the Lord shall be many* (Isaiah 66:16 KJV).

In these end-times it is important that our lives remain chaste. As we allow the sword of the Lord to rightly divide the word of truth, the enemy will have no foothold in us. God's holy Word will arise in this hour to divide between wheat or tare, sheep or goat. Lukewarm lovers will fall by the droves. To those who are humble and of a contrite spirit, the Lord will entrust His sword. You, Simeon, are a mighty company of warriors to wield the sword of the Lord. Seek first the kingdom of God and His righteousness—this must be your battle cry. The fear of the Lord must take the foreground of your heart. Do not entertain the spirit of the world or carnal means of justice. If you do so, you will be found fighting against the Lord. No one wants to be found at the end of the sword of the Lord when judgment comes. *The slain of the Lord will be many* (Isaiah 66:16). Those who have not heeded wisdom and lived a chaste life for the Lord will be found wanting in the balance. Render your heart, dear Simeon, and the Lord will reward with His heavenly sword.

> *Think not that I am come to send peace on earth: I came not to send peace, but a sword* (Matthew 10:34 KJV).

The Lord will bring division to every profane thing. His Word will draw the dividing line in the sand. We must choose now with whom to align ourselves.

## THE CITY GATES

This symbol exemplifies one of Simeon's most tragic downfalls. Read Genesis 34:1-31. Simeon and Levi took revenge into their own hands. Notice this scripture does not state that they sought God. Verse 7 says they were grieved and very angry. Simeon and Levi had a just reason to be angry. What happened to Dinah was a devastating blow to their family. One thing to learn of Simeon and Levi is that they both deeply feel love and pain. When they see someone hurting, it grieves them. They will take on that pain and carry it, so much so that they can make it into a cause. Where Simeon and Levi went wrong is they didn't give this situation over to God. They allowed their quick tempers to rule them and took matters into their own hands. Whenever you try to "help" God out and He didn't call you to action, you will always end up in a mess. What do you allow in your gates: the King of glory, or anger, unforgiveness, pride, etc.?

> *Lift up your heads, O ye gates; and be ye lift up, ye everlasting doors; and the King of glory shall come in* (Psalm 24:7 KJV).

O Simeon, allow the King of glory into your gates. Lift up the eyes of your heart, the very gate of your soul; let the radiant splendor of the King of Kings and the Lord transform you from the inside out. No flesh can glory in His presence. Leave your cares, impetuous nature, jealousy, and striving on the outside of the gate. You alone have the authority over what comes in and out of your gates. You should be watchful over both the eye and the ear gates. Brethren, quickly uproot the profane guile of the flesh from your gates. Embrace love, truth, and mercy. If you want a true visitation of the King of glory, surrender your will in sincerest brokenness, and He will come in all His glory. He wants to reveal His glory to you.

> *Enter into his gates with thanksgiving, and into his courts with praise: be thankful unto him, and bless his name* (Psalm 100:4 KJV).

When Simeon comes into the gates of the Lord with thanksgiving, he has already assured victory for himself. Praise is an atmosphere breeder. In the atmosphere of praise, Simeon will excel when surrendered.

> *Open to me the gates of righteousness: I will go into them, and I will praise the Lord.* (Psalm 118:19 KJV).

The gates of righteousness are open to all who hunger and thirst after righteousness. Simeon finds his place of dominion within the gates of righteousness, for he is not only a hearer of the Word, but also an effectual doer of the Word.

## JACOB'S PROPHECY

> *"Simeon and Levi are brothers; their swords are implements of violence. Let my soul not enter into their council; let not my glory be united with their assembly; because in their anger they slew men, And in their self-will they lamed oxen. Cursed be their anger, for it is fierce; And their wrath, for it is cruel. I will disperse them in Jacob, and scatter them in Israel* (Genesis 49:5-7).

Jacob's prophecy was directly referring to the incident at Shechem. When Jacob refers to them as brothers, he's not referring to them in the natural; he's referring to their sin. They were "brothers" or "united" in the spirit of anger and murder. The King James Version says: "instruments of cruelty are in their habitations." We mustn't allow unclean spirits to dwell in our habitations. We are the temples of the living God. Anger, wrath, unforgiveness, murder, judgment and cruelty had taken up habitation within the temples of Simeon and Levi. Jacob cursed these strongholds in Simeon and Levi when he said, "cursed be their anger." If you belong to either one of these tribes, you must be careful not to let the sun go down on your anger. Repentance will draw you back into the habitation or dwelling of God. Anger and unforgiveness drive you away because they have no place in perfect love.

Jacob had to separate these two tribes. He spiritually discerned that when they were united in that sin, they would easily be drawn into all kinds of mischief. God separated them in the placement of the tabernacle and also in the allotment of cities. Simeon's inheritance was with the tribe of Judah. There are some people in ministry that God in His foreknowledge separates. He foresaw the familiar spirits that would cause these two tribes to go astray. Simeon and Levi both have powerful anointing and callings, but together they bring each other down. Moses does not prophesy over Simeon in Deuteronomy Chapter 33. The Word does not directly explain why either. To understand why you must look at what was spiritually taking place in the tribe of Simeon at that time.

Read Numbers 25:1-16. Zimri's (a Simeonite) sin was so appalling in that he had the gall to continue in his idolatry after God devastated Israel with a plague that killed 24,000 people. He showed no fear of God. His rebellion was so blatantly defiant against God. The Word makes God's feelings clear toward rebellion and idolatry.

> *For rebellion is as the sin of witchcraft, and stubbornness is as iniquity and idolatry* (I Samuel 15:23 KJV).

God's call to Simeon is to be his bondslave. When he is in loving obedience to the Father, his gift of hearing draws him into the throne room. Simeon is in grave danger when his spiritual ears aren't nailed to the Master's door. He eagerly indulges in rebellion through his strong will that leads him into witchcraft.

Countless times I have witnessed Simeonites who are dominated by witchcraft, divination, and deaf and dumb spirits—all stemming from rebellion. When we insist on manipulating circumstances and people to achieve our desires, we fall prey to all kinds of demonic activity. If you are dwelling in darkness, your ability to hear from God will either be distorted or nonexistent. This is a truly devastating blow for the destiny of Simeon. Your zeal and passionate love of God will also diminish when rebellion rules your heart. Deception will masquerade itself as the voice of God. Some may truly believe that they are hearing from God, when in truth they are entertaining their own flesh. When this occurs, a deaf and dumb spirit arises, coupled with divination, as these spirits take dominion.

Read Acts 16:16-18. With the spirits of divination and deaf and dumb spirits also comes a mocking spirit. The tone of this girl's proclamation is thick with a mocking spirit. The spirits of divination, mockery, and lying are some of the most guile in nature. They point also to witchcraft. Pride is often the root of these spirits. Zimri's pride and divination is what ultimately killed him. Divination is when you divine something. In other words, you set yourself up as an authority independent of God's authority. The Father is looking for a people whose spiritual senses are fine tuned to His voice. We must be expectant to hear, know, and beat as one with our Father's heart. As His children, we must be in tune to know the patterns and rhythms of His heartbeat. This is the call to every true Simeonite. Repentance will bring you back into intimacy and freedom in Christ.

## REPENTANCE BRINGS RESTORATION
## OF DESTINY FOR SIMEON

Simeon's journey of transformation began with suffering.

*And he turned away from them and wept. But when he returned to them and spoke to
them, he took Simeon from them and bound him before their eyes* (Genesis 42:24).

Simeon was Jacob's second eldest son. For him to be shackled before his younger siblings
was probably quite humbling. Why would Joseph choose to imprison him? In all likelihood
he was a ringleader of Joseph's demise many years prior. Joseph in his wisdom was testing
Simeon, to see if he had any true remorseful repentance. This "test" was to determine
whether or not Simeon had acknowledged his zealous nature, which had grown to full-
blown jealousy and cruelty. God was looking to see if Simeon would crucify this old nature.
The Father desired to fashion or transform him from an instrument of cruelty to one of
peace, humility, and ultimately, zealous love. It was in that prison cell that I believe a radical
transformation of the soul took place within Simeon. The ugly truth of his rebellious,
jealous, and cruel nature had come full circle. He knew his sentence was deserved. It was
there he called out to God. It was there that he was still and quiet and could "hear" his God
speak to him. Unfortunately, it often takes the school of hard knocks for not only
Simeonites but all of us to hear God. Simeon came to the end of himself, acknowledged his
sin (repented), and walked into his destiny.

The lost books of the Bible contain the testimonies of each one of the sons of
Jacob. While I cannot conclude these testimonies are the infallible word of God, I do believe
that they can confirm the character (and its flaws) within each tribe. They are helpful in
understanding the gifts, facades, and even sometimes the heart of each son of Jacob.

### THIS IS THE TESTIMONY OF SIMEON: [1]

Simeon, the second son of Jacob and Leah. He becomes jealous of Joseph
and is an instigator of the plot against Joseph. These are the words of
Simeon, the things which he spoke to his sons before he died, in the
hundred and twentieth year of his life, at which time Joseph, his brother,
died. 2 For when Simeon was sick, his sons came to visit him. And he
strengthened himself and sat up and kissed them, and said: 3 **Hearken**, my
children, to Simeon your father and I will declare unto you what things I
have in my heart. 4 I was born of Jacob as my father's second son; and my
mother Leah called me Simeon, because God had **heard** her prayer. 5
Moreover, I became strong exceedingly; I shrank from no achievement nor
was I afraid of ought. For my heart was hard, and my liver was immovable,
and my bowels without compassion. 6 Because valor also has been given
from the Most High to men in soul and body. 7 For in the time of my
youth I was jealous in many things of Joseph, because my father loved him
beyond all. 8 And I set my mind against him to destroy him because the
prince of deceit sent forth the spirit of jealousy and blinded my mind, so
that I regarded him not as a brother, nor did I spare even Jacob my father. 9
But his God and God of his father's sent forth His angel, and delivered him
out of my hands. 10 For when I went to Shechem to bring ointment for the
flocks, and Reuben to Dothan, where our necessaries and all our stores,
Judah my brother sold him to the Ishmaelites. 11 And when Reuben heard
these things he was grieved, for he wished to restore him to his father. 12
But on hearing this I was exceedingly wroth against Judah in that he let him

go away alive, and for five months I continued wrathful against him. 13 But God restrained me, and withheld from me the power of my hands; for my right hand was half withered for seven days. 14 And I knew, my children, that because of Joseph this had befallen me, and I repented and wept; and I besought GOD that my hand might be restored and that I might hold aloof from all pollution and envy and from all folly. 15 For I knew that I had devised an evil thing before God and Jacob my father, on account of Joseph my brother, in that I envied him. 16 And now, my children, hearken unto me and beware of the spirit of deceit and envy. 17 For envy ruleth over the whole mind of a man, and suffereth him neither to eat nor to drink, nor to do any good thing. But it ever suggesteth to him to destroy him that he envieth; and so long as he that is envied flourisheth, he that envieth fadeth away. 18 Two years therefore I afflicted my soul with fasting in the fear of God, and I learnt that deliverance from envy cometh by the fear of the Lord. 19 For if a man flee to God, the evil spirit runneth away from him and his mind is lightened. 20 And henceforward he sympathiseth with him whom he envied and forgiveth those who are hostile to him, and so ceaseth from his envy.

In Simeon's testimony he deeply repented for his jealous and cruel nature. Repentance will always unleash destiny. Rebellion, jealousy, and self-centeredness will tie God's hands from moving in our lives. A broken and contrite spirit He will not despise. He gives His grace to the humble, but resists the proud.

## SIMEON IN TIMES OF REVIVAL

*And when Asa heard these words, and the prophecy of Oded the prophet, he took courage, and put away the abominable idols out of all the land of Judah and Benjamin, and out of the cities which he had taken from mount Ephraim, and renewed the altar of the Lord, that was before the porch of the Lord. And he gathered all Judah and Benjamin, and the strangers with them out of Ephraim and Manasseh, and out of* **Simeon***: for they fell to him out of Israel in abundance, when they saw that the Lord his God was with him* (II Chronicles 15:8-9 KJV).

*And they break down the altars of Baalim in his presence; and the images, that were on high above them, he cut down; and the groves, and the carved images, and the molten images, he brake in pieces, and made dust of them, and strewed it upon the graves of them that had sacrificed unto them. And he burnt the bones of the priests upon their altars, and cleansed Judah and Jerusalem. And so did he in the cities of Manasseh, and Ephraim, and Simeon, even unto Naphtali, with their mattocks round about* (II Chronicles 34:4-6 KJV).

True revival consists of sincere repentance, which involves tearing down high places and altars we have exalted in our lives. I believe the tribe of Simeon inherited a seed of righteousness from their father Simeon, stemming from his transformation in prison while in Egypt. Simeonites gifted with innate ability to hear God will always be among the first in a mass call for revival. A true passionate hearer of God will always hear the Holy Spirit calling His people to intimacy and holiness.

*Therefore repent and return, so that your sins may be wiped away, in order that times of refreshing may come from the presence of the Lord* (Acts 3:19).

Repentance not only unlocks your hearing, dear Simeon, but releases revival! You are passionate carriers of the flame coming to and from the throne room of Heaven to the earth to light the hearts of man ablaze for the Father's glory. The New Testament has evidence of this as well.

Read Luke 2:25-33. Whether or not this Simeon belonged to the actual tribe or was just a namesake is not known. I personally believe that he was from this tribe. Whatever the belief, the spiritual picture painted here in Scripture is clear and holds vital insight for not only the tribe of Simeon but for all believers. We are defined by our God-given names, and in this text he demonstrated his namesake by accurately hearing in the spirit that his Messiah had finally come. Not only did he recognize Yeshua, but he also accurately prophesied Messiah's ministry by saying, "A LIGHT OF REVELATION TO THE GENTILES, and the glory of Thy people Israel."

This is the true prophetic evangelistic call of every Simeonite. They herald the kingship of Messiah Yeshua wherever they can. Simeonites are gifted in "publishing the good news" and are sensitive to the moving of the Spirit where soul-winning, miracles, and deliverances are concerned. The passionate zeal for souls, infectious love for God, and their keen sense of spiritual hearing enables them in this calling as prophetic evangelists. No one better demonstrated this than Simeon Peter.

There was no disciple or apostle more colorful or zealous than Peter. While the Bible doesn't directly state that he is from the tribe of Simeon, its internal indications are undeniable. Known for his fiery character and quick impetuous nature, he clearly defines a true Simeonite. His life and ministry illustrated this. In the book of Matthew 4 we find him eagerly following God. It's more than eagerness; it is zeal that defined him time and again for better or worse. His zeal is even better displayed in the following scriptures:

> …and when the disciples saw Him walking on the sea, they were frightened, saying, "It is a ghost!" And they cried out for fear. But immediately Jesus spoke to them, saying, "It is I; do not be afraid." And Peter answered Him and said, "Lord, if it is you, command me to come to you on the water." And He said, "Come!" And Peter got out of the boat, and walked on the water and came toward Jesus (Matthew 14:26-31).

What *chutzpah* (Yiddish word, meaning "nerve")! Notice Peter responded to Yeshua by His command. He responded with his God-given gift of hearing. The other disciples were probably thinking: "He's *mashugana* (crazy, nuts)! What is Peter thinking? There's no way I'm getting out of this boat." A brazen fearlessness is one of the most endearing (sometimes frustrating) qualities Simeonites possess. The next verses also demonstrate a Simeonite's nature as well.

> But seeing the wind, he became afraid, and beginning to sink, he cried out, saying, "Lord, save me!" (Matthew 14:30).

Though Peter was most often times fearless, he inwardly struggled with insecurities within his faith. He, like many of his tribe, had the gumption but needed to become focused on the Savior. It is neither one's ability, nor the hype of the moment, but on seeing and hearing the Master, whatever stormy sea he or she is walking on. This is wisdom for all of us, to have the Savior in view always and listen for that still small voice, no matter what stage in life we are in.

Peter's zealous love and keen sensitivity was evident by his relationship with God. Read Matthew 16:13-19. Peter, like Simeon in the temple, recognized Yeshua as Messiah. How did Peter know Yeshua was the Messiah, the Son of God? He heard the Father, which came from knowing him intimately, just as Yeshua taught him. Peter, a passionate hearer, knew by experience that Yeshua is Lord. That is how every true Simeonite knows Him.

Peter's frailties were no different than any other Simeonite. His quick-tempered nature often got the better of him.

> *Simeon Peter therefore having a sword, drew it, and struck the high priests slave, and cut off his right ear; and the slave's name was Malchus. Jesus therefore said to Peter, "Put the sword into the sheath; the cup which the Father has given Me, shall I not drink it?* (John 18:10-11).

How well the impetuous nature of Simeonite is displayed. Peter cut off the slave's ear, the very thing Peter is called to be in the Body. So what does this story tell us? Peter's ears had grown dull of hearing. His sensitivity (as well as the other disciples') had grown faint during Yeshua's greatest hour of need. He needed the disciples to be sensitive to the Spirit. That is why he said in Luke 22:46: *Why are you sleeping? Rise and pray that you might not enter into temptation.*

Yeshua spoke volumes when he made this comment. Why are you sleeping? He is saying this to the Church today. Why are you sleeping? If our spiritual senses are dormant, we open ourselves to all kinds of temptation and unnecessary warfare. It might be possible that if Peter had been alert and had his ears fine-tuned to the throne, he might not have denied Yeshua. It is somewhat comical Peter used a sword, the very symbol of Simeon. His spiritual sense of hearing was sleeping in the garden.

Peter went on to become one of the most influential disciples in the early church. Three thousand souls came to Yeshua from his first sermon alone. He went on winning many souls, healing the sick, delivering the afflicted, and performing many signs and wonders in the name of Yeshua. Peter's ministry fully embodied the calling of every Simeon.

## SIMEON PROSPERS UNDER THE GUIDANCE OF JUDAH

The tribe of Judah often motivated and provided guidance for many of the tribes. Simeon is one of them. They eventually were absorbed into Judah and shared an inheritance with them.

> *And all the villages that were round about these cities to Baalathbeer, Ramath of the south. This is the inheritance of the tribe of the children of Simeon according to their families. Out of the portion of the children of Judah was the inheritance of the children of Simeon: for the part of the children of Judah was too much for them: therefore the children of Simeon had their inheritance within the inheritance of them* (Joshua 19:8-9 KJV).

When Simeon was absorbed into the tribe of Judah, they did not lose their identity. They still functioned as a tribe by the whole but were aided by Judah's encouragement and resources. Together in battle, Judah and Simeon were invincible.

Read Judges 1:3-4, Under the guidance of praise (Judah), Simeon was restored. They were referred to by King David as "men of valor," as they often fought for him. When the "ears" of the Body link up with the government of praise (Judah), their hearing comes in sync with the harmonies of Heaven. They are to discern the Spirit's call to intimacy, repentance, and the cry for souls. Dear Simeon, it is my earnest prayer that as you join the government of praise, you are released into your destiny as the zealous hearer of God, whom we, the Body of Christ, so desperately need. Keep your ears nailed the doorpost of the heart of Yeshua. For when the Savior comes knocking, you'll surely hear His voice, calling you unto Himself.

> *As many as I love, I rebuke and chasten: be zealous therefore, and repent. Behold, I stand at the door, and knock: if any man hears my voice, and opens the door, I will come in to him, and will sup with him, and he with me* (Revelation 3:19-20 KJV).

Dearest Simeon, your zealous Bridegroom King is knocking upon the door of your heart. His eyes are full of fire and His heart burning with holy jealousy for you to become a chaste, wise virgin ready for His return. Do not be foolish and miss your appointment with the King. *Knock, knock, knock*…does not your spirit leap upon hearing the Master call? *Knock, knock, knock*…the end is near. Will your hear? *Knock, knock, knock*…How will you answer Him?

## KEYS TO THE KINGDOM RELEASED BY HEARING

The Father is longing to release Simeon into the fullness of his destiny and dominion. He chooses to release this by Simeon coming to Him as a humble and zealous hearer. Dear Simeon, there are secrets of the Father's heart that He has called you to release in the earth. Your keys to the kingdom lie within your God- given tool for intimacy, your spiritual ears. There are sound frequencies of both Heaven and hell that only your fine-tuned ears can discern. You are a valuable and priceless treasure to the Father and the Body of Christ.

> *Put me like a seal over your heart, like a seal over your arm. For love is as strong as death, jealousy is as severe as Sheol; Its flashes are flashes of fire, the very flame of God. Many waters cannot quench love, nor will rivers overflow it; If a man were to give all the riches of his house for love it would be utterly despised* (Song of Solomon 8:6-7).

Bind yourself, Simeon, to your Bridegroom King. He is a zealous lover. His love was so zealous for us that He gave His own life. Not even Sheol could keep Him. He has given you the keys to the kingdom and true dominion through your ability to hear. Cling to the lover of your soul and savor His every word of passionate and zealous love for you.

## PRAYER OF REPENTANCE AND DESTINY
## FOR THE TRIBE OF SIMEON

Dear Lord, my Bridegroom King, I come before You to lie at your feet and incline my ears to Your every word. Your Word is life and love, likened unto a two-edged sword that divides between flesh and spirit within me. Gracious King and Lover, may my ears be forever nailed to your heart's door. Father, open my ears. I want to hear what You are saying. I repent of all stubbornness, jealousy, cruelty, and rebellion that has muffled and even, at times, deafened my hearing. Make me an instrument of peace. May your glory permeate my habitation in You. Forever change me, Lord. As I leave the prison walls of my hatred and bitterness behind, I focus on your loveliness. Your beauty has raptured my heart. You are my jealous lover.

Holy Spirit, stir the flame of first love. May apathy never extinguish its holy flame. Set me ablaze to be an all-consuming wildfire who melts the hardest of hearts and draws the prodigals back to You. Stir up, Holy Spirit, the gifts of healing, signs, and wonders. Most of all, refine me into a sharp sword in King Yeshua's hand, invading the darkness. Break and mold this vessel of honor. Place me on Your wheel, Creator. You have fashioned me with a specific destiny hidden in the depths of Your heart. Father, help me to be patient as You fashion me in Your likeness. When I grow impetuous, draw me with cords of love, casting out my idolatry and fear. Then I ask You to fill the void in me. I surrender my vessel for You to fill. Would You then pour me out as a drink offering for Your service? In Your precious name, Yeshua, I pray, Amen.

---

[1] Rutherford H. Platt, Jr. (Edited by), *The Forgotten Books Of Eden,* (New York, N.Y.: Alpha House, 1926), Pages 224-225.

# CHAPTER 4
# LEVI: THE PRIESTLY BRIDE

The Father created mankind for one purpose alone: intimacy. The heart of our Father and our heavenly Bridegroom is to have a people separated unto Him for the sole purpose of worship.

> *But an hour is coming and now is, when the true worshippers shall worship the Father in Spirit and in truth; for such people the Father seeks to be His worshippers. God is spirit, and those who worship Him must worship in Spirit and in truth* (John 4:23-24).

Marriage embodies the picture of intimacy. There is no greater union than marriage. For this reason God chose to demonstrate this through this tribe, even in the meaning of their name.

## THE NAMING OF LEVI

> *and she conceived again, and bare a son; and said, "Now this time will my husband be joined unto me, because I have born him three sons," therefore was his name called Levi* (Genesis 29:34 KJV).

Levi means "joined" or "attached." The reference implies that of a matrimonial union. Prophetically, this is what the priestly Bride says to her Bridegroom. This is the song in every true Levite's heart. In fact, it is their mandate for living!

Read Ephesians 5:22-32.

## BE SUBJECT

The phrase "be subject to" does not mean dominated but rather a form of honor and worship. A mature Levite who has been liberated from the bonds of religious striving knows that being "subject" is obedience stemming from intimacy. God uses the marriage union in the natural in this Scripture to tell of a deeper mystery, which is the union of the heart. We have become "one flesh" with Yeshua. When His flesh (or the veil) became rent, He forever sealed us as His priestly bride.

> *Since therefore, brethren, we have confidence to enter the holy place by the blood of Jesus, by a new and living way which He inaugurated for us through the veil, that is, His flesh, and since we have a great high priest over the house of God, let us draw near with a sincere heart in full assurance of faith, having our hearts sprinkled clean from an evil conscience and our bodies washed with pure water* (Hebrews 10:19-22).

The term "draw near" is the definition for the Hebrew name *cohen* or "priest." We are to draw near to the Lord, as a bride would her husband in full assurance and faith, for this is true intimacy: love without fear.

You see, Beloved, Yeshua went back to a garden and wrestled with an ancient serpent. His pure lovesick passion for His bride caused Him to pour out His life in the greatest battle for love mankind has ever known. Just before He went into the Garden of Gethsemane, he prayed this prayer at the Passover Seder:

*Jesus spoke these things; and lifting up His eyes to heaven, He said, "Father, the hour has come; glorify Your Son, that the Son may glorify You, even as You gave Him authority over all flesh, that to all whom You have given Him, He may give eternal life. This is eternal life that they may know You, the only true God, and Jesus Christ whom You have sent. I glorified You on the earth, having accomplished the work which You have given Me to do. Now, Father, glorify Me together with Yourself, with the glory which I had with You before the world was"* (John 17:1-6).

Our Beloved Yeshua fought relentlessly so that you and I might be restored to full fellowship with the Father so that Yeshua Himself would be betrothed eternally to His priestly Bride. Yeshua wrestled against the façade or lie that we are separated from the love of God. The debt was canceled and the facades were torn down. As He gave up His last breath entering behind the veil, His precious body was torn. Read Matthew 27:50-52.

You see, beloved, there is NO SEPARATION between you and I and the Father. There is no separation in His glorious habitation of love. He bids us from His heavenly garden. We are His bridal flowers: precious, beautiful, fragrant, and costly. A Levite's calling is to bid others back to the Garden, for they have the revelation that we can never ever be separated from His love. The sealing comes from the fountain of His blood and is empowered by His glory. Beloved, you are a sealed fountain, a garden enclosed, set apart for the Master and Creator of the Universe! Cease from doubting that you are loved. Tell that façade of rejection, fear, or shame to go in Yeshua' name. May love be revealed, may you be revealed as His glorious Bride, the treasured possession of your Father God! We are forever joined, abiding in the Savior's love, to the destiny of Abba's heart. May He breathe upon your garden today and awaken you to true love!

*Who will separate us from the love of Christ? Will tribulation, or distress, or persecution, or famine, or nakedness, or peril, or sword? Just as it is written, "FOR YOUR SAKE WE ARE BEING PUT TO DEATH ALL DAY LONG; WE WERE CONSIDERED AS SHEEP TO BE SLAUGHTERED." But in all these things we overwhelmingly conquer through Him who loved us. For I am convinced that neither death, nor life, nor angels, nor principalities, nor things present, nor things to come, nor powers, nor height, nor depth, nor any other created thing, will be able to separate us from the love of God, which is in Christ Jesus our Lord* (Romans 8:35-39).

## "PRESENT TO HIMSELF THE CHURCH IN ALL HER GLORY"

The hour is nigh, beloved, when we shall be presented to our Bridegroom. The glory of God is housed within us. This verse points out the very nature and character of God's manifest presence within the Church. Psalm 45 says the King's daughter (the Bride of Christ) is "all glorious within." This scripture is indicative of Yeshua's return and His spotless Bride being presented to Him in all her glory. Indeed we are truly all glorious within. We are called to purity. The tribe of Levi gains its strength from its purity and devotion to God. Purity is one of its greatest strengths. We are all transforming into the perfection and beauty of His holiness so that we may become that bride for whom He so desperately yearns.

The primary calling and destiny of every Levite is both to embody and impart the message of being housed with His glory. They are called to carry the weight of God's house, His *K'vod*. Within the tribe of Levi we can see the Lord using this tribe as a presentation of the Bride to the Church. It is not self-promotion, "Look at me, look at me, I'm so holy." Instead, a Levite, in his call to separateness and purity, says, "Look at Him (Yeshua)! Be transformed by the washing of His Word and be holy."

*K'vod* is the Hebrew term relating to the heavy weight of God's glory, being His very nature. It is for this reason Levi is chastened for purity in the Beloved. Flesh cannot touch the glory of God, for flesh itself is a continually decaying façade. Yeshua is the incorruptible seed. Let us abound in the fruit of repentance, for this is true purity. Purity is not based on works, but rather is birthed from a circumcised heart, being desperate and poor in spirit and purified by fire. A mature Levite has taken the benefits of the chastening of Lord by applying the sword of the Spirit to circumcise the facades of the flesh. True purity is enabled by grace, coming through the cleansing work of the blood. A pure life in Yeshua is one that is lived abiding in the Cross. It has been transformed by the resurrection power and glory in the union of the Cross.

## THE GEMSTONE OF LEVI

As a testament of the work of the Cross, Abba has given Levi an appropriate stone. The gemstone of Levi is the carbuncle, more commonly known as the garnet. The garnet is a deep, blood-red color—almost black. Mystics of old believed that the garnet warded off evil spirits, impurity, and bad dreams. Hebrews 12: 24 (NIV) states: "To Jesus the mediator of a new covenant, and to the sprinkled blood that speaks a better word." The garnet serves as a reminder not only to the tribe of Levi but to everyone whose sins are atoned for that our foe is defeated once and for all. What a powerful promise for Levi! The color of the stone also points back to the time when the priests would make the sacrifices for Israel's atonement. We no longer need to make sacrifices, as the final sacrifice, Yeshua, the spotless lamb, has been offered once and for all. The garnet's deep color also speaks of the mysteries that God has entrusted Levi with in His Word.

Levi's gemstone was located on the first row (from right to left) in the third position. It was worn directly over the high priest's heart. As His priestly bride, dear Levite, know that you always possess the Bridegroom's heart. Levites live, love, and learn from deepest intimacy. If you are from this beautiful tribe, know that you are defined and propelled by the union of the heart. Levites are a company of passionate laid-down lovers who are marked by God to profoundly encounter Him. Moses, Isaiah, and Ezekiel, amongst scores of others from this tribe, had lifestyles of radically transformational encounters with God.

Levi's existence is in large part defined by face-to-face encounters with the Lord. One does not come face-to-face with someone and remain unaltered. Picture, if you will, two lovers. First they are standing on opposite sides of the room. How intimate do you think they feel with each other? Can they encounter one another well at such a distance? Of course not! They move closer, now holding hands—more intimate, yes, but distractions can still come between them. Now picture the two lovers eyeball-to-eyeball, nostril-to-nostril, sharing the same breath, and heart-to-heart. This is what a true face-to-face encounter looks like. In this place of encountering Him we are vulnerable, stripped away of all defenses and made acutely aware of His holiness. My dear brother and sister Levite, this is where God is calling you to live. As His bride we are a walking PDA (public display of affection)!

The garnet's origin comes from the Latin word: *granatum*, as in *pomum granatum* ("pomegranate," literally "apple having many seeds").[1] The garnet is similar in color to the pulp of the fruit. The high priest's robe had pomegranates sewn onto it. I feel this further confirms that the garnet is the stone for Levi. Levi is a first-fruits company. The term "first fruits" means to be the first choice, separated, and consecrated. By no means does this term infer any elitism but rather an act of worship. We want to give Abba the best of our worship, time, service, and, ultimately, our whole lives. "First fruits" also implies selflessness. An offering is given freely, no attachments. Abba was and is looking for a people whose lives are given freely to Him, wholeheartedly, no strings attached. The servant nature of Levite is the essence of their call to selflessness, faithfulness, and long-suffering. This is a type and shadow of the Bride of Yeshua and her call to be a first fruits company, the Priestly Bride consecrated to her Beloved High Priest, Yeshua.

Levite is also a cultivator of first fruits. This is displayed in the gifting as a teacher with a foundation of an apostolic mantle. Levites cultivate first fruits within the Body of Christ by building precept upon precept in the Word, adhering to a doctrine of righteousness grounded in the law of love.

> *These are the ones who have not been defiled with women, for they have kept themselves chaste. These are the ones who follow the Lamb wherever He goes. These have been purchased from among men as first fruits to God and to the Lamb* (Revelation 14:4).

Within the heart of every Levi is a righteous abandonment of the profane in their pursuit after the Beloved. To try to separate or rebuke them for this would be deadly to their very identity. Their nature is formed in the purity of the matrimonial union. Like Isaiah, they are instinctively aware of how undone they are in their human frailties and facades in the light of Love Himself (Isaiah 6). This is where the very circumcision of the heart begins—with the revelation of who He is, the purity of His nature.

## LEVI NOT NUMBERED

As a first-fruits company, Levi was not numbered, further confirming their call to separateness.

> *The Levites, however, were not numbered among them by their father's tribe. For the Lord had spoken to Moses, saying, "Only the tribe of Levi you shall not number, nor shall you take their census among the sons of Israel. But you shall appoint the Levites over the tabernacle of the testimony, and over all its furnishings and over all that belongs to it. They shall carry the tabernacle and all its furnishings, they shall take care of it; they shall also camp around the tabernacle"* (Numbers 1:47-50).

God did not number Levi for a few reasons: 1) He called them to be set apart in order to minister to Him; 2) Levites are intercessors. Their function was to intercede for all the tribes, especially during times of war. They were not to engage in battle naturally, but supernaturally through prayer.

> *…for the weapons of our warfare are not of the flesh but divinely powerful for the destruction of fortresses* (II Corinthians 10:4).

As a Levite, one must never engage in a spiritual battle in one's own flesh. Sometimes our own understanding, motives, and souls must be purged with fire before becoming an effective intercessor entrusted on the battlefield. A Levite's immaturity can lead to not only their own casualties on the battlefield, but also those they carry in intercession. Therefore, dear Levi, submit yourself to the fire of God; seek first the kingdom of God and His righteousness. Your greatest victories will come through your greatest surrender to the Cross. Intercession must come through the Cross and nothing less. At a time when Satan's schemes are grossly rampant, you are called to guard your "place of abiding"[2] in intercession in the purity of the Cross. Dear Levi, it is only from a place of abiding that you and I can ever hope gain a place of intercession. We lose battles through the legal license of sin and the self-life that we have not surrendered through the Cross.

3)Abba knew of Levi's impetuous tendency to defend a righteous cause. In His infinite wisdom, He knew if they engaged in a physical battle, they would be detoured from their spiritual responsibilities and ultimately lose sight of their call. Abba must be Levi's defense; they cannot have any other. 4) Abba was their inheritance.

*At that time the Lord set apart the tribe of Levi to carry the ark of the covenant of the Lord, to stand before the Lord to serve Him and to bless His name until this day. Therefore, Levi does not have portion or inheritance with his brothers; God is his inheritance, just as the Lord your God spoke to him* (Deuteronomy 10:8-9).

## SYMBOLS

Abba loves to speak great mysteries though pictures and symbols. Levi has many. The most commonly recognized is the breastplate worn by the high priest.

## THE BREASTPLATE

*And Aaron shall carry the names of the sons of Israel in the breastplate of judgment over his heart when he enters the holy place, for a memorial before God continually. And you shall put in the breastplate of judgment the Urim and the Thummim, and they shall be over Aaron's heart when he goes in before the Lord; and Aaron shall carry the judgment of the sons of Israel over his heart before the Lord continually* (Exodus 28:29-30).

The breastplate of the high priest is a beautiful picture of intercession and worship. The breastplate holds the twelve different stones on which are engraved the names of the tribes of Israel, joining Manasseh and Ephraim under the name of Joseph (onyx stone). The breastplate stones were positioned in birth order, reading them from right to left (as is the Hebrew language). When someone introduces their children, they usually introduce them from oldest to the youngest. No child is favored over another in a healthy family unit; each is loved and treasured for their uniqueness. This is true of our Heavenly Father. The breastplate is one of the most beautiful symbols God gives to us, showing His deep love and care for us. Exodus 28 mentions the breastplate as a token of judgment. As a mediator, Aaron carried his brethren upon his heart when he came before God. With sincerest humility and compassion for his brethren, flawed or faithful, he carried this token of intercession on him perpetually. While in the Holy Place, Aaron would lift his fellow living stones to the Father. He heard both the cry of the Father and the needs of His children. The glory of God would then illuminate each priceless living stone, revealing the character and beauty of the Father, their sins (flaws), and their uniqueness in the kingdom of God.

Yeshua, our great High Priest, carries each one of us on His heart. As a Levite myself, I have many times during intercession been reminded by the Holy Spirit of the picture of the breastplate. God would illuminate a particular tribe's stone, representing the one for whom I was interceding. It is so moving to know He cares for each one of us so deeply.

Levi's calling is that of a lifestyle of intercession. The role of an intercessor is one of selflessness. It is not one of hyped prayer for men to see. We carry the burden of prayer day and night. Ministry compels a Levite, drawn from our intimacy with Abba. One of the great intercessors of modern day (whom I believe was a Levite) was Rees Howells. If you are called to intercession, and especially if you're a Levite, I strongly urge that you read the book about his life, *Rees Howells: Intercessor.*[3] It dramatically changed me, my view, and my life of intercession.

The tribe of Levi is also identified with symbols of the furnishings from the tabernacle in which they served. The insight is rich and brings much freedom for Levi as well as all believers.

## THE LIFE AND CALLING OF LEVI REVEALED
## THROUGH THE TABERNACLE FURNISHINGS

*And I heard a loud voice from the throne, saying, "Behold, the tabernacle of God is among men, and He shall dwell among them, and they shall be His people, and God Himself shall be among them"* (Revelation 21:3).

We come to Yeshua as tabernacles in which He dwells. He is the way, the truth, and the life. I was taught by a messianic rabbi who had studied the tabernacle extensively. In his studies he discovered that the three compartments of the tabernacle were given names, which translated were: the outer court, called *the Way*; the inner court, *the Truth*; and the Holy of Holies, *the Life*. Yeshua said:

*I am the way, the truth, and the life; no one comes to the Father, but through Me* (John 14:6).

Hallelujah! Amen! To GOD be all glory!

## THE WAY: THE OUTER COURT

There were two furnishings in the outer court: the brazen altar and the bronze laver. Both furnishings speak of cleansing and refining to Levi.

## THE BRAZEN ALTAR

Read Exodus 27:1-7. Sacrifices were made upon the brazen altar. We no longer offer sacrifices of animals, but that of a pure heart. When sacrifice is born of human striving, it is a vile, profane stench in the nostrils of Abba. Levi, take care that you do not offer sacrifices out of a works mentality.

*For thou dost not delight in sacrifice, otherwise I would give it; Thou art not pleased with burnt offering. The sacrifices of GOD are a broken spirit: A broken and a contrite heart, O GOD, Thou wilt not despise* (Psalm 51:16-17).

The Father delights in our brokenness. How does brokenness occur within? It transforms us as we lay our lives before Him in total abandon, despite our desires and dreams, shortcomings, achievements, and fears. We must daily die to the flesh. The flesh is opposition to the Spirit, so we must kill it every time it takes opportunity within us. Brokenness is the sincerest form of devotion. This is a prerequisite to any Levite and his or her high calling of intimacy.

*I urge you therefore, brethren, by the mercies of God, to present your bodies as a living and holy sacrifice, acceptable to God, which is your spiritual service of worship* (Romans 12:1).

*But to this one will I look, to him who is humble and contrite of spirit, and who trembles at My word* (Isaiah 66:2b).

To be "contrite of spirit" is to be truly humble. An immature Levi will struggle with a religious spirit. A religious spirit will entail false humility, spiritual pride and elitism, fear of man, performance agendas, and rejection. This thread runs throughout the spiritual flaws in Levi's fleshly facades. God provided the brazen altar as a picture of sacrificing all that hinders holiness. The main purpose of the brazen altar speaks of repentance and redemption.

Repentance is the way to freedom. It is the way to the Way, Yeshua. Levites are not only reminded of their personal need for repentance but their mandate to call people to repentance.

Levites are very "black-and-white" people, seeing things in either the extremes of sin or holiness, darkness or light. Levites will not only make this demand of themselves but others as well. A word of caution to you, my fellow Levites: Take heed to remember the grace and mercy of the Savior. Bow low in heart and mind and do not become judgmental and harsh, even if your beliefs and discernment are right. Always seek to portray the Father's heart with compassion.

## THE BRONZE LAVER

Read Exodus 30:18-21. According to Jewish commentaries the bronze laver consisted of bronze mirrors.[4] When the priests came to wash their hands and feet, they could look into the bronze laver to see how to cleanse themselves. What does the bronze laver represent for us? It represents the Word of God. When we truly look (not glance) intently into the Word of God, we see what we need to be cleansed of.

> *For if anyone is a hearer of the word and not a doer, he is like a man who looks at his natural face in a mirror; for once he has looked at himself and gone away, he has immediately forgotten what kind of person he was. But one who looks intently at the perfect law of liberty, and abides by it, not having becomes forgetful hearer but an effectual doer; this man shall be blessed in what he does* (James 1:23-25).

Take note of this portion of the text: *So they shall wash their hands and their feet that they may not die.* Why do you suppose God would say this? To answer this, you have to realize what the washing of the hands and feet symbolized. It wasn't just a ritual. Its meaning is deep and poignant for us. Hands represent our service to God. Whatever we put our hands to do must be done for God's glory. The Psalmist expresses this point better:

> *Who may ascend into the hill of the Lord? And who may stand in His holy place? He who has clean hands and a pure heart. Who has not lifted up his soul to falsehood, and has not sworn deceitfully* (Psalm 24:3-4).

Our service to God must be clean, our hearts and mouths honest. The feet represent our walk. Our walk not only affects us, but others as well. Don't our feet publish the good news of the gospel? That being said, our walk must be blameless and upright so that the testimony of Christ is not tainted by sin.

The brazen altar and bronze laver together represent three ways God cleanses us from the flesh: the water, the fire, and the blood. The water and the fire are both types of the Holy Spirit, and the blood is the sacrifice of Yeshua that paid our debt of sin. What does the Bible say the three witnesses are? The water, the fire (the Spirit), and the blood. All three of these elements are in the outer court: the blood on the altar, the fire from the altar, and the water from the bronze laver. Levite is drawn to the three witnesses as catalysts for revival. The blood, a call of repentance; the water, Spirit baptism; and fire, refinement and the empowering of the Spirit.

## THE INNER COURT:
## THE TRUTH THE TABLE OF SHOWBREAD

Read Exodus 25:23-30. There were actually twelve loaves of the bread, one for each of the tribes of Israel. The loaves were all on the same level and balanced. This symbolized both the unity of the Body and equality. Each served its purpose, and each was equal. What a beautiful picture for the Body of Christ. Levites are called both to intercede for and to keep this unity in the Body. The bread itself is referring to Yeshua; he is the Bread of Life. He is the Word. Levites are called to teach, to bring fresh bread, hot from the ovens of Heaven, to the Body. They are gifted to teach the oracles of God. Levi gains strength from the Word. Always seek for a fresh word from Him alone.

## THE MERCY CALL

It is important to note that many of the furnishings were made of acacia wood. The crown of thorns Yeshua wore came from the acacia tree. It is known for its thorny boughs and beautiful, yellow, fragrant flowers. To a Levite, this is a mercy call in intercession. Moreover, it is a call to live as a laid-down lover of God and His creation. Beloved, mercy triumphs over judgment! When Yeshua went to the Cross wearing the crown of thorns, it spoke of His mercy and compassion. His mind and His heart are always founded in mercy. This adornment declared that he was a King who rules and reigns in mercy. Though you carry, my dear Levi, the righteous judgments of God, remember that it is the law of love you serve. When we lay aside our own judgments, facades, and agendas and serve one another in love and unity, then victory and liberty can come! Ask Abba to circumcise your heart with His mercy.

The fragrance of the acacia tree speaks of the fragrance of mercy. It is always sweet. I pray earnestly that the fragrance of mercy consume your life and ministry. Mercy brings balance to believers, resulting in unity and sound doctrine. For this reason, dear Levi, you must be made whole—no anger, unforgiveness, and religious judgment; those things are vile to the Father. As an intercessor, it is pivotal that you are made whole so that the fragrance of mercy will draw the lost, unite the Body of Christ, and captivate our loving Father. Allow His mercy seat to be established in your life.

## THE ALTAR OF INCENSE

Read Exodus 30:1-8. The Altar of Incense reiterates Levi's call to intercession and worship. Prayer is a lifestyle of intimacy, not ritual. God longs for the sweet incense of our worship. The lampstand, altar of incense, and the table of showbread identify mainly with the calling for Levi. These furnishings also reinforce Levi's call to purity and intimacy.

Incense is a type and shadow of the offering of emotions. Emotions offered up in sincerity become the catalyst that enables a believer to enter the Holy Place. The Word says, "With all who are sincere, you are sincere" Psalm 18:26 (CEV). Do not hide your emotions—God knows them anyway! Take Moses: a fellow Levite who honestly poured out his emotions of self-doubt, fear, and anger to the Lord. In the Book of Psalms we see David pouring out his heart before the Lord. They both had one vital key: the glory. They knew the Father's nature. The glory of God is the very nature of God whereby His grace and heart is revealed to us. Both men offered fragrant lives like incense in sincere and raw, honest emotions. The Father is not afraid of your honesty. In fact, He welcomes it. He desires a pure offering of incense, fragrant surrender.

> *He shall put the incense on the fire before the Lord, that the cloud of incense may cover the mercy seat that is on the ark of the testimony, otherwise he will die* (Leviticus 16:13).

It has been said in Jewish commentaries that the fragrance of the incense could be smelled as far as the territory of Dan. We are the fragrance of Christ. Levi is the distinct fragrance in the Body of Christ; Levites are called to impart the fragrance of intimacy and devotion by their lives and ministries. Their fragrance can either attract or repel others according to the condition of the heart. Levi must take care not to allow flies of religion and striving into his emotions and relationship with God. You are a beautiful and treasured fragrance of worship to the Father. Allow yourself to be broken and spilled out before Him!

> *But thanks be to God, who always leads us in triumph in Christ, and manifests through us the sweet aroma of the knowledge of Him in every place. For we are a fragrance of Christ to God among those who are being saved and among those who are perishing; to the one an aroma from death to death, to the other an aroma from life to life. And who is adequate for these things?* (II Corinthians 2:14-16).

## THE AVTINUS FAMILY

The Avtinus family was a Levitical family who specifically had charge of the incense within the Temple.[5] Exodus 30:34 mentions only three spices for the incense. There were actually a combination of eleven resins and spices, the salt of Sodom, Jordan amber, and one secret ingredient.[6] The Avtinus family was uniquely marked for keeping the secret ingredient within the incense called the *Maaleh Ashan*. They never revealed what the *Maaleh Ashan* was. It was their belief that the *Maaleh Ashan* should be kept a secret as not to fall into the hands of idolaters. Without the *Maaleh Ashan* ingredient, incense would dispense in a horizontal manner, scattering randomly and quickly diminishing. With this rare secret ingredient, however, incense would rise in a tall vertical column. Fragrant worship must remain vertical, meaning it must rise to God alone. It must be free from idolatry. Prophetically speaking, I believe the secret ingredient *Maaleh Ashan* is about always keeping the one thing the one thing.

> *One thing I have asked from the LORD, that I shall seek: that I may dwell in the house of the LORD all the days of my life, to behold the beauty of the LORD and to meditate in His temple* (Psalm 27:4).

Where the Avtinus family prepared the incense is equally compelling. Located in the southern portion of the Courtyard of the Temple, just above the Water Gate, was the Avtinus Chamber where the incense was carefully prepared.[7] The location of the Avtinus Chamber reveals an exciting mystery for Levites today. Being that it was located above the Water Gate directly ties into the calling of Levites who serve as revivalists in the final outpouring of the Holy Spirit! Dear brother and sister Levite, as we keep the *Maaleh Ashan* (the one thing always the one thing) we are entrusted to oversee what, I believe, is the end-time move of God: the glory covering the earth (Hab. 2:14). Dear Levi, our *Maaleh Ashan* is habitation. Settle for nothing less!

## THE LAMPSTAND

Read Exodus 25:31-40. The almond bulbs and its flowers signify the budding of Aaron's rod. This is truly meaningful for Levi. The tribes had turned against Moses and Aaron (Numbers 16-17). God showed both His covenant and His favor upon the house of Levi in the midst of treachery and uprising when He caused Aaron's rod to bloom and not the other tribes. Whenever your enemies are pursuing you, dear Levi, remember: When you are in right standing with God, He will always cause your rod to blossom.

The lampstand also represents that Levi is a light to all with whom he comes into contact. He is ever ready with a word of encouragement or revelation to bring light in the midst of darkness. The light also stands for the many times Levi stands for truth, whether it is popular or not. He often stands alone in his walk. Dear Levi, always remember to follow that inner light, Yeshua. Do not be swayed by men. Take your stand for righteousness in humility and the strength of heart with which God has gifted you.

The wicks for the lampstand were made from old priestly garments. Levi cannot rely on tradition and the way the Spirit has moved formerly. Don't live by old works. Realize

Abba's kingdom is in the here and now. He might have moved previously before in one way, but that doesn't mean He always will move that same way. Also, you mustn't take pride in past accomplishments in God. Get out of any performance agendas and join the Father in what He is doing in this moment. Everything is in subjection to the refinement of the Spirit, including your gifts and calling(s). He is always doing a new thing in and through you. Just trust Him.

The budding almond branches on the lampstand also speak of Abba's faithfulness to Levi. God watches over His Word to perform it.

*The word of the LORD came to me saying, "What do you see, Jeremiah?" And I said, "I see a rod of an almond tree." Then the LORD said to me, "You have seen well, for I am watching over My word to perform it"* (Jeremiah 1:11-12).

Levi lives in fellowship with Yeshua by abiding in the habitation of His Word. The Word is the meat and drink to every Levite. If he is not getting fed pure manna and fresh water, he becomes spiritually malnourished. Levites are designed by Abba (as are all of us) to exist in the eternal habitation of His Word. They expressly live this truth out as a lifestyle of intimacy. This foundation is built upon the rock Himself, the foundation Yeshua, the Word that became flesh (the façade buster!). He is the living habitation of the Father's Word to us. As we abide in Him, His Word abides in us, thus conforming us to the Father's will and heart. Read I John 1: 1-15.

## THE HOLY OF HOLIES: THE LIFE, THE ARK OF THE COVENANT

Read Exodus 25:10-22. The Ark of the Covenant has special meaning for the tribe of Levi. The Levites were called to carry the Ark. The Ark represents the glory of God. Levites are called to be carriers of the glory. The glory will follow both their lives and ministries. Within the Ark was Aaron's rod: God's promise to Levi that He is their defense and also a symbol of leadership. The tablets on which the law was written symbolize Levi's calling to teach the oracles of God. In the same way, the pot of manna represents the fresh and living word that Levi must always attain by intimacy in God's presence. The Ark of the Covenant is also known as the Ark of the Testimony. Levites are called to steward the testimony of God's miraculous provision, encounters, and revival (manna in the Ark).

A special note: All the temple articles were portable, meaning God is longing for us bring what these furnishings symbolize into everyday life. The Outer Court and its refining is an everyday process. The Table of Showbread calls a Levite to be balanced in doctrine, having a fresh word from Heaven every day. Offering intercession and worship is not just a Sunday morning or conference occasion. It's an everyday lifestyle.

The Mercy Seat over the Ark of the Covenant speaks of a balance of grace and mercy found in the glory. Without the blood, which Yeshua shed for us, sprinkled upon the Mercy Seat, you and I would be subject to judgment. All have sinned and fallen short of the glory. Therefore, it is mercy that beckons us all to enter in to the Holy of Holies with boldness! It is important to note the Mercy Seat was already in place with the Ark of Covenant at the time Moses was given this furnishing. The Mercy Seat did not come into full effect, however, until Yeshua came and shed His blood. In other words, Yeshua became the provision and plan for mercy even though the Mercy Seat was already there, beckoning the Israelites. They could not obtain it in the law (Mount Sinai). It was after Yeshua came that He beckoned us all to Mount Zion (His grace) whereby we obtain mercy! An Ark without the Mercy Seat would be full of a law of commandments that are impossible to keep. The only way we can lead holy lives and be true carriers of the glory, the Ark of the Covenant, is through the mercy of God! Anything other than this would be works of religious pride. We cannot obtain righteousness in ourselves for that is striving. We were created to abide in the Ark, only by means of the Mercy Seat! Dear Levi, the Lord is calling you into a habitation of His Ark through His lavish mercy!

## JACOB'S PROPHECY

> *"Simeon and Levi are brothers; Their swords are implements of violence. Let my soul not enter into their council; let not my glory be united with their assembly; Because in their anger they slew men, And in their self-will they lamed oxen. Cursed be their anger, for it is fierce; And their wrath, for it is cruel. I will disperse them in Jacob, And scatter them in Israel* (Genesis 49:5-7).

Anger and unforgiveness grow like a cancer if not dealt with. For this reason, the Word says not to let the sun go down upon your anger and to be angry but sin not (Ephesians 4:26). Other than the religious spirit, anger and unforgiveness are the main strongholds within Levi. Levi, like his brother Simeon, was quick to rush to the cause of his sister, Dinah. Neither brother truly sought the heart of God nor their father Jacob's wisdom to deal with the matter. They foolishly chose to avenge wrongdoing on their own. A warning to every Levi: When you try defending a cause, no matter how righteous or just it may seem, if you fail to seek God, you are in grave danger of grieving the heart of God and possibly forgoing your destiny. Moses, like any other Levite, struggled with this constantly too. His quick-tempered nature got the better of him a few times. When he slew a man in Egypt, when he threw down the two tablets, and when he struck the rock twice are three instances. No cause is worth damaging your testimony for Yeshua, dear Levi. If anger and unforgiveness have taken over your habitation, then repent so that God may restore you to be an instrument of peace.

## MOSES' PROPHECY

> *And of Levi he said, "Let thy Thummim and thy Urim be with thy holy one, whom thou didst prove at Massah, and with whom thou didst strive at the waters of Meribah; Who said unto his father and to his mother, I have not seen him; neither did he acknowledge his brethren, nor knew his own children: for they have observed thy word, and kept thy covenant. They shall teach Jacob thy judgments, and Israel thy law: they shall put incense before thee, and whole burnt sacrifice upon Thine altar. Bless the Lord, his substance, and accept the work of his hands: smite through the loins of them that rise against him and of them that hate him that they rise not again"* (Deuteronomy 33:8-11 KJV).

### "LET THY THUMMIM AND THY URIM BE WITH THY HOLY ONE"

The Thummim and Urim mean "light" and "perfection." Yeshua's light and perfection is constantly working out the flaws in Levi, bringing forth the beauty of His holiness. It is a call to integrity for Levi. The Thummim and Urim were stones that were cast as lots when the priest would carry them. It was a way of bringing discernment and clarity to a situation. The Thummim and Urim prophetically illustrate the innate gifting of keen discernment and wisdom within every Levite.

### "WHOM THOU DIDST PROVE AT MASSAH, AND WITH WHOM THOU DIDST STRIVE AT THE WATERS OF MERIBAH"

Read Exodus 17:1-7.

*This is the water of Meribah; because the children of Israel strove with God, and he was sanctified in them* (Numbers 20:13 KJV).

The children of Israel were a real motley crew. Moses failed to rise above their murmuring and complaining, knowing how they angered God, and to bring blessing. God was testing the character of Moses. The character of Levi is always tested in times of great fire and trial. This is especially true because of Levi's apostolic calling. Anger tears down, but love builds up. Moses could not deny his quick temper (denying the flesh) and thus did not walk in the fullness of his authority. Know, fellow Levi, God may call on you to bring forth sweet waters out of the desert, despite the conditions of the hearts of others. Levi, you must lead by example, popular or not, without religious pride or self-satisfaction. Obedience is one faithful act of surrender after another that will breed the atmosphere of miracles. It is not our works that bring the supernatural, but rather the surrender to the will of God, allowing His Spirit to move within us. You may be the source of someone's great miracle. Do not give the enemy an opportunity through your flesh and so hinder the Spirit's moving. Your obedience will bring forth sweet waters in a time of drought. Abba may call on you to be an oasis in someone's desert.

## "WHO SAID UNTO HIS FATHER AND TO HIS MOTHER, I HAVE NOT SEEN HIM; NEITHER DID HE ACKNOWLEDGE HIS BRETHREN, NOR KNEW HIS OWN CHILDREN"

The calling of every Levite is one of great sacrifice. In pursuit of a true intimate relationship with God, Levi is often asked to forsake what he holds dear. He must know that earthly things can tie him down. Sometimes jobs, relationships, and possessions can become idols. Levi must sometimes sacrifice to an extreme level, and this is often misunderstood by loved ones and friends. However, compromise is a grievous thing to Levi because of his call to purity and separateness. There is a balance, and finding it requires seeking God whole-heartedly. This verse essentially marks the call of separation from the world and to God for Levi. Yeshua said:

*He that loveth father or mother more than me is not worthy of me: and he that loveth son or daughter more than me is not worthy of me* (Matthew 10:37).

Something isn't precious until we are made aware of what it costs us. Levites are aware of the cost upon their lives. They value the sacrifice and see it as their life-long call to worship and separateness. There is no cost too great for intimacy with the Beloved, for He paid the ultimate cost: His own life. How could we not give Him ours in return?

*Listen, O daughter, give attention and incline your ear: Forget your people and your father's house; Then the King will desire your beauty. Because He is your God, bow down to Him* (Psalm 45:10-11).

## "FOR THEY HAVE OBSERVED THY WORD, AND KEPT THY COVENANT. THEY SHALL TEACH JACOB THY JUDGMENTS, AND ISRAEL THY LAW"

This scripture speaks of Levi's calling to teach the Word. The Bible was transcribed from generation to generation by Levite scribes (for the most part). God dispersed Levi throughout all the tribes when the inheritance was given. This was done so that the Israelites would have a source of constant wisdom, revelation, and prayer coming from this tribe. God is careful to whom He entrusts His Word. Take this to heart, Levite. He is ready to give the oracles from His heart as long as you remain faithful and pure to Him. He has placed within you a word of holiness and freedom but also the law of love. I charge you, fellow Levi, to be an unashamed workman diligently keeping, applying, and teaching the Word of God.

## "THEY SHALL PUT INCENSE BEFORE THEE"

This portion of the prophecy specifically relates to the calling of intercession for the tribe of Levi. True and pure intercession is first wholeheartedly made with our lives. The sweetest incense you and I can ever offer comes from a sincere heart, a yielded and purified will and emotions. We are the fragrance of Christ. A true priestly bride knows that power is not found in works; that alone would be a prideful stench to the Father's nostrils. Rather, it must be a sweet fragrance of surrender. As pure incense rising before the throne, fellow Levi, you must choose the better portion as Mary of Bethany did. God is calling you to a life of unconditional and radical surrender. It is from this place alone one should make intercession to the Father. Prayer rendered in religious pride and works is not only a stench to the Father but completely ineffective. Levites today are called to a harp-and-bowl lifestyle of intercession and worship. Know that your broken life moves the heart of God, defies and confronts pride of many, thwarts hordes of hell and darkness, and ushers in the return of the King! Know who you are, brother and sister Levi. When you are free of facades of your flesh, you are a pungent fragrance, full of the glory of God!

## "AND WHOLE BURNT SACRIFICE UPON THINE ALTAR"

Levites are called to lead radical lives of surrender and obedience. Your song, dear Levi, is this, from S. Sundar Singh's, I Have Decided to Follow Jesus:[8]

I have decided to follow Jesus; No turning back, no turning back.
Though I may wonder, I still will follow; No turning back, no turning back.

The world behind me, the Cross before me; No turning back, no turning back.
Though none go with me, still I will follow; No turning back, no turning back.

Will you decide now to follow Jesus?
No turning back, no turning back.

> *These are the ones who have not been defiled with women, for they have kept themselves chaste. These are the ones who follow the Lamb wherever He goes. These have been purchased from among men as first fruits to God and to the Lamb* (Revelation 14:4).

The surrender of a Levi is a continual daily sacrifice of will, preconceived ideas, emotions, ministry, and desires. It is a life marked often by being lonely, misunderstood, sometimes chastised by ignorant spectators, and painfully aware of frailties. However, it is most certainly WORTH IT! It is through the eye of the needle, the straight and narrow way that the Lord calls a Levite to bow low continually and be a perpetual sacrifice to Him. Rejoice! There are infinite and eternal rewards, brethren! The chief and most precious reward is that we have an eternal habitation with Him and His house! Hallelujah!

Sometimes, brother and sister Levi, it seems as though the Lord has stricter requirements for you or is often chastising you more than others. Sometimes He indeed does, but what you must recognize is that He is hallowing His name and His kingdom in you. You carry the Ark of the Covenant—He does not assign that task lightly! We are entrusted with the oracles of God that man might know Him! So when a fiery trial comes your way or painful chastisement of the Lord, surrender joyfully!

### "BLESS, THE LORD, HIS SUBSTANCE, AND
### ACCEPT THE WORK OF HIS HANDS"

Hands represent service or, in a Levite's case, servanthood. The calling of every leader is first and foremost servanthood. A Levite's call is to be a servant to God first, then his fellow man. Servanthood is a great strength of Levi. When he serves God in purity, he is blessed in all he does.

### "SMITE THROUGH THE LOINS OF THEM THAT RISE AGAINST HIM
### AND OF THEM THAT HATE HIM THAT THEY RISE NOT AGAIN"

The tribe of Levi was never allowed to engage in battle. God was to be his defense. When Levi looks outside the protection of God (his own strength or to men), he is compromising. Being joined to God means you are joined to His protection. He is your Adonai T'sveout (Lord of Hosts). Whatever battle you face, know He goes before you and has promised victory as you trust Him. He is your vindication alone.

## THE FACADES OF LEVI

Read Numbers 16:1-33. Korah's rebellion was a very grievous offense to God. He was a Levi, set apart to minister to God. Korah struggled with a jealous and gluttonous spirit, both stemming from a religious spirit. He was not content in the position where God had placed him. He desired his own glory. His rebellion not only cost him his own life but also some of those from the tribe of Reuben. Sometimes our rebellion not only leads us into spiritual death but others into spiritual death as well. Hidden agendas must be purged by the fire of God. This fire comes from the altar of Heaven, where He takes the coal and purges our uncleanness. If you have a hidden agenda, come before the throne of God and allow Him to undo you.

Read I Samuel 2:12, 17, 22-25, 27-33. Eli is typical of a Levite who gets so caught up in the duty of ministry that he ignores his own household. This is evident of a religious spirit. Eli was so caught up in his priestly duties that he ignored the fact that his sons were going straight to hell! We must take authority over our house before our house takes authority over us! This is so true of the Body today. Why do think America has such a stronghold in the areas of immorality? It is because the priests of the home have not taken their rightful place. Whether you are in a notable place of authority or not, there are no excuses when it comes to sin. Eli's sons assumed because they had a place of power, they could get away with all kinds of lascivious acts. Nothing is hidden from the eyes of God.

Read Leviticus 10:1-9. Nadab and Abihu's offering of strange fire was a grievous thing to God. They were both priests separated unto God. Their sin was that of religious pride. We cannot approach God in a flippant manner. He is a holy God. Nadab and Abihu's motives were both profane and self-gratifying. They chose to offer up what they desired, not bothering to seek God concerning their offering. Their self-importance, drenched in their religious pride, killed them. A religious spirit will kill destiny. God resists the proud, but He gives His grace to the humble.

Read II Samuel 6:1-8. Human effort and striving cannot touch the glory of God. Uzzah was killed because of His blatant irreverence for God. He tried to help God out. Trying to touch the glory with fleshly agendas is profane. God will not allow His glory to be tainted. To strive in human performance is a religious spirit. Doing so will kill the anointing. Ministering to God is for an audience of one. Anything contrary to this is profane and vain. The Pharisees in Yeshua's day had the same agenda of self-importance. Don't view ministry as if you are doing something great for God. Rather, view ministry as an overflow of your communion with Him. Dear Levite, beware of the leaven of the Pharisees.

*...for I say unto you, that except your righteousness shall exceed the righteousness of the scribes and Pharisees, ye shall in no case enter into the kingdom of heaven* (Matthew 5:20).

## THE GOLDEN CALF INCIDENT

Read Exodus 32. This chapter of Exodus is very interesting. It contains both the flaws and strengths of the tribe of Levi. Aaron, pressured by the people, makes a very unwise decision: to entertain the people's desires. His first mistake was that he didn't seek God. Secondly, Aaron bowed to the fear of man rather than the fear of the Lord. Worst of all, he led his people into idolatry. Aaron's most grievous mistake is that he became disconnected from his primary ministry as a priest to the Lord. He neglected to "draw near" (which is what the word priest means in Hebrew) to the lover of his soul. Instead, he foolishly chose the fear and praise of man.

*The fear of man brings a snare, but he who trusts in the Lord will be exalted* (Proverbs 29:25).

The fear of man will always give birth to bondage and idolatry. Aaron allowed the people to intimidate him rather than standing for truth. Fear is the opposite of perfect love. We know that the word says, "Perfect love casts out all fear" (I John 4:18). When we fear man, we do not fear the Lord. We mustn't allow the fear of man or anything to diminish the flame of our first love. To do so is compromise. Falling prey to the intimidation of man is a thread running consistently throughout this tribe. It is always coupled with compromise. Compromise is the breeding ground of apathy and lukewarm love toward God.

Moses, on the opposite end of the spectrum, was fervent both in his love for God and stand for truth. Notice that Moses was on the mountaintop seeking God. When Levi stays on the mountaintop of the Lord's presence, not only is he communing with Him, but he is gaining discernment and insight into the very heart of God. Moses took the role of an intercessor, despite the harlotry of the people. True intercession goes beyond personal persuasions. It goes to the heart of the matter. Compared to his brother, Aaron, Moses' stance was born of true purity and passionate love of God. When Moses called the congregation of Israel to repentance, the tribe of Levi was the first to answer the call. Levi, despite its faults, is sensitive to the call of repentance because of their deep desire for God.

## THE ZADOK PRIESTHOOD VS. THE AARONIC PRIESTHOOD

The Bible makes it clear that God desires that the priesthood be set apart unto Him. God's original intention was to have a kingdom of priests. Because of the golden calf incident, the Lord chose the tribe of Levi. He chose them because they abandoned all idolatry. The tribe of Levi went astray when they became involved in the agenda of personal ministry and ignored their true relationship as priests. The whole purpose of the priesthood was to have a people separated unto Himself for the sole purpose of worship. In fact, it is the very heart of the Lord to raise up an end-time kingdom of priests. Whether you are from the tribe of Levi or not, your main calling is to be transformed into that priestly bride. If you are a Levite, your calling is to live a reckless, abandoned life of love and devotion to the Lord, which provokes the Body of Christ to intimacy and holiness.

Over time the Aaronic priesthood lost sight of their calling. The Aaronic priesthood, though useful, became wrought with striving because of facades that were attached to their worship, how they viewed ministry, the calling, themselves, and the Lord Himself. Zadok priests rely on the grace afforded by the rest of the Lord, stemming from their fellowship with the Father. Their ministry and lives are lived by "being" rather than "doing." They are laid-down lovers who allow the Spirit to turn the light on and search the innermost parts of their hearts. Allow Yeshua to break the facades that hinder you from transforming from an Aaronic priest to a Zadok priest, for this is who you truly are.

Read I Samuel 2:31-35.

## "AN OLD MAN WILL NOT BE IN YOUR HOUSE FOREVER"

This reference speaks of religion and getting caught up in the mundane. The Aaronic priesthood, instead of being joined to the heart of the Lord, seeking only to minister to Him, began to place importance on the duty of ministry rather than the heart of it. Unchecked, it grew into idolatry of massive proportion. Our relationship with God is meant to be vertical, not horizontal. It is the Holy Spirit's job to minister to the people. Because the Aaronic priesthood had gone astray from their calling, God sought out a new priesthood, the Zadok priesthood. Read Ezekiel 44:10-14.

## "BUT I WILL RAISE UP FOR MYSELF A FAITHFUL PRIEST WHO WILL DO ACCORDING TO WHAT IS IN MY HEART AND IN MY SOUL…"

God was looking for a priesthood who would hear His heartbeat, and He found it in the Zadok priesthood. Zadok means "righteous." Why was Zadok righteous? He stayed close to the heartbeat of the Father. He focused on ministering to God and not for him. Zadok saw what the Father was doing and gladly joined Him in it. This is why the Zadok priesthood was faithful to King David. They discerned that Spirit rested on David and that he was appointed by God to lead Israel. Most importantly, the Zadok priesthood knew the difference between the holy and profane.

> *Moreover, they shall teach My people the difference between the holy and the profane, and cause them to discern between the unclean and the clean* (Ezekiel 44:23).

Zadok could teach the difference between the holy and profane and discern the difference between the unclean and the holy because of his intimacy with God. To discern and teach without agenda and criticism requires living and walking in the Spirit. The only way to walk in the Spirit is to be intimate with Yeshua, to seek the Fathers heart, and join Him in His work. This is the difference between the Aaronic priesthood and the Zadok priesthood. Verses 17-18 talk about the priest wearing linen garments and not wool. Linen is a fabric that breathes, whereas wool causes one to sweat.

When Levi is in performance agenda, he is not clothed in his linen garments (righteousness) but rather the wool garments of striving, pride, and man pleasing, drenched in the sweat of human effort. When we rest in God and His work, there is no striving. This is where Levi must stay. In the rest of God, dear Levi, you cease to live; Yeshua lives in you, as you minister to Him out of pure love. Striving and performance agendas stem from fear. You are, in essence, denying God's ability to save (the name of Yeshua means "salvation"), while continuing to strive in idolatrous self-sufficiency. God is not concerned with the sweat of human effort but rather the condition of the heart.

> *These are the sons of Zadok, who from the sons of Levi come near to the Lord to minister to Him* (Ezekiel 40:46 b).

> *…then they shall not go out into the outer court from the sanctuary without laying there their garments in which they minister, for they are holy. They shall put on other garments; then they shall approach that which is for the people* (Ezekiel 42: 14).

God leaves specific instructions in His Word. If Levi's inheritance is the Lord Himself, then possessing the call of the Zadok priesthood is found within the call not only of separateness, but the call of unity. As Levites, we are hidden in Christ in plain sight. We are walking billboards of a call of separation from the world to be joined to the Father. It is important not to throw the baby out with the bathwater, dear Levi brethren. In Temple times, priests would change their priestly garments after making sacrifices and when interacting with others outside the Temple. You must change your clothes when fellowshipping and ministering to the people. As ministers of reconciliation we must be all things to all people (I Cor. 9:19-23). The Samaritan knew this truth where both Levite and priest failed (Luke 10:30-37). Neglecting to minister from a place of relational intimacy can wound and repel those we are meant to minister to. A gospel without intimacy is ineffective.

Read I Corinthians 9:19-23. Becoming all things to all people, Levi, is the call of humility and abiding intercession combined. This is the essence of Messiah's ministry. We must be transformed into that perfect breastplate, a balanced mediator between God and man. So, brothers and sisters, know when to change your clothes.

## FORERUNNING REVIVAL

A forerunner is one who goes before to lay the groundwork for things, events, and people to come. For the tribe of Levi, being a forerunner is the essence of the apostolic call in which they move. Just about every Levite the Word mentions was a forerunner in some fashion. Scripture and history are full of Levitical forerunners who birthed revivals and movements, delivered nations from slavery to inheritance, rebuilt the Temple, scribes who penned the infallible Word of God, and those who prepared the way for Messiah. Levites are some of the most prominent and prolific forerunners throughout history! It is the radical "blind yes" of a consecrated Levite that makes him or her a forerunner. After the golden calf incident, Moses, the first Levite forerunner, says to Israel, "Whoever is for the LORD, come to me!" Out of all the tribes, only the tribe of Levi forsook idolatry and began a revival submerged in repentance.

Read Exodus 32:25-29. The same brave forerunning spirit resounded in the heart of John the Baptist, a Levite. John, set apart from the womb, lived a life of no compromise. One simple little life of a laid-down lover made way for the Savior of the world!

> *And he will turn back many of the sons of Israel to Lord their God. And it is he who will go as a forerunner before Him in the Spirit and power of Elijah, TO TURN THE HEARTS OF THE FATHERS BACK TO THE CHILDREN, and the disobedient to the attitude of the righteous; so as to make ready a people prepared for Lord* (Luke 1:16-17).

Dear Levite, your surrender not only impacts your own life but can be a generational catalyst that expands beyond your lifetime. Your faithfulness is not trivial but valued and precious to God. Though you may be unpopular, misunderstand, and peculiar, God has ordained that you should lead the way in the end-time hour and make way for His return. Know your divine destiny and run with it! You hear the Bridegroom and recklessly run after Him in abandoned passion, thereby infecting many others to do the same.

> *Draw me after you and let us run together!* (Song of Songs 1:4a).

## INTIMACY AND THE PLACE OF DOMINION FOR LEVI

Levi's place of dominion is his separateness to God. The Beloved is calling you to His *chuppah* (wedding canopy). He so desires to meet you in that secret place. He is calling you to a new realm of intimacy, joined to Him in a holy matrimonial union. The *chuppah* represents His glory over you. Read Hosea 2:19-20, II Corinthians 11:2, and Song of Songs 2:4-5.

The *chuppah* is a place of abiding in the Bridegroom and the Father. It is the deepest place of intimacy, even the very chambers of His heart. When we come into a place of abiding, we cease from striving. The Father's heart is for you to be joined to Him in the place of abiding.

> *Just as the Father has loved Me, I also have loved you; abide in My love. If you keep My commandments, you will abide in My love; just as I have kept My Father's commandments, abide in His love* (John 15:9-10).

Levi, God has appointed a time for you to come up to the mountain and meet with Him. There is a burning bush waiting for you, ready to challenge your ideals of who you think God is and who you are. Make it the one cry of your heart: "God, show me your glory!" When you do, know that God Himself will be revealed and a transformation of drastic proportions will occur from within. It is the Bridegroom's cry, dear priestly Bride, for you to be all glorious within. Draw near to your husband, Yeshua, under His glorious *chuppah*. He is waiting with arms wide open for you.

### "WHAT KIND OF HOUSE WOULD YOU BUILD FOR ME?"

What kind of house would you build for Me? This is the pressing question on our Father's heart. This question is the commission of every Levi. Abba's chief desire for His creation is worship. Ezekiel 9 describes men who cried out against the abominations in the temple. Isaiah 66:1-6 reiterates this point. It is the Zadok priesthood God is calling forth in this hour to arise and cry out against the abominations in His holy temple. Yeshua said His Father's house would be a house of prayer for all nations (Mark 11:17).

We have yet to see the full glory of Abba's house revealed, due to a serious need of housecleaning. Holiness adorns the house of the Lord. Levi, Abba has called you in His infinite love and mercy to stand for truth and to teach the oracles of His heart. Draw near to Him in faithfulness, emptied out of every profane and idolatrous thing that hinders your priestly matrimonial union with Him. He is jealous for us with holy jealousy. He does desire to use you, but only if you are clothed in true humility. By example you are called, to display the image of priestly Bride separated for these end times. Take time for serious introspection. Be like Isaiah and allow God to undo your every desire, mindset, and motive.

### BUILDING THE HOUSE OF THE LORD

> *Jesus answered and said unto him, "If anyone loves Me, he will keep My word; and My Father will love him, and We will come to him, and make Our abode with him"* (John 14:23).

It is the utmost passionate desire of a Levite not to only build the house of the Lord, but to inhabit the house of God. Habitation is the deepest form of intimacy you and I can possess. Through habitation we find the original and chief intention of the Father's heart: He's seeking for a people who will dwell with Him. This is what Adam and Eve possessed before the Fall. Before His return, Yeshua will call His Bride to return to the Garden and find habitation. Abba loves to visit His children, but the purpose of visitation is to lead us into habitation. Habitation is the abiding presence of the Father. It is His very glory in its fullness restored to you and I as those who house Him!

So what does it mean to build the house of the Lord and how does Levi partake of such a glorious promise? We cannot attain to habitation through religious works but through a life of sincere repentance, keeping the Word of God, abandoned worship, and surrender. Holiness befits the house of the Lord (Psalm 93:5). A Levite who is caught up in works of religion, striving, and offense will only serve God in a limited Aaronic priesthood. He or she will forever circle Mount Sinai, bound to a list of do's and don'ts, trying to prove love to God and man. They will see glimpses of glory and maybe even have glorious visitations from the Lord, but the saddest thing is that they will never fulfill their destinies if they have decided to camp at the wrong mountain. Though Moses had a foretaste of habitation, he never crossed over into true habitation.

A Levite must know that the foundation of the God's house is in Christ alone. No matter how awesome your ministerial duties may seem, if you neglect to enter into the Zadok priesthood, you'll never enter into habitation at Mount Zion.

So how do we possess habitation? How do we become a temple not made with human hands but a living, breathing possession where God himself abides? We keep the Word of God hidden in our hearts, applying it daily to our lives. We allow the bronze laver of God's Word to mirror in us what we need cleansing of. In the brazen altar we sacrifice our wills; upon the table of showbread we are aligned and receive fresh bread from Heaven. Rising from the altar of incense we offer our fragrant aroma: prayer. In the radiant light of His lampstand we abide, as the illumination of His Spirit transforms us.

The veil has already been torn. Do you see your great High Priest beckoning you into the Holy of Holies? Oh, what glory to see the Ark of His Covenant! Oh, what greater glory to have it dwell within us, beloved! His glory is incorruptible. As we abide in Him and His Word, He and the Father will draw us into an everlasting habitation with Him! Does not your spirit leap from within that we mere humans, abiding in our frailties, can be given such an incomprehensible grace? My answer is *yes we can* and *yes we must*! For such is our inheritance. It is for this very reason you and I were made to possess His house. A child does not live outside his Father's house in a secondary residence, born to shame and reproach. No! We are first-class citizens of Heaven! We are not orphans, void of affection and homeless, but heirs to habitation! Ezra possessed a true passion for habitation. He was consumed with the rebuilding of the house of the Lord. Make it your passion, fellow Levi, to rebuild the house of the Lord.

## THE ROLE OF CHIEF MUSICIANS AND SINGERS

*Now these are the singers, heads of fathers' households of the Levites, who lived in the chambers of the temple free from other service; for they were engaged in their work day and night* (I Chronicles 9:33).

Amongst this radiant tribe are some of the most powerful worshippers and intercessors of our day. One vital way Levites serve the Lord is through worship, specifically harp-and-bowl worship. Levites often share this place with the tribe of Judah. Together they both possess an unparalleled passion for habitation. Their infectious love and devotion draws many into the throne room of God, releasing an open Heaven and pulling down strongholds in high places with their radical, surrendered worship. Both in the time of David and Solomon, Levites simultaneously served alongside their brother Judah and released the manifest Shekinah glory and power of God. Moses and Miriam led Israel forth in worship and changed the status of the whole nation of Israel. Likewise, many a Levite and priest have offered melodies of Heaven that have moved the heart of Almighty God. In our present time God is raising up houses of prayer in which He is restoring true Levitical worship. These houses of prayer are paving the way for the King of Kings in their diligent pursuit of the kingdom. If you are a Levi, ask the Lord how He would call you to build His house in this end-time hour.

Read II Chronicles 5:7-14. When you and I offer undefiled worship void of the flesh and its striving, it is like putting out the welcome mat for the glory of God. A broken and poured out priestly Bride is whom the Lord is seeking to serve in His courts. When unbridled and full of liberty, songs of infinite love and praise begin to rise to Heaven and God's throne moves! Do not take lightly how you offer worship. Worship is not a show, it's a lifestyle. Intercession is not a pious duty in which you are doing God a great service, it's communion. No flesh can glory in His presence.

Isaiah, also a Levite, caught a revelation to which we would be wise to adhere to. He was in the throne room of Heaven, beholding the Lord and all His holiness, and was undone. Isaiah was acutely aware of his fallen human nature. He saw the King high and lifted up, the very train of His robe filling the temple, and had an encounter that forever changed him. Seek the Lord, dear Levi, to catch a living revelation of Him in His holiness. When this revelation brings an undoing, engage in worship. It is my sincere belief, brother Levi, that as we do, we will enter into glorious habitation and thus build His house!

## CROSSING OVER INTO HABITATION

Read Joshua 3:1-17. When the Israelites crossed over the Jordan, it was a foreshadowing of when we as believers cross over from visitation into habitation. When we cross over into habitation we fully come into our inheritance found in Christ. Notice that the priests were to go ahead of the people. The Lord often calls a Levite to go ahead of others, for they are like pioneers (an apostolic calling), preparing the way for the Lord. Secondly, notice that Joshua asked the priests who carried the Ark to go to the edge of the water and stand still. God is calling you, Levi, to the edge of the waters of life that flow from His throne. In the waters you meet Him, as you stand in a place of stillness and great purity. It is a place of no striving, for flesh cannot enter into the glory of God, and more importantly, it cannot enter into habitation. From this place the Lord does mighty wonders, both in and through you, brethren Levi. You are given the charge of carrying the Ark of the Lord. It is not a small task, nor is it to be taken in a flippant manner, but it must abound in the fear of the Lord, righteousness, humility, and absolute love. You are the living oracle of the Word of God, carrying the mandate of the King of Kings. Appointment awaits you in the waters of life. Abba is calling you to the Jordan. Will you accept this appointment to cross over into habitation? Dear priestly Bride, will you be ready in the hour the Father calls you to enter into habitation?

## PRAYER OF REPENTANCE AND DESTINY
## FOR THE TRIBE OF LEVI

Abba, I long to abide and to be joined to You under your *chuppah*. Show me your face, Abba. I desire only You. I so desperately need You, my one true Love. Reveal to me the deep mysteries of who You are and who I am. Take me to my mountaintop, where my burning bush will confront me with the reality of who You really are. Consume me in that rapturous blaze of Your glory. Refine all dross and lead me to the Cross. Purge me deep within, to the very core of my being. I repent of the leaven of the Pharisees. I lay my life on Your brazen altar. Wash me with the bronze laver of Your Word. Deliver me of performance agendas. I repent of being religious. Help me not to get caught up in the mundane ritual of ministry, but rather may I be consumed in ministering only to You. May my ministry to the Body be an overflow of my communion with You. Fashion me into a pure Zadok priest. Give me discernment between the holy and profane. Slaughter the religious cows in my beliefs. Destroy every golden calf. Deliver me from anger, bitterness, and unforgiveness. Heal me, O Healer, and I will be healed. Restore me to my place of destiny in You, my Beloved. Under your wings I take refuge. Hide me in Your Holy Place. Restore me in Your love. Transform me into that priestly bride for whom You desperately long. Release the oracles of Your Word from within me. May I always seek and stand for truth, no matter the cost. My life is Yours. In Yeshua's name, Amen.

---

[1] Oxford Dictionaries, "Oxford Dictionaries. Oxford University Press.

http://www.oxforddictionaries.com/us/definition/american_english/garnet (accessed July 08, 2015).

[2] Norman Grubb, *Rees Howells Intercessor* (Fort Washington, Pennsylvania: Christian

Literature Crusade/Lutterworth Press, 1952) Page 64. Rees Howells would gain places of intercession through the work of abiding in the Cross.

[3] Norman Grubb, *Rees Howells Intercessor* (Fort Washington, Pennsylvania: Christian

Literature Crusade/Lutterworth Press, 1952).

[4] Rabbi Ariel Hargis. "Preparation for Praise and Worship: Series I" Ephraim and Judah

International home group study; Rabbi Hargis referenced Midrash Tanchuma, Pikudei 9 about bronze mirrors, Lakeland, FL September 8, 1995).

[5] The Temple Institute, "The Temple Institute," *International Department of the Temple

Institute,* March 19, 2015, https://www.templeinstitute.org/incense.htm

[6] Yoav Elan, "Beis Hamikdh Topics," *Beis Hamikdash Topics Blogspot,* Feburary 17.

2014, Accessed March 19, 2015, http://beishamikdashtopics.blogspot.com/2014/02/preparation-of-incense-and-view-of.html .
8 S. Sundar Singh, *I Have Decided to Follow Jesus,* Public Domain.

[7] V. Chris and Thomas M. Tinney, Sr "The Book (stick) of Levi,"

Acessed March 19, 2015, http://www.academic-genealogy.com/ancientgenealogylevi.htm

# CHAPTER 5
# JUDAH: THE GOVERNMENT OF PRAISE

*Praise the Lord! Praise God in His sanctuary; Praise Him in His mighty expanse.*
*Praise Him for His deeds; Praise Him according to His excellent greatness. Praise Him*
*with trumpet sound; Praise Him with harp and lyre. Praise Him with timbre and*
*dancing; Praise Him with stringed instruments and pipe. Praise Him with loud cymbals;*
*Praise Him resounding cymbals. Let everything that has breath praise the Lord. Praise*
*the Lord! (Psalm 150:1-6).*

If the kingdom of God is righteousness, peace, and joy, then praise is its government. God's kingdom is built on love. The kingdom of God is within us. We are ruled by our love for God. The precepts of the kingdom are built on relationship. God has ordained that Judah would rule. So what is God saying through this tribe? He is saying that He establishes His kingdom through Judah, even to the meaning of the name.

## THE NAMING OF JUDAH

*And she conceived again and bore a son and said, "This time I will praise the Lord."*
*Therefore she named him Judah. Then she stopped bearing (Genesis 29:35).*

Judah means "praise." Within this tribe you will find some of the most intimate lovers of God. Judah's existence flounders apart from the throne room. Their very being is immersed in the fabric of praise and worship. They constantly live and strive (in rest) for the manifest presence of God. The Body of Christ would do well to learn from this beautiful tribe.

## WHAT IS TRUE PRAISE?

True praise is a great exhortation, a lifting of another (or something) in esteem, ascribing honor, worth, a recognition of majestic lordship. In order to offer true praise to the Lord, we must bow low so that He is exalted in sincerity. So in order to truly praise, we must possess humility and sincere love.

*But let the brother of humble circumstances glory in his elevation (James 1:9).*

When we decrease, the Father and His kingdom increase. Praise is magnification. For believers, praise is magnification to the utmost extreme!

## BE MAGNIFIED BY LYNN DESHAZO[1]

I have made You too small in my eyes, oh Lord, forgive me
and I have believed in a lie, that You are unable to help me
But now, oh Lord, I see my wrong, heal my heart and show
Yourself strong, and in my eyes and with my song, oh Lord,
 be magnified.

Be magnified, oh Lord, you are highly exalted
and there is nothing You can't do
Oh Lord, my eyes are on You
Be magnified, oh Lord, be magnified

I have leaned on a wisdom of men, oh Lord, forgive me
and I have responded to them instead of Your
light and Your mercy
But now, Oh Lord, I see my wrong, heal my heart
and show Yourself strong and in my eyes
and in my song, oh Lord, be magnified.

When we bow low, laying ourselves down, we are exalting His majesty. In essence, it is a true picture of throne room worship. The Word says that we are seated in heavenly places with Christ (Ephesians 2:6). How is this possible? As we bow low, we come to truly abide in His nature as we die to our own. This is how a humble man glories in his elevation (James 1:9). We glory in whom we belong to; it is the praise of His lordship. God created for Himself a people who, with their simple lives, express just this. The tribe of Judah is full of passionate lovers whose ultimate destiny is the throne room of God.

## THE GEMSTONE OF JUDAH

The gemstone of Judah is the emerald. The emerald is a deep green color. Emerald is the most valuable type of beryl. The emerald's intense green color is the color of life. We know that we have life and life more abundantly in and though Christ (John 10:10). Yeshua Himself is from this tribe. We see that He is our cornerstone, that perfect emerald. Praise is also associated with the color green because of its connection to new growth and the earth. Therefore, this stone is very fitting for the tribe of Judah. It can also be seen as a symbol of healing (trees of healing for nations) and abundance (in wealth, favor).

*And the one who sat there had the appearance of jasper and ruby. A rainbow that shone like an emerald encircled the throne.* (Revelation 4:3)

In Revelation 4:3 the apostle John illustrates a beautiful picture of throne room worship and habitation. First, he describes Yeshua as one who "had the appearance of jasper and ruby". Jasper is the gemstone of the tribe of Benjamin and ruby the gemstone of the tribe of Reuben. John then depicts an emerald rainbow that encircles the throne. This beautiful mystery speaks of how we, the Bride composed priceless living stones, are *echad* (Hebrew for one) with our Bridegroom. The mystery is not just speaking of Benjamin (jasper) and Reuben (ruby) but rather from the youngest son Benjamin to Reuben the firstborn. In other words, Scripture is speaking of all the tribes.

The emerald rainbow puzzled me for some time. Why is it a rainbow? Gemstones refract light. A prismatic rainbow can be seen depending on how the light catches a stone. Gemstones will also refract even more prismatic light and color from surrounding gemstones. Yeshua is the exact representation of the Father. He radiates the Father's glory (nature). We are to be so one with Him that there is no differentiation between Bride and Groom! In my opinion this is by far one of the most exquisite pictures of intimacy found in habitation.

*"I have given them the glory that you gave me, that they may be one as we are one. I in them and you in me—so that they may be brought to complete unity...* (John 17:22-23 a).

This mystery also alludes to Jacob's prophecy in Genesis 49:8 "*Judah, your brothers shall praise you. your father's sons will bow down to you...*". It is describing Yeshua who embodies the emerald rainbow being worshiped from His throne! O what wedded bliss with have seated with our Bridegroom in heavenly places!

## THE SYMBOL

The symbol of Judah is the lion. The lion speaks of many characteristics of this noble tribe. The lion has three stages to its growth and maturity: infancy, adolescence, and adulthood.

## INFANCY

Cubs take six to seven months to be weaned. Over 80% are killed or die before reaching adolescence.[2] In Judah's infancy, you can see the makings of a great leader. David's early training ground came through being a lowly shepherd boy in his father's fields. It was there the Holy Spirit nurtured him as a worshiper, warrior, and great patriarch of our faith. Leadership without wisdom and maturity is likened unto a young cub. A cub lacks the knowledge and strength of an adult. This is why they die off so quickly. Judah in his infancy, though showing leadership ability, cannot reign until he learns to fight, feed, and nurture himself in throne room praise. He must replenish his own strength and capabilities, drawing on the strength and ability of the Savior. Many a Judah (and other young believers from other tribes) has faltered and even died spiritually due to immaturity.

Leadership takes a lifetime to be developed. Seeking the nourishment and counsel of another mature Judah or Levi is needed for a young Judah's development. A cub is just learning to eat, walk, and be in unity with the rest of his pride (clan). When he prematurely ventures out, Judah is detrimental not only to himself but to others as well. He is clumsy, making many mistakes in learning the timing and move of the Spirit. He is often whiny, lazy, and prideful. It takes great discernment, unconditional love, and patience to aid Judah into maturity. In this stage of a Judah's growth Abba is laying the foundation of a leader. He lacks deep revelation although he shows immediate signs of a powerful prophetic nature and ability. He can be loud, brash, offensive, and even annoying to some. This cycle is ended and maturity begins through the school of the Spirit, often through brokenness. During this time, Judah must stay close to nurturing fathers and mothers of the faith with Spirit-led insight and unconditional love.

## ADOLESCENCE

Adolescence is a curious, hard, and bittersweet time for Judah. Much "pruning" takes place in this stage. During this time, shifting and some of the greatest seasons of chastening by the Father come. Judah is in a hard place because he is no longer a cub. While he has gained his chomps (ability to chew on revelation), he is not yet ready to be king. David himself proved to be a leader with his victory over Goliath. However, he was not ready to be king. No doubt he was a strong warrior and a powerful worshipper. David's obvious charisma and anointing was known to many. He lacked, however, the humility, wisdom, and mature character to reign as Israel's king. So God, in his loving-kindness toward David, used affliction and mistakes to chasten David to his true identity: a man after God's own heart.

Disney's *The Lion King*, a popular children's movie, has poignant truths for Judah. In the story, Simba, the young lion, sings a song called, "I Just Can't Wait To Be King."[3] Cute and light-hearted as it is, this is the very way an adolescent Judah thinks and is motivated. He is no longer satisfied with the milk of the Word. He longs for deeper revelation and worship and even begins to venture out prophetically. What hinders him is brokenness. He thinks he is ready to rule, but he isn't. True, he has been through much breaking and hard lessons already, but he still lacks the brokenness and servanthood to be a true ruler. At this stage, Judah must be careful not to intimidate others with his strong and fierce, warrior-like nature. Doing so could wound others and hinder his destiny. Other temptations prevalent during this stage is worry, insecurity, and the spirit of offense. What hinders you in this stage, Judah, may cost you destiny and dominion. In your infancy, you were given a greater grace. During your adolescence you are given some responsibility. Always remember that bowing low is the key to ruling and reigning with Christ.

> *Can you hunt the prey for the lion, or satisfy the appetite of young lions, when they couch in their dens, and wait in their lair?* (Job 38:39).

During this time Judah is truly being fashioned as an expert in war. His appetite for the prophetic and to worship is his food day and night. Have you ever noticed how adolescents can practically eat you out of a house and home? They have an increase in appetite because of this crucial time of accelerated growth. Judah, my word to you is to get so desperate, so hungry for God that your hunger and thirst for righteousness becomes the driving force in this time. Let no one spurn your worship. Cling to the Father, spend time at His feet, and pour out your whole being. For it is in the quiet place of His love that He will answer you and fill you with every good thing.

> *For thus says the Lord to me, "As the lion or the young lion growls over its prey, against which a band of shepherds is called out, and he will not be terrified at their voice, nor disturbed at their noise, So will the Lord of hosts come down to* **wage war** *on Mount Zion and on its hill"* (Isaiah 31:4).

The term "wage war" in Hebrew (*tsaba*) means: to do military service, to do a sacred service, and to wait upon The Lord. These are your marching orders, young Judah. Your worship is sacred unto the Father and your praise powerful. As you learn to quiet your spirit and allow the Spirit to teach you lessons of servanthood and brokenness, He can then entrust you with His kingdom. It is through this time of adolescence that your God-given roar is developed.

## HOW JUDAH DEVELOPS HIS ROAR!

For Judah to develop his roar, he must allow the spirit of the Lord to roar through him.

> *Thus says God the Lord, who created the heavens and stretched them out, who spread out the earth and its offspring,* **who gives breath to the people on it, and spirit to those who walk in it** (Isaiah 42:5).

Dear Judah, the first thing you must do to develop your roar is allow the Spirit of God to breathe upon you. You must be born of Spirit and not the flesh. A roar made in the flesh is a useless and pitiful cry of vanity. The Hebrew word for breath in this verse is נשמה *neshamâh* (pronounced nesh-aw-maw'). It means, "a puff, a wind that is angry, or a vital breath, a divine inspiration, a blast." It is directly tied to the work of the Holy Spirit; as we see in this verse, He gives us His Spirit to show us how to walk before Him.

Secondly, Judahs must begin to connect with their God-given sound. What is their God-given sound? First, it is important to note where their God-given sound comes from. A Judah's roar comes from the throne room. It is birthed and cultivated in praise. Your roar is developed as you draw near to the Lord; bowing low, you exalt His majesty. It is only then that you can gain victory over the enemy.

> *The young lions roar after their prey, and they seek their food from God. When the sun rises they withdraw, and lie down in their dens* (Psalm 104:21-22).

In an open vision the Lord gave me a beautiful picture about how to gain victory. I believe it holds insight for us all, but for Judah it is especially pertinent. I saw before me a great battle. The battlefield was at the foot of a mountain in a valley. The armies of Heaven and hell were gathered there. What was seemingly strange was that in the middle of the battlefield the Lord had pitched a tent for His Bride. There He had provided a lavish King's feast (His banner over us is love). There was also a couch for His Bride to rest upon. Yeshua went to war against the enemy, while His Bride was resting and feasting.

I give this illustration to say this: When the Lord is lifted up in battle, you come into a place of absolute victory. As Judah is feasting upon Him and resting in Him, he prevails. To engage in this battle any other way would leave you, Judah, weary, prone to burnout, and out of the perfect will of the Father. Communion coupled with the rest of the Lord is your high place of anointing, Judah. Take note of the lions in the scripture above. First they found their God-given roar, next they sought God for their food, and then they feasted at the Lord's Table. The battlefield is where the Lord spreads His table before you. Third, when the sun arises, they withdrew. In other words, when you see Yeshua (the Son/Sun of Righteousness) arising in the brilliance of His glory, you withdraw for victory is imminent. He is bringing breakthrough! Lastly, you retire to your den—Shiloh, which is Christ, your rest! Certainly David, a Judah, knew this well when he offered this song of praise:

*The Lord is my shepherd, I shall not want. He makes me to lie down in green pastures; He leads me beside still waters. He restores my soul; He guides me in paths of righteousness for His name's sake. Even though I walk through the valley of the shadow of death, I fear no evil; for Thou art with me; Thy rod and Thy staff, they comfort me. Thou dost prepare a table before me in the presence of my enemies; Thou has anointed my head with oil; my cup overflows. Surely goodness and mercy shall follow me all the days of my life, and I will dwell in the house of the Lord forever* (Psalm 23:1-6).

## ADULTHOOD

There is a sound coming from the throne. Legion upon legion of demons flee at this deafening sound. It shatters the darkness and melts the hardest of hearts. One note from this sound has the ability to free nations, bring restoration to the ancient ruins of ages past, and usher in the coming of a long-awaited King. What is this sound that causes hordes of demons to beg for mercy and transforms the cold hearts of many?

Picture an exceedingly great army rising from the earth, an army indispensable in power and beauty. The warriors are nameless and faceless, seeking no glory of their own. On the frontline come the most fearless and dreadful warriors. It is not their mere strength that makes their enemies cower, it is their brokenness. Radiant in beauty, they sing a song of love which moves the heart of their Bridegroom King and Creator to return for them. Processing forth in colors, sounds, and movements not even yet heard or seen in angelic companies of Heaven, they move their Lover, the Bridegroom King, and Abba Father, stirring their heart strings. Moving into the frontline in battle array, which at first looks like wedding attire to the untrained eye, these warriors arise with one sound: A MIGHTY ROAR!

Judah, you are approaching your finest hour. It is through you that God expressly chooses the sound of Heaven to arise from. The only way this sound can be developed in you is through true brokenness. Whatever hinders perfect love and its holy song arising in and through you, repent of it. For when and as you do, you will provoke, in absolute laid-down love, your brothers and sisters in Christ to arise to their true place of dominion. When the lion reaches adulthood, he is ready to rule. He has weathered many battles, trials and great suffering, and has come out victorious yet humble.

Judah, it is by laying down your own kingdom and glory that you can truly receive your inheritance in Yeshua, the government of praise. Upon maturity, you make powerful leaders in the areas of worship, the prophetic, administration, and warfare. The commission from the throne is for you to carry a governmental anointing of praise. Judah, your appointment in the throne room awaits you. The Father's chief desire is that you make His throne room your habitation. Your key to habitation is to bow low.

## THE COUNTERFEIT LION: SATAN

Read I Peter 5:8-9. For everything God has created that is holy there is a profane counterfeit. This scripture states, "*like* a lion," meaning Satan is no more than an imitator, a mere copycat. His deceptive guise is not blatant but very crafty and enticing. For this reason, the Word tells us to be sober and on alert. God has given Judah a keen sense of smell in the spirit. He can always smell out the pretenders and thieves. Over time, this develops into a true prophetic gifting and calling for Judah. When Judah's sense of smell wanes, it is because he is neglecting the throne room worship (a holy aroma) and therefore is prey to Satan.

## YESHUA, THE LION OF THE TRIBE OF JUDAH

Read Revelation 5:5-6. Yeshua, the Lion of the tribe of Judah, is longing to roar as never before. Within His deafening roar, life and death hang in the balance. His roar explodes with resurrection power to His saints and brings death to all things profane. In Him and through Him all victory lies. When you are in the heat of battle, picture Him arising on your behalf and waging war! The victory is already won—it's a done deal! Read Isaiah 42:13 and Exodus 15:3.

## THE LORD ROARS FROM ZION

Read Joel 3:16-17. The Messianic reign of our King is imminent and very soon. His fame will soon be known through all the earth, for the knowledge of the glory is appointed to usher in His return. Zion is His dwelling place. He is not only zealous for His habitation (Zion/Jerusalem), but that we should enter into it. His roar is unparalleled in power and majesty. When He roars, He shall align all things. Suddenly, His kingdom will be established. His roar is weighty, both in glory and absolute authority, for He has been given this by His Father.

## JACOB'S PROPHECY

> *Judah, your brothers shall praise you; Your hand shall be on the neck of your enemies; Your father's sons shall bow down to you. Judah is a lion's whelp; From the prey, my son, you have gone up. He couches, he lies down as a lion, And as a lion, who dares rouse him up? The scepter shall not depart from Judah, Nor the ruler's staff from between his feet, Until Shiloh comes, And to Him shall be the obedience of the peoples. He ties his foal to the vine, And his donkey's colt to the choice vine; He washes his garments in wine, And his robes in the blood of grapes. His eyes are dull from wine, And his teeth white from milk* (Genesis 49:8-12).

## "JUDAH, YOUR BROTHERS SHALL PRAISE YOU"

Judah means "praise." This scripture establishes this fact and confirms Judah's role of leadership. This does not imply idolatry but rather a tribute to Judah's God-given gift of leadership and destiny. As believers, we need to encourage each other in our gifts and callings. Affirming the destiny of others is crucial to coming forth in our own. This verse also speaks of the honor placed on this tribe.

Judahs possess a very charismatic nature, which, like a magnet, draws people to them. We see this displayed in Yeshua when He was on the earth. Crowds flocked to Him. Also, after David's early victories the women of Israel praised him saying, "Saul has slain his thousands, and David his ten thousands" (I Samuel 18:7). What causes people to be drawn to a Judah? The glory of God stirs up absolute love and absolute hate. We see this displayed in Yeshua's and David's day, when they had both those who followed them faithfully, loved them, and praised them and also those who persecuted them and sought for their lives. It is important to know how to use this charisma (glory) correctly. If it is used in pride, your fall will come. However, when a Judah walks in humility, many are drawn to run after the Beloved with them (Song of Songs 1:4). Your charisma must be used to draw others into the throne room. Worship implies an attraction to something or someone. Judah attracts people to the throne room and ultimately to the Lord.

### "YOUR HAND SHALL BE ON THE NECK OF YOUR ENEMIES"

Praise is a powerful tool in spiritual warfare. Furthermore, it is vital for true victory. When we are focused on Yeshua, knowing that He has already paid the price, we know victory is assured. The tribe of Judah was known for being experts in war. Why is this? Judah first went forth in praise into battle.

Read II Chronicles 20:1-27. Praise is the most effective battle plan we can engage in. The Word says to draw near to God first (James 4:7). When we draw near in praise and worship we are seeking Him and His will. Praise is a mighty weapon that brings breakthrough. This passage further confirms this truth.

Strangulation is the primary way a lion kills his prey. It is Judah's deafening praise and surrender in worship that strangles our enemy, Satan! A lion knows the exact method of attack. The neck is a place of strength. When strangling his prey, the lion shuts off the life-source of its victim. In spiritual warfare it is the same. We go after the strong man (the neck) and thereby take down the head (Satan). The tribe of Judah receives this direct plan of attack through praise. It took Israel three days to carry off all the spoil! Now that is a monumental victory!

### "JUDAH IS A LION'S WHELP; FROM THE PREY, MY SON, YOU HAVE GONE UP; HE COUCHES, HE LIES DOWN AS A LION, AND AS A LION, WHO DARES ROUSE HIM UP?"

As a skillful warrior, Judah was seen as intimidating to many. Praise is very intimidating to the enemy. Our praises announce and establish that the kingdom of God has come, thereby thwarting the enemy's kingdom. The enemy is terrified of pure, surrendered worship. A lion's whelp implies that Judah in his infancy shows promise of being a great warrior. Though he is not yet ready for the immensity of great battle, he can still be intimidating, despite his immaturity. When Judah is called a lion's whelp, he is given the charge to grow in strength and ability to become that strong and intimidating warrior. Praise will also intimidate or provoke jealousy in other believers who are immature and scoff at the pure worship Judah is called to give. Stay humble, dear Judah, whether you are favored or persecuted. You do not want to give the enemy a legal right for any reproach you may suffer. God will vindicate you as you place Him first in all things.

### "THE SCEPTER SHALL NOT DEPART FROM JUDAH, NOR THE RULER'S STAFF FROM BETWEEN HIS FEET, UNTIL SHILOH COMES, AND TO HIM SHALL BE THE OBEDIENCE OF THE PEOPLES"

God has established His government in and through Judah (praise). Judah's calling to government speaks of leadership, administration, and motivation to the Body. Judah is called to be a motivator. Judah pushes others to move into their destiny. Wherever God is moving, you will always find Judah leading the way. Judah motivates through encouraging and praising others. As mentioned earlier, they can be very charismatic in nature. People are automatically drawn to them. Judah will operate in the motivational gift of exhortation. Their exhortation can come through music, dance, the prophetic, and their leadership. Judah's leadership abilities stem from a governmental anointing. They often move in the supernatural this way also. This scripture states that the scepter shall not depart from Judah. This means the kingdom of Yeshua, the Lion of the tribe of Judah, is eternal. It knows no end.

Shiloh has several different interpretations. Christians believe that Shiloh is the Messiah (Yeshua). In the Hebrew it means, "place of rest." It was also a city in the territory of Ephraim, where the Ark first rested in Israel until the time of Eli.

Read Hebrews 4:1-11. In the throne room, Judah comes into his "place of rest." In the presence of God every worry, burden, and battle subsides. When Judah is not in the throne room of God, he is not at rest. His very nature lives for the manifest presence of God. His meat and drink is worship and intimacy with the Father. One thing you will learn of Judah: he is either worshipping or worrying. When we worry, our focus has taken a detour away from Yeshua. Our souls enter a state of unrest, and anxiety begins to dominate. Judah, seek first the Kingdom and His righteousness and cast all your cares upon Him for he cares for you.

## "AND TO HIM SHALL BE THE OBEDIENCE OF THE PEOPLES"

God has ordained that Judah would have the anointing and mantle of authority. He expressly speaks His kingdom purpose through their lives and ministries. Judah carries this authority not only into the kingdom of God, bringing motivation and administration to the Body, but to the darkness also. As you yield fruits of repentance and obedience to Christ, you are given the ability to reign with Him. He has been given the golden scepter of Heaven to this tribe. Within His scepter, we find that the government of praise is all about intimacy and carrying out the kingdom mandates of Abba's heart. The dynamic of praise and worship brings an order to the spiritual atmosphere within the Body of Christ. It is God's ordained way; the Father chooses to bring unity, peace, and balance.

Ultimately this portion refers to Messiah (though all of this prophecy does), that man is subject to his Lordship. Yeshua's obedience to die upon the Cross afforded complete lordship. Demons, principalities, and Satan himself are subject to Christ. Read Philippians 2:9-13.

## "HE TIES HIS FOAL TO THE VINE, AND HIS DONKEY'S COLT TO THE CHOICE VINE"

The foal and the donkey imply work or labor, humility, and servanthood. A vine represents life, fruitfulness, and growth. The verse states, He ties his foal to the vine…. God is saying, "Judah ties his life, ministry, worship—the essence of who he is—to a fruitful place. Tie your labor to the fruit of the Spirit. When you labor, make sure it is in the attitude of servanthood and true humility. For when you do, you will experience growth, joy, and fulfillment in My kingdom. When you tie yourself to unfruitful things that do not promote My kingdom, you will find pride, self-serving, fear, despair, and stunted growth."

Judah tying himself to a fruitful vine is tying himself directly to the nature of Christ, which is the essence of abiding. Judah can come into abiding in Christ successfully through bowing low.

Read John 15:1-8. A beautiful example of this is with your brethren of the tribe of Ephraim. The joint of Ephraim is supplying the spiritual marrow to the tribe of Judah by representing the Father in Ephraim's own calling to abide. The donkey's colt, is a picture of the relationship between Judah and the tribe of Issachar (who camped in the wilderness together). Issachar's symbol is the donkey, who carries the mantle of humility. God will often tie us to other tribes, whose innate spiritual giftings and DNA help us to overcome our weaknesses. How glorious for us to lay down our lives, that we might build the glorious temple of Living Stones. Amen!

### "HE WASHES HIS GARMENTS IN WINE, AND HIS ROBES IN THE BLOOD OF GRAPES. HIS EYES ARE DULL FROM WINE, AND HIS TEETH WHITE FROM MILK."

This portion has a twofold meaning. Judah wears the garment of praise. His robes are not only of righteousness but of kingly honor and majesty. Wine is a symbol of joy and the Holy Spirit. Praise is always washed in joy perpetuated by the Holy Spirit. The garment of praise lifts the heavy burdened spirit of both the wearer of that garment and those with whom he or she comes into contact. Praise is contagious! It is the very thing that broke Paul and Silus's chains in prison. Likewise, praise breaks chains and fetters of those who sit in darkness.

Read Isaiah 61:1-7. Through the mantle of praise, Judah brings the ministry of reconciliation and restoration. Praise is a life source bringing new growth and healing to whatever it touches. It brings times of refreshing and great joy. Praise is vital to restoration, for it is through praise that our focus is returned to God, our hope renewed, and a strengthening which empowers to our lives. This is why Judah is so vital to the Body of Christ.

On the other side of the coin, wine is also a symbol of worldliness. The world offers a counterfeit wine, intoxicating to many; it lures many a soul into compromise. We are not to be drunk with the world's wine. Drunkenness impairs one's judgment. For Judahs this is detrimental because it hinders their discernment and ultimately cripples their ability to rule. Their spiritual eyes cannot be "dull from wine" that the world has to offer. Doing so blinds them from being spiritually receptive and thus open for attack to the enemy.

Judah must be cautious not to be intoxicated with mammon. The spirit of mammon will lure you away from intimacy. Mammon brings fear, causing you to doubt God's provision. This can lead to a spirit of poverty. Judah, if God has given you the kingdom, then provision is within the kingdom purposes. You can unlock these treasures through the intimacy of your worship. Stay childlike in faith and in your worship.

Teeth are a sign of maturity and the ability to chew on revelation and truth. Judah must continually seek for a deep revelation from God's Word. Linking up with Levi would ensure this and provide him wise counsel. God is calling Judah to chew on deep revelation. Revelation from God's Word coupled with worship is a powerful weapon. This is why Judah and Levi are indispensable to each other. It is the marriage of worship and praise (harp) and intercession (bowl) that brings a balance to God's end-time House of Prayer. While ministering at a 24/7 House of Prayer in Jerusalem, I saw the beauty of this unity in the Spirit. I could truly sense Abba's pleasure of this unity.

This portion also clearly reveals the second coming of Christ. Yeshua was buried with His bloody tallit (Scripture says He folded it a certain way, as is the custom to fold a prayer shawl in a prescribed manner). When He returns, He will be wearing that same bloody tallit as a sign of indignation and judgment to His enemies and vindication for His Father's kingdom and His Bride. Read Isaiah 63:1-4 and Revelation 19:13.

## MOSES' PROPHECY

*And this regarding Judah; so he said, "Hear, O Lord, the voice of Judah, And bring him to his people. With his hands he contended for them, And may You be a help against his adversaries* (Deuteronomy 33:7).

### "HEAR, O LORD, THE VOICE OF JUDAH"

This verse translates to, "Hear, O Lord, the voice of praise." God is ever-present when His praises ascend from out of pure hearts. It also implies, "hear the prayer of Judah." Our supplications are continually arising to the throne room, to the very heart of God. His ear is attentive to the cry of His beloved ones. As you, Judah, bow low, the Lord will answer you in His lovingkindness. Know that your surrender will always afford you an audience with the King. Read Psalm 10:17 and Psalm 17:1-3.

Read Psalm 20:1-9. King David was intimately acquainted with the Lord. David's consuming passion was His Bridegroom. He knew that the Lord heard him. When David released a pure, repentant, and honest cry to the Lord, he always got God's attention. He knew to release a sound that would move the heart of the Father. The tribe of Judah is a company of passionate worshippers who know how to possess the ear of their Bridegroom. When they do, they often render an open Heaven, for God has made a covenant with them to answer them.

## "AND BRING HIM TO HIS PEOPLE"

This also has a twofold message. It is an appeal to Judah in the natural to call Israel and its people, to return home, to make *aliyah*. It is also a call to the Church to unite with Israel, to love her, pray for her, and befriend her. God blesses those who bless Israel. In essence this the emergence of the One New Man. Read Ezekiel 37.

Secondly, Judah, as a leader, is called to bring people to the throne room, even to the depths of the Father's heart. God placed a charismatic nature within Judah to accomplish this. People are either drawn or repelled to the Father's heart, depending on the condition of their own hearts.

## "WITH HIS HANDS HE CONTENDED FOR THEM, AND MAY YOU BE A HELP AGAINST HIS ADVERSARIES"

Judah, as an expert in war, defends his brethren with great passion. It is the heart of every Judah to protect their "pack." They are fiercely defensive of those whom they love. When Judah looks to God for a battle plan, he is invincible. It is this strength that is intimidating to the enemy. Over and over in David's psalms he reiterates his need for guidance in deliverance from his enemies. Worship is a secret place where Judah can go in the heat of battle. Praise is both a weapon and a refuge. This scripture also makes reference to Yeshua, the Lion of Judah, going to battle on our behalf.

## THE FACADES OF JUDAH

If praise is the character and driving force of Judah, then pride is his Achilles heel. Pride is the one thing that will separate us from the throne room. It was in the throne room that Lucifer pronounced his declaration of pride and rebellion against God.

Read Ezekiel 28:12-18. Before his fall, Satan, a.k.a. Lucifer, was one of the most beautiful creatures in Heaven. He was specifically created by God for the purpose of worship. Lucifer was adorned with every precious stone. Music, praise, and worship were etched into the fiber of his very being. Worship entails adoration, beauty, and the ecstasy of love from another. Lucifer sought his own worship. This became his undoing: the need for self-worship and pride. Satan was consumed in his pre-Fall magnificence, which led to his apostasy through pride and self-exaltation against the Father. Satan's driving passion is to be worshipped.

*And he said to Him, "All these things will I give, all these things will I give You if you fall down and worship me"* (Matthew 4:9).

*But you have said in your heart, "I will ascend to heaven; I will raise my throne above the stars of God, and I will sit on the mount of assembly in the recesses of the north. I will ascend above the heights of the clouds; I will make myself like the Most High"* (Isaiah 14:13-14).

When we begin to delve into an unholy self-love, pride, and even self-pity, we are in direct opposition to what we are created for: worship. We enthrone what we worship. Take a close look. Is the King of Glory enthroned in your heart, or is self-exaltation, pity, and rebellion enthroned? It was Satan's rebellion to enthrone himself and set up his own kingdom that brought his demise. How can it be any different for us? We have all heard the saying, "pride goes before a fall" (Proverbs 16:18), but do we internalize these deadly ramifications to our spirit man, and, more importantly, our intimacy with the Father? It is only logical that Satan would try to steal from Judahs the very area of their strength: the intimacy of worship. If the enemy can distract and lure you into his devices of self-love, pride, despair, and rebellion, he can detour you from throne room worship.

## THE SPIRIT OF OPPRESSION

*The garment of praise for the spirit of heaviness* (Isaiah 61:3 KJV).

Judah carries the mantle of praise. Whatever is the source of your strength and calling is the very gateway the enemy will come and attack. The enemy seeks to weaken and eventually completely annihilate our source of anointing. Praise uplifts the spirit of whomever and whatever it touches. Many times throughout the Book of Psalms we find David crying out to God to uplift him. He knew that through praise, the spirit of heaviness, i.e., oppression, would lift.

> *Why are you in despair, O my soul? And why have you become disturbed within me?*
> *Hope in God, for I shall yet praise Him, the help of my countenance, and my God*
> (Psalm 42:11).

Take this to heart, Judah, when you feel downtrodden and hopeless: Lift your eyes toward Heaven and praise. For it is through your praise Heaven is opened and the dark clouds of heaviness and oppression are lifted. Whenever you sense heaviness, begin to praise and alter the spiritual atmosphere.

## THE LUST FOR POWER

A common thread in leadership is a lust for power. It is a major temptation, especially to the tribe of Judah although not exclusively to them. The lust for power has roots within the spirit of pride. In fact, it is the deepest source of pride there is. This combination is deadly to the destiny of Judah. If the enemy can gain a foothold in both of these areas, he can rob you of your destiny, peace, and joy. Repentance and humility are the keys to freedom that bring restoration. Scripture gives many examples for Judah's instruction and restoration.

## JUDAH AND TAMAR

Read Genesis 31:1-26. Judah's lust for power caused him to abuse young Tamar. His pride overtook him. He chose to magnify a need of self-gratification through a spirit of pride which dominated his soul. When a Judah magnifies his need for power, he is denying his authority to rule righteously as a king.

## A FAULT WITHIN THE FAMILY LINE

This is the first indication of the degradation of the Judah clan. Judah ventured outside the family and, in doing so, was away from the wisdom and counsel of loved ones. For this reason I feel in my spirit there is something important to note, otherwise it would not have been mentioned. Judah's troubles began when he was outside of the counsel of his family. This is true of the Body of Christ as well. Though there are times of God-ordained separateness (always Spirit-led), there is a vital connection and even nourishment within the family of God. Throughout this passage the family is falling apart through its own lust for power. What was the key thing that led to its degradation? I believe it began with pride, coupled with a lust for power; this was Judah's demise.

Judah's sons were blatantly drenched in motives of pride and lust for power. It was particularly demonstrated through the second son, Onan. This pompous young lad had no regard for anything or anyone other than himself. He took his position as a means of self-gratification, where he should have stepped in with humility and integrity. Instead, he viciously shamed Tamar through his impenitent pride and self-whim. The apple did not fall far from the tree because Onan's father, Judah, instead of being a patriarch of integrity, sought his own self-preservation. Not only did he withhold his third son, but he had relations with Tamar, thinking she was a harlot. His driving passion was not sexual lust (although this does play a part in the sin), but a lust for power. This lust for power is embedded in motives of building one's own kingdom and a misuse of dominion. It is a common fault within someone spiritually immature who holds a place of authority. It is even more deadly with those who have grown in wisdom and integrity. This can be seen within the lives of David and Solomon.

## DAVID: FLAWED YET FAITHFUL

The lust for power never begins as an obvious and blatant display of pride. It chooses, rather, a backdoor of deception, thus deceiving many. The most deadly ploys of Satan are always backhanded and unassuming. David was no exception to this rule. He, too, was lured through the enemy's devices.

Read I Chronicles 21:1-4, 7-30. David had just returned from the heat of battle with the Philistine giants where he achieved a glorious victory. No doubt the praises of man were ringing loud in his ears, and his confidence as both warrior and leader solidified. David, like many a leader, allowed the praises of man to dilute the need to give glory to the Lord for victory won. With his defenses down, he became easy prey for Satan's web of deception.

## "THEN SATAN STOOD UP AGAINST ISRAEL AND MOVED DAVID TO NUMBER ISRAEL…"

His senses were tuned in to the flesh and his own pride rather than the Holy Spirit. David faltered when he neglected to bow low and bestow all praise and glory to the Father. It is the pride of life that snares us so easily.

Satan lured David through David's own pride and lust for power. In verse 3, David is warned through Joab, a gentle yet poignant nudge of the Holy Spirit. David, in his arrogance, ignored the wisdom of his servant and enforced his powers as king to his own glory and self-gratification. It was a grave mistake and devastating blow that cost 70,000 men their lives. Whether we are in an obvious position as leaders or not, we must keep in mind that leadership is a place of absolute servanthood. Leadership in the truest sense is meant to be selfless, meaning that our own ideals and hopes are put to death and that we seek His kingdom and His righteousness in all matters. David, known for being a man after God's own heart, grieved the Father when He neglected one thing—worship. His focus was not on the Father, and thus the web of deception and devastating folly began. When we neglect our sole purpose, which is to worship the Father in spirit and in truth, we too are easy prey for Satan. God, in His love, chastens us and brings us to a place of restoration and wholeness. David saw this, but not without first paying a great price. Many times our sins have lasting ramifications on not just ourselves but others.

This story truly displays the beauty of repentance tied with pure worship. It is only when David began to turn in sincere repentance that God began to reverse His judgment. One thing especially to note was that not only did David repent, but He came to the Lord in sackcloth, spurring on his elders to do likewise. This is pure leadership. It is born of pure worship, servanthood, and vulnerability. Judah, this is your place in leadership. Another thing to note is that David was adamant about paying for Ornan's threshing floor. David knew the keys of repentance and worship. He knew it would not be a true sacrifice unless it cost him something.

Whenever you falter, know that you lead by first being a servant, taking the worshipper's true place of bowing low. Restoration, a mighty revolution of repentance, and true worship can be born in your place of brokenness.

> *Thus says the Lord, "Heaven is My throne, and the earth is my footstool. Where then is a house that you can build for Me? And where is a place that I may rest? For My hand made all these things, thus all these things came into being," declares the Lord.* **"But to this one will I look, To him who is humble and contrite of spirit, and who trembles at My word"** (Isaiah 66:1-2).

> *O Lord, my heart is not proud, nor my eyes haughty; Nor do I involve myself in great matters, or in things too difficult for me. Surely I have composed and quieted my soul; like a weaned child rests against his mother, my soul is like a weaned child within me. O Israel, hope in the Lord from this time forth and forever* (Psalm 131:1-3).

David puts in best in Psalm 131:1-3. I feel he must have sung this song or one like it after this hard lesson. Remember, Judah, that first and foremost God chooses your brokenness. He chooses true worship.

## LUST FOR POWER THREATENS A KINGDOM AND FAMILY LINE

Read II Samuel 11-12. Yet again in this story, the folly of lust for power came after a time of victory. David was in his palace, basking in great victory and, yet again, neglecting to bow low, when he sees beautiful Bathsheba. David fell prey to the lust for power, just like his forefather, Judah. Once again the family line is threatened due to pride and the lust for power. He is already primed for deception and ready for the lust of power to take territory. Forbidden pleasures flourish under the lust for power. They eventually bring a deviation from destiny that blinds and then robs us of eternal purpose and hope. David most likely assumed that, as king, he had rights and even privileges to gratify his every whim—a grave deception for leaders. So he lures Bathsheba through his position, fame, and power as king to his chambers. In his greed, he desired her for himself; but he has one problem: Bathsheba's husband, Uriah. Now Uriah, being a faithful, sincere, and valiant warrior and servant of the king, does as he is commanded. David, all the while, knows he must be rid of Uriah in order to gain possession of Bathsheba. So he does the unthinkable and places Uriah on the frontline, where he knows Uriah will be killed.

David displayed an abominable failure of character and leadership. He traded his God-given position of authority for a cheap thrill of sexual pleasure and, most grievously, a lust for power. Position is never a means for adulterating the kingdom. Yet this is what David chose. He chose in his pride to exercise what he thought was his "right." We must take great caution to what we may think are our so-called "rights." Yet again, God sends a prophet, this time Nathan, to pinpoint the root of David's arrogance (12:1-4, 7-12). Nathan targeted the very core of David's soul and thus called David to repentance. David's sin once more did not meet without consequence, for his firstborn of Bathsheba God chose to take. David and Bathsheba's sin cost another human being his life and destiny. God was faithful to bring restoration and new life once true repentance came, thus resulting in the birth of Solomon. Psalm 51 is David's prayer of repentance and his cry for restoration. Read Psalm 51:1-12.

## SOLOMON: THE KINGDOM, HIS STRENGTH AND FOLLY

Read I Kings 11:1-14. Solomon began his reign as a lover of God, pure in pursuit and motive. It mentions in this portion that: *the God of Israel, who had appeared to him twice…*. Solomon experienced the very *Shekinah* glory of God. He knew firsthand the power of intimacy, worship, and love. Therefore God gave him the deep gift of revelation of wisdom. Wisdom without intimacy leads to pride and sets the stage for the lust for power to rule and reign. It was Solomon's insatiable desire of pride, lust for power, and women that detoured and eventually diminished his true calling as a worshipper. He was drawn into all kinds of debauchery and idol worship through foreign women and their idols.

The lust for power is the breeding ground for spiritual harlotry. If it can divert your affections, it can abort your calling as a throne room worshipper. This was Solomon's demise. He never saw destiny fulfilled, and more importantly, never grew into a true intimate lover of God. The lust for power tries to abort the dominion of the government of praise in Judah. The government of praise is the rightful inheritance and dominion of every Judah. For in this dominion, they inspire vibrant, passionate, jubilant, and pure praise, which draws the Body of Christ into the very chambers of our Bridegroom King and establishes the kingdom of God.

## YESHUA: TEMPTED BUT TRIUMPHANT

Read Matthew 4:8-11. Yeshua lived and ruled (and still rules) from His place of dominion. Dominion was the very thing Satan was trying to get Yeshua to give up. He tempted Him with a lust for power. Note that Satan offered Yeshua *all the kingdoms of the world, and their glory*. What Satan was offering was a counterfeit dominion. He can never offer true dominion. When Yeshua was tempted by Satan, He responded to the devil with these words: *Be gone, Satan! For it is written,* "YOU SHALL WORSHIP THE LORD YOUR GOD, AND SERVE HIM ONLY."

Yeshua, the Lion of the tribe of Judah, responded back to the enemy in a thundering roar of worship! The truest sense of dominion is found in worship. Therefore, when Yeshua made this declaration, he was restoring us back to the Father: *You shall worship the Lord your God, and serve Him only.*

## REDEMPTION THROUGH THE BLOODLINE OF JUDAH

The Bible gives us many illustrations of redemption that came through the bloodline of the tribe of Judah. Ultimately, the Redeemer of the world, Yeshua, came through this line. The picture of redemption first began with Jacob's son Judah. Read Genesis 37:25-28.

Read Genesis 44:14-34. Though imperfect, Judah's plea to his brothers to sell Joseph rather than kill him was an act of redemption. It was through selling Joseph that Judah began his own journey of redemption and refining, as well as his brothers'. In essence, God used Judah as a source of redemption for the family. Later in time of famine, Judah arose again as a leader of the family and pleaded to Joseph, whom he formerly sold into slavery, for the redemption of Benjamin. Judah's second cry for redemption came from a place of true brokenness and repentance, unlike the first time. The purest sense of redemption is always born of humility, compassion, and love. Judah's act of love showed true maturity and a change of heart. When Judah lives in a place of true brokenness, humility, and repentance, he can then bring redemption to many.

## BOAZ: THE KINSMEN REDEEMER

Boaz is a type and shadow of Christ. His calling as a kinsman redeemer reveals truth to us all. As a righteous man of impeccable character, nobility, and compassion, he ransomed Ruth and Naomi from poverty, shame, and their hurtful past. The tribe of Judah, carrying the heart of Yeshua, the kinsmen redeemer, often manifests this heart in pastoral leadership. Read Ruth 3:7-10 and Ruth 4:1-6, 9-15.

## PRAISE: JUDAH'S RIGHTFUL PLACE OF DOMINION

*Bless ye The Lord, all ye His hosts, ye ministers of his that do his pleasure. Bless the Lord, all his works in places of* **dominion**: *bless the Lord, O my soul* (Psalm 103:21-22).

Judah, it is your worship that restores your rightful dominion and releases true kingdom authority. Settle for nothing less than intimacy, intimacy, intimacy! Your true identity and spiritual DNA is comprised of pure worship. You can't exist without it. Without you leading the way, the Body of Christ would be robbed of the keys to worship. You possess the heart of David, to be a people after God's own heart. God has given you the authority to unlock the government of praise in spiritual high places and see an open Heaven released! This is your high calling. Run to the battle with the high praises of God upon your lips, a contagious love that infects lukewarm lovers to be ablaze, and roar into the darkness that Yeshua, the Lion of the tribe of Judah, is on the throne! In you, Judah, are the prophetic voices, dancers, musicians, and instruments of praise God is releasing in this end-time hour! Awaken, O sleeper, and let the light of His glory shine upon you (Ephesians 5:14). May He awaken you to songs of Heaven! As you rest in your bed at night, may you hear Him singing songs of deliverance over you! You are so precious, beautiful, and needed. Arise, O Judah, to the roar of Abba Father's heart. The militant drums of Heaven are sounding a war cry for you. Take your place at the frontline. It is your time!

## THE DESTINY OF JUDAH
### RELEASING THE HOLY ROAR: THE CRY OF CONSUMMATION

*Let heaven and earth praise Him, the seas and everything that moves in them. For God will save Zion and build the cities of Judah, that they may dwell there and possess it. And the descendants of His servants will inherit it, and those who love His name will dwell in it* (Psalm 69:34-36).

In this end-time hour the tribe of Judah will possess a holy roar. This holy roar is known as the cry of consummation. Consummation is the work of completeness. It is in this work of fulfillment whereby the kingdom is established through the government of praise. Consummation for us as believers is the coming union of the new Heaven and new earth. Eye has not seen, nor has ear heard, all that the Father has prepared for those who love Him. What He has prepared for us is an eternal habitation with Him.

*Let not your heart be troubled; believe in God, believe also in Me. In My Father's house are many dwelling places; if it were not so, I would have told you; for I go to prepare a place for you. And if I go and prepare a place for you, I will come again, and receive you to Myself; that where I am, there you may be also* (John 14:1-3).

Yeshua spoke these words during the Passover Seder. He was telling the disciples (and us) that he was going away, but when He returned, He would consummate our marriage to Him. The

Jewish wedding is profoundly prophetic for us in this hour. To understand where we are as His Bride and where we are going, we would do well to study the Jewish wedding.

The Cup of Praise was the both the fourth and the final cup in the Passover Seder. It is also known as the Cup of Consummation and the Cup of Elijah. During a Jewish wedding reception, bride and groom adjourn to the wedding chamber, a secluded room, and consummate the marriage. It is known as the *yichud*.[4] If the bride bleeds, she is truly a virgin and a suitable mate for the groom. Now for us as the Bride of Christ, this is not a literal sexual consummation but a spiritual one. Before the work in the Garden of Gethsemane and Calvary, we were indebted by the harlotry of our sin. We were not pure, but through the Blood of Christ, we are declared the pure virgin Bride.

The Hebrew word for "consummate" is *temimah*. Hebrew studies reveal that the numerical value of *temimah* is 495, and the numerical value of Sarah (the mother of our faith, Abraham being our father) is 505. These two numbers equal 1,000. This is the most perfect consummation of numbers. The millennial reign of Messiah will be for 1,000 years. It is the fullness of consummation that He and His bride would enter into an eternal habitation in their Father's house! Yichud: איסור ייחוד *issur yichud*, seclusion) is what we have been in for 2,000 years. The Word tells us that 1,000 years is a day. We are approaching—if not in—the third day. In either case, we live in the Third Day, who is our resurrected Yeshua! The third day is Yeshua's consummation of resurrection power. This is what the tribe of Judah is mandated to cry out for. May the Lord release the holy roar within you, O mighty tribe of Judah. For when you roar, you are not only crying out for consummation but for habitation of the Lord's house.

## KING DAVID'S INFINITE PASSION FOR THE LORD'S HOUSE

Read Psalm 132:1-5. King David's greatest passion was habitation. Because of bloodshed, the Lord did not permit David to build His house, but rather Solomon would build it. Every Judah has a consuming passion for the Lord's house. Judah precedes Levi by carrying the cry of consummation. Once a marriage is consummated (Judah), the bride and groom enter into habitation. Judah builds the Lord's house in praise. This why Judah was given the government of praise. In Psalm 26, we see David's passion for the Lord's house:

> *LORD, I have loved the habitation of thy house, and the place where thine honour dwelleth* (Psalm 26:8 KJV).

## THE WILDERNESS OF MAON

> *Saul also and his men went to seek him. And they told David: wherefore he came down into a rock, and abode in the wilderness of Maon. And when Saul heard that, he pursued after David in the wilderness of Maon* (I Samuel 23:25 KJV).

When Saul was in hot pursuit of David, where did David run? He ran into the habitation of the Lord (wilderness of MAON, meaning "habitation")! David knew who his refuge was. He knew that only in a place of habitation of the Lord was he safe from His enemies. The secret place of every Judah is the house of the Lord. In times of testing and great warfare, run to the safety found in habitation! The enemy cannot touch you in the Lord's habitation. There is no greater shelter than the holy habitation of the Most High. The Lord appoints a wilderness for us all. His purpose is that we run into His holy habitation. What a glorious promise indeed for all of us!

## JUDAH AND THE RESTORATION OF THE FALLEN TABERNACLE OF DAVID

*How lovely are Thy dwelling places, O Lord of hosts! My soul longed even yearned for the courts of the living God* (Psalm 84:1-2).

There is a yearning, even a desperate cry within the heart of every true worshipper. It is Judah whom the Father has ordained to stir up this yearning for the courts of the Lord. The cry of the Father's heart is for us to know and live in the reality that we are sealed for His courts.

*Lord, who may abide in Thy tabernacle? Who shall dwell in your holy hill? He who walks with integrity, and works righteousness, and speaks truth in his heart* (Psalm 15:1 KJV).

God is calling His people to a place of abiding. Abiding requires sincerity of heart and purpose. Judah, this is the Father's call for integrity in your life, ministry, and, most importantly, your worship.

*In that day I will raise up the fallen booth (tabernacle) of David, and wall up its breaches; I will also raise up its ruins, and rebuild it as in the days of old* (Amos 9:11).

God is rebuilding His tabernacle. It is the tabernacle of David that God uses to bring restoration—the very place where the Ark rested. He chooses the tabernacle of David to be His resting place. Before we can truly see His Ark, His glory resting in His tabernacle, He must first bring restoration to it. Repentance and true worship are the keys to restoring His resting place. We will only begin to see His glory manifested amongst us when we return to true worship. I believe it is within the heart of the Father to restore the fallen tabernacle of David in our day. We are truly living in the end times. He will return to take up His throne, and His throne is built on our worship. Judah is the instrument of restoration for God's resting place. Judah has the innate ability and calling to restore end-time worship.

*A throne will be established in lovingkindness and a judge will sit in the tent (tabernacle) of David; moreover, he will seek justice and be prompt in righteousness* (Isaiah 16:5).

*"After these things I will return, and I will rebuild the tabernacle of David which has fallen, and I will rebuild its ruins, and I will restore it, in order that the rest of mankind may seek the Lord, and all the Gentiles who are called by my name," says the LORD, who makes these things known from old* (Acts 15:16-18).

King Yeshua will rule from His holy throne. He will rule His people under the government of praise with justice and His loving-kindness. The restoration of the tabernacle of David is a true sign of the return of Yeshua.

*God is known in Judah; His name in Israel. And His tabernacle is in Salem; His dwelling place also in Zion. There He broke the flaming arrows, the shield, and the sword, and the weapons of war. Selah* (Psalm 76:1-3).

## PRAYER OF REPENTANCE AND DESTINY
## FOR THE TRIBE OF JUDAH

Hear, O God, the cry of Your servant. I hunger and thirst for You alone. I long for Your dwelling place. I yearn to abide in Your presence all the days of my life. Create in me a clean heart, O God, and renew a steadfast spirit within me. Let the bones that Thou hast broken rejoice. I thank You, God, for your chastening. In Your perfect love, You refine me, mold and break me. You are my chief desire. In Your presence there is fullness of joy, and at Your right hand are pleasures forevermore. God, I want to know the true pleasures of Your heart, Your very throne room. Fashion me into a man/woman after Your own heart. My heart's desire is to be in tune with the rhythm of Your very heartbeat. I want to join in Heaven's song of love. Cause me to hear and be in tune with the symphonies coming from the throne room. May I resound with Your praise every day of my life. Develop a holy sound, a holy roar within me.

Break me of my pride. Forgive me for enthroning my own self-love, worry, and self-pity instead of worshipping the beauty of Your holiness. I know this has grieved you Abba, and I humbly repent of it. I thank You, that in Your grace and loving-kindness to me, You restore Your tabernacle within me. I long for Your Ark to rest within me. Return me to my rightful place of dominion. Return me to the government of praise. Help me to rule with a servant's heart, bowed low, forever giving You all glory and praise. Perfect Your praise within me. I long for You to be my resting place, my Shiloh. May Your scepter never depart from me. Teach me in the way I should go. I will forever praise You. I love You, my Bridegroom King. Be enthroned within my heart. In Yeshua's name, Amen.

---

[1] Lynn DeShazo, *Be Magnified* (Colorado Springs, CO: Integrity's Hosanna! Music 1992), https://www.weareworship.com/us/songs/song-library/showsong/2423 .

[2] David MacDonald, *The Encyclopedia of Mammals* (New York, NY: Facts On File, 1984), Page 31.

[3] John, Elton, Tim Rice, Hans Zimmer, Carmen Twillie, Jason Weaver, Jeremy Irons, Nathan Lane, Ernie Sabella, Joseph Williams, and Sally Dworsky. *I Just Can't Wait To Be King, The Lion King Original Motion Picture Soundtrack*. (Los Angeles, CA Buena Vista Pictures Distribution, 1994.) Track 11.

[4] Gal Einai, "Gal Einai," *www.inner.org*, March 13, 2014,

# CHAPTER 6
# DAN: THE VOICE OF JUSTICE

*Righteousness and justice are the foundation of Thy throne; Loving-kindness and truth go before Thee. How blessed are the people who know the joyful sound! O Lord, they walk in the light of Thy countenance* (Psalm 89:14-15).

God is calling His end-time people to walk in His righteousness and justice. Righteousness and justice are the very foundation of His throne. As worshippers, this is a vital key to unlocking the mysteries of Heaven and His throne. When we walk according to the laws and precepts of the Father's heart, we can find true freedom and justice. The Father has endowed Dan as the voice of justice for the Body. Within this tribe you will find a people whose heart's cry is to see God's justice restored. Danites are freedom fighters, deliverance ministers, counselors, teachers, mighty warriors, and great voices of discernment to the Body of Christ.

## THE NAMING OF DAN

*Then Rachel said, "God has vindicated me, and has indeed heard my voice and has given me a son." Therefore she named him Dan.* (Genesis 30:6).

Dan means "to judge, vindicate, and to bring justice." God is longing to release the voice of justice within the earth. The tribe of Dan has long been a subject of mystery, debate, and intrigue. I urge you to seek God regarding His heart for the tribe of Dan. Justice is defined as: "the maintenance or administration of what is just especially by the impartial adjustment of conflicting claims or the assignment of merited rewards or punishments; the administration of law; especially: the establishment or determination of rights according to the rules of law or equality; the quality of being just, impartial, or fair; the principal or ideal: righteousness; the quality of conforming to the law; conformity to truth, fact, or reason; correctness."[1]

The cause of justice and freedom is the driving force within every Dan. They are relentless in their stance for truth, righteousness, and justice. In Yeshua, all things are embodied and perfected. We cannot obtain justice in our own strength. Our human natures are too flawed and weak to endure God's righteous judgments. For this reason, we must live our lives where God alone is our Judge and source of true righteousness.

## DAN'S BIRTH AND RACHEL'S HEARTACHE

*Now when Rachel saw that she bore Jacob no children, she became jealous of her sister; and she said to Jacob, "Give me children, or else I die." Then Jacob's anger burned against Rachel, and he said, "Am I in place of God, who has withheld from you the fruit of the womb?" And she said, "Here is my maid Bilhah, go in to her, that she may bear on my knees, that through her I too may have children." So she gave her maid Bilhah as a wife, and Jacob went in to her. And Bilhah conceived and bore Jacob a son. Then Rachel said, "God has vindicated me, and has indeed heard my voice and has given me a son." Therefore she named him Dan* (Genesis 30:1-6).

Dan's birth was a pivotal moment within Jacob's family. Rachel, Jacob's true beloved, was barren. She was so grieved that she said to Jacob, *Give me children, or else I die.* Unable to bear children herself, Rachael gave Bilhah to Jacob as a wife to bear children for her. Bilhah was treated more like a slave, having no true voice or rights of her own. In Hebrew, *Bilhah* means "troubled." There are two dynamics that played into the birth of Dan—Rachel's joy and Bilhah's troubled soul. For Bilhah, it meant being bound to a man who never loved her. Moreover, she was enslaved to her selfish mistress, Rachel. She was a servant with no voice for freedom. On the other hand, Dan's birth brought both hope and justice for Rachel. God heard her cry and brought vindication through Dan's birth. Dan's spiritual DNA carries a consistent cry for freedom, vindication, and to bring justice. Justice, many times, is birthed through great troubles in our lives.

There was much warfare and turmoil that formed the identity of Dan. Dan's very nature is wrapped in the dynamics that surrounded his birth. Rachel was favored and thus most likely spoiled and prone to idolatry (read Genesis 31: 22-42), secretive, deceptive, and selfish. Bilhah, having no true identity herself, was enslaved to birth Jacob's children, who never loved her either. She was oppressed and bound in pain and hopelessness. Bilhah's spirit was consistently crying out for freedom. Both mothers would form the character of Dan. Dan's very nature was a contradiction. Within Dan we see a tug of war for freedom vs. idolatry, pain vs. selfishness, secretiveness, deception, and hopelessness. God is sounding His shofar to release Danites into their true identity and freedom in Him.

## THE GEMSTONE OF DAN

The gemstone for Dan is the blue sapphire. It is a deep, midnight blue color. The sapphire has been known both for its connections with Heaven (the throne especially) and God's law.

Read Exodus 24:10-18. One of the strongest manifestations of God's glory came when He gave Moses the law. It says that the area under His (God's) feet was like a pavement of sapphire. According to the Talmud, the Ten Commandments were written on two perfect cubes of sapphire.[2] Some believe that the sapphire came from the throne of God itself. God's law is inscribed on our hearts. Continually in Scripture, the connection between the law and the throne is identified with the gemstone of sapphire. What does this reveal to us? God was revealing Himself as the Great Judge and Lawgiver over Israel.

Verse 11 states: and *they beheld God, and they ate and drank*. This is truly a rich nugget of truth from God's Word. While they were beholding the beauty of God, they were satisfied. They ate and drank of Him and His goodness. God wants us to partake of Him and His Word (law) and become fully satisfied. He must be our meat and drink. His judgments are true and just. His law brings freedom as it transforms us into His likeness. It is vital for Dan to no longer sit as a judge of others, but to behold the beauty of the Great Judge, our loving Father. It is better we fall into the judgments of His hands than our own or others. He judges with perfect love that transforms us into our destiny in Him. Dan, the charge given to you from God is to stay connected with His throne. His precepts and laws are the only thing that can satisfy you. The sapphire symbolizes Dan's call to the truth and to always be grounded in God's Word. When God brings forth His law, He brings a work of transformation. Read Psalm 119:1-8.

Look into the mirror of His Word, to release your transformation and destiny. His holy law brings liberty (James 1:22-25).

## THE SYMBOLS

Dan has two symbols: the snake/scales of justice and the eagle. Both symbols reveal mysteries of Dan. The eagle was the captain tribe symbol given to Dan.

### THE SNAKE AND THE SCALES OF JUSTICE

The symbol of the snake/scales of justice for Dan has been a source of contention, controversy, and confusion. The identity and destiny of Dan has been shrouded in mystery and debate for ages. God's heart is for revelation that frees Dan, not chaos that confuses him. The serpent has long been a seen as a symbol of Satan. It was in the Garden he first appeared and deceived Adam and Eve to forgo their intimacy and dominion. A serpent is seen as sly, deceptive, crafty, and deadly. It also carries the connotation of fear. This symbol was not meant as a snare for Dan, but rather a warning. Within the tribe of Dan, you will find a consistent thread of idolatry, mystery, deception, judgment, criticism, and even the spirit of anti-Christ. This symbol serves as a red flag to Dan of his facade(s). It is not meant to accuse, displace, or discourage them.

On a good note, the serpent is also known for wisdom. Yeshua himself said to be as wise as serpents but harmless as doves (Matthew 10:16). The serpent's nature is one of craftiness, a device of warfare which, when tempered with love and humility, can be used strategically by Dan. The scales of justice represent Dan's call to justice and righteousness. Like Simeonites and Levites, they are passionate about causes for truth.

## THE SCALES: A CRY FOR JUSTICE

Read Deuteronomy 25:13-16 and Proverbs 1:11. The scales of justice indicate Dan's innate, God-given character of wisdom, counsel, understanding, and discernment. They weigh a matter in their spirit. A wise Dan will not be quick to speak, but be slow to judge, weighing the matter and revealing the counsel of Abba, the Great Judge and Lawmaker. The scales are also a symbol of balance. Danites carry an ability to bring balance when they themselves are balanced by the Word and Spirit of God. Dan must not add to or take away from the scales the Lord has set. A Dan must have not only balanced scales, but honest ones, for true justice should be pure, without deceit. Selfishness, speculation, rejection, and an unrefined desire for vindication brings imbalance to your scales, Dan. The tempering of the Holy Spirit is crucial to appropriating balanced scales.

## THE EAGLE

During the time of Moses, the symbol was changed to the eagle. I believe it was changed because of the travail of the Father's heart to bring the tribe of Dan into freedom, for He alone embodies the scales of justice.

*It was for freedom that Christ has set us free; therefore keep standing firm and do not be subject again to a yoke of slavery* (Galatians 5:1).

The eagle speaks of redemption for Dan in that he no longer has an identity tied to deception. God chose restoration and healing for Dan through this very symbol. It has often been used as a symbol of freedom.

Dan, when you free yourself from the yoke of judgmental and critical spirits and idolatry, you release the fetters that bind you. Your freedom lies within the very intimacy you possess with the Father. His call to you is to abide, to become a habitation of His justice. When we strive in idolatry and self, we enslave ourselves to the deception of the flesh. The heart of the Father for you, Dan, is to be a true disciple of your Beloved. Read John 8:31-32.

The eagle is known for its strength and nobility. It is the also one of the four living creatures that surround the throne. Again this reiterates the call for Dan to align his heart and will to the throne.

Read Malachi 4:2. Yeshua came to bring healing, to bind the brokenhearted, and to set captives free. This is a beautiful picture for Dan. He is girding you up on His wings. In the shadow of His wings you find rest, healing, and hope renewed. Let Him restore you in the resting place of His love.

Read Isaiah 40:28-31. God has endowed the tribe of Dan with this supernatural promise of strength and rest. When you are weary, trust Him to carry you. If you are weary, take time for introspection. You may be striving and fighting against the very rest God desires you to have. Striving entails fear and lack of trust. The Father longs for Dan to come up higher, above the storm, and view the earth from Heaven's vantage point. Abide in the rest He has called you to, Dan.

Read Psalm 103:5. Every good thing is found in our intimacy with the Father. From times of intimacy, we are renewed like the eagle. God is calling you, dear Dan, to fly! He's called you to a life of freedom! His judgments are for you and not against you. For within His judgments lie the freedom and rest you desperately long for!

God is summoning His eagles! He is looking for a people who long to go to new heights with Him. What He is calling you to, dear Dan, is a place of habitation. When storms come, His call to you is to rise above. Come past the thunderstorms and turbulent winds. He wants to draw you to His very throne, where your strength is renewed like the eagle.

During all of my years in ministry I have observed that those from the tribe of Dan can be very guarded emotionally. Sometimes they can appear cold, aloof, and even mean-spirited. Often times Danites are gravely misunderstood because of these behaviors. There are times it's because of their keen sense of discernment that they sense danger, so they react defensively toward others. Other times it's a case of rejection, stemming from offense. The most common way this manifests is through the tongue. Danites tend to have quite the forked tongue and can wound many. These tendencies always stem from a hurtful past.

It is important as Dan's brethren that we love unconditionally and help them in their restoration without judging them also. When we feel unsafe, we build up walls to shut others out, even God. Because Dan has these tendencies, they can be very independent and headstrong in nature. Usually someone with a strong gift of discernment, when immature, can be judgmental, critical, and intimidating. Real love does not bring fear or intimidation, but rather intercedes and confronts the stronghold. Dan, allow your brothers and sisters in Yeshua to bring restoration. Most importantly, let your Beloved in! He's knocking on the door of your walled garden. He wants to come into you, His glorious garden, and restore you. In His strength and unfailing love, He alone will rebuild you and enable you to trust again.

## JACOB'S PROPHECY

"*Dan shall judge his people, as one of the tribes of Israel. Dan shall be a serpent in the way, a horned snake in the path, that bites the horse's heels, so his rider falls backward. For Thy salvation I wait, O Lord*" (Genesis 49:16-18).

## "DAN SHALL JUDGE HIS PEOPLE, AS ONE OF THE TRIBES OF ISRAEL"

The Father's heart is always to have mercy triumph over judgment. His greatest desire is for communion with us. Judgment comes when idolatry draws us away from intimacy with Him. The book of Judges is riddled with stories of God's love and redemption for Israel and their harlotry through idolatry. He is a jealous lover. We become like what we chase after. When we strive and compromise, we in essence deny ourselves of our glorious inheritance in the Beloved: communion. In an act of tough love, the Father handed Israel over to their adulterous lovers (idols). They quickly forgot His deliverance from Egypt. So God allowed the Israelites to be overcome by their enemies because of their spiritual adultery.

Read Judges 2:11-17. When Israel began to cry out to God, He brought deliverance through judges (verses 16-18). Justice was designed by God to bring deliverance and ultimately redemption. Now several tribes served as judges during this time, but it was Dan who was endowed with the calling. God sought Dan to be a redeemer to His people through his tool of intimacy: justice. How does justice relate to intimacy? True justice stems from righteousness. It fights for and brings restoration to the afflicted. Our Beloved, Yeshua, brought justice through sacrificing His own life. He forever eradicated the penalty of sin even though we were guilty in our transgressions against Him. Yeshua, the embodiment of true justice, knowing the cost or penalty of wrongs owed, obtained freedom for us through laying down His own life. This is the most profound act of love and justice. We rightfully deserved the penalties of sin, but God's justice triumphed over sin, death, hell, and the grave and forever bound us to His love and courts for eternity! Amen! Hallelujah! He desires so passionately to restore communion with us. This is the very heart of justice: restoration. There is no greater act of love than redemption. The calling of the tribe of Dan is to see justice restored to God's glorious creation. In fact, it is their driving passion! They are mighty deliverance ministers whose pursuit of truth awakens the slumbering Bride of Christ and challenges her in love and humility to righteousness.

## "DAN SHALL BE A SERPENT IN THE WAY, A HORNED SNAKE IN THE PATH IS, THAT BITES THE HORSE'S HEELS, SO HIS RIDER FALLS BACKWARD"

This portion of the prophecy is quite interesting. It has a twofold meaning that reveals both the strength and facade(s) of Dan. On a positive note, this can be interpreted as Dan's calling in warfare. Dan can use both his discernment and craftiness as a tactic of warfare and deliverance for the Body. He will often use the unassuming way to counterattack the enemy because he sees from Heaven's vantage point. As an eagle, He flies above the storm, above the carnal realm, and thereby receives a true picture of the spirit realm. Dan has very keen discernment and can rightly divide truth when surrendered to God. When the heart of Dan is tied to the Father's heart and will, he is unstoppable. Because of his intimacy with the Father, he discerns the judgments and decrees that proceed from the throne. With this ammunition, he can, in humility and wisdom, devise a Spirit-led strategy of victory for himself and others in times of warfare. It is especially helpful during counsel and deliverance ministry to have a Dan present. For this reason, Danites are valiant and strong warriors. They see keenly with no inhibitions, partiality, or hype. Like Levites, they are quick to discern character and motives of the heart. It is very difficult to deceive Dan when he is sold out to God. Intimacy with the Father, coupled with sincere humility, is the key to your greatest asset, Dan. Surrender any critical shortcomings and offenses so that the Father might freely use you as a loving instrument of justice for His kingdom.

Dan can use craftiness to deceive, manipulate, and wound others. The serpent was very crafty in the Garden and thereby deceived Adam and Eve. It is the enemy's desire to use Dan as a weapon of warfare as well. When idols of heart hold you captive, Dan, you open yourself up to the anti-Christ spirit. If unchecked, this can lead you to completely forego your destiny. Be wise of the enemy, for he is ever present to ensnare you through idolatry of self, critical spirits, offenses, and judgmental spirits. Commit your life's purpose to bowing low in loving devotion to the Father.

## "FOR THY SALVATION I WAIT, O GOD"

God is longing to release His salvation to and through the tribe of Dan. Though you have been pressed in on every side, Dan, you will surely see the salvation of your God. He is your knight in shining armor, ready to rescue you from idols of the heart and your hurtful past. He longs to restore justice to you. Though you have been afflicted and misunderstood, Yeshua is longing to rebuild your ancient ruins. He longs to renew your strength so you might soar in His Spirit as the mighty eagle that you truly are. Divorce yourself from the facade of the flesh. The enemy has lied to you and caused you to believe and live a lie that you are separated from communion with your Beloved. His blood has already ransomed you from the death sentence brought by your idolatry. His heart is crying and bleeding for your freedom. So arise and shake off the dust! Put on your beautiful garments of salvation! Come and soar in His salvation for you!

## MOSES' PROPHECY

*And of Dan he said, "Dan is a lion's whelp that leaps forth from Bashan"* (Deuteronomy 33:22).

Moses' prophecy to Dan speaks of a riddling paradox.

(A)He was referring to Dan's immaturity like that of Judah's in infancy as a lion's whelp. When immature, Dan, like Judah, can find himself in a miry pit of his own pride's doing. Dan's folly of pride lies with the idol of self and judgmental spirit. This is where the anti-Christ spirit will seek territory within Dan.

(B)He was portraying a role not given to him by God. Dan was trying to portray or be a mere copycat of Judah, the lion. I feel this portion of the prophecy especially notes the anti-Christ spirit. The spirit of anti-Christ is given a foothold when we give into the deception of idolatry of the heart. Idols of the heart deny and oppose the true glory of God, seeking their own glory and throne. That is essentially what Satan will do when the anti-Christ comes on the scene. The spirit of anti-Christ is already present and has been for quite some time.

Read I John 4:1-6. The Holy Spirit is wooing and compelling you, Dan, to take on the spirit of Christ. The true spirit of Christ is one who identifies with the Cross through obedience, and true humility.

Read I Peter 4:12-13. This is your commission, Dan. I urge you to seek to have the fruit of repentance and the Spirit within in you. This will combat the anti-Christ spirit that seeks to snare you. When you seek to put on Christ each day, living as a new creation in Christ, the enemy will lose ground. The anti-Christ spirit opposes the very glory/nature of God within you. It is idolatry of the heart that is the anti-Christ's breeding ground. It is our self—the "I factor," self-made agendas, ideals, and habits—that detours the kingdom's purpose within us: intimacy. Dan, when you decide to live in a place of absolute laid-down love for Yeshua and your brethren, the enemy will have no hold on you. Seek first His kingdom and His righteousness, for in doing so, you will release justice not only to yourself but those around you.

(C)The next thing that seems out of place is that it mentions Bashan. Bashan was a territory that was inhabited by Gad on the east side of the Jordan. Prior to Joshua's conquest of the land, it belonged to the Amorites. It was known for its idolatry and giants that dwelled therein. So Moses, when he prophesies, is saying that Dan is immature (a lion's whelp) leaping into all forms of idolatry such as that of the Amorites. This is a warning of facade(s) for Dan to avoid, rather than an accusation. In greater essence, this prophecy serves as a call to repentance and deliverance for the tribe of Dan. He is questioning Dan. *Why are you associating yourself in idolatry in a territory where I have not placed you, immaturely going into all forms of bondage that negate your true calling of justice?* Dan neglects his calling and communion when he denies his God-given tools of intimacy: wisdom and justice. When we cling to foolishness, we separate ourselves from the Father and the abundant life He freely offers. Foolishness detours destiny; wisdom propels it.

Read Proverbs 1:20-23. Wisdom is the voice travailing and pleading with the hearts of God's people. Wisdom is a voice that God sends to His people to guide their way. The sad thing is some have completely hardened their hearts by forsaking one of God's most precious gifts, wisdom. God is pleading with our hearts to hear His voice, to stay close to His heart. This is your battle cry, Dan: to wage war against the enemy. The battlefield is in your mind and emotions, the soulish realm. The Father has assured victory for you. Do not be deceived by Satan's devices against you. He is the guilty one whose desire is to detour you from intimacy and true freedom in Christ. Let heavenly wisdom guide you into the Father's rest and delight for you.

*The integrity of the upright shall guide them...* (Proverbs 11:3 AMP).

## SAMSON: THE STRENGTHS AND FACADES OF DAN

Israel had strayed far from intimacy after the death of Joshua. Their idolatry was the source of their harlotry. Separated from His people because of their sin, God longed to restore His people back to Him through judges. Some succeeded, but only for a short time. Again and again, Israel would revert back to idolatry, disregarding the great love and deliverance of the Father. As I noted earlier, many tribes served as judges during this time. I have to wonder where the tribe of Dan was during this time. More importantly, why did Dan not pursue his calling to judge during Israel's blatant apostasy? When an enemy has a stronghold within you, you are unable to discern his tactics. Oblivious, you get detoured by the whims of your flesh, and thereby become deceived regarding your true calling to intimacy and righteousness. Dan was ensnared with its own idolatry, just as the other tribes were. The enemy, through sly devices, often diverts us though idolatry so that when he is working all manner of evil schemes, no one is able to discern them.

I believe this was the depravity of the tribe of Dan. While in the arms of idolatrous lovers who ensnared their hearts, they were unable to discern the mass deception the enemy was planting in the hearts of their brethren. In my opinion, if Dan hadn't been deceived at this time, he would have not only discerned his enemy, but brought true justice and righteousness to Israel. Toward the end of this saga, Samson arises as a deliverer. His life embodies the story of every Dan.

## THE BIRTH, CONSECRATION, AND CALLING OF SAMSON

Read Judges 13:1-5. Samson was born of a barren woman. What is interesting to note is that every time God spoke to a barren woman and she was visited by an angel, she was promised to birth a deliverer. Some examples are: Samson, Joseph (Rachel was not visited by angel but was barren for a long time), Samuel, John the Baptist, and Yeshua (Mary not barren, but a virgin). The outcry of justice was ringing loud in the spiritual realm at the time of the Book of Judges. The Father was seeking for a deliverer out of the tribe of Dan, and He found such a person with Samson.

It is interesting to note that Samson's father's name was *Manoah*, which means "rest" in Hebrew. This is a beautiful and deep nugget for Dan and all of us. God chose to birth justice through His rest. True justice is not anxious, but arises from the peace and reliable assurance that truth and restoration will be administered. Dan, when you rely on God's rest, He will always bring you the justice and wisdom you so eagerly seek.

## THE NAZARITE VOW: SEPARATENESS AND INTIMACY

The Nazarite vow was one of separation and holiness to God. It was a distinction from idolatry and a call to truth. This was the seal of the calling of Samson (see also Numbers 6:1-8). The vow was simple: *Now therefore, be careful not to drink wine or strong drink, nor eat any unclean thing. For behold, you shall conceive and give birth to a son, and no razor shall come upon his head.* A vow of separateness invokes a dedication to truth and righteousness, which, above all, should stem from intimacy.

## "BE CAREFUL NOT TO DRINK WINE OR STRONG DRINK"

This is a call away from the influence of sin and its idolatry. Idolatry's intoxicating lure enables our spiritual senses to become impaired. When our senses are impaired, we are unable to discern and function to our full capacity. It is Satan's scheme to impair Dan's (or anyone's) judgment in order to lure them away from communion. This was his scheme in the Garden of Eden, and it is no different today.

## "NOR EAT ANY UNCLEAN THING"

We have a choice to make. There are two different feasts we can choose to attend. Both require a price to be paid. Both require your life. One, however, is distinctly different from the other. The Father's invitation is for us to come and dine. His feast is compared to no other. He has left nothing undone. All is prepared and ready for us to partake of. You see, the enemy has a counterfeit feast. It's not real. It won't satisfy our spiritual hunger. The counterfeit feast is contrary to the very reason for which we were created: to glorify God and to enjoy Him forever. When we feed on the garbage of the flesh, we chase after profane wind and feed on it. We find ourselves weary from the toil and striving when we willingly subject ourselves to idols of the heart. There can be no true peace, joy, or rest until we find His resting place.

The wedding feast of the Lord is completely different. At the King's table we find this peace, this joy. His table is abundant and plentiful with the choicest foods. We lack no good thing. We can become truly satisfied. Here at the wedding feast of the Lord, we are in harmony with the Father, for our lives are surrendered to Him in completely abandoned obedience. The counterfeit feast holds no comparison to our King's feast. First, look at the menu: Garbage! Yuck! The rottenness and guile of the flesh cannot fulfill us. It is contrary to our purpose as God's creation. We are King's kids. We are royalty because of the blood of Yeshua. We are partakers with Yeshua and His righteousness!

Dan, the Father is beckoning you to His wedding feast. Choose to be like the wise virgins and prepare yourself for the wedding feast that awaits you! How is this accomplished? When we repent of idols and leave the counterfeit feast behind, when we return to our Beloved with all of our hearts, seeking His restoration, we are made whole.

## "NO RAZOR SHALL COME UPON HIS HEAD"

This portion yet entails another beautiful view of consecration. Consecration is not a mere religious act. It is meant to be act of worship in sincere humility and dedication. Hair or head coverings often symbolized the glory and Yeshua as our covering. God desires for us to truly surrender, for in doing so, His glory, His very nature, becomes our covering. This covering was not only a sign of separateness but of protection. When the enemy sees the glory of God, he is disabled from his tactics. Our strongest tactic of warfare is our communion with the Father. For this reason, God spoke to Samson to never cut his hair, for if he obeyed, his intimacy would ward off the enemy. Then he would be victorious.

## SAMSON'S MINISTRY: HEIGHTS AND PITFALLS

Read Judges 13:24-25. Consecration and separation are always accompanied by the empowerment of the Spirit of the Lord. Samson was nurtured by the Spirit and wisdom. Every Dan must acknowledge his call to intimacy: Justice was formed in and by the very glory of the Lord, just as with Samson. Samson's separateness was the very school of the Holy Spirit by which he was trained for the eventful day he would deliver his people. I encourage you, Dan, to take on the spirit of what the Nazarite vow meant for Samson.

When you fully take to heart the call of intimacy within the spirit of this vow, you will be able to fully engage in your destiny in Christ.

## AN UNCONVENTIONAL DELIVERER

Read Judges 14:1-10. Samson, being schooled by the Spirit, would become a mighty deliverer. The methods he achieved it by were not conventional in any form. This is the true mark of the tribe of Dan. Remember Jacob's prophecy, *Dan shall be a serpent in the way, a horned snake in the path that bites the horse's heels, so his rider falls backward.* A true Dan will never take the obvious line of attack of his enemy. He will skillfully and decisively assess his enemy, strategize the unseen vantage point, and thereby defeat his enemy. Samson's unconventional tactics followed his life and ministry repeatedly. Judges 15 further reiterates Samson as a mighty but unconventional deliverer. This is the embodiment of what Yeshua said: to be as wise as a serpent (Matthew 10:16). Wisdom and discernment are the true weapons of every Dan.

The heights of Samson's ministry relied on his consecration, strength, discernment, and ability to judge. His heroic acts of strength and deliverance are unparalleled and go beyond natural ability. It is clear that his strength and victories could only be achieved supernaturally. His pitfalls related primarily to the facade(s) of every Dan: idolatry, which clouds judgment. A disconnect occurred for Samson when he became intoxicated with idolatry through his own impulsive desires of the flesh. Early on in Samson's ministry, we see his hunger for pleasures of the flesh coupled with an immature ability to handle his calling with humility. He relied too heavily on his ability, which proved to be his arrogant downfall (Chapter 16). The idol of self arose within him, snaring and blinding him to truth and righteousness. God used Samson, in spite of his shortcomings, to deliver Israel from the Philistines, but it came with a grave cost: his own life.

Samson, I believe, side-stepped the fullness of his destiny. Though he may have tasted a portion of it, I don't believe he found the fullness of dominion and destiny. His hunger for the flesh and idolatry was stronger than his hunger for holiness. Idolatry is a beguiling mistress that entices us to forgo the very intimacy for which we were created. This was the case with Samson, when he allowed Delilah to seduce him into compromising his destiny. His enemies overtook him, simply because he allowed his complacent pride and idolatry to rule his heart.

*And she said, "The Philistines are upon you, Samson!" And he awoke from his sleep and said, "I will go out as at other times and shake myself free!" But he did not know that the Lord had departed from him. Then the Philistines seized him and gouged out his eyes; and they brought him down to Gaza and bound him with bronze chains, and he was a grinder in prison* (Judges 16:20-21).

## "BUT HE DID NOT KNOW THAT THE LORD HAD DEPARTED FROM HIM"

Idolatry so ensnared the heart of young Samson to the point that he did not know when it had separated him from intimacy with the Father. When he revealed his secret to Delilah, he broke his covenant with the Father, his Nazarite vow. In doing so, he broke his consecration, for it was the very source of his strength.

## "THEN THE PHILISTINES SEIZED HIM AND GOUGED OUT HIS EYES"

Samson lost his spiritual sight long before he lost it in the natural. The disconnect was made when he chose idolatry and separated himself from that inner voice of justice. When Dan separates himself from his inner voice of justice through idolatry, he is in grave danger of foregoing his destiny.

Read James 4:4-12. Spiritual adultery catapults us into realm of confusion and fear, which, if unchecked, can result in spiritual death. The Lover of our soul is zealous for a pure and humble Bride. Dan, the greatest weapon you can possess is drawing near to God, bowing low, and heeding wisdom. Submit to the mercies of the only righteous and true Judge, GOD. His judgments are pure and life-giving; His mercies are new every morning for you. Divorce yourself from spiritual adultery, which impairs your judgment and keeps you from your true beloved, Yeshua. Repentance and intimacy will draw you back into destiny and dominion. Samson, humbled by the repercussions of his own idolatry, arises to be a mighty deliverer. Read Judges 16:22-31. Though flawed, he becomes a great hero of our faith.

> *And what more shall I say? For time will fail me if I tell of Gideon, Barak,* **Samson**, *Japheth, of David and Samuel and the prophets, who by faith conquered kingdoms, performed acts of righteousness, obtained promises, shut the mouths of lions, quenched the power of fire, escaped the edge of the sword, from weakness were made strong, became mighty in war, put foreign armies to flight* (Hebrews 11:32-34).

## IDOLATRY DETOURS JUSTICE

Read Leviticus 24:10-16, 23. In this passage, a son of Israel—a Dan—lost his life and destiny when he cursed his Creator. The tongue can either serve as a weapon of warfare and freedom or it can serve as the implement of death for the tribe of Dan. This man proudly defied his Creator, neglecting that inner voice of justice and thereby sealing his fate. Dan, the tongue (voice of justice) is meant to bring you into your place of dominion and destiny. For when you herald the justice of the Lord, you release the spirit of freedom into the spiritual atmosphere. When you hurl insults, fleshly judgments, and curses, you insult the very glory of God's creation. You must learn to tame that forked tongue. Your tongue, your very voice, was meant to speak of the glorious judgments and precepts that proceed from the throne. Learn to tame the tongue by being Spirit-led in your discernment and counsel, remaining humble and always abiding in love.

Read James 3:2-11. We are a people of unclean lips. Isaiah found his words to be full of guile. Therefore he cried out to the Lord. Read Isaiah 6:5-7. We must allow the Lord to come and undo us from the guile of our tongue. Dan, come before the throne and allow the Lord to cleanse your lips and heart. He longs to restore you as His habitation. Repentance will restore you as the voice of justice you were created to be.

## THE SEVENTH LOT

Read Joshua 19:40-48. God has ordained Dan to possess the seventh lot as their rightful inheritance. The seventh lot is a beautiful prophetic picture; the number seven represents God's perfection. Dan, however, did not come into God's perfection for him. At this time they were one of the largest tribes, yet they lost their territory due to the Amorites.

Read Judges 1:34. If Dan was so great in number and strength, why did the Amorites overtake them and cause them to forego their inheritance? The reason was their tendency toward idolatry. Dan did not bind the spiritual strong man in his spiritual house and was thus overtaken by his enemy.

Read Matthew 12:29, 43-45. A people robbed and plundered is a travail that I've been hearing from the Father's heart. We the "saints," the "redeemed," allow our inheritance to be stolen by the enemy. We leave the door of our hearts unlocked and wide open for him to come in. We put out a welcome mat for the thieves to enter and take our priceless possessions. Dan, your heritage, who you are in Christ, cannot be taken lightly.

Read Judges 18. Dan settled for less than he was created for. Chapter 17 tells of Micah, an Ephraimite also prone to idolatry, and a Levite whom he made his priest were both led into idolatry. Dan, then seeking his own gain, plundered Micah for his idols and overtook and conquered Laish (Judges 18:27-29). Once they obtained it, they set up the graven image in it (Judges 18:30-31).

Dan's spiral into obscurity started when they neglected to conquer their enemy completely because of compromise in their own hearts. Thus Moses' prediction was fulfilled. It is believed that they settled in Bashan, thus further fulfilling the prophecy. From this scripture on, we hear precious little of Dan. He is not even mentioned among the other tribes in Revelation 14. Some scholars say he is a lost tribe with no identity of his own. I, however, do not believe this. Dan is not lost. The Father never loses His children. For this reason, I feel God has a remnant of Dan awaiting their salvation. I believe Jacob's words to Dan, *For Thy salvation I wait, O Lord*, are waiting to be fulfilled. God is longing to restore His justice to Dan. It is His utmost desire that Dan takes possession of his seventh lot, God's perfection, found only by surrendering his all to the Father.

## THE MOLTING PROCESS OF DAN

Read Isaiah 40:26-31. Eagles will often enter a molting process in advanced years. It often takes place in a valley or low place. The eagle will begin to lose all its plumage, strength, vision, appetite, which could possibly result in death. Before reaching maturity, Danites themselves go through a spiritual molting process. We see this example in the life of Samson displayed very clearly. God brings us all to the valley to cause us to wrestle out those inner demons and soul wounds that keep us from soaring into the heights of the kingdom of love.

## JUDGING YOURSELF UNWORTHY TO WORSHIP

One day in worship during a "valley" season of my life, the Lord spoke very clearly and said to me, "You've judged yourself unworthy to worship and thus judged yourself unworthy to rule." Valley times are times of crises of belief, where facades at the deepest core are revealed, confronted, and challenged by perfect love to be shed. Facades must be shed like that layer of plumage of the old appearance we have had of others, God, and ourselves. A look into the mirror of God's Word will cause us to see truth. Rejection can keep one from judging or discerning through the Father's eyes. Rejection robs us of our inheritance of sonship. When we see ourselves outside of the family, this is an orphan spirit. This facade must be shed before ascending into true identity in Christ.

At times there are a number of eagles molting in the valley, pecking at each other, sometimes even resulting in killing one another. Take care, dear Dan, not to peck your fellow brethren while they, too, are undergoing a painful transformation. Do not misjudge what the Lord might be doing in another or yourself. Valley times bring transformation. We must look upward to our Maker, the Author and Finisher of our faith, for in the valley, we discover who our Great Shepherd is. If your vision is failing, ask Yeshua to renew your vision.

Read Hebrews 12:1-3. Older eagles who have gone before will often drop fresh meat down and screech as if to encourage the failing birds below. Our faithful Father has sent saints who have gone on before us to testify of the fullness of Christ and the victory and hope from past experiences they have obtained through their previous "molting" experiences. It is vital to surround yourself with the voice of hope and with the meat of the Word during times in the valley.

Another characteristic of the molting process is that the eagle's beak will have a calcium buildup that becomes very painful, so much that they begin to peck at their beaks to rid themselves of the buildup. The beak is the Danites' sense of spiritual perception, which, by sin or old wounds, can become tainted. The false buildup must be pecked away; painful it might be, but necessary for life! Your sense of perception is one of your greatest tools of intimacy, Dan, so allow the metamorphosis!

The eagles will often times lay up on a high rock or place to soak up the light of the sun and gain strength. What a picture of you, Dan! Lay yourself upon the Rock, which is Christ, and let the rays of His glory renew you! Do not be weary in well doing, dear Dan, for your heavenly Father has promised absolute victory in the light of His Son. Look upward to the glorious rays of His countenance, for your vision shall be restored. Rise up, O Dan, in the Father's perception, look through His eyes, soar on His wings, and let Him carry you to new heights of love!

## DAN AND THE BUILDING OF THE TABERNACLE

Read Exodus 31:6. Oholiab was ordained by God to help build the tabernacle in conjunction with Bezalel, who was from the tribe of Judah. It is a beautiful picture of how co-laboring with others works in the kingdom. Justice (Dan and the administration of God's justice), partnering with Judah, the government with praise, helps to build the habitation of the Lord. God longs to bring restoration to the whole house of Israel. Within the tribe of Dan you find those gifted in learning and the arts. The Father longs to build His name and heart, His very likeness, within you Dan, His habitation.

## LET JUSTICE ROLL: THE HOPE OF DOMINION RESTORED TO DAN

> *But let justice roll down like waters and righteousness like an overflowing stream* (Amos 5:24).

There is a mighty river whose streams make glad the city of our God, and they are flowing with justice for the tribe of Dan (Psalm 46:4)! The current of God's mighty river is rolling with precepts and judgments proceeding from the very throne of God.

> *…now shall not God bring about justice for His elect, who cry to Him day and night, and He will delay over them? I tell you that He will bring about justice for them speedily* (Luke 18:7-8 a).

The heart of the Father is to restore this mighty tribe of valiant warriors, voices of justice and discernment, skilled workman, counselors, and fighters of freedom, righteousness, and truth. Dan, your hour of redemption has come. Yeshua is arising with healing in His wings for you. His call is for you to soar in His judgments and in the precepts of His love. So arise, Dan, from the dust! Awaken to the cry of your Beloved, calling you out of the darkness of idolatry and into the chambers of His heart. His love alone will restore you as His glorious creation!

## PRAYER OF REPENTANCE AND DESTINY
## FOR THE TRIBE OF DAN

Abba Daddy, I long for Your righteous judgments instead of my own carnal wisdom and flawed judgments. Oh, how I love Your commandments, for they are righteous and true, forever enlightening my heart to serve You! Come and restore my broken wings. I long to soar in the heights of the kingdom of love. I repent of being judgmental and serving idolatrous lovers. By Your Spirit enabling me, I tear down every idol and altar I have enthroned within my heart. Let Your justice roll over my soul. I bow low to the laws and precepts of Your heart. I surrender the cold exterior around my heart. Restore me to become a beautiful garden that You, my Beloved, may come in and enjoy Your fragrant spices, wafted upon my praises. Truth, wisdom, and justice are the longings of my most inward being. Cause them to awaken me to perfect love. I cast off negative mindsets, hurt, and offenses that hinder Your justice from within me. I long for Your courts, where Your justice draws me into Your chambers. Establish me as the voice of justice, so I truly am forever aligned with Your throne. In Yeshua's name, Amen

---

[1] "Justice." Merriam-Webster.com. Accessed April 10, 2008. http://www.merriam-webster.com/dictionary/justice.

[2] Rabbi Ariel Hargis. "Shavuot Conference" (Ephraim and Judah International Messianic Congregation; Dallas, TX. June 2, 1995).

# CHAPTER 8
# NAPHTALI: THE DOE SET FREE!

*Though the fig tree should not blossom, and there be no fruit on the vines, though the yield of the olive should fail, and fields produce no food, and there is no cattle in the stalls, yet I will exult in God of my salvation. GOD is my strength, and He has made my feet like hinds' feet, and makes me walk on my high places* (Habakkuk 3:17-19).

The heart of the Father is for all of His glorious creation to come into freedom. The tribe of Naphtali resounds with the very heartbeat of freedom from the Father. How appropriate that following Dan, the voice of justice, God would ordain the birth of Naphtali, whose passion is to bring liberty in Christ to the captives. Among the ranks of this noble tribe you will find great warriors, intercessors, counselors, deliverance ministers, and spiritual fathers and mothers who are ordained to birth the sons and daughters of God into their dominion and destiny.

## THE NAMING OF NAPHTALI

*And Rachel's maid Bilhah conceived again and bore Jacob a second son. So Rachel said, "With mighty wrestlings I have wrestled with my sister, and I have prevailed." And she named him Naphtali* (Genesis 30:7-8).

Naphtali means "to wrestle." Their name is synonymous with their nature both in their strength and facade(s). To wrestle means "to struggle, contest, to strive with arms extended, as two men, who seize each other by the collar and arms, each endeavoring to throw the other by tripping up his heels and twitching him off his center."[1]

Jacob's family was engaged in an intense wrestling match prior to the birth of Naphtali. Animosity, jealousy, and hurt drove friction between Leah and Rachel. Both sisters felt justified in their causes against one another. They were competing for the affection of their husband. It was no secret that Jacob's deepest affection was upon fair Rachel, but he was loyal to Leah for, after all, she had borne him four sons, a triumph and validation for Leah. After the birth of Judah, Leah became barren, thus heightening the tension within the family. Rachel, still barren, cried out to her husband to take her concubine so she could birth children for her. Rachel then obtained justification through the birth of Dan and flew her long-awaited victory banner with the birth of Naphtali. This wrestling proved to be what defined the character of Naphtali.

I believe that there was a great wrestling match in the heavens at this time. This battle went far beyond what the natural eye could see. God was warring for the identity and destiny of a company of deliverers who would intercede for and become spiritual midwives to His beloved creation. Satan, seeing the glory of God fashioning within the nature of Naphtali, sought to bring confusion and destruction, even abortion to this mighty company of deliverers. This wrestling can still be found within every Naphtali until he awakens to his rightful place of intimacy and dominion within the kingdom of love.

Take in mind that Bilhah, still subservient to an overbearing and selfish Rachel and bound to Jacob, who she knew did not love her, felt alone, rejected, and even imprisoned by her circumstances. Her cries for freedom were continually going up before the throne day and night. All of these dynamics set the stage for the birth and identity of Naphtali.

Then from the throne proceeded a loud clap of thunder with lightning, the holy shofar heralding the birth of Naphtali. A deliverer was born that would resonate the liberty of the kingdom of love! The angels rejoiced with the Father and Yeshua, wildly celebrating the arrival of this beautiful creation. Liberty had been birthed into the family of God, the house of Israel!

Meanwhile, Satan sat sulking, numb in his defeat, so he devised a master plan to ensnare and hopefully thwart this deliverer, Naphtali. His plan was simple: Turn Naphtali's innate, God-given place of dominion—to wrestle against darkness—into a detour from his destiny. So he thought to himself, "Hmmm, what if Naphtali is distracted through his own wrestling within himself? What if he is destroyed through striving, perfectionism, and control? Yes, that would work! He would ignore his weapons of warfare by engaging in this mass redirection of self, caught in a miserable web of his own undoing. I am a genius! Defeat Naphtali with the very thing that is meant to free him."

> *For we do not wrestle against flesh and blood, but against the rulers, against the authorities, against the cosmic powers over this present darkness, against the spiritual forces of evil in the heavenly places* (Ephesians 6:12 KJV).

The vital key for Naphtali (and all of us) is that when he wrestles, he must be in a place of abiding in the Father. Scripture states: *Submit therefore to God. Resist the devil and he will flee from you. Draw near to God and He will draw near to you* (James 4:8). When engaging in warfare and intercession, it is strategic not only to be in communion with the Lord, but to be in absolute lovesick awe of our Bridegroom also. As we abide in Yeshua, we magnify Him, and all grows dim in the light of His presence. When we turn our focus onto our battle, our enemies, or even our tactics of warfare, we come into striving. It is striving that will draw us away from communion. The greatest weapon of warfare is intimacy! The Beloved's greatest desire for us is to know him and abide in him and the Father.

Naphtali, do not engage in battle unless you are abiding in the Lord. Striving manifests in forms of confusion and formulas and agendas contrary to the Father's heart that are drenched in fear. It is Satan's desire to pull you away from abiding through striving. For Naphtali, this includes warring in his flesh, perfectionism, and even control. Satan will even seek to deceive you into thinking that it is for the kingdom of God. God is not in a model of warfare conceived in formulas of works that neglect the heart of worship, first and foremost! If Satan can lead you on a wild goose chase, detouring you away through a counterfeit of what true wrestling is meant to be, he can than prevent you from entering into the fullness of Christ: abiding.

Many an intercessor and deliverance minister can be deceived by the enemy through formulas and striving. This often results in believers becoming burnt out or even flakey. Ministry is an overflow of our communion with the Father. Striving and perfectionism can spiral into behavioral patterns of control and eventually the Jezebel spirit. When the Jezebel spirit ensnares you, Naphtali, its goal is to abort both your destiny and dominion. Its devices are sly and unassuming. The spirit of control is rooted in the Jezebel spirit. Jezebel's agenda was to control everything and everyone, no matter whom it hurt. This wrestling, which is meant to be your strength, can serve as your death sentence when you are not in pure communion with the Father.

Read Revelation 2:20-23. When we tolerate the spirit of control, we open ourselves up to all kinds of idol worship, sickness, mind control, and witchcraft. The Jezebel spirit leads us into acts of immorality against the Lover of our soul, Yeshua. To be free of this spirit, we must come into sincere repentance and let go of our need to control or be controlled.

Jezebel seeks to usurp true authority and dominion of a believer. Many believers who play the authority card seek to control the Church. What actually takes place is all kinds of abuse and even spiritual rape. To demean someone's life and calling is to demean Creation of God's glory within them. True spiritual authority is becoming whom we truly are in Christ, serving the Lord and one another in love and humility in the fullness of our dominion. God is sounding the call of deliverance to Naphtali and the entire Church to divorce itself from

Jezebel and her tactics. Jezebel opposes the true bride of Christ. She is the apostate church. Jezebel opposes your destiny, dear Naphtali. When you feel tempted to strive, engage in perfectionism and control, draw near to the Father in repentance and bow low. In doing so, you will ensure victory as you wrestle against the darkness meant to ensnare you.

## THE GEMSTONE OF NAPHTALI

The gemstone of Naphtali is the diamond. The diamond's symbolism speaks many oracles to this beautiful tribe. It is the hardest gemstone and is even used to cut other gemstones. This can serve both as a strength and facade(s) for the tribe of Naphtali. The sharpness of Naphtali's "diamond" can cut away impure motives, idolatry, fear, or anything that hinders perfect love within himself and his fellow living stones. When tempered with love, Naphtali can be used as an instrument of restoration. God desires to use Naphtali to bring His perfection to His priceless living stones.

The danger Naphtali must be on guard for is not allowing his carnal nature of perfectionism and control to wound his brethren. When Naphtali engages in his own agenda of perfectionism, he can cut and wound his brothers and sisters in Yeshua. Bowing low is pivotal, dear Naphtali. For when you seek the Father's heart with no sense of striving or agenda, you become a mighty tool in His kingdom of love!

The diamond also speaks of the charisma and beauty of Naphtali. The diamond is one of the most desirable gemstones. Its brilliance and beauty has been desired the world over. The very nature of Naphtali attracts many. They are very friendly and hospitable. They have the gifting of hospitality, coupled with a comforting, parental nature. God desires to shine His beauty, His glory, through you. Though you may be a diamond in the rough, He longs to chisel away all that hinders perfect love from abiding in you. Allow His spirit to cut away your imperfections, for He is that perfect diamond! When He is done with you, He will turn you in every direction to refract His glory!

## THE SYMBOL OF NAPHTALI: A DOE SET FREE!

Naphtali's symbol of the deer speaks of their call to bring liberty to the captives and the call to intercession, especially in the area of birthing, and includes an apostolic and prophetic mantle. Scripture also paints the deer as a symbol of intimacy for Naphtali.

### CALL TO INTERCESSION

*The voice of the Lord shakes the wilderness; the Lord shakes the wilderness of Kadesh. The voice of the Lord makes the deer to calve and the strips of the forests bare, and in His temple everything says, "Glory!"* (Psalm 29:8-9).

### "THE LORD SHAKES THE WILDERNESS OF KADESH"

Kadesh was a wilderness within the territory of Naphtali. Kadesh in Hebrew means "sanctuary." God is longing to build His sanctuary within Naphtali. His greatest longing is to bring them into His holy habitation of Himself. The Father has ordained that Naphtali not only come into their freedom though habitation but give birth to sons and daughters through intercession.

### "THE VOICE OF THE LORD MAKES THE DEER TO CALVE"

It is the voice of the Lord that causes and calls Naphtali to become spiritual midwives, mothers, and fathers to the Body of Christ. Naphtali, upon hearing the Word of God, will conceive, deliver, and nurture the family of God. In essence, the calling of Naphtali is apostolic in nature. They build the kingdom through prophetic intercession and wrestling/warfare. Not only will they give birth to the revealing of God's sons and daughters, but they are also called to nurture them into a place of habitation.

Read Romans 8:19-25. The very connotation of wrestling speaks of the calling of intercession for the tribe of Naphtali. In this wrestling, a birthing takes place. It is a wrestling for the identity of the Father's priceless "living stones." God is longing to reveal the true identity of His creation. He is longing to reveal what Adam and Eve knew in the Garden: absolute habitation. He longs to draw His creation back to His Garden, back to intimacy. He has ordained Naphtali to aid in the birthing of the true identity of His creation. God has gifted Naphtali to know and feel the birth pangs of the Spirit. Naphtali, when surrendered to the Holy Spirit, will reverberate the groaning of creation. The essence of their calling is in this portion of the passage: *in hope that the creation itself also will be set free from its slavery to corruption into the freedom of the glory of the children of God. For we know that the whole creation groans and suffers pains of childbirth together until now.*

This is your mission, dear Naphtali, your battle cry. God is longing to free His creation from the corruption of the flesh and bring them into their true identity of His glory. The key for you, Naphtali, is to stay bowed low in the place of laid-down love for your Master and your brethren. Striving, control, and perfectionism are in opposition to this work of His glory. They are counterfeit attributes, a mere façade of holiness and a form of godliness that denies the power thereof. Naphtali, you are a mighty instrument of freedom and restoration. He has a strategic placement for you within the kingdom of love. Be sensitive to His calling.

## "AND THE STRIPS OF THE FORESTS BARE"

It is through the wrestling with sin that God uses Naphtali and strips the forest bare. All sin must be stripped and laid bare through repentance before the revealing of God's glorious creation. Take it to heart, Naphtali. When God uses you as an instrument of sonship, He will first strip all your fleshly facades of sin. Profane agendas, pride, and bitterness will prevent you from being an instrument of reconciliation to the kingdom of love.

## "AND IN HIS TEMPLE EVERYTHING SAYS, "GLORY!"

Everything within the habitation of God will reflect His glory. We were created for habitation. Sin has separated His creation from habitation. It is the calling of intercession of Naphtali that brings liberty to God's creation held captive to sin and birthed into the glory of God!

## A PICTURE OF INTIMACY

*As the deer pants for the water books, so my soul pants for Thee, O God. My soul thirsts for God, for the living God* (Psalm 42:1-2).

There is a desperate cry coming from a Bride whose heart and destiny is forever sealed for a Bridegroom King and His eternal courts of love. God has chosen you, dear Naphtali, to resound a desperate cry of hunger and thirst for the Beloved. God will use your wrestling, which will evolve into the desperation of a lovesick bridal spirit. Those who hunger and thirst after righteousness will be filled. As you cry out with deep, desperate longings for the Groom, you will entice your Lover with passionate and holy worship. Allow this thirst for His water brooks flowing from the throne, and become a contagious lover that infects the entire Body of Christ!

## LIBERTY TO THE CAPTIVES

*Then the lame will leap like a deer…* (Isaiah 35:6).

When we think of the deer, we think of it leaping with the greatest of ease and freedom. Liberty in Yeshua is just as free and beautiful as the deer leaping upon the mountains and hills. Naphtali is endowed with the prophetic mantle of liberty. Where sin and darkness abound, God is calling you, Naphtali, to bring His freedom. Your innate intercessory nature of deliverance shatters the darkness and brings restoration to the afflicted. The Father longs to release His healing and deliverance through you.

The heart of your deliverance and counseling ministry is sonship. In order to be a good father or mother of the faith you must first be a son or a daughter. Ask the Holy Spirit which areas that the orphan spirit is holding you captive. When you have broken free from the slavery/orphan mindset you will begin to walk in dominion as a father/mother of the faith. God has ordained that you would impart the father's (or mother's) blessing to His Creation.

## JACOB'S PROPHECY

*Naphtali is a doe let loose, He gives beautiful words* (Genesis 49:21).

*Naphtali is a doe let loose that bears beautiful fawns* (KJV).

### "NAPHTALI IS A DOE LET LOOSE"

Jacob's prophecy reverberates Naphtali's call to liberty. First and foremost, the Father's heart cries out for Naphtali to obtain freedom for himself. Whatever holds you captive, Naphtali, surrender in repentant honesty to the Father. He loves you so much, and it grieves Him when you are bound in any way. Whether it is striving, perfectionism, fear, or control, surrender your shortcomings to Him. He is ready and faithful to deliver you!

Another notable characteristic of the deer is that it holds no gallbladder. One who has no gallbladder is unable to hold bitterness or guile. Naphtali, do not allow the bitterness or the guile of past hurts to hold you prisoner. When you are bitter, not only are you held captive, so are your captors. The stronghold of a Jezebel spirit is birthed when we cannot release the bitterness of the past and those who have controlled us. Release yourself and them through forgiveness and repentance and become that vessel of liberty you truly are!

### "HE GIVES BEAUTIFUL WORDS AND BEARS BEAUTIFUL FAWNS"

Though these translations interpret the prophecy differently, they both have the same meaning. What Jacob was referring to was the paternal gifting within Naphtali. Their words bring comfort, counsel, and direction to the Body. Naphtali's gift of encouragement, whether it be through counsel or prophecy, speaks of the reproductive nature of God within this beautiful tribe. Naphtali's words reproduce the longing of the Father's heart for His creation. When Naphtali seeks to minister from the place of abiding in Yeshua, he gives forth beautiful words that reproduce life and hope in his brethren. This prophecy also further confirms the apostolic nature of this tribe. One way the Father builds His family is through the spirit of liberty and encouragement found within Naphtali. This verse also speaks of how Naphtali through their calling to be counselors will disciple many.

## MOSES' PROPHECY

*And of Naphtali he said, "O Naphtali, satisfied with favor, And full of the blessing of the Lord, take possession of the sea and the south"* (Deuteronomy 33:23).

## "O NAPHTALI, SATISFIED WITH FAVOR AND FULL OF THE BLESSING OF THE LORD"

Wherever there is liberty, there is favor and blessing. When Naphtali walks in the fullness of who he is and is intimately engaged with his Beloved, he not only receives (and brings) liberty, but favor follows him as well. Cease from all striving Naphtali; allow God Himself to perfect and liberate you, for in doing so you will find great favor in the eyes of your King.

## "TAKE POSSESSION OF THE SEA AND THE SOUTH"

In the natural Naphtali was given the inheritance of the south, which is the Galilee region of Israel God has called for you to possess it. When God calls us to possess our rightful inheritance, he desires for us to possess all His promises, destiny, and dominion granted to us within that inheritance. Our true inheritance is Christ-likeness. The Galilee was the very region Yeshua primarily ministered in while He was on earth. I am privileged to have been to this region and found the glory of God is heavily tangible. It is a true treasure that the Father bequeathed this land to you, Naphtali. Take time and meditate on the scriptures of Yeshua's ministry within the Galilee area. I feel as you do, you will find a great wealth of the Father's love and insight for you and your ministry.

## THE FACADES OF NAPHTALI

### THE DEER HELD CAPTIVE

> *...and from the daughter of Zion all her beauty is departed: her princes are become like harts that find no pasture, and they are gone without strength before the pursuer* (Lamentations 1:6 KJV).

The beauty of His glory diminishes when Naphtali allows the enemy to bring him into captivity. Satan is the hunter, ever ready to ensnare you with his deadly devices of deception. His mission is to rob you of your destiny and dominion. The deer is a frequently hunted animal. I believe Satan seeks to hunt, capture, and destroy you, Naphtali, because you are a liberator. If he can snare you, then you are unable to set captives free.

The nature of the deer can sometimes be fearful in nature. Fear is a snare to many; it can serve in two ways to Naphtali: (a) He can either be intimated/afraid, or (b) He can use the tactic of intimidation/fear to others. Both characteristics will hinder perfect love within you. *Hinds Feet on High Places* by Hannah Hurnard is a wonderful tool to overcome fear and come into true identity.[2] I especially recommend it to this tribe.

Read II Timothy 1:7. Often times when we have meditated on this scripture, we have interpreted it to mean that fear should not hold us prisoner from perfect love. We are right in interpreting it this way, but we must also think of it in the context that we should not cause others to be held captive by fear. Intimidation and control are two of the most common snares of leadership within ministry.

> *Then spake Jesus to the multitude and to his disciples, Saying, "The scribes and the Pharisees sit in Moses' seat. All therefore whatsoever they bid you observe, that observe and do; but do not ye after their works: for they say, and do not. For they bind heavy*

*burdens and grievous to be borne, and lay them on men's shoulders; but they themselves will not move them with one of their fingers"* (Matthew 23:1-4 KJV).

I have seen an alarming trend within the Church that is grounded in control and the Jezebel spirit. When we lead others, our calling first and foremost is to serve out of love, not agendas, formulas, and vain ego trips. As spiritual parents to the Body, you must encourage people to hear the Shepherd for themselves. When you impose your opinions and insight (in a fleshy selfish manner, not Spirit-led) on others, you deny the Body the chance for intimacy. Intimacy is based on relationship. Your spiritual children will be needy, clueless to their identity, and fearful if you rob them the right to hear God for themselves. A good parent knows when and how to cut the apron strings. A marriage relationship is two parties in loving communion with one another—not three. You do not want to be the overbearing mother-in-law, hindering the marriage of your spiritual children. Control is an attempt to lord over another with your will. This opposes the heart of God. Your calling is to birth the revealing of the sons and daughters of God. If you see someone in error, intercede for them and give counsel only when led by the Spirit according to the will of God.

When you control someone, you deny them the responsibility and pleasure of their journey in Yeshua. I have personally experienced those from the tribe of Naphtali who, however well-intentioned, control and suppress the Body they were meant to liberate. There is no place for dictatorial, controlling natures in the kingdom of love. Even our loving Father gives us a free will; give your brethren the same free will the Father freely gives to you. Behaviors of control found with the Church today are nothing more than charismatic witchcraft, similar to the destructive shepherding movement of the 1970's. Our main calling is to worship our Beloved and serve one another in love.

> *Therefore, I exhort the elders among you, as your fellow elder and witness of the sufferings of Christ, and a partaker also of the glory that is to be revealed, shepherd the flock Of God among you, exercising oversight not under compulsion, but voluntarily, according to the will of God; and not of sordid gain, but with eagerness; nor yet as lording it over those allotted to your charge, but proving to be examples of the flock. And when the Chief Shepherd appears, you will receive the unfading crown of glory* (I Peter 5:1-4).

## "HER PRINCES ARE BECOME LIKE HARTS THAT FIND NO PASTURE"

When the enemy leads you into a place of fear, striving, perfection, bitterness, and control, there is no pasture for you to graze. Separated from your pasture (your place of rest in the Beloved), you are easy prey to your hunter, Satan. When you are unable to graze upon your pasture, you become spiritually malnourished, which can result in spiritual death. Seek always for your Beloved Shepherd and His pasture for you. In Him alone you find rest and nourishment for your weary soul. When you venture away from His pasture, you will find your strength gone and be privy to the attack of your pursuer, Satan.

## WATCH OUT FOR THE TRAPS!

> *The Lord your God is angry, and on every street corner your children lie helpless, like deer trapped in nets* (Isaiah 51:20 CEV).

Your children, your spiritual offspring, are helpless and open to attack when you fall for the enemy's snares he has laid for you. This is a bleak departure from your strength as a mighty deliverer and gifting as an intercessor. Be on the alert at all times. When idolatry, fear, and shortcomings captivate you, you become prey to your enemy.

Read Judges 1:33. When we neglect to drive out what ensnares us, we subject ourselves to all kinds of unnecessary suffering and bondage. Because Naphtali neglected to drive out the Canaanites, they became captive and thus enslaved to them. This is an erroneous detour of destiny for you, dear Naphtali. When the Holy Spirit reveals a stronghold within you, be quick to repent and be set free of it. The Father longs to bring His liberty to and through you!

## THE SPIRIT OF ABORTION

To wage war against our enemy, we must know his battle plan and tactics. The scheme of the enemy is to abort the revealing of God's glorious creation. Naphtali, your marching orders are to thwart the spirit of abortion against the family of God. Seek the Father for strategy against this evil scheme. God will enable you from the place of abiding, intimacy, and intercession to overthrow this deadly demise of creation. You are the mighty warriors that the Father has entrusted in the nurturing care of His creation. Mighty moves of revival, restoration, and repentance will come through your birth pangs of intercession. Strategically, He will place you to assist the birth canal of Heaven and see the revealing of His children into the kingdom of love. This is no small task, therefore submit to God in sincere humility and love as He places you for this end-time work.

## BARAK: THE RELUCTANT WAR GENERAL

Read Judges 4 and 5.

> *Now she sent and summoned Barak the son of Abinoam from Kadesh-napthali, and said to him, "Behold, God, the God of Israel, has commanded, 'Go and march to Mount Tabor, and take with you ten thousand men from the sons of Naphtali and from the sons of Zebulun. And I will draw out to you Sisera, the commander of Jabin's army, with his chariots and his many troops to the river Kishon; and I will give them into your hand.'" Then Barak said to her, "If you will go with me, then I will go; but if you will not go with me, I will not go." And she said, "I will surely go with you; nevertheless, the honor shall not be yours on the journey that you are about to take, for God will sell Sisera into the hands of a woman." Then Deborah arose and went with Barak to Kadesh* (Judges 4:6-9).

Barak's reluctance caused him to forego the fullness of dominion and destiny. Though he was a mighty and heroic general, he shrank in fear at the time of battle. This fear is a consistent thread running through the tribe of Naphtali. Instead of boldly confronting and wrestling with his enemy, he relied on the comfort zones of his flesh by asking Deborah to accompany him. God, through the prophet Deborah, gave Barak the battle plan for victory. His reluctance caused him to forego the fullness of the glory God desired for him.

The stronghold of fear seeks to detour and even abort the calling of God on our lives. Take note, Naphtali, not to shrink back in fear when your moment of destiny arises. Know that your strategies and marching orders lie in the heart of your King when the time of battle comes. You were created to bring liberty to the captives, to be a doe set free by living example! I urge you to settle for nothing less than the purpose for which you were created.

Barak goes on to be a mighty liberator of Israel (Judges 4:10-16) and, just as Deborah prophesied, he sees the victory through the hands of a woman (17-23). In Judges 5, alongside Deborah, he proclaims a mighty victory song over Israel's enemies, and they live in peace for forty years. This mighty, heroic general proclaimed the victories of God through prophetic song. Within the tribe of Naphtali, you find many a prophetic singer who heralds the proclamation of liberty to the captives. Barak is mentioned in Hebrew 11:32 as one the great heroes of our faith. Though timid, he still managed to aid Israel in one of the greatest deliverances of his time.

## THE UNSTOPPABLE DUO OF NAPHTALI AND ZEBULUN

Read Judges 4:6 and Judges 5:18. God ordained certain relationships, and the duo of Naphtali and Zebulun is one of them. Positioned around the tabernacle and originating from two different camps, Naphtali and Zebulun were side by side. Their camaraderie is a beautiful picture of unity in the Spirit. They warred together in an undeniably powerful way, intimidating many a formidable foe. During the time of battle, they would rely on each other's strengths and compensate for the other's facade(s). At the battle of Kadesh, they displayed one of their mighty acts of bravery and unity. Sacrificing their own lives, they relentlessly overcame their enemy.

Read Matthew 16:24-25. Naphtali and Zebulun were able to obtain victory because the fought from a place of abiding. They fought from Kadesh—the place of sanctuary. When we are abiding in Yeshua, we deny our flesh, letting it die with all of its ambitions and corruption. Through this process, we can obtain fullness of victory in Yeshua. These two beautiful tribes are the perfect combination in the Spirit: Naphtali, the mighty wrestler who births the revealing of creation through intercession, and Zebulun, a fisher of men who longs to save and restore them. Wherever there is a battle for the souls of men, you will find these two noble tribes.

Read Isaiah 9:1-4. God is proclaiming His liberty to the land of Naphtali and Zebulun. He is restoring their inheritance and place of dominion. Yeshua fulfilled this prophecy when he spent a good portion of His ministry in the Galilee area. From personal experience, there is a tangible deposit of God's glory in this region. It is a region of restoration. The ministry of Naphtali and Zebulun both share the ministry of restoration.

## NAPHTALI IN THE NEW TESTAMENT

*In Joppa there was a follower named Tabitha. Her Greek name was Dorcas, which means "deer"* (Acts 9:36 CEV).

*Tabitha* in Aramaic, corresponding to the Hebrew translation *tsebiah*, is "a female gazelle." In Greek her name is Dorcas, which means "deer." Both names confirm her identity as a Naphtali. The passage goes on further to confirm her as a Naphtali both in character and in spiritual gifting(s): *She was always doing good things for people and had given much to the poor.*

Tabitha displayed her gifting through a hospitable and a nurturing nature. The tribe of Naphtali possesses the gift of hospitality and caring for the poor and afflicted. It is the parental nature of the deer that we see fulfilled in this beautiful disciple of Yeshua. In verse 37 she becomes ill and dies. The believing community called for Peter to come and pray in faith that she might be restored.

*But Peter sent them all out and knelt down and prayed, and turning to the body, he said, "Tabitha, arise." And she opened her eyes, and when she saw Peter, she sat up* (Acts 9:40).

This verse may seem simple upon reading, but it is profoundly prophetic for the tribe of Naphtali. Bear in mind her name, Tabitha, which means "deer." Peter calls out to her to arise, to awaken from slumber. This is what the Father is saying to you, Naphtali. "My deer, arise; awaken to Me, to My love, and to My freedom. Come forth in resurrection power and glory. I desire your beauty. Awaken to be both liberated and a liberator in My kingdom of love."

This miracle goes on to bring further liberation as it states in verse 42: *And it became known all over Joppa, and many believed in God.* Through Tabitha's miracle of liberation, many souls became liberated from sin. Her death and resurrection birthed many souls into the kingdom that day. Naphtali, see how infectious liberation can be? How explosive a power and glory that lies within you to transform and reveal the Father's sons and daughters of glory!

## LIBERATION BRINGS DESTINY AND DOMINION TO NAPHTALI

Arise, O mighty Naphtali, awaken from your slumber. May the glory of God lying dormant within you awaken and call you forth into liberty! You are a doe set free! In the mighty name of Yeshua, I release you to your destiny in the Father's heart. You are a gazelle whose destiny is to leap over the mountains and valleys of sin, death, hell, and the grave! Resurrection power lives within you! So come forth, O mighty ones who wrestle against darkness. Arise, you instruments of restoration and repairers of the breach. Take your place in the delivery room of Heaven, for the sons and daughters of God are crying out to be birthed into glory! You shall come forth as the intercessors, prophetic singers, and heralds of liberty for these end times. This is your moment of destiny. Now is the hour of your awakening to truth and love!

Your destiny and dominion lie within your very nature. Your God-given ability to wrestle, to overcome, is what draws you to the throne. It is the charge of your loving Father that you should obtain favor and blessing through abiding in Him.

The Beloved is yearning to bring you into His place of habitation. He yearns so desperately to behold the beautiful diamond you truly are. Cease from striving, perfectionism, fear, and control and come into the Father's restful abiding He has preordained for you.

*Hurry, my beloved, and be like a gazelle or a young stag on the mountain of spices* (Song of Solomon 8:14).

Cry out to your beloved, Naphtali, for His quick return. Prepare yourself as a wise and chaste virgin ever ready for the wedding that awaits you.

## PRAYER OF REPENTANCE AND DESTINY
## FOR THE TRIBE OF NAPHTALI

As the deer pants for the water, so my soul longs for You! I am desperate and lovesick for You, my beloved Yeshua! As the deer runs to her home, Master I run to Your throne! My striving and perfectionism won't do! I long to abide in You, in a place of true habitation of Your glory. I repent of not abiding in perfect love. I have made fear my master. I repent of my need to control and be controlled. Release me into the liberty of Your perfect love and cast out my fears. I long for You. Chisel away at this diamond in the rough. I trust You to transform me into a diamond of incandescent beauty and brilliance that shines for Your glory alone. Cause me to leap over the mountains of sin and death in my life. Position me in Heaven's delivery room to liberate Your creation and see their revealing to glory! Restore me in Your Kadesh, Your sanctuary for me. In humble surrender I pray, Amen.

---

[1] "Wrestle", Merriam-Webster.com. *Merriam Webster Dictionary Online*, Accessed August 5, 2008, http://www.merriam-webster.com/dictionary/wrestle

[2] Hannah Rose Hurnard, *Hind's Feet On High Places* (London; Christian Literature Crusade, 1955).

# CHAPTER 8
# GAD: THE HABITATION OF GOD'S FORTUNE

*But I have built a house of habitation for thee, and a place for thy dwelling forever* (II Chronicles 6:2).

Our Father and Yeshua's chief desire is habitation. Habitation is the sole reason the Father redeemed His glorious creation. What He wants you and I to know is that He longs for us to join Him in the work of habitation. Habitation is not an overnight phenomenon. The work of habitation is built on a journey laden with much suffering, many mistakes, healing, rebuilding of the ancient ruins of our past, and a conquest of our fears and stubborn will. The Father's desire for true habitation is for the kingdom of perfect love to take up residence within our hearts. Habitation is our journey to come into the fullness of the kingdom.

Habitation is a revealing of identities: God to us and whom we truly are in Him. Our ultimate destiny and place of dominion is found within the habitation of God, the greatest intimacy we are created to possess. The Father longs to reveal to and through Gad that he is the habitation of God's fortune. If anyone of the tribes ever struggled with their identity and knowing his place within the kingdom, it is Gad. Gad is a beautiful tribe of mighty warriors, evangelists, workers of miracles, revivalists, and evangelistic prophets. The treasures of habitation are found within Gad. In fact, the Father chooses to release His treasures through Gad to the Body. A great wealth of wisdom, prophetic insight, faith, and passion for souls is found with this endearing tribe.

## THE NAMING OF GAD

*When Leah saw that she had stopped bearing, she took her maid Zilpah and gave her to Jacob as a wife. And Leah's maid Zilpah bore Jacob a son. Then Leah said, "How fortunate!" So she named him Gad* (Genesis 30:9-11).

Gad means "fortunate, fortune, to invade, to overcome, a troop." The name of Gad has many wondrous revelations for this tribe. These definitions speak of the oracles of the Father's character in each Gad's identity.

(A)Fortunate: The promise of God's Word and presence is that Gad should dwell in true prosperity. Gad is endowed with God's favor and blessing from the place of habitation.

*Beloved, I pray that in all respects you may prosper and be in good health, just as your soul prospers* (III John 1:2).

The Father has called Gad to mirror and obtain true prosperity within their souls and livelihood. Favor is not an automatic thing for Gad. He usually obtains it after much suffering, soul searching, repentance, and discovery of identity. Dear Gad, you are a beautiful reflection of God's favor. It is your calling to release this upon the Body as well. You carry the mantle of favor in areas of spiritual prosperity, health (miracles of healing), finances (restoration), and with men. The further you pursue the heart of the King, the more you will find His favor. True favor comes from dwelling in the habitation of the Lord. It is by dwelling within the perfect will of the Father's love and destiny for you that you obtain favor.

(B)Fortune: The promise of God's fortune to Gad is the very seal of his identity, which lies within God's glory. Gad, when you discover the identity of God Himself (as He reveals Himself, face-to-face and heart-to-heart), your identity is revealed also.

> *In Him all the treasures of* [divine] *wisdom* [comprehensive insight into the ways and purposes of God] *and* [all the riches of spiritual] *knowledge and enlightenment are stored up and lie hidden* (Colossians 2:3 AMP).

In Yeshua alone lie the depths of the glory and nature of God. Picture this: Out on a vast ocean are many people, some wading in the shallow end, many dog-paddling or floating on the surface, all having a good time. Then there are a very rare few who go deep-sea diving. They go diving to seek for treasures at the very bottom of the ocean. This is the picture of the Church today. Some are wading, staying safe in their traditional and religious boxes, and some content to play on the surface of the water, having a good time in the Lord, but there is no depth to them. They are caught in the thrills and fads of charismatic happenings. Considerably smaller are those who go deep-sea diving into the realms of God's heart. This remnant is not satisfied with the mundane religious life.

Diving deeper into the depths of God can many times be unpopular (and costly) because it challenges religious thinking. As you come deeper into intimacy with the Beloved, you must become more and more (eventually completely) dependent on Heaven's breathing apparatus, the Holy Spirit. Those who brave the deep waters find rich truths and revelations of Yeshua. This is the revelation I long to impart to Gad. The Father wants to take you on a great adventure of exploration where you find Him and yourself. He has so many treasures and mysteries He is longing to unlock and release within you! You are His fortune, a jewel of great price!

> *And they shall be mine, saith the Lord, in that day when I make up my jewels; and I will spare them, as a man spareth his own son that serveth him* (Malachi 3:17 KJV).

Dear Gad, you were once a lost treasure, but now the Father has found you and longs to bring you into the fullness of your destiny. Allow God to reveal Himself to you as you surrender your shortcomings of self-doubt. Read Isaiah 33:6 and II Corinthians 4:6-7.

(C)Invade: Gad must take special notice to his surroundings. The enemy is ever present, trying to steal, kill, and destroy. The enemy's devices against Gad lie within his very quest for identity. Satan will try to snare you with insecurity, self-doubt, and the fear of failure. Arm yourself brethren with the truth of the God's Word and who it says you truly are.

Read I Thessalonians 5:4-8. The Father has assured you victory and refuge in the warmth of His embrace. Seek His heart and will, as it will serve as a great defense against your enemy. Jacob's prophecy to Gad will further speak of how the enemy tries to invade Gad.

(D)Overcome: The Father has assured the tribe of Gad victory even through the very meaning of their name. It is within your spiritual DNA to overcome every snare the enemy has laid for you. What an awesome promise! Arm yourself with the assurance that the victory is already yours! Defy the enemy and his lies with God's promise that you have overcome. Read 16:33, John 2:13-14, and Revelation 7:11.

(E)Troop: Gad is a force to be reckoned with in times of battle. When relying on God's strength, they are fearless, bold, and aggressive warriors, especially in regards to the souls of men. "Troop" defines Gad in their true militant cadence in which they invade darkness. A troop also implies the unity of this tribe. When tempered by the Spirit, their unity affords them the offensive attack on the enemy. Gad is often gifted in areas of spiritual warfare, deliverance, and intercession with an evangelistic, prophetic thrust. This mighty band of warriors is empowered by the Spirit of the Lord to overcome the enemy's troop as they abide in the Lord.

> *For by Thee I can run upon a troop; and by my Lord I can leap over a wall* (Psalm 18:29).

## THE GEMSTONE OF GAD

The gemstone of Gad is the jacinth or Hebrew *leshem*, "ligure." It was the seventh stone in the high priest's breastplate because Gad was the seventh son of Jacob. This has a special meaning for the tribe of Gad. God's perfection (the number 7) is longing to radiate in and through you, transforming you into your destiny. Smith's Bible Dictionary says, "ligurite is a crystallized mineral of a yellowish or apple-green hue found in Liguria…'jacinth' is identical to the Hebrew term *leshem*."[1]

Revelation 9:17 states that "the breast-plates of jacinth" are of hyacinth color, the dark blue iris color. It is the bluish-iris color that is more popularly adopted for the tribe of Gad. I have also personally adopted this view for the sole reason of God's call to habitation for the tribe of Gad. God has unique ways of displaying His destiny within us in small details that speak profound mysteries. This rich, beautiful hue speaks of Heaven and of Gad's call not only to habitation, but also to identify with the temporal nature of this present life. When Gad views Yeshua in the light of Heaven and the eternal promises of Heaven, he not only overcomes the enemy but is drawn into intimacy with his Beloved.

Read Psalm 8:1-5. When Gad considers the wondrous eternal works of the kingdom, he is given hope and reassured of his destiny in the Beloved. As we bow low, remembering the frailty of our human frame in comparison to the glory of God, we realize that our own righteousness is as filthy rags. Abba desires Gad (and all His children) to know is that the facade(s) of the human frame can be made glorious when we become truly humble and worship with a sincere heart. Gad's call to worship is to recognize and live his life by this principle. It is the Father's passion for you to abide in the light of Heaven. Heaven is the only true reality.

> *For our citizenship is in heaven, from which we also eagerly wait for a Savior, Christ Jesus; who will transform the body of our humble state into conformity with the body of His glory, by the exertion of the power that He has even to subject all things to himself* (Philippians 3:20-21).

Gad, you were created in the very likeness of the King of Glory Himself. You are royalty and a citizen of Heaven. It is imparted to you to be a living revelation of Heaven and to bring this revelation to the Body. When the enemy comes in with his lies of insecurity, past mistakes, and shortcomings, remind yourself and him that you are inscribed in the Book of Life (Eph. 2:1-7).

Realizing that we are no longer bound by sin will free us to come forth as the priceless living stones we truly are. The corruption of the flesh is a façade that deceives and detours us away from our true identity in Christ. God, who was rich in His mercy, freed us from this decay and called us to His love, His very glory! For this reason we can rest assured we are seated in heavenly places, that we are King's kids! The work of the Cross afforded us with such an inheritance of grace and mercy, which propels us into our true kingdom identity. Take this to heart, dear Gad, treasure the gift of salvation within you every day. For from this salvation you were brought near to the King of love and been freely given a glorious inheritance!

## THE SYMBOL OF GAD

The nomadic nature of Gad defines his life and ministry. Long after the Israelites settled, Gad, along with Reuben and the half tribe of Manasseh, remained nomads. They were shepherds by nature, desiring rich, plush, green grazing land and found it within the eastern Jordan region. Gad proved to the boldest of the tribes in this conquest, leading the way. Appropriately, the symbol of Gad is a picture of three tents.

## THE WORK OF THE CROSS DISPLAYED WITHIN GAD

Picture this: the center tent is in the foreground, and the other two to the left and right of it in the background. Upon viewing this image of the three tents, it forms a Cross. These three tents speak of the Cross and habitation through the work of the Cross. This is Gad's call: to live in the complete work of the Cross.

> *For the word of the cross is to those who are perishing foolishness, but to us who are being saved it is the power of God* (I Corinthians 1:18).

The power of the Cross enables you, Gad, to overcome and come into a place of habitation with the Father. Resting in the work of the Cross, by allowing its work to have a habitation within you, births you into your true identity in Yeshua. The Cross is your protection and a work of completion to your soul.

> *But may it never be that I should boast, except in the cross of our Lord Jesus Christ, through which the world has been crucified to me, and I to the world* (Galatians 6:14).

The only thing we can be sure of and boast of is the Cross. The power of the Cross is the only enablement we should seek for our lives. Relying on our own strength and abilities is self-reliant pride that disables the work of the Cross and alters destiny. Gad falters when he neglects to boast only in the Cross. When He boasts of his own self-reliance and strength, he fails miserably. The Father desires you, dear Gad, to come into the fullness of the Cross of Yeshua for your life. Read Colossians 1:19-20.

## A WANDERER

Read Numbers32:1-15. Gad is a wanderer, looking for habitation. The tents speak both of the folly and the destiny of Gad's lifelong quest. Gad's carnal nature is that of a wanderer seeking always for greener pastures. This wandering and dissatisfaction can cause Gad to forego his destiny if it is not dealt with. The phrase "gad about" stems from the nomadic nature Gad is known for. In his immaturity, Gad will often wander through relationships, jobs, churches, and fellowships, looking for a quick fix to satisfy him. What he often finds, however, is a demise of destiny leading to his undoing.

One of the primary facade(s) of Gad is that he often will settle for less than God's perfect destiny for him. This is why the picture of the tents serves as a warning to Gad as well. When Gad settles in a land that the Father has not ordained for him, he finds himself in all forms of hurt, unnecessary warfare, and confusion. In fact, it is the enemy's prime tactic against Gad to have him settle in the camps of confusion, causing him to graze upon the land of his own foolish desires. This tactic of Satan can result in spiritual death for the tribe of Gad. Later on, we will discuss how this fully plays out in Scripture.

Gadites tend to be very flighty and (or) flakey in their immaturity. Their desires often cause them to become delusional in their understanding and discernment. Like Simeon, they are easy prey to the spirit of divination. Relying on the truth of God's Word and wise counsel will aide Gad in deliverance from these facade(s). God does not want to extinguish your adventurous spirit Gad, but refine it. His Spirit led you into the adventures He has planned for you.

## THE HABITATION OF GOD'S FORTUNE

*O Lord, I love the habitation of Thy house, and the place where your glory dwells*
(Psalm 26:8).

The glory of God is the very fortune God longs to bring to Gad as he abides in perpetual habitation. We all house the glory of our Creator. The Father is summoning the tribe of Gad to seek his true fortune within himself, the glory of God. The keys to the treasure chests of Heaven are repentance and intimacy. When Gad ceases from his wandering and settles in his rightful inheritance of habitation, he discovers these treasure within.

Read Psalm 84:1-2. Dwelling places in Hebrew is the word *mishkan*, meaning "tabernacle." In this reference, tabernacle is actually plural so it would read: *How lovely are Thy tabernacles*. The tabernacle was a tent and a temporal dwelling place.

*Yet you do not know what your life will be like tomorrow. You are just a vapor that appears for a little while and then vanishes away* (James 4:14).

Our lives our temporal, but we forever anticipate the eternal dwelling place of God. God is saying, "How lovely are My tabernacles in which I abide!" Gad must consistently yearn and seek the courts of the Lord, for his very livelihood depends on it! There is a yearning from Heaven for us to dwell in His courts eternally.

Read II Corinthians 4:16-18. The tribe of Gad's gifting, to see things on earth as temporal and the things of the Spirit as eternal, cause them to be a people of great faith. In fact, Gad is endowed with a great measure of the gift of faith. He communes with God in faith and even carries the mantle of faith to the Body. This tribe's gift of faith accompanies their calling to signs, wonders, miracles, mighty deliverances, and salvation. This is the very key to their evangelistic prophetic calling.

## JACOB'S PROPHECY

*"As for Gad, raiders shall raid him, but he shall raid at their heels"* (Genesis 49:19).

### "RAIDERS SHALL RAID HIM"

The KJV says, Gad, *a troop shall overcome him: but he shall overcome at the last.* Jacob is referring to Gad's tug-of-war within himself. Even his name implies "invade." Troops of insecurity, double-mindedness, and fear of failure war within the soulish realm of every Gad. It is this multitude or troop that seeks to devour Gad. That "troop" is Gad himself; he is his own worst enemy. These characteristics are the cause of Gad's wandering nature.

Satan seeks to engage Gad in the battlefield of the mind and his own shortcomings. The enemy seeks to destroy Gad's gift of intimacy: faith. He will try to cause you to lose faith in your identity in the Beloved and, more importantly, His ability to save you. Satan's devices of self-condemnation will divert Gad from the path of the revelation of God within. The key to overcome, dear Gad, lies within the Cross of Yeshua and His sufferings, for from that place is your identity revealed and victoriously won! Read Romans 8:1-2.

## "BUT HE SHALL RAID AT THEIR HEELS"

The work of the Cross is truly the work of habitation. It is the only way to victory and restoration of identity. If we engage in the battlefield of the mind without pursuing the work of the Cross and its power to save, we end up defeated, striving, lost, and confused. Resurrection glory lies within the Cross; therefore it is vital, Gad, that you cling to it. The Cross will put to death the old man, which seeks to snare your identity and steal your hope of salvation. Your old man (flesh) is a lie that masquerades your true identity and destiny. Your identity lies within the saving grace and glory of the Cross.

Read II Corinthians 3:3-9, 16-18. I charge you, Gad, to look into the face of God and see His mirrored reflection within you, the reflection of the Cross. To behold His glory is to behold the fullness of the Cross. Only this reflection can transform you through the work of grace that enables you. The veil of the flesh, with its condemnation, disables our true identity. The Cross enables the work of transformation and freedom by bringing conviction and rending apart the veil of the flesh and its condemnation. Read Colossians 1:20-22.

## MOSES' PROPHECY

*And of Gad he said, "Blessed is the one who enlarges Gad; he lies down as a lion, and tears the arm, also the crown of the head. Then he provided the first part for himself, for there the ruler's portion was reserved; and he came with the leaders of the people; he executed the justice of the Lord, and His ordinances with Israel"* (Deuteronomy 33:20-21).

## "BLESSED IS THE ONE WHO ENLARGES GAD"

The Father is longing to enlarge Gad. He enlarges Gad through the work of habitation, by building their faith and revealing their hidden identity.

*Enlarge the place of your tent; stretch out the curtains of your dwellings, spare not; lengthen your cords, and strengthen your pegs* (Isaiah 54:2).

Blessing and honor belong to God alone who grants favor and fortune to the habitation of Gad. It is the revelation of the Father Himself that causes Gad's tents to become enlarged. Clinging to the façade of the flesh and its false beliefs will weaken and eventually diminish the dwelling place of Gad. Gad, you must be careful who and what you allow in your tents. Satan's lies will cause the infrastructure of your soul to reap decay and even spiritual death. Repentance and intimacy will enlarge your tent. Make it your soul's passion and mission to allow the King of glory to enter your dwelling place. Yeshua is the true habitation we must seek. Through His transformation glory, you are made complete, restored, and filled with His love and glory.

*But you shall seek the Lord at the place which the Lord your God shall choose from all your tribes, to establish His name there for His dwelling, and there you shall come* (Deuteronomy 12:5).

The name of Yeshua: literally *salvation*, is established within us when we have surrendered our lives to Him. It is His saving power in grace that enables us to abide in Him, to live and move and have our very being. Let the saving power of His name be forever branded upon your dwelling place. Read Revelation 21:3.

### "HE LIES DOWN AS A LION, AND TEARS THE ARM, ALSO THE CROWN OF THE HEAD."

This portion of the prophecy speaks of Gad's identity in warfare and their tactics. Gadites can possess the same boldness and gallantry as the tribe of Judah. Judah serves as a powerful influence to many tribes. God chose Gad to emanate the war-like nature of Judah. David himself took notice of these mighty warriors. The nature of Gad is very impressionable (good or bad). They are chameleons, like Reuben, but motivated to do so for different reasons. The primary reasons for this are Gad's insecurity and his very pliable nature. Gad will seemingly take on characteristics of other tribes. Gad is a wanderer, searching to find himself. He tries on many hats before coming to rest in his own gifting and calling. Gadites may try many different religions, habits, jobs, or relationships when insecure.

Read I Chronicles 12:8, 14-15. The tribe's fierce warlike nature caught the attention of King David. It was their relentless spirit that caused him to see them in this light. The scripture also says that they were *as swift as a gazelle*. They are swift to run to the cause of freedom and deliverance of their brethren, much like Naphtali. The tribe of Gad identifies with similar aspects of warfare in Moses' prophecy: (A) He lies down as a lion, (B) he tears the arm, and (C) the crown of the head.

### "HE LIES DOWN AS A LION"

The meaning of this portion is two-fold for Gad. It can be interpreted both as a call to rest in the Lord and also the laziness of Gad. On a positive note, God is calling Gad to engage in battle from the place of rest in the Lord only. Engaging from God's rest affords us not to strive in our own abilities or tactics, but to fight with Gad's heavenly weapons of war: faith and habitation. Rest is born out of true habitation. When Gad is at rest, he is abiding in the kingdom's plan laid out before him, knowing that only in Yeshua is victory assured. Faith is also born of rest and habitation. When our hope is set on the Author and Finisher of our faith, we relinquish self-doubt, fear of failure, and the lies of the enemy. This prophecy also serves as a warning to the tribe of Gad. Moses is referring to the incident in Numbers 32:6-9:

> *But Moses said to the sons of Gad and to the sons of Reuben, "Shall your brothers go to war while you yourselves sit here? Now why are you discouraging the sons of Israel from crossing over into the land which God has given them?"*

The laziness of Gad is very apparent in this scripture. For this reason Moses warns against this in his prophecy.

### "HE TEARS THE ARM"

The arm is known as a symbol of strength. The Father has granted Gad to know the source of strength of his enemies and thereby attack it. Once Gad tears the arm of his foes, they are defenseless, thus Gad achieves his victory. Whereas Dan goes from behind, taking the unassuming tactic of warfare, Gad will engage in a complete frontal confrontation and assault on the enemy.

### "AND THE CROWN OF THE HEAD ALSO"

The crown of the head symbolizes authority. Gad, when tempered by the Spirit in love and humility, will foresee and expose the hypocrisy and falsehoods within his enemy's authority or dominion. The very source of the enemy's power is overthrown by Gad's keen discernment and militant strength.

### "HE PROVIDED THE FIRST PART FOR HIMSELF FOR THERE THE RULER'S PORTION WAS RESERVED"

Moses was referring directly to Gad's engagement in the land of Jordan. I feel this prophecy further confirms Gad's influence in the conquest. This prophecy also has a reference to the tribe of Benjamin. Jacob's prophecy states, *In the morning he devours his prey and in the evening he divides the spoil.* Gad sought out his own portion for himself and his pleasures, not taking into account the Father's desires. It is this insatiable hunger that drives Gad to graze for what he thinks are greener pastures. This selfish desire can lead him into confusion and sin when unrepentant. Gad must overcome his immature wanderings that detour his destiny in order to adventure into the habitation of God's fortune reserved for him.

### "HE CAME WITH THE LEADERS OF THE PEOPLE; HE EXECUTED THE JUSTICE OF THE LORD, AND HIS ORDINANCES TO ISRAEL."

The tribe of Gad is gifted with a prophetic discernment similar to that of Dan. His insight will often bring justice to the afflicted and freedom to the captives. They are often gifted in deliverance ministry with a prophetic and evangelistic thrust. Elijah, a Gad, brought justice to Israel through his prophetic ministry.

## THE FACADES OF GAD

There are three main idols of the heart that lead Gad away from his rightful place of habitation: gluttony or a wantonness spirit, a sedentary or lazy spirit, and lying spirits (divination that leads to grave delusion). The Father's heart's cry is for Gad to be free of all three in order to come into the fullness of destiny and dominion He has for them. Each one of these is the root cause of Gad's wandering ways.

## GLUTTONY OR A WANTONNESS SPIRIT

This spirit is greedy. It isn't satisfied with what God provides. This would describe some of Gad's wandering and always looking for greener pastures. We need to look to Yeshua to fulfill us. He is our source for everything we need.

> *The soul of the sluggard desireth, and hath nothing: but the soul of the diligent shall be made fat* (Proverbs 13:4 KJV).

Gad begins to wander when his voracious appetite of the flesh begins to control him. Gluttony and wanton are driving spirits. Driving spirits will cause us to come into a depravity of the mind and spirit. When these spirits take over the habitation of Gad, he loses sight of his true fortune in Christ. I implore you, dear Gad, to become content in your Beloved. Only He can satisfy you.

> *Not that I speak in respect of want: for I have learned, in whatsoever state I am to be content* (Philippians 4:11).

Gad, through these spirits driving him, becomes fattened on enticements of the flesh. These enticements are unhealthy and even detrimental to the purpose for which he is predestined. I like to call these enticements "junk food." Often junk food sounds much better to us than that "healthy stuff." Gad becomes malnourished when he feasts on junk food. Malnourishment will cause his growth in Christ to be stunted. Instead, he should feast on the fruits of the Spirit, God's character. Our hunger must be a holy hunger and not a profane one.

Sincere desperate hunger and thirst for God really brings a manifestation of the glory. Desperation is so pleasing to God. He delights when we wait upon Him. He is the only one who can satisfy our souls.

*Blessed are they which do hunger and thirst after righteousness: for they shall be filled* (Matthew 5:6).

The key for you, dear Gad, is to seek first the kingdom of God. When this becomes your sole pursuit, the work of habitation begins within. Seeking first the kingdom will prove to be your most valuable weapon against these spirits. Gad, you will truly become a habitation of God's fortune when you to seek first the kingdom and His righteousness. Read Matthew 6:33-34.

## A SEDENTARY OR LAZY SPIRIT

To settle for less than you were created for is truly a grievous thing to our Father. Gad, when your appetite guides you to foreign pastures, it detours you away from the Father's heart and will cause you to become despondent and numb to the calling on your life. Spiritual apathy is compromise that draws you away from habitation. It is a spirit of slumber that can sometimes lead you into spiritual death of your destiny. God wants you, precious Gad (and all of us), to engage in His work in us and through us. Our relationship is a two-way street and requires responding to the Father's voice.

Sometimes Gad can become despondent because of cares of this world or hurts. The most common is the fear of failure. Sometimes we are inactive because we are paralyzed with fear due to past mistakes. This so grieves the Father. He loves you so much, and He wants you to join Him in the work He is doing in you. Gad, your past has been paid for by the precious blood of Yeshua. True, you cannot rely on shortcomings, but in His strength and Spirit you can overcome.

## LYING SPIRITS AND DIVINATION

When Gad allows the idols of gluttony and lazy/sedentary spirits full reign, he then spreads out the welcome mat for lying spirits and divination, which will lead to the grave delusion of his soul and mind. Gad's wandering free spirit, when immature, will lead him far from the kingdom of love. The infantile wanderings of Gad are likened unto those of the prodigal son. Read Luke 15:13-24.

Gad, your facade(s) will lead you off the path of destiny and cause you to squander your inheritance: the habitation of God's fortune. When you dine on the husks that swine partake of, you lose your holy hunger for the banqueting table of Heaven. The Father will often give us over to our own desires. This comes with a grave price.

Read II Thessalonians 2:1-11. If we continue on the path of our desires and laziness, we can buy into any lie the enemy has to offer. During the conquest of the land, when God was allotting the inheritance, the Gadites, while influencing Reuben and the half tribe of Manasseh, sought a land for their own desires and not God's. They sought to appease their own willful desires instead of coming into the perfect will of God for their lives. This caused these tribes to settle for less than their destiny. God does redeem them later, as we see the land of Gilead, which overflowed with healing balm.

## ELIJAH: THE PROPHET OF GOD'S FORTUNE

Elijah fully embodied the nature of every Gad. His calling as a prophet to Israel beautifully portrayed his evangelistic prophetic mantle. Elijah was a true son of the tribe of Gad in the way he performed many signs and wonders and fiercely opposed Jezebel and the prophets of

Baal. He also identified himself with the facade(s) of Gad's insecurity, fear of failure, and other shortcomings. Elijah, though flawed at times, is a hero of great faith and embodied the habitation of God's fortune that he truly was.

## A GREAT MAN OF FAITH

> *Elijah was a man with a nature like ours, and he prayed earnestly that it might not rain; and it did not rain on the earth for three years and six months. And he prayed again, and the sky poured rain, and the earth produced its fruit* (James 5:17-18).

Elijah's ministry was the abundance of signs, wonders, and miracles. Though at times his faith wavered, he proved himself to be a habitation of great faith. Elijah boldly defied Ahab because of his prideful apostasy to God, and he prophesied a drought (I Kings 17:1). He went after the crown of the head of Ahab's polluted authority and tore it down.

His faith was in His Creator, and His destiny for Israel. When faced with insurmountable odds, this lion-faced warrior didn't even flinch. In full assurance of faith, Elijah prayed that God would withhold rain, and He did. Elijah went on to perform many miracles, signs, and wonders: the miracle of oil and flour, raising the widow's son from the dead, fire upon the altar, etc. This same fortune of faith lies within the tribe of Gad today. Their ministry is followed by many signs, wonders, and miracles, demonstrating the spirit of Elijah that rests on them.

## ELIJAH CONFRONTS JEZEBEL AND THE PROPHETS OF BAAL

Read I Kings 18. Ahab named Elijah, "a troubler of Israel" (verse 17). Elijah then ferociously exposed Ahab and his sins to God and the nation of Israel. He openly scorned the false authority of Ahab and Jezebel. He also exposed the heart condition of Israel when he said, *How long will you hesitate between two opinions? If God is God, follow Him, but if Baal, follow him.* Elijah demonstrated both his calling as a prophet and revivalist. As a prophet he rebuked Israel for their apostasy, and as a revivalist he desired to bring them back to the Father.

> *And he will turn back many of the sons of Israel to the Lord their God. And it is he who will go as a forerunner before Him in the Spirit and power of Elijah, TO TURN THE HEARTS OF THE FATHERS BACK TO THE CHILDREN, and the disobedient to the attitude of the righteous; so as to make ready a people prepared for the Lord* (Luke 1:16-17).

This is the true mark of every Gad. Elijah was an evangelistic prophet in that he sought to return the hearts of the children of Israel to the Father. He then mocked the blatant sorcery, adultery, and guile of Jezebel and her prophets. Elijah became that mighty troop against the hordes of hell ensnaring Israel at that time. After the futile attempts of the prophets of Baal, Elijah called upon God.

Read I Kings 18:36-39. Elijah demonstrated a sincere and compassionate heart of a revivalist when he cried to the Father, *Answer me, O GOD, that Thou art God, and that Thou has turned back their heart again.* Gadites today carry the same Elijah spirit in times of revival. They carry a great mantle and burden for souls with an evangelistic, prophetic thrust.

## ELIJAH WANDERS FROM THE HABITATION OF GOD

Read I Kings 19-1-4. Jezebel's sinister attack shook his faith and disillusioned him from the truth of God's salvation for him. It momentarily called him out of identity. He had just witnessed a mighty miracle and saw his own people return to God. Elijah began to wander when he allowed intimidation, insecurity, and control to minister to his mind. He allowed the troop of self-doubt and fear of failure to invade him. Disillusioned by these circumstances, he ran from the very greatness and glory of God within him.

Read I Kings 19:9-13. Elijah had been taken over by his own insecurities, fear of failure, and self-reliance, so much so that it caused him to want to take his own life. This proved to be a detour from the Father's ultimate destiny for Elijah. Though he was an absolute lover of God, he feared his own greatness, which withheld victory for himself and the conquest of Jezebel and Ahab. God then handed it down to Elisha, an Issachar, who got the job done. He went on to perform almost double the amount of miracles as Elijah. Elijah was a wonderful hero of our faith who came shy of completely possessing his fortune (riches of God's glory, destiny, and dominion) of habitation.

This is important lesson for every Gad to learn. There comes a moment in your walk with God when He calls you into the fullness of habitation. If you run away from what you fear, even your own greatness, you will miss out on God's perfect plan for your life. Surrender your shortcomings of self-doubt and allow God to reveal Himself to you as His glorious creation. When you truly begin to bow low and search for the hidden treasures of God's glory within you, you then become the great habitation of God's fortune you really are. Cease from your wandering and settle into your destiny created by your loving Father. Once you settle into your rightful inheritance and truly possess it, you will flourish overnight in the courts of God. You are His glorious habitation—where His glory dwells. Dear and beloved Gad, come into the Father's rest and delight. In His Kingdom of love you will lack no good thing. He will supply all the riches and fortune of His kingdom.

*And my God shall supply all your needs according to His riches in glory in Christ Jesus* (Philippians 4:19).

## THE TREASURES OF DESTINY AND DOMINION RELEASED TO GAD

Read Isaiah 33:20-24. Gad, my dearest brethren and priceless living stones, the Father chooses to build His holy habitation in you. Enter into His rest, for therein lies the hidden treasures of glory and His fortune. I charge you to cease from your striving and wandering. How lovely are you, dear Gad, the dwelling place of the Most High God! Your tent shall no longer be folded, your stakes never pulled up, and your cords never to be torn apart again. Look up, dear Gad, to the heavens: Your rightful abode is the Creator of life Himself. He has removed the reproach of your many wanderings and drawn you unto Himself, His glorious and most beloved habitation of His fortune!

## PRAYER OF REPENTANCE AND DESTINY
## FOR THE TRIBE OF GAD

Heavenly Father, I long for Your abode! Draw me with cords which cannot be broken! Many times I have wandered away from Your habitation of fortune for me. I repent, Father, for grazing in pastures of my own foolish desires. Turn me, and I shall be turned, O God, in your loving-kindness and great mercy to habitation once again! Awaken my glory; reveal the hidden treasure of my identity, of my Creator God within me! I relinquish my foolish desires, inadequacies, and delusions. Forgive me for buying into the strong delusion of my own wandering. Purge me deep, purge me quickly of the enticements of my decaying, gluttonous flesh. Cause righteousness and truth to spring up from my innermost being. Drive my stakes deep into the soil of Your Word. Stretch out my tent that it might become a habitation of Your fortune in which You and I abide. Longing and awaiting the eternal purpose of betrothal and intimacy to You, My precious Bridegroom, I pray, Amen.

---

[1] William Smith, *Smith's Bible Dictionary* (London, England; 1863), Public Domain.

# CHAPTER 9
# ASHER: THE SPRING OF JOY!

*All my springs of joy are in you* (Psalm 87:7).

Joy is a kingdom principle. It is the enlightenment of hope, the very radiance of blissful lovers, and the renewing of strength to the weary in soul and body. The kingdom of Heaven is heavy laden with everlasting joy. It is an eternal spring gushing out of our Father's heart. All of our joy is found through abiding in our Beloved. Yeshua is the exact representation of the Father's joy. Joy is the abundance of the Father's presence to our internal habitation. In Yeshua we have been given life abundant, a life of joy!

> *The thief comes only to steal, and kill, and destroy; I came that they might have life, and might have it abundantly* (John 10:10).

Joy is the overflowing essence of Yeshua Himself. It is the very abundance of His glory. The foundations of both Heaven and earth were created with abundant springs of joy eternal. Joy is the sustaining power of our glorious salvation. It was the Father's master plan to design a jewel of great price who would both display and release true joy. So He fashioned Asher after His very likeness to be a reflection of His joy in the earth.

Asher is the spring of joy in our Father's Kingdom of love. How appropriate that after the birthing of the habitation of God's fortune through Gad that the Father would bring a wellspring of everlasting joy into His kingdom in Asher! This exuberant tribe infectiously permeates the Body of Christ with their joyous nature. Whenever God is throwing a party, you will surely find Asher in the midst of it. Asher longs, breathes, and exists for the joy of the Lord. It is the very core of their being and spiritual DNA. Among this jubilant tribe you will find a people who are sustained and propelled by the joy of the Lord. The joy of the Lord is their destiny and inheritance. Asher imparts revelation, anointing, rich dainties from the Word of God, revival, and intercession through the spring of joy within him.

## ASHER: THE SPRING OF JOY

A spring is a natural resource within the earth that brings life-giving substance. Joy is like a spring that leaps up at the response to God's love. This is true of the tribe of Asher. Their spirit leaps up in extreme joy to the Father. Asherites are gifted with a special empowerment through the joy of the Lord to bring anointing, healing, nourishment, and provision to the Body. There are many springs of joy waiting to be released in and through the tribe of Asher.

## A SIGN OF COMPLETION AND NEW BEGINNINGS

Asher, as the eighth son of Jacob (and the sixth son of Leah), holds a special place in the family of God. Eight is the number of completion and new beginnings, and Asher is a sign of this covenant to the house of Israel. Joy, one of the fruits of the Spirit, is very essential to us as believers. It is what completes our hope and is present in every new beginning the Father has ordained for us! Each new day dawns with the hope of a new beginning for us as we dwell in the joy of the Lord! The joy of the Lord is the completion of the work of perfect love within our hearts. We would all do well to tap into the natural resource of God's joy within our brethren Asher.

## A SOURCE OF NOURISHMENT TO THE BODY

*Then he said to them, "Go, eat of the fat, drink of the sweet, and send portions to him who has nothing prepared; for this day is holy to our Lord, Do not be grieved, for the joy of the Lord is your strength"* (Nehemiah 8:10).

The Father is longing to unleash a wealth of anointing and joy in these end times. Asher is strategically planted within the Body for Christ to bring strength, nourishment, and refreshing in turbulent times. Oil is a very valuable source. Within this beautiful tribe you will find a great spring of the oil of joy, coming fresh from the olives trees of Heaven. He has reserved you, dear Asher, to provide much comfort, healing, strength, and provision through your God-given tool of intimacy: the joy of the Lord! Precious Asher, you are the very pleasure and delight of your Creator and to all with whom you come into contact!

## THE NAMING OF ASHER

*Then Leah said, "Happy am I! For women will call me happy." So she named him Asher* (Genesis 30:12).

Asher means "happy, joy, to be joyful, to rejoice, abundance, jubilation." Asher is the very celebration of God's love expressed in human form. There are countless references to joy within Scripture. It is very much tied to the presence of God, worship, and intimacy. All of Heaven resounds with the anthem of joy of the Father's love for us. He has appointed Asher to resound this anthem through his life and ministry.

For the kingdom of God is not eating and drinking, but righteousness and peace and joy in the Holy Spirit (Romans 14:17).

Joy is one of the key building blocks of the kingdom. As a priceless living stone, Asher is a vital building block within the temple of the Lord. The Beloved expressly desires you, my brethren Asher, to come into His kingdom and the fullness of His joy. Joy is your very life source, nourishing you as the priceless habitation that you are.

## THE GEMSTONE OF ASHER

The gemstone of Asher is the agate. The agate is a beautiful stone of many earth tone colors such as browns, greens, yellows, rusts, etc. Agate is fashioned in the hollows of volcanic rocks. A volcano's lava structurally changes whatever form it touches. This is true of the joy of the Lord. The character and nature of Asher is formed through intense fire of the Holy Spirit. It is the process of the heat and pressure that forms rings or bands of color around the agate stone. With each testing and trial, the Holy Spirit refines the character of Asher to bring forth layer upon layer of the beauty and character of God. Asherites, with their many layers and colors, are very unique, intriguing, and pleasurable people. They beautifully display the character and many layers of the Father's joy. Within this glorious tribe you will find layers of revelation, knowledge, and understanding.

## ASHER'S CALL TO THE EARTH

The earth tone colors speak of Asher's call to the earth. Asher is called to release revelations of Heaven's joy within the earth. God revealed to me that creation was founded upon two principles: rest and delight. It was on the seventh day that man was created. You and I were created according to these two principles: rest and delight. The tribe of Asher mirrors the Father's rest and delight in their lives and ministry. They resound the Father's delight in creation through the very joy they possess.

It excites them immensely to see and aid their brethren to come into the fullness of joy in the Father's plan. This passion for creation is joyfully resonated in their lives and ministries. Asherites are by far the most people-oriented tribe out of the twelve. There is not a person they meet that they do not consider an instant and sincere friend. Asherites, most often times, are very sincere and faithful in their friendships. They bear the brethren up with great joy through their intercession and unfailing friendship. They tend to be impartial, loyal, and endearing souls as they minister the Father's joy to everyone they touch. Asherites will often carry both mercy and exhortation motivational gifts.

## REFINING THROUGH SUFFERING

It is the intense heat of suffering that builds the layers and character of Asher. Suffering with each trial forms each band of glory and joy within Asher. Asher grows in joy from strength to strength.

> *How blessed is the man whose strength is in Thee; in whose heart are the highways to Zion! Passing through the valley of Baca, they make it a spring; the early rain also covers it with blessings. They go from strength to strength; every one of them appears before God in Zion* (Psalm 84:5-7).

## "HOW BLESSED IS THE MAN WHOSE STRENGTH IS IN THEE"

How blessed is Asher whose strength is in the Father! Joy is built over a lifetime of intimacy with the Father. Hardship molds layer upon layer of the unique intimacy, gifting, and calling of every Asher.

> *Consider it all joy, my brethren, when you encounter various trials, knowing that the testing of your faith produces endurance. And let endurance have its perfect result, that you may be perfect and complete, lacking in nothing* (James 1:2-3).

This scripture is the anthem of every Asher. Dearest Asher, allow your sufferings to bring about His perfection in you. His joy will sustain you in your trials. The joy of the Lord, as it builds strength, will afford you the endurance to run the race. Your ultimate prize is Christ-likeness. Welcome the transformation that suffering brings you.

## "IN WHOSE HEART ARE THE HIGHWAYS OF ZION"

Zion is the highest place of praise. It represents the ultimate and glorious habitation for which we were all created. It is through joy, Asher, that you come into habitation. The Father builds the highway of holiness in your heart by the refining work of joy. Not only does God choose to build His highways to Zion through joy, but He calls you to emanate by example this crowning aspect of God's nature—His joy and delight—to His Bride.

## "PASSING THROUGH THE VALLEY OF BACA, THEY MAKE IT A SPRING"

Baca is known as the valley of tears. This is a beautiful picture of intimacy for the tribe of Asher. In the lowest valley and darkest night of your soul, God chooses to bring you into a radical transformation. It is in the very place that you begin to pour your tears (and yourself) out in complete abandon that you find the substance of true joy. True joy is not a fleeting work of hyped sensationalism, but a building of life experiences and suffering. It is in the valley of Baca that the Father causes you, my dear Asher, to become a spring. Your heart leaps up from the ground of your frail human frame to find intimacy through the joy and strength of the Lord. Asher, you are a walking spectacle of the glory of God and how suffering produces eternal joy to you and all you encounter.

### "THE EARLY RAIN ALSO COVERS IT WITH BLESSINGS"

The early rain is the symbol of outpouring. Asher is called to intercede and bring forth mighty outpouring from the Father's heart. There are storehouses of outpouring pregnant with joy and anointing that Asher unleashes. From this he carries great blessing, freedom, restoration and inner healing to his fellow living stones.

### "THEY GO FROM STRENGTH TO STRENGTH; EVERY ONE OF THEM APPEARS BEFORE GOD IN ZION"

This scripture is the very seal of the identity of every Asher. The anvil of suffering births the truest form of joy, for joy produced through suffering is the fruit of faith, and passion tested to the core. This process produces an eternal spring of joy, an incorruptible seed of abiding in the nature of Christ. For it was the joy set before Him that calls us all into habitation with Him!

Read Hebrews 12:2. It is the spring of joy within Asher that enables him to come into habitation. Going from strength to strength is to go from joy to joy, from suffering to suffering, for suffering is transformed to joy in the light of the Son! Allow the enduring work of joy to have full reign within you. In doing so, you will be drawn into the King's chambers with great exceeding joy!

## THE SYMBOL OF ASHER

The symbol of Asher is the olive tree. Asher's symbol of the olive tree holds a plethora of revelation. Their symbol not only entails the actual tree, but also the olives and the oil produced by the tree. The olive tree has been indigenous to Israel since the time of Canaan. It is a vital source for Israel's economic prosperity today. The territory of Asher was known for their cultivation of the olive tree. Many products come from it, such as wood, oil used for cooking, beauty products, medicinal compounds, and, of course, the olives themselves, which are a vital and favorite part of many Israelis' diets. The olive's importance in everyday life in both ancient and modern Israel represents just how vital Asher is to the kingdom of God.

### THE OLIVE TREE

The olive tree itself is one of the sturdiest and most fruitful trees grown in Israel. Though it does not flourish overnight, it is a great symbol of strength and revelation to the tribe of Asher.

Read Psalm 52:6-9. Asher is that green olive tree that flourishes in the courts of the Lord. The olive tree grows best on rocky soil preferably near the ocean (most commonly the Galilee region). It takes a great deal of perseverance to grow an olive tree for this reason. Asher's life and testimony is often built during rocky times. He must seek always to glean strength from his God-given tool of intimacy, the joy of the Lord. Also, the rocky soil also serves as a warning to Asher. Asher is called to release great revelation. If he is not rooted in truth, he can easily become unbalanced. I urge you, dear Asher, to be like the Berean Jews (Acts 17:11 NIV). Seek always to rightly divide the Word of Truth, for as you do, your roots will run deep into the soil of God's Word and kingdom plan for your life. It is very easy for Asher to be carried away by the thrills of charismatic revelations, manifestations, signs, and wonders. Seek the Holy Spirit's counsel always, my dear Asher, to provide you with balanced truth in the areas of revelation and doctrine. Levi would serve as a good mentor to you (when led by the Spirit), holding you accountable to the balance of God's word.

Read II Timothy 2:15. An olive tree without stable roots is useless and produces no fruit. If Asher neglects to plant himself in sound truth, he is in danger of foregoing his destiny. Joy and revelation, two of Asher's greatest assets, will not be able reproduce—if they are not rooted in good soil. Asher must take special care not to get caught up in the glitz of charis-mania and sell himself for cheap thrills. True balance graces him to endure suffering and to discern false doctrine and vain whims. When we fully embrace the workings of the Holy Spirit, God calls us to step outside of the box of religion. However, Asher's tendency can be to step too far out of that box.

Read Hebrews 6:7-8. It is vital for the growth and the endurance of the olive tree to be frequently plowed, breaking up the fallow ground. If a young tree is neglected, older trees will then boost up a great many shoots from the roots all around the parent stem; it is then pruned. This is truly prophetic for the tribe of Asher. Asher's older brethren provide the stability and push for him to come into maturity. Wisdom will expose these false roots that hinder the maturity of young Asher. It is also vital for water to freely flow to the roots from the earliest rain and greatly enrich the soil. Tapping into the power of the testimony from the early rains (revivalists past) prepares Asher to receive the new waves of outpouring coming while providing wisdom to avoid error. It is that early rain that continually identifies and propels the ministry of every Asher.

## YESHUA IN THE GARDEN OF GETHSEMANE

Read Luke 22:39-44. I have been to the Garden of Gethsemane in Israel and felt an overwhelmingly sweet presence of the Lord. It is located on the Mount of Olives and in the Garden are olive trees, some of which have been growing for over 2,000 years. The first part of this verse mentions that it was customary for Yeshua to go to the Garden. I feel the Garden of Gethsemane is a meaningful place for all believers, but especially for the tribe of Asher. Amongst the olive trees Yeshua poured out His cry of suffering to the Father. Yeshua, surrounded by the symbol of joy (the olive tree), found comfort and strength to embrace the Father's will. It was also in the Garden that he began to take on our suffering through immeasurable travailing intercession for us.

As you fix your gaze upon your Bridegroom King, Asher, He will strengthen you with everlasting and unspeakable joy that is full of His glory. He bore your suffering, shame, and sin. In the Garden of Gethsemane He betrothed His love to you as He drank the cup of the Father's will for you. Gethsemane means, "the oil press." With sin and suffering pressing Him on every side, Yeshua became that "oil press" which produced eternal joy! What a phenomenal promise for you, dear Asher!

Read I Peter 4:12-14. A revelation of His glory awaits all those who share in the sufferings of Yeshua. When we allow the oil press of life to truly produce a lasting revelation of the kingdom, we are revealed as the true sons and daughters of Abba's glory! It is the pressing of suffering in the cause of Yeshua that brings growth. The works or hype of religion and flesh bring only self-exaltation, which is fleeting and profane. Asher, take to heart that your Bridegroom identified with and bore your suffering to reveal His glory and to birth your identity as an eternal spring of joy within His kingdom.

## OLIVES: THE FRUIT OF JOY

The olive speaks of the fruit of joy within every Asher. Olives are most commonly harvested by shaking the base of the tree. Through much "shaking," Asher produces his God-given tool of intimacy. God will often shake Asher from his false beliefs, revealing the true fruit of the Spirit. The fruit of joy takes time and patience to produce. True joy is never automatic or hyped, but borne of the true nature of the Father.

Asher, allow God to shake your ideal of who you think He is and who you think you are. God's shaking will cause you to come to repentance. Many are disillusioned with the concept of repentance, as if it carried a foreboding shadow over us. True repentance brings freedom and comes from conviction, not condemnation. Repentance will produce the fruit of joy in our lives if we partake of the redemption and intimacy it affords us. Therefore, I urge you, Asher, to bear forth fruit in keeping with repentance. Read John 15:1-8.

## OLIVE OIL: THE OUTPOURING OF THE HOLY SPIRIT

Oil is a symbol of the anointing. Asher must always seek to abide in the place of anointing. Oil was very crucial in biblical times for the anointing of kings and priests, for offerings, medicinal purposes, and for nourishment. For this reason Asher is very crucial to the Body of Christ. Oil was used for the Temple lampstand, which lit both the wilderness tabernacle and the Temple. Asherites spread light through their joyful and infectious nature that emanates from within them. They dispel darkness through the mantle of joy they carry. Their joy and laughter is their greatest tool in warfare. Asherites can laugh in the presence of his enemies as God sustains them with joy. As a source of healing, they are the oil poured out upon the wounded. Asher's merry heart is like a good medicine. .

*A joyful heart is good medicine, but a broken spirit dries up the bones* (Proverbs 17:22).

The Father's covenant promise to Asher is the joy of the Lord (the wine), the anointing (the oil), and revelation (food). Asher is especially connected with the work of the Holy Spirit and is often at the center of outpouring. His livelihood is crucially dependent with intimacy in the Holy Spirit. Read Joel 2:19, 24-29.

A daily-crucified life in Yeshua brings the outpouring of the Spirit. Obedience invites the Holy Spirit to come with the rain and the new wine, to cleanse and fill us. In order for the work of the Spirit to remain pure (the oil), Asher must crucify his flesh. Flesh contaminates the oil, and, if gone unchecked, can thoroughly pollute it, making it stagnant and worthless. Take special care, Asher, to surrender any hype or compromise. Repentance and intimacy will ensure a pure flow of the anointing in your life.

## JACOB'S PROPHECY

*"As for Asher, his food shall be rich, and he shall yield royal dainties"* (Genesis 49:20).

## "HIS FOOD SHALL BE RICH"

*Jesus said to them, "My food is to do the will of Him who sent Me, and to accomplish His work* (John 4:34).

Asher, the Father is inviting you to eat of the golden manna from His hand. In His presence He prepares a table before you that far outweighs your human expectations. He has reserved revelation from the breadbaskets of Heaven just for you. The Father's substance for you is eternal and life-giving. Your food is to do the will of the Father. Its ingredients are His glory, love, and revelation of Himself. He is the only true nourishment that can sustain in times of suffering. Come to His table, He longs to commune with you and share in the choicest foods.

## "HE SHALL YIELD ROYAL DAINTIES"

This portion of the prophecy speaks of Asher's call to nourish the Body of Christ with the revelation that they receive from the Father. They are teachers and intercessors. Whereas Levi is a teacher whose thrust is focused primarily on intimacy, repentance, and holiness, an Asher's teaching ministry is centered on encouragement, mercy, the work of the Holy Spirit, and revival. Asherites are revelatory teachers of the Word. When they are grounded in truth, they can feed the Body with rich delicacies of revelation. Asherites must take special care also not to have stale bread. The ovens of Heaven are forever producing new revelations of the Father's love to His children. This portion also speaks of Asher's giving nature. It is his passion to see his brethren nourished with rich revelation and joy. Rueben will give out of love, and Asher will give out of his need to make others happy. Asher's own life is a royal dainty fresh from the royal kitchen of Heaven for the Body of Christ. Sweet and enticing royal treats—edifying words—proceed from the mouth of Asher.

## MOSES' PROPHECY

*And of Asher he said, "More blessed than sons is Asher; May he be favored by his brothers, and may he dip his foot in oil. Your locks shall be iron and bronze, and according to your days, so shall your leisurely walk be"* (Deuteronomy 33:24-25).

*And of Asher he said, Let Asher be blessed with children; let him be acceptable to his brethren, and let him dip his foot in oil. Thy shoes shall be iron and brass; and as thy days, so shall thy strength be* (Deuteronomy 33:24-25 KJV).

## "MORE BLESSED THAN SONS IS ASHER; MAY HE BE FAVORED BY HIS BROTHERS"

Joy is the abundance of our Father's love for us. Blessing is naturally derived from joy. The easy-going nature of Asher causes him to be favored by his brethren. It is the countenance of the Father's joy upon Asher's life that makes him so delightful. These happy-go-lucky souls bring sunshine wherever they go. They are often the life of the party because of their engaging nature. Blessing and favor also come to Asher because of his ties to the anointing and the Holy Spirit. The spring of joy within Asher brings life to him and all those around him.

*For he who finds me finds life, and obtains favor from God* (Proverbs 8:35).

This is referring to the wisdom of God, Asher's key to abundant life. Wisdom will give Asher the balance and direction to his life.

## "MAY HE DIP HIS FOOT IN OIL"

This is the direct tie to Asher's dominion in the earth. The anointing calls you into true spiritual authority when yielded to the Holy Spirit. I urge you, Asher, to walk in the anointing always. When you step in the flesh or hype, your revelation becomes stale and your joy no more than hyped emotion. You then walk out of your dominion and into confusion. The depths of the Father's heart are calling to the deep spring of joy within you. Compromise is your enemy and snare. Passionately seek the truth of God's Word and heart for you. Walking outside of the anointing leaves you as an open target for the enemy and false doctrine. To walk in the anointing means to walk daily by the Spirit. Your connection to the Holy Spirit is vital to your intimacy and very existence.

Read Galatians 5:16-18. It is by walking in the Spirit that you can produce the fruit of the Spirit. When you walk in your own ways, Asher, you walk away from allowing the fruit of the Spirit, and especially the fruit of joy, to be produced in your life. This is such a detriment to your destiny.

Read Ephesians 5:8-16. Walking in the anointing means not walking in your own strength, abilities, or ideals. It is the essence of the Spirit-led life. Your calling, dear Asher, is to walk in the joy of the Lord. Come to the end of yourself and arise in the light and glory of your Beloved. Awaken from your slumber, O Asher, for He is calling you to walk in His joy!

Read Zechariah 4:6. It is amazing that God speaks this to Zechariah when he receives the revelation of the golden lampstand in Heaven. Verse 3 says, *also two olive trees by it, one on the right side of the bowl and the other on its left side.*

Could it be that these two olive trees are the picture of the Jew and Gentile in the midst of the suffering servant Himself, Yeshua? Romans 11 speaks of the Jew and Gentile being one in Christ and its relation to the olive tree. We all have obtained joy by being grafted into the Christ. When we are dependent on the Lord and one another to become the One New Man in Him, we will see tremendous outpouring and anointing. The Gentile is in need of the Jew to come into the fullness of his anointing, and the Jew is in the need of the Gentile for the fullness of his anointing. We can gain so much from each other when we are balanced and empowered by the Spirit. This is a special promise to Asher indeed, to see himself grafted into the whole house of Israel. In the midst of the lampstand Asher is enabled by the Spirit, not his own might or power, to walk in the oil of joy perpetually.

## "YOUR LOCKS, SHOES, OR GATES SHALL BE IRON AND BRONZE"

Moses' prophecy concerning Asher's iron and bronze locks, shoes, and gates, has a two-fold meaning. Iron and bronze are both drawn from the earth, again reiterating their call to the earth. Asher's consecration (locks) must be strong, uncompromising, leaning on the righteousness of the Beloved to complete and perfect him. His walk (shoes) is enabled by the Spirit to overcome his enemies. Asher must seek to walk in the anointing and not compromise destiny. The joy of the Lord provides Asher both strength and discretion for his soul. This noble tribe is graced with the strength within the gates of his heart to guard against intruders (compromise, idolatry, and complacency) that would steal his intimacy (joy).

On one hand, iron and bronze can be interpreted as a sign of strength with the tribe of Asher, yet another picture of the joy of the God is to be their strength. Asher derives his strength from their God-given tool of intimacy, empowerment, and supernatural ability. Iron and bronze are symbols of an unwavering spirit and purpose within the tribe of Asher. Asher's joy and anointing is the enabling weapon of warfare in their spiritual walk.

Read Jeremiah 1:8. Joy is a force by which Asher can resist the enemy. Through the Spirit's enabling, you can both offensively and defensively engage in the battle. When your gaze is fixated solely upon your Beloved and not your situation or your enemy, it will become a bulwark of impenetrable strength to you.

Iron and bronze were often used in the building of the tabernacle from the time of wilderness tabernacle of Moses, and Solomon's and Herod's temples. Asher prophetically serves as a source of great strength and stability to the Body of Christ, who, when led by the

Spirit, enable themselves and others in joy to stand as a strong and empowered temple of the Living God.

Iron and bronze are also repeatedly mentioned in Scripture as a sign of judgment. When Asher neglects his source of strength, he subjects himself to judgment afforded by his own rebellion. It is the compromise of people-pleasing and self-indulgence that leads Asher astray. Iron is often seen as a sign of rebellion and idolatry. Many times when we trust in our own strength, we put on a happy face, disillusioned by our own self-reliance, idolatry, and ignorant pride.

Dear Asher, take special care not to trust in your own resources or strength. The joy of the Lord alone is your source and empowerment to overcome. Anything less would be profane idolatry, causing you to forego the riches of strength provided by the joy of the Lord.

Read Isaiah 48:4-5. Asher indulges in idolatry through the sin of complacency, thus not confronting his enemies. Compromise causes one to indulge in one's selfish desires or those of others, regardless of truth. When Asher disconnects himself from the Spirit-led life, he is lured into the deadly demise of destiny. Compromise brings us into bondage; it blinds us from the Father's heart and will. Asher, take care not to allow compromise to lead you away from your Father's glorious destiny for you. Pacifying others or yourself at the expense of truth will hinder the fullness of joy in your life. You may be satisfied temporarily, but repercussions always come when you give in to idolatry and willful desires. Be on alert not to indulge in the fantasy of making everyone happy at your own soul's expense. Be a kingdom builder by actively pursuing the pleasure of your King and heavenly Father. Anything short of this would be a grievous pitfall for you and bring unnecessary suffering.

## "ACCORDING TO YOUR DAYS, SO SHALL YOUR LEISURELY WALK BE"

*Happy are thy men, happy are these thy servants, which stand continually before thee, and that hear thy wisdom* (I Kings 10:8 KJV).

*Thou wilt make known to me the path of life; In Thy presence is fullness of joy; In Thy right hand are pleasures forevermore* (Psalm 16:11).

Wisdom is the way to joy, the sustaining power of every believer. The wisdom of the Holy Spirit is the foundation for the Spirit-led life. When Asher walks in the ways of wisdom, not leaning to his own understanding, he is afforded life and joy everlasting in the Beloved. His walk becomes carefree of burdens, and suffering becomes an adventure in the school of the Holy Spirit. Dear Asher, seek always to walk on the path of life (wisdom). For when you walk in the path of wisdom, your life will become a joyous place of habitation in the Beloved, where His hope eternally leads you to His pleasures for you.

## THE FACADES OF ASHER

Read Judges 5:17 and Judges 1:31-32. Asher continually engaged in a non-confrontational manner in the areas of warfare and possessing their inheritance. This proved to be a demise of destiny for them. Their complacent nature caused them to make very little impact on Israel's history, and as a result, they didn't possess the fullness of identity and dominion to which the Father called them. For the tribe of Asher, this failure to drive out the Canaanites proved fatal to Asher's promise of dominion. It is urgent, therefore, my brethren, to possess the fullness of your identity in Yeshua by actively pursuing the Father's battle plan for your life. Another way to be complacent is not to confront sin or idolatry when the Holy Spirit convicts us of it.

## THE PURSUIT OF HAPPINESS CAN LEAD TO IDOLATRY

The pursuit of happiness is something we all commonly seek after. What we don't know is that sometimes it can lead us into idolatry. The tribe of Asher are peacemakers. Their pursuit of happiness with all men could sometimes lead them into idolatry. Sometimes in the process of trying to make everyone happy or bless them, we can compromise pleasing God in exchange for the approval of man. It is important to side with the Father's heart, not pacifying self and others.

Asher's tendency to make everyone happy, placating their own desires, causes them to spiral into confusion and idolatry. We must be able to stand on the truth of God's Word, unwavering, without coming into a compromise in our souls. Warfare must be Spirit-led and must always come from a place of abiding in the Lord. Asher must take care not to compromise in a situation just because something is easy or popular. To allow oneself to be deluded by thinking we must make everyone happy can cause our own soul to come into bondage and lose the joy of the Lord.

When we confront sin or engage in battle (through rest and intimacy), we become free, and His joy can then be released. Placating to others' desires never brings true joy, but rather an appeasement to the idolatry in one's heart. My dear Asher, the way to victory is to be connected to the anointing, the very oil of joy within you. The Holy Spirit will provide discernment and direction in times of testing and battle. I strongly urge you to arm yourself with the truth of God's Word and actively pursue the kingdom work at hand. As you connect yourself to the olive tree of Heaven and its vast oil supply, you will be empowered to confront idolatry in yourself and others in love. Settle for nothing less than pleasing your heavenly Father, for in doing so you will release the deepest springs of joy! You are called to be history makers and pioneers in areas of revelation, revival, outpouring, and intercession. Spring forth, O Asher, into the Father's kingdom plan He is releasing in this hour.

## ASHER IN THE NEW TESTAMENT

Read John 7:37-38. In Yeshua alone we find the eternal spring of joy. His presence continually overflows with joy and salvation. When Yeshua made this declaration, it was during the Feast of Tabernacles (Feast of Booths, see Verse 2). Tabernacles, a feast of great joy, celebrating the harvest (a.k.a. the Feast of Ingathering) has types and shadows of the Wedding Feast for believers today. It was said of this feast: *He who has not witnessed the rejoicing at the water-drawing huts (booths) has, throughout the whole of his life, witnessed no real rejoicing*.[1] It is also referred to the season of our joy. Yeshua came and tabernacled among us.

> *And the Word became flesh, and dwelt among us, and we saw His glory, glory as of the only begotten from the Father, full of grace and truth* (John 1:14).

Yeshua declared Himself as Messiah when he said, *If any man is thirsty, let him come to Me and drink. He who believes in Me, as the Scripture said, 'From his innermost being shall flow rivers of living water.* During the Feast of Tabernacles they hold a water libation ceremony. The water libation offering was added to the festival offerings in order to give thanks for the prior year's rain, a petition to God for more rain and to picture the great outpouring of Holy Spirit.

Yeshua is declaring to you, Asher, that He is that well of salvation. He has become your spring of joy! Asher, He has come to tabernacle in you. Yeshua is the season of your joy! From Him alone, you draw wells of salvation. Become thirsty, desperate even for the heart of your Beloved. He is longing to reveal Himself to you as the eternal spring of joy. Yeshua paid it all so that you, Asher, would have joy eternal. He became the water libation poured out for you! What an awesome promise this is for you, dear Asher.

## ANNA, THE SPRING OF JOY WITHIN THE TEMPLE

*And there was a prophetess, Anna the daughter of Phanuel, of the tribe of Asher. She was advanced in years and had lived with her husband seven years after her marriage, and then as a widow to the age of eighty-four. She never left the temple, serving night and day with fasting and prayers. At that very moment she came up and began giving thanks to God, and continued to speak of Him to all those who were looking for the redemption for Jerusalem (Luke 2: 35-38).*

Anna is a beautiful example of the tribe of Asher in the fullness of their destiny and calling. She was in intercessor and prophetess who rightly proclaimed Yeshua when she recognized that salvation and joy had come to tabernacle with her people. As any true Asherite, she heralds that the spring of joy (Yeshua) had come to bring deliverance to His people. Anna rejoiced, for she knew that her many years of intercession and travail had been rewarded in the Messiah's birth.

The tribe of Asher joyfully heralds the message of salvation to all. They declare and decree that salvation is the true way to joy, found only in Yeshua, the Messiah our Lord. As intercessors, they pursue the Father's heart for the joy of salvation to be restored to the kingdom and revival.

## A VITAL CONNECTION TO THE TEMPLE

Asher's spiritual DNA and identity is directly tied to the temple. Anna was in the temple when she made her declaration that the Messiah, the spring of salvation, had come to her people Israel. The tribe of Asher is tied to many things in the temple: the anointing oil, the showbread, and olive wood for the furnishings. With such strong ties to the temple, it is apparent that the tribe of Asher is crucial to the body of Christ.

## ASHER PROVIDES THE SHOWBREAD FOR THE TABERNACLE

Asher was responsible for baking the twelve loaves of showbread in the tabernacle. This is a beautiful picture of revelation. Asher is ever ready with a word of revelation, fresh from the ovens of Heaven. Come forth Asher, with the heavenly loaves of showbread, for within you lay deep mysteries to catapult the Body into revival. With a word of encouragement always on your lips, speak forth those rich delicacies to your brethren, for in doing so you stir them to revelation of the Beloved and His joy for them. Mighty, mighty words are longing to spring forth from within you—words that bring great impact and change! You have been given the recipes of revelation, which nourish and adorn the Bride of Yeshua. Within you is growing the bread of life, Yeshua Himself, imparted to His creation, restoring them to the Creator!

## THE SUPPLY OF OIL

Asher, your everlasting supply of oil supplies joy that sustains and rejuvenates the glorious temple of God. You are so needed and vital to your fellow living stones. For within you, my dear Asher, lies the eternal spring of joy gushing up within the temple of the living God. You are the outpouring to a parched people needing desperately the oil of joy you possess. To the lampstand you provide oil (anointing), which causes the flame of the Holy Spirit to burn brighter within the souls of men. Your oil is the agent that conducts the fire of God to burn brighter. May your oil never run dry, may it overflow, eternally producing anointing, joy, and empowerment and illuminating the temple of Living Stones in your Father's house!

## ASHER AND THE TWO CHERUBIM

Read I Kings 6:23-29. The tribe of Asher provided the olive wood for the two cherubim in Solomon's Temple. Here is profound prophetic significance for Asher. Asher provides deep revelation of communion. What hovers above the wings of the cherubim? Just above the wings of the cherubim, the mercy seat of the Father is bidding us to commune with Him. Abba's extreme joy is communion! He is beckoning you, Asher, beyond the mercy seat, into the realms and mysteries of His heart! Come lay on His chest as He imparts indescribable glory and joy to you!

## ASHER RESTORED AS THE SPRING OF JOY

Spring up, O Asher, from the four corners of the earth, the Spirit is wooing you. All of the Father's eternal springs of joy are found in you. The chasms of the deep are waiting to explode with joy unspeakable within you! Awaken to the love of God calling you as the revelation of His joy is expressed into all the earth. Awaken unto your glorious inheritance in your Beloved! Do not slumber; do not sit complacently under the world's lure or the pursuit of happiness. Run after your Bridegroom King! He is the eternal spring of joy waiting to erupt from the depths of you!

Walk into the deep pools of transformation glory and joy laid up for you. Your walk will become leisurely as you seek to live in His joy and rest. Cease from striving and know He is God. You are the infinite expression of the Father's pleasure in the earth. Awaken to your destiny and possess your rightful dominion through the joy of the Lord!

## PRAYER OF REPENTANCE AND DESTINY
## FOR THE TRIBE OF ASHER

Abba Daddy, I joyfully come before You! I spring up in complete abandon and reverential fear to Your love and acceptance of me! I repent of pursuing fleeting carnal happiness instead of Your eternal joy for me. Forgive me for appeasing myself and others at the expense of Your destiny for me. Teach me what pleases You! Free me of the obstinate attitude, which has hindered me from communion with You. I repent of allowing my oil to become stagnant and my bread stale. You alone supply me with fresh oil and bread from Heaven. Knit my desires to Your desires. I want to bring you pleasure. You are my soul's one true joy! Without You, I have no substance. I am empty and desperate without Your touch, God. Come, Holy Spirit, and sustain within me the revelations of my Father's love and will. Teach me the truth of His Word. Cause me to be a living source of revelation to My Father's creation. Spring up, O well of joy within my soul! Cause my roots to grow deep within Your Temple, that I might eternally be a green olive tree in the house of my God. In Yeshua's name I joyfully pray, Amen.

---

[1] *The Babylonian Talmud, Sukkah 53a-b.* Public Domain.

# CHAPTER 10
# ISSACHAR: THE HUMBLE BURDEN BEARER

*Blessed be the Lord, who daily bears our burden, the Lord who is our salvation* (Psalm 68:19).

The Father has called us to walk in His rest and delight. Walking in His rest and delight is central to communion and intimacy with God. Burdens can hinder us from experiencing the fullness of His love. It grieves Him when we carry burdens that hinder our communion with Him. More often than not, we try to enter into His love or things pertaining to His kingdom by our own striving.

The key to entering into the fullness of the kingdom is to bow low by recognizing that Yeshua bore your burdens. If we could bear our own burdens, we wouldn't need a Savior. It is His grace that enables us to trust Him to bear our burdens for us, for this the very work of salvation. The frailty of the human nature is to strive, as Adam and Eve did in the Garden. Trusting in this frailty separates us from communion with the Father, and we do not enter into His rest and delight. Focusing on the saving power of Yeshua will afford us to live in a perpetual state of His rest. This is a vital key to seeking the kingdom. He became the suffering servant who bowed low to bare our burdens.

Read Isaiah 53:1-5, 12. The Father in His great love and compassion sent to us a humble burden bearer, our Beloved. There is no care, worry, shame, or sin that our Beloved cannot bear. If anyone can identify with the sufferings of this world, it is Yeshua. Take everything to Yeshua; He alone knows the depths of our hearts and the suffering of our souls. He became suffering by taking on all of our sin and shame. He bowed low, foregoing His kingly majesty so that He might win His Bride back to the kingdom of love.

## BOWING LOW AS A KINGDOM PRINCIPLE

The word *bare* in Hebrew is *nasa* or *nacah*, meaning "to raise, lift up, bear, carry, wear, take, accept, be lifted up, be raised, to be elevated." Yeshua wonderfully fulfilled all of these: He raised us up from the miry pit; He carried the Cross (our sin); He bore our shame and sufferings; He took away our reproach. Through Him we are accepted, lifted up, and elevated to our kingdom place of dominion: our heavenly Father's heart!

The concept of bowing low is a vital kingdom principle we all must seek to live out. It bids us to lay down our kingdoms, ideals, and agendas and to then lift up, extol, and/or magnify the manifest character of God and His glory within us. In order for Yeshua to carry the weight of His Father's kingdom and glory, He first had to bow low and be clothed in true humility. This is the calling of every Issachar. The Father has endowed them to wear, as a sign to the Bride of Yeshua, garments of humility and servanthood. These garments, though humble in nature, are majestic. Divine majesty and royalty are both built on the concept of bowing low, for with humility comes honor and elevation from our Father. Royalty is tied to the nature and redemption of every Issachar. It is their very seal of favor and glory from Heaven itself. Yeshua laid down His own glory and took upon Himself our sufferings, for it was the weight of the Father's kingdom that He was ultimately meant to bare. In bowing low, He was exalted. A true Issachar daily lives by the precept of bowing low. In order to carry the glory of God and His kingdom, we must make bowing low a lifestyle.

> *But let the brother of humble circumstances glory* [the position of bowing low-emphasis mine] *glory in his high position* (James 1:9).

The tribe of Issachar embodies the character of Yeshua as a humble burden bearer. They were created to display the attributes of Yeshua, who came as a lowly servant but was exalted to glory. Among this noble tribe you find a people of great strength of character and body, whose will is tied to the Master. Within Issachar you will find prophets, seer(s)/dreamers, pastors, and administrators with an apostolic mantle. They are kingdom builders whose hearts and hands are never slothful. It is the prime joy of every Issachar to be about their Father's business.

## DOING THE FATHER'S WORK HIS WAY

*Jesus gave them this answer: "I tell you the truth, the Son can do nothing by himself; he can do only what he sees his Father doing, because whatever the Father does the Son also does. For the Father loves the Son and shows him all he does. Yes, to your amazement he will show him even greater things than these* (John 5:19-20).

This verse should be the theme song of every Issachar's heart. An Issachar's ears and heart is forever tied to the throne. Issachar is always busy about his Father's business. Every Issachar knows that the true meaning of servanthood is based upon intimacy. For Issachar, servanthood is not a matter of legal obligation to duty but the joy of fulfilling the desires of their Beloved. The meaning of servanthood often gets distorted with striving, perfection, and a false belief of forced submission. Be careful, dear Issachar, not to allow the enemy to distort your place of intimacy: servanthood. There are snares within Church doctrine today that lead to bondage brought on by a legalistic view of servanthood and performance mindsets. To crucify them, we must feast on the beauty of God, which will free us from these false beliefs. Issachar, God is sending you an invitation to daily sup with Him at His banqueting table. He is your substance and reward. No good thing will He withhold from you as you walk uprightly before Him.

## THE NAMING OF ISSACHAR

*Now in the days of wheat harvest Reuben went and found mandrakes in the field, and brought them to his mother Leah. Then Rachel said to Leah, "Please give me some of your son's mandrakes." But she said to her, "Is it a small matter for you to take my husband? And would you take my son's mandrakes also?" So Rachel said, "Therefore he may lie with you tonight in return for your son's mandrakes." When Jacob came in from the field in the evening, then Leah went out to meet him and said, "You must come in to me, for I have surely hired you with my son's mandrakes." So he lay with her that night. God gave heed to Leah and she conceived and bore Jacob a fifth son. Then Leah said, "God has given me my wages because I gave my maid to my husband." So she named him Issachar* (Genesis 30:14-18).

Issachar means "wages, for hire, servant, [and] his reward will come."

*The wicked earns deceptive wages, but he who sows righteousness gets a true reward* (Proverbs 11:18).

Leah's journey was wrought with much striving and suffering to earn Jacob's love. Her womb had been shut up after the birth of Judah, leaving her only Gad and Asher through her handmaid whom she gave to Jacob. Her wrestling with Rachel came to a climax over the affections of Jacob and bearing him children. Leah's lonely heart was looking for more than a dutiful *Baali* (master, husband), but rather an affectionate *Ishi* (a husband, Beloved).

*"Therefore, behold, I will allure her, Bring her into the wilderness and speak kindly to her. Then I will give her vineyards from there, and the valley of Achor as a door of hope*

*and she will sing there as in the days of her youth, as in the day when she came up from the land of Egypt. It will come about in that day," declares the Lord, "that you will call Me Ishi and will no longer call Me Baali* (Hosea 2:14-16).

Leah's heart was crying out for intimacy with Jacob. She wanted to be loved passionately and not out of duty. When Hosea prophesied, "*you will call Me Ishi and will no longer call Me Baali,*" it was the bleeding heart of the Father to have His people love Him intimately and not out of legal duty or religiosity. It was this persistent longing within Leah that conceived and gave birth to Issachar. This trait was inherited in his spiritual DNA. Issachars are persistent pursuers of the Kingdom.

## FOR HIRE

The connotation of the word *husband* is often tied with the "breadwinner" or the "wage-earner" for the family. Yeshua paid a debt we could not: the wages of sin (Romans 6:22-23; 11:34-36).

Read I Corinthians 6:19-20. Yeshua became our servant for hire. He paid the wages of sin and death. What a wonderful promise for Issachar! He paid it all with His blood! He is your Bridegroom of Blood who has removed the guilty stains. As far as the east is from the west, so far has He has removed your transgressions. The façade of the flesh is a deceptive wage, but abiding in the redemption and righteousness of Yeshua is our ultimate reward!

## THE REWARD LAVISHED UPON ISSACHAR

Read Isaiah 40:10. Your deliverer has come, Issachar! He is bringing His reward with Him! What is His reward? It is His glory, His manifest nature, which He is longing to lavish upon you. It is the Father's chief desire that you carry His glory as the reward, the prize of your life!

> *Thus says the Lord, "Restrain your voice from weeping and your eyes from tears; for your work will be rewarded," declares the Lord, "And they will return from the land of the enemy"* (Jeremiah 31:16).

Dear Issachar, God has seen your tears and suffering. Your diligent faithfulness has never gone unnoticed. Rejoice, for God Himself will reward you with His love and glory!

## THE CALL TO THE HARVEST

### "NOW IN THE DAYS OF WHEAT HARVEST"

Issachar was conceived during the time of the wheat harvest. This has profound prophetic significance for this tribe. Issachar is always found in the harvest field. He is plowing, planting, or reaping for the Kingdom.

> *He was saying to them, "The harvest is plentiful, but the laborers are few; therefore beseech the Lord of the harvest to send out laborers into His harvest"* (Luke 2:10).

Issachar's spiritual senses are forever tuned into the laboring in God's harvest. With their prophetic and apostolic insight, they are able to carry kingdom-mandated workloads. Issachar's spiritual gifting entails the innate ability to oversee and administrate also. They carry the burden of the work of the ministry upon their backs. They are the spiritual workhorses in the kingdom. An Issachar always gets the job done.

## THE GEMSTONE OF ISSACHAR
### ISSACHAR: THE MAJESTIC SERVANT

The gemstone of Issachar is the amethyst. It is in the quartz family and known for its rich, deep purple to deep violet color. Its color and stone often carry the symbolism of royalty, majesty, and kingship (Job 40:10).

The Father adorns those whose hearts and lives are bowed low. If anyone out of the tribes makes a lifestyle of bowing low, it is the noble tribe of Issachar. Their humble nature is the prerequisite to bowing low. Yeshua often taught on how vital humility is to the Kingdom.

*Blessed are the poor in Spirit, for theirs is the kingdom of heaven* (Matthew 5:3).

Blessed are those who have chosen to make bowing low a lifestyle, for from such yielded hearts the Father will bring immeasurable rewards of kingdom and understanding of His glory and bequeath His immeasurable love! A humble servant is always primed to hear the voice of the Lord. For this reason, I believe, God ordained Issachar to camp with Judah, to be a constant reminder of pure humility. Jacob even mentions this connection in his prophecy to Judah, saying: *And his donkey's colt to the choice vine.* Jacob was calling on the innate gifting within Issachar of humility to help Judah overcome their façade of pride. What a beautiful picture of unity and love for the tribes! When we support our brethren (rather than judging them) and bow low to serve the kingdom fully, we come into our true identity as a fully functioning Body in Christ! When Issachar and Judah are tied to the Vine (Yeshua), they glean the innate character of God, edifying one another by His very glory!

A great leader truly fulfills his destiny when he views his position as an opportunity to serve out of love and devotion. Leadership wanes and becomes profaned when agendas, vanity, and lack of perspective are dominating us. A true minister must serve from intimacy and communion with God. When tainted with facades of fleshly man-made ideals and agendas, one lacks the ability to purely see the vision that the Father has for His kingdom. God has graced the tribe of Issachar with innate spiritual DNA to perpetually bow low. It is for this very reason the Father has entrusted them with a prophetic apostolic ministry. The most unlikely and unassuming in demeanor possess the true persona of a prophet. The Father chooses them to defy the more seemingly obvious charismatic and dynamic traits some associate with the office of the prophet.

### AMETHYST: THE DREAM STONE

*Amethyst*, or *Achlamah* in Hebrew, was known as the "dream stone." In connection with this word is the Hebrew word for dream *chalam*, meaning to dream prophetically. Because of their humility, Issachar's ears and eyes are tuned into the kingdom. They hear the Majestic One's voice and spring into action out of pure and humble devotion. As a prophet the tribe of Issachar also can serve as a "seer." Prophets of old and present often had dreams and visions.

Read Joel 2:28-29. The difference between visions and dreams determines the seasoning or spiritual maturity of the prophet. A mature prophet has learned that his ability to accurately hear and see the Word of God requires bowing low.

## THE SYMBOL OF ISSACHAR

The donkey is the symbol for the tribe of Issachar. Often referred to as the "beast of burden," the donkey is rich in symbolism. The lowly state of a donkey reiterates the call to bow low. It speaks of their servant-nature, hard work ethic, strength, stubbornness, and humility.

## THE UNASHAMED WORKMAN

*Be diligent to present yourself approved to God as a workman who does not need to be ashamed, accurately handling the word of truth* (II Timothy 2:15).

The concept of the unashamed workman holds vital instruction for us all, but especially for the tribe of Issachar. An unashamed workman is diligent in heart and in service. The donkey is known as a loyal workhorse. As a prophet, Issachar must rightly divide the Word of Truth. They are loyal to God's Word in administrating and proclaiming it. Issachar often will take a logical, no-nonsense approach in his prophetic gifting. They are not easily caught up in hype or thrills and are not easily bought. It is their administrative apostolic call to the prophetic that urges them to be based on sound doctrine of God's Word.

A workman is prosperous when he inclines his ears to God's wisdom. Issachar must heavily rely on the wisdom and counsel of God in order to be a pure prophet. When stubborn, set in his own ways or traditions of men, he can become tainted with the familiar, and thereby be ensnared by the misdirection of the flesh and its desires. When God formed creation, wisdom was His counselor. A master workman will follow the voice of wisdom in all they do. This is true of the tribe of Issachar. Read Proverbs 8:30-35.

## THE EARS AND VOICE OF A PROPHET

The donkey's distinct long ears and braying are attributes found within every Issachar. A donkey's ears are considerably larger than that of a horse. Their ears help them pick distinct and distant noises. A true Issachar, when surrendered to God, can pick up the faintest whisper in the spirit realm. They are uniquely designed by God to hear the still, small voice of God. They can also detect the enemy from afar off. An Issachar's solemn spirit and wisdom causes them to abide in pure prophecy, aiding them to hear precisely into the spiritual realms.

In like manner, a donkey's bray is very distinct. It can seem harsh, but it gets the attention of the listener. This is the prophetic gifting within Issachar. Unassuming they may be, without frills or charismatic persuasion, yet speaking profound mysteries of the Father's heart. A donkey's bray is also a sign of warfare or warning, repelling its adversary by its loud sound. Their prophetic voice resounds into the spiritual realms, speaking life to the mandates of the Father's heart and death to the plans of the enemy.

## BALAAM AND THE DONKEY

Read Numbers 22:1-41. "If God could use a donkey, He can use me," has become a common cliché in Christian/prophetic circles. It is easy to misinterpret this passage and its meaning. God was targeting the pride and rebellion of Balaam by using the donkey as a symbol of bowing low.

*...but he received a rebuke for his own transgression, for a mute donkey, speaking with a voice of a man, restrained the madness of the prophet* (II Peter 2:16).

Issachar is a perpetual reminder to the Body of Christ of this principle. Because of their unassuming mannerisms that are a contradiction to the more accepted charismatic demeanor of a prophet; they go undetected to most (even themselves). It is vital to the Body to receive our brethren Issachar. Though his words may be simple, he speaks deep chasms of the Father's heart. Humility is by far the qualifier of the heart of any true prophet (pride being a disqualifier). It is Issachar's God-given attribute of quiet humility that confronts the pride in the hearts of men.

## THE DONKEY AS A SYMBOL OF MAJESTY

The donkey has often been the symbol of humility and servanthood. In ancient times, however, it was a sign of nobility, authority, and majesty. Ownership of many donkeys was a sign of God's blessing. The Bible often specifies whether a person rode donkeys since this was used to indicate a person's wealth in much the same way luxury cars do today. Humility is bankable wealth in the kingdom. It always pays to bow low.

The donkey is most commonly pictured carrying a pregnant Mary with Yeshua to Bethlehem. Yeshua's triumphant entry into Jerusalem on the back of a donkey speaks volumes of prophetic significance to the tribe of Issachar. Yeshua was declaring His kingship as the suffering servant who bowed low.

Read Matthew 21:1-11. Yeshua made his triumphant entry as King in humility. He came as a servant King, bowed low, carrying the burden of His Father's kingdom. His heart and life was focused upon the Father's burden for creation. Yeshua did not assume a political stance as some had hoped he would. He came as a lowly servant, carrying only for the burden of the salvation for mankind. It is this calling that is sent out to every Issachar.

The Father has ordained workloads of kingdom mandate for you to carry, dear Issachar. He has placed His Word within you, to bear His creation on your heart day and night. Carry your burden from a perpetual state of bowing low. Know that none of your righteousness, agendas, striving, or idols will help you bear you burdens. It is the place of abiding in God's grace and glory that equips and enables you, Issachar, to fulfill your destiny as Heaven's humble burden bearer.

God's heart is to bring the restoration of true servanthood. Sometimes servanthood in the Body of Christ has meant lowering of status, browbeating and belittlement, and a false requirement of submission to abusive authority figures. The enemy has planted a deception that links servanthood with slavery: submission that brings abuse, belittling, bitterness, and even shame. Just as a donkey can be mishandled by the abuse of its master, so it is with the ministry of servanthood. A donkey will buck at an abusive master. There are those in the world and even the Church who use doctrines of authority to abort the true meaning and purpose of servanthood. Servanthood, in a true biblical kingdom mindset, is meant to be an elevation, as well as a sign of pure leadership.

Read Matthew 20:25-27 and Matthew 23:10-12. False beliefs and false doctrines are birthed out of a lack of knowledge of God's Word and love. God is longing to bring elevation to the hearts of humble, bowed-low servants who have been faithful to His kingdom. These false beliefs must end in order to have a true Yeshua preached to a dying world. It is time for the Church to lay aside her ego and false doctrines that bring abuse and idolatry. The "shepherding movement" is a prime example of this false doctrine.

God brings His reward to those who are bowed low, forging the glory of men who share in the sufferings of Christ. True leadership is a calling to servanthood. If you feel the need to fulfill your own desires and ambitions or crave recognition, examine your heart! You may be laying yourself open to a false doctrine that abuses others in ministry. When pride and agendas enter into the picture, God's glory moves out. No flesh can glory in His presence. An effective minister is one who shares daily in the sufferings of Christ, denying his or her flesh and looking to the Father for His kingdom plan.

## JACOB'S PROPHECY

*"Issachar is a strong donkey, lying down between the sheepfolds. When he saw that a resting place was good, and the land was pleasant, he bowed his shoulder to bear burdens, and became a slave at forced labor"* (Genesis 49:14-15).

### "ISSACHAR IS A STRONG DONKEY"

Read II Corinthians 12:9-10. Issachar, you are endowed with a supernatural gifting of strength in your body, character, heart, and spirit. The key to this strength is not your own self-sufficiency but rather relying on God's strength to be perfected in you.

God's strength is made perfect in your weakness when you surrender your striving and will. Issachar, your will is strong and unwavering. This can work for or against you. Humility of heart is the key to your strength. Self-sufficiency is your snare, dear Issachar. It can become a striving that causes your will to become stubborn and contrary to the Spirit of God. Brethren, when we recognize that when we are at our weakest, Yeshua's glory enables us through the abiding work of His Cross. It is through the Cross, Issachar, that you are perfected in weakness. The glory of grace is the redemption of our weakened human frailties. It is only by grace that we can be sustained and glorified as His priceless living stones.

Read Romans 15:1-3. Issachar, you were born with this innate spiritual strength to carry in a Christ-like manner the burdens of the kingdom and souls of man. It is your honor, to the renown of Yeshua, to be that humble yet majestic burden bearer. This is your very seal of dominion and claim to the inheritance of God's glory on your life, Issachar! Rejoice, for the glory of God and His limitless grace is your strength. What a promise! What a destiny! What a righteous heritage that has been bestowed upon you!

### "LYING DOWN BETWEEN THE SHEEPFOLDS"

This portion of prophecy is two-fold for the tribe of Issachar. It is Issachar's call to the prophetic, as well as a call to rest in the Beloved. He is identified in the context of a sheepfold, symbolically speaking of his prophetic pastoral anointing. The sheepfolds are on the heart of every Issachar. Their calling is that of an administrative anointing, which appeals to many because of their humble servant-like heart. Issachar is a "regular Joe." He may not carry the charisma of a Judah, but he warms the heart of many with the sincerity of his character. Issachar's sincerity of heart and humble nature draws the broken and the lost. They become everything to everyone. It is their intensive motivation of working the Father's kingdom His way that causes them to labor with great love, no matter the cost. Issachar foresees the lost sheep going astray from the fold of the ninety-nine and goes after the one sheep with great perseverance of heart and purpose.

In a two-fold meaning, the sheepfold imagery reiterates a call of rest. Every prophetic administrative anointing must have the foundation of God's rest. When Issachar tries to strive for his own agenda or perfectionism, he is grossly led astray from the kingdom plan the Father has laid before him. Nothing we do in ministry or our personal walk with God can be born from our striving. Servanthood comes from resting in our Beloved and intimacy with Him. The glory of God cannot fellowship with our striving and performance mechanisms. The lost are sensitive to and even repelled by our performance agendas for one primary reason: Self-made programs are religious and deny the work of grace. Self-sufficiency, tied with a stubborn will, is a deadly cocktail for Issachar, for when he indulges in the flesh, he denounces his call to bow low. This is a diminishing of his dominion and intimacy with the Father

While in Israel, I went to Ein Kerem with a sister in the Lord. The glory of God was very present that day. It seemed as though it reverberated through the air and nature itself. We could hear the music of Heaven joining with creation and felt the Father's heart very near to us. We went to this little valley, full of blossoming almond trees. Even they seemed to speak of the glory and rest of the Lord. As we traveled down the path, we saw a large donkey lying in the way. He was so still, I thought he was dead. However, when we got closer, he rose up, bowed low, and let us pass him. He then proceeded to go back to his deep state of rest. It was then that God spoke to me concerning the tribe of Issachar, that this was a prophetic sign for them. The almond tree is also prophetic, a symbol of God keeping His Word to us.

> *The word of the Lord came to me saying, "What do you see, Jeremiah?" And I said, "I see a rod of an almond tree." Then the Lord said to me, "You have seen well, for I am watching over My word to perform it"* (Jeremiah 1:11-12).

My dear Issachar, when you are in a state of rest in the Beloved, you will see His Word performed in glorious measure. The sleeping donkey, who appeared to be almost dead, was a symbol of Issachar's calling, which is about death to self and about abiding. As we die to the striving within, we truly come into our Father's rest. Abiding is a willingness to die to our will and rest in perfect love.

Issachar, it is from a place of rest that you must hear and declare the Word of God. Anything less could lead to a misguided sense of direction or even false prophecy. How beautiful a promise to you when you rest in His love! His words would resound to and through you. He watches over His Word when we are in a place of abiding.

### "WHEN HE SAW THAT A RESTING PLACE WAS GOOD, AND THE LAND WAS PLEASANT, HE BOWED HIS SHOULDER TO BEAR BURDENS, AND BECAME A SLAVE AT FORCED LABOR"

This portion can be taken two ways: Issachar's call and motivation to serve, abiding in God's rest, and the danger of Issachar being manipulated or taken advantage of because of his sensitive servant's heart. The serving motivation is the very passion of their intimacy. When led by the Holy Spirit, it exemplifies the nature of Yeshua Himself. Yeshua bowed His shoulder to bear our burden of sin, shame, and sickness. The caution or danger for every Issachar is not to allow others to control or take advantage of their kindly servant's heart. If one is pushed into slavery or forced labor, it can create resentment. The key for you, Issachar, is to only do what you see your heavenly Father doing and abide in His rest, delighting as you go about His kingdom business. Anything less will lead you into striving, perfectionism, and even victimization through abuse.

### MOSES' PROPHECY

> *And of Zebulun he said, "Rejoice, Zebulun, in your going forth, And, Issachar, in your tents. They shall call peoples to the mountain; There they shall draw out the abundance of the seas, and the hidden treasures of the sand"* (Deuteronomy 33:18).

### "REJOICE, ZEBULUN, IN YOUR GOING FORTH, AND, ISSACHAR, IN YOUR TENTS"

God is making a distinction between the callings of these two closely knit tribes. They were raised together, not too far apart in age, and were camped together in the wilderness. Their bond was made in the Spirit, so it is not surprising that Moses mentions them together in this prophecy. Zebulun, as we will learn in more detail in the next chapter, has the call and heart for missions and traveling abroad. Issachar, on the other hand, is the laborer who works to keep things running on the home front.

Issachar, being the workhorse, knows of the tasks in the field and on the home front that are required of other soldiers and laborers. Issachar's nature is one of sacrifice for others, for this is their focus in relation to servanthood. Hype and charismatic thrills do not move an Issachar. He is solely focused on the kingdom workload before him. An Issachar is a practically-minded individual, motivated by his heart to serve with integrity.

## "THEY SHALL CALL PEOPLES TO THE MOUNTAIN"

Issachar would be more of a pastoral/ administrative prophet, while Zebulun would be more of a mercy motivated prophet. Unified in the Holy Spirit, they call God's people to His mountain, a place to meet and hear the word of God.

## "THERE THEY SHALL DRAW OUT THE ABUNDANCE OF THE SEAS, AND THE HIDDEN TREASURES OF THE SAND"

Issachar and Zebulun are called to the sea of humanity. They both carry a unique prophetic gifting. It is to the sea of humanity that Issachar hears a kingdom mandate that brings freedom, accomplishing the will of the Father. He is drawn to the deep things of God's kingdom plan for creation through his servanthood.

Read Psalm 78:1-3. The depth of the Father's heart is calling out to you, Issachar. Hear the deep sayings of His heart for you and creation. The treasures of His glory are held within you. It is your bray that draws His people back to His heart. The riches of His glory and wisdom are laid up for you to tap into and share with humanity. His very nature is waiting to be revealed to you! The Father longs to unearth those treasures in the sand that you have sought after in desperation, long awaiting your revealing as a son or daughter of His glory!

## THE FACADES OF ISSACHAR

## THE MARTHA SYNDROME

Read Luke 10:38-42. The Martha syndrome involves striving, perpetuated by a works mentality. Martha was neglecting her first and foremost call—worship. It is a common snare within the Church today to get caught up in service-related activities that epitomize the Martha syndrome. Servanthood is based on worship, not works. Many times as believers we can become deluded by the pursuit of service, thinking we are doing kingdom work. When service neglects the call to bow low and hear the Father, it becomes a form of bondage.

Issachar, this is a snare that can steal your intimacy and cause you to become burnt out! You are easy prey, like Martha, who also became snared by it. Your chief call, as with any believer, is to be a worshipper. Yeshua is your reward; the Father's glorious kingdom is your inheritance!

Sometimes our busy work can cause us to detour from our ultimate destiny as lovers of the King! The essential thing is for us to stay at the feet of our Lord in lovesick wonder and fervent worship. When we do serve, we do so from this perspective of being at the feet of Yeshua, clinging to His every word. The influence of a strong Judah would aide as reminder of worship to the tribe of Issachar. The Martha syndrome causes one to neglect our call to abide in God's rest and delight for us.

## LIES OF UNWORTHINESS

Lies of unworthiness are a common snare to the tribe of Issachar. Because of their humble nature, they can tend to take on feelings of unworthiness when they do not dwell on the truth of Abba's heart for them. Unworthiness is a false façade that will try to masquerade through hurt, bondage, self-pity, and negative self-image. An Issachar's tender nature can be easily manipulated and thus detoured through this façade. It is important that we rest in the knowledge of our heavenly Father's words of love to us. The Bible tells us we are fearfully and wonderfully made (Psalm 139:14). Recognizing that we are the treasured possession of the Creator frees us from feelings of unworthiness. We house the beauty and glory of God. If we are indeed formed in His image, we are His beautiful reflection expressed in the earth. Read II Corinthians 3:17-18.

## DRIVING SPIRITS AND PERFECTIONISM

Driving spirits and perfectionism cause an Issachar to become numb to his innate godly character. These spirits detour Issachar from the Father's kingdom plan for them. Often times these spirits manifest in workaholic behavior within Issachar. This can be in the secular workplace, in ministry, and even home life. This is a vanity of the heart that comes to deceive Issachar.

Read Ecclesiastes 1:13-15. Walking in our own earthly wisdom or self-sufficiency will cause driving spirits and perfectionism to take control over us. This is deadly to our call as worshippers. Even kingdom mandates can be profaned when we allow these things to take over our lives. Take care, Issachar, that whatever you do is to His glory. When you are carrying a burden, even if God gave it to you, carry it only from a place of bowing low and abiding in the rest of God.

## STUBBORNNESS BRINGS DETOUR TO DESTINY

*But My people did not listen to My voice, and Israel did not obey Me. So I gave them over to the stubbornness of their heart, to walk in their own devices. Oh that My people would listen to Me, That Israel would walk in My ways! (Psalm 81:11-13).*

Stubbornness has long been associated with the nature of a donkey. For the tribe of Issachar it can be both strength and facade. As a facade, stubbornness detours the destiny of any of us. Stubbornness is an unrelenting of the will. When Issachar is set on his own agenda or old ways, he becomes a stubborn donkey, therefore causing his spiritual senses to become dull and diverting him. Sometimes the enemy will even cause Issachar to be stubborn for a right cause but for the wrong reason. If self-sufficiency, pride, feelings of unworthiness, and rebellion lure your senses, dear Issachar, they will produce a stubbornness that brings you into idolatry. Idolatry happens when we go after our own desires.

When stubbornness has a grip, God will give you over to those desires. He is greatly grieved when we ignore the work of grace (empowered by the Cross) and choose our self-reliance and desires. Stubbornness is the most serious deception to you, Issachar, because it draws you away from bowing low and abiding in the rest of God. The enemy's snare can be subtle, but when enticed by the deadly seduction of stubbornness, we can forego fulfilling the fullness of our destiny in the Beloved. A broken and contrite heart God will never despise, but a prideful and stubborn will oppose the heart of the Father and grieves Him so.

*But they refused to pay attention and turned a stubborn shoulder and stopped their ears from hearing (Zechariah 7:11).*

Stubbornness will dull the hearing of any prophet. Your key to intimacy and your very identity is your call to bow low. When you disconnect from your calling, stubbornness takes over, dulling your heart and hearing. Your prophetic calling is then tainted with a selfish and profane agenda. Repentance and bowing low will draw you back into truth and intimacy.

Read Romans 2:5. Unchecked, stubbornness will deny you your inheritance. Do not be deceived, brethren, for a little yeast leavens the whole lump. Even the slightest twinge of stubbornness, if we are unrepentant, can cause us to forego destiny. God is merciful, loving, and kind. Relinquish your right to be right. Humbly submit to God your self-sufficiency, and He will lift you up!

Stubbornness as a strength can serve as wisdom to the tribe of Issachar. They are not easily swayed, so sometimes their stubbornness is a testimony of God's wisdom in them. Stubbornness can be a form of insight and unrelenting passion for truth within Issachar. It may not be popular, dear Issachar, but if you stand for truth in humble and broken love, be assured that God rewards such faithfulness. It may cause you persecution to stand against the wiles of hype or false doctrines, but trust the seer ability within you, who innately detects both holy and profane. Do so always from a state of bowing low, for you are a chosen vessel of His glory. It is the strength of God that perfects you and graces you for destiny.

## ELISHA: GET THE JOB DONE!

Elisha is a picture of an Issachar in the fullness of his dominion and identity. His strength of spirit and character defined him as well as his ministry. There is much to glean from this beautiful Issachar! Read I Kings 19:13-21.

## THE PROPHET IN THE FIELD

*So he departed from there and found Elisha the son of Shaphat, while he was plowing with twelve pairs of oxen before him, and he with the twelfth* (I Kings 19:19).

Elisha met destiny in the harvest field. Every true Issachar will find his destiny in the harvest field. It was in the harvest field, as Elisha was pulling twelve pairs of oxen, that Elijah found him to impart his mantle and destiny. I feel the twelve pairs of oxen hold prophetic significance for this tribe. Elisha finds purpose and calling by carrying the load of his brethren (the twelve tribes of Israel) in his heavenly Father's harvest field. Purpose of mission will passionately move any Issachar. Elisha follows with a divine purpose, but not without cost. Elisha, proving to be a true Issachar, weighs his cost, leaves both father and mother, and follows Elijah. He knew that God Himself was his reward and that God had "hired" him (Elisha) with a holy calling. Elisha then sacrifices the oxen, symbolizing that we cannot carry the burdens of our brethren in our own strength. Issachar, in order to carry the workloads of your Father's kingdom, you must lay aside your own soulish strength to carry any burden. The glory of God is the enabling grace to carry anything the Father has purposed you to carry.

## THE DOUBLE PORTION

Read II Kings 2:1-14. Elisha received a double portion of Elijah's mantle. It was his divine workload that thrust him into destiny and fullness of dominion. He went on to perform twice as many miracles as Elijah. Upon his death, he was buried in a tomb where his bones held enough glory to resurrect a dead man from the grave! This makes the amount of miracles twice that of Elijah, a double portion indeed (Elijah—16, Elisha—32!).

The double portion anointing or mantle has become a popular subject in charismatic circles. Though we generally get the meaning of this scripture, do we really know the depths of it? I was pondering on these thoughts when God poured out some revelation to me.

God revealed to me that the fullness of the double portion mantle was dependent upon abiding in His rest. Notice that Elisha speaks to Elijah and says, "Yes, I know, be still." Elisha was abiding in the Father and His workload; he was not moved by circumstance or insecurity as his mentor, Elijah. He patiently awaited not only a mantle but a destiny that was tied to Elijah (the prophetic calling). Furthermore, he was being fashioned to release a destiny of great freedom for the nation of Israel.

Elisha can also been seen as a type and of Yeshua. John the Baptist (the Spirit of Elijah) was awaiting Yeshua at the river Jordan. Elisha represents the fullness of power contained in the double portion anointing. He did not achieve this by his own means of striving, but rather by daily living in a state of bowing low, waiting for the workload of Heaven. Yeshua's ministry was marked with sincerest humility (being poor in spirit) and his daily abiding in the Father. Yeshua said, "I do nothing apart from what I see my Father doing." Allowing our agendas and striving methods to die calls us into God's rest. Yeshua obtained his workload from the Father through being intimate with Him. It sprang from His communion. There is no load we can carry in our human strength. Elisha was a powerful man of God, mainly because he daily lived by the precept of bowing low. His abiding released him into his true identity and dominion through his God-given lifestyle of intimacy.

Effective ministry stems from abiding in Christ. When we abide in His nature, the miraculous, prophecy, and soul-winning becomes the byproduct of just being in His presence. Elisha went on to defeat Jezebel and worked many miracles, signs, and wonders, all from the state of bowing low. He was an effective prophet because of his humility and ability to rest in the Lord. He proved he was a true son of Issachar upon receiving Elijah's mantle.

Read II Kings 2:12-13. Elisha did not cross over into destiny and dominion until he fully accepted the mantle of humility. By tearing his clothes, he was tearing away his old garments of striving, stubbornness, and perfectionism. God is calling you, Issachar, to tear off these filthy rags in order to receive the fullness of your double portion mantle! God has an appointment with you, dearest Issachar, in the harvest field. He longs to bequeath you with a heavenly workload. He primarily wants to commune with you.

## HUMILITY AND SERVANTHOOD RELEASES DESTINY AND DOMINION FOR ISSACHAR

Read John 13:5-7, 13-15. Yeshua displayed his kingship through both his humility and servanthood. The regal robes that adorned Him were worn inwardly. Bowing low catapults you, dear Issachar, into dominion. Humility and servanthood are the keys to unlocking your true spiritual authority in Christ. The royal robes of humility and servanthood are the kingdom's true majesty defined.

> *Tell me, O you whom my soul loves, where do you pasture your flock, where do make it lie down at noon?.. "If you yourself do not know, most beautiful among women, go forth on the trail of the flock, and pasture your young goats by the tents of the shepherds"* (Song of Songs 1:7-8).

As your Bridegroom, the Shepherd King is calling to you as His Shulamite to rest in Him and receive His burden for the souls of man. The cry of His heart is to restore souls to their place of rest in Him. You are called, dear Issachar, to bring them to their rest in the Beloved! In His sheepfolds He will bring you into the fullness of His rest and delight for your weary soul. Never forget that your brokenness and humility of heart captivates the Lover of your soul. In fact, it moves Him! You are a sign of the humble yet majestic servant exalted to glory. This is your honor; wear it well!

You are destined for the greatness of your heavenly Father's joyful heart toward you. His goodness and greatness is your reward. Issachar, you have been hired to be a shining example of a true burden bearer. Set your hand to His plowshare. He has a harvest field ripe and ready for you! Your humility and lowly state pleases Him! Continue to be poor in spirit, for the wealth of His kingdom is yours!

## THE PRAYER OF REPENTANCE AND
## DESTINY FOR ISSACHAR

I bow low before you, my King. I want to meet You in the sheepfolds, where You call me to relinquish the burdens of my soul. Draw me into a perpetual place of Your rest and delight. Fashion me into a servant solely at Your service, my beautiful King. You have become my reward, the very prize of my life! I choose to believe Your acceptance of me and leave behind the façade of unworthiness. Call me into truth of who I am in You. Clothe me in humility of heart and soul, that I might be one with You. I repent of my striving and perfectionism. Quiet my heart to be still and know You alone are God. Transform my heart to be a true servant, devoted out of pure love and not duty. Be my Ishi, O Lord. I repent of seeing and serving you as my Baali. Transform my stubbornness into a passionate, undivided heart. Open the eyes of my heart and my understanding, that I might be truly poor in spirit. I bow low and receive Your kingdom mandate for my life. Like Elisha, I abandon everything and receive your prophetic and apostolic burden for my brethren. Call me to serve you and them in all humility and the sincere love You desire. I bow low so that you may be high and lifted up. I receive your call to abide in Your rest and delight. I love you, O most lovely King! In Yeshua's most lovely name above all names, Amen.

# CHAPTER 11
# ZEBULUN: THE HAVEN FOR SOULS

*Then they cried to the Lord in their trouble, and He brought them out of their distresses. He caused the storm to be still, so that the waves of the sea were hushed. Then they were glad because they were quiet, so He guided them to their desired haven* (Psalm 107:28-31).

Yeshua is our most desirable haven. He is our place of rest, our refuge, our ever-present help in times of trouble. In the midst of the storms of life He is the haven for our weary souls. It is His earnest desire for us to make Him the eternal habitation of rest. Resting in knowledge of Him as Savior affords us the refuge we seek after. The name *Yeshua* literally is "our salvation." Let it become the tower of strength and refuge you need. His name and His nature is the lighthouse on the sea of life. Yeshua is the Prince of Peace in whom we find rest and safety. Whatever the storm that rages within, we must always remember: In the arms of Love we are safe and secure. Yeshua is our sanctuary in travail, tragedy, or triumph.

*For You have been a defense for the helpless, a defense for the needy in his distress, a refuge from the storm, a shade from the heat; for the breath of the ruthless is like a rain storm against a wall* (Isaiah 24:5).

The tribe of Zebulun is called to be the haven for the souls of men. Amongst this virtuous and endearing people you will find great fishers of souls for the kingdom. Zebulun carries the mantle of peace and missions. Within them you will find diligent hearts who are great prophets, teachers, and missionaries who carry a burden to rescue the souls of man. Their burden and longing for souls is unquenchable. The beauty of the Prince of Peace radiates from each beautiful soul within this tribe.

## ZEBULUN CALLED TO THE CHASMS OF THE DEEP

*In the beginning God created the heavens and the earth. The earth was formless and void, and darkness was over the surface of the deep, and the Spirit of God was moving over the surface of the waters. Then God said, "Let there be light," and there was light* (Genesis 1:1-3).

Creation was formed by the very nature of God's glory. The deep chasms were formed with His wisdom, and the treasures of His heart lie hidden therein. He longs for us to seek His treasures found within the deep chasms of His nature. Zebulun is such a seeker. The Father is calling unto the depths within us to enter into the depths of His heart where He longs to reveal His glory. For Zebulun, this is their call to intimacy: discovering the depths of the nature of God and treasuries of His wisdom. They are intimate seekers of truth, thinking and feeling very deeply. *Deep unto deep* is more than a spiritual metaphor; it is a longing from the very heart of God. Zebuluns are deep-sea divers of the kingdom of God whose souls and very identities are unlocked as they pursue God and His mysteries. Whether it is the sea of humanity or the depths of the Father's fathomless heart of love for them, their spiritual DNA is connected to the sea. May we all discover the treasures hidden within the love of God.

# THE MEANING OF THE NAME

*Leah conceived again and bore a sixth son to Jacob. Then Leah said, "God has endowed me with a good gift; now my husband will dwell with me, because I have borne him six sons." So she named him Zebulun (Genesis 30:19-20).*

Zebulun means "gift, honor, dowry, dwelling, sacrifice." Zebulun derives its name from these Hebrew root words: *zebed* (gift), *yizbeleni* (honor), and *zibhe* (sacrifice). Leah received her heavenly gift, her dowry from Heaven, where God showed her honor for the sacrifices she made of her heart through the birthing of Zebulun. Her soul came to rest in God. Zebulun's birth was the continuation of God's call to rest for us with Issachar. Dwelling in the haven or safety of the Beloved enables us to receive the dowry of Heaven.

## ZEBULUN AND GOD'S GIFT

Read Luke 11:13. The Father, in His infinite kindness, earnestly longs to bestow gifts upon His children. It brings Him extreme joy just to make His children happy! Childlikeness is the key to receiving gifts from the Father. Simple and pure faith moves our Abba to shower us with His gifts. His greatest gift to us is His Son and the Holy Spirit. He knew that we needed the Holy Spirit to lead us to Himself and our Beloved Bridegroom. Zebulun is in tune with the gift of salvation and the workings of the Holy Spirit.

The gift of salvation was by far the most costly gift we can ever hope to receive (Romans 3:23-25). It is the gift of salvation that enables us to return to the Garden of God. We can never earn our salvation, which is why it is a gift. None of our striving will earn God's love or make us righteous. In light of Zebulun's calling to missions and rescuing souls, they are empowered by this very revelation. It is the deepest longing of every Zebulun that all would receive the free gift of salvation. Not only do they long to see others receive salvation, but they are key mentors of discipleship, establishing the work of salvation. They are earnest fishermen whose nets are always extended and hearts always open to comfort storm-tossed souls.

Read Hebrews 6:4-5. The gifts from our Father were meant to be a way to enter into His delight for us. Zebulun, in touch with his heavenly gift, comes into the fullness of his identity by pursuing the Father and His gifts. Zebuluns themselves are great gifts bestowed upon the Body of Christ for our delight. Zebuluns are peacemakers who pursue peace because it is their mandate from God. Their fellowship and ministry is a heavenly gift to all who cherish such beautiful souls of the kingdom.

*The mind of the prudent acquires knowledge, and the ear of the wise seeks knowledge. A man's gift makes room for him and brings him before great men (Proverbs 18:15-16).*

The gifts and callings of God make room for destinies we are meant to possess. Intimacy is the key to entering into the fullness of our gifts. Zebulun is abundantly endowed with spiritual and natural gifting(s) in the areas of the prophetic, teaching, wisdom, counsel, writing, and many others.

## THE DOWRY OF ZEBULUN

Dowry, or *mohar* in Hebrew, was a price paid for one's bride by the bridegroom. The *mohar* is paid to the bride's father as an agreement before the bridegroom can receive her in marriage.[1] The dowry sealed the betrothal in ancient wedding customs, distinguishing this word from the Hebrew meaning of מַתָּן, *mattān*, meaning "gifts." Strong's further explains it as being "clothed."

What does it mean to be clothed or endowed? Could being clothed with God be our very dowry from Heaven?

> *And the man and his wife were both naked and were not ashamed* (Genesis 2:25).

> *Then the eyes of both of them were opened, and they knew that they were naked; and they sewed fig leaves together and made themselves loin coverings. They heard the sound of the LORD God walking in the garden in the cool of the day, and the man and his wife hid themselves from the presence of the LORD God among the trees of the garden. Then the LORD God called to the man, and said to him, "Where are you?" He said, "I heard the sound of You in the garden, and I was afraid because I was naked; so I hid myself." And He said, "Who told you that you were naked? Have you eaten from the tree of which I commanded you not to eat?"* (Genesis 3:7-11).

In the Garden of Eden Adam and Eve were clothed with the very nature of God, and because of this, they did not know shame. Their very identities were fashioned through the manifest nature of God. Upon the fall of Adam and Eve, there began a tearing away of intimacy. The stripping of their clothing of God's nature occurred, and they knew they were naked. In order for creation to be restored and clothed again with the Father's glory, Yeshua came and paid the ultimate dowry: His own life.

Read John 19:28-30 and Matthew 27:51. The enemy's primary tactic is to separate us from the identity (or dowry) we each possess inwardly, the glory of God.

> *For indeed in this house we groan, longing to be clothed with our dwelling from heaven; inasmuch as we, having put it on, shall not be found naked. For indeed while we are in this tent, we groan, being burdened, because we do not want to be unclothed, but to be clothed, in order that what is mortal may be swallowed up by life. Now He who prepared us for this very purpose is God, who gave to us the Spirit as a pledge* (II Corinthians 5:2-5).

The Father desperately longs for His children to return to Him and walk with Him in the cool of the day. His heart is ravaged with longing for us. It bleeds for His children to be restored to Him. Take time and pull on Abba's heart strings. He longs to reveal His dowry for you.

Read Revelation 3:18. Zebulun, I urge you to be in touch with the refining work of the Spirit. The glory of God (the gold) is revealed within you as you surrender to this work of transformation. The garments of salvation are indeed being clothed with the dowry of God. What a beautiful promise for you, dear Zebulun. He has chosen you not only to be clothed in your heavenly dowry, but to call others to do the same.

## ENDOWED WITH HONOR

True honor is bestowed upon humble hearts and lives who heed the voice of wisdom. Zebulun's very nature is endowed with honor because of their passion for the wisdom of God. They are seekers of truth, who dig deep for answers, whether it is within Scripture, themselves, humanity, or pursuing the heart of God.

Read Proverbs 3:15-17. The Father designed us to seek after honor through worship by seeking His wisdom. Honor is given to all who inherit the kingdom of Heaven though it is not achieved on the broad way but rather the straight and narrow. The path of wisdom brings us life, thereby possessing true intimacy and holiness in Yeshua. Zebulun innately knows that wisdom will bring him honor because it is a tool of intimacy for him. They are intimate seekers to the treasuries of wisdom and kingdom. Seeking after God's wisdom also helps us to show honor to others.

## THE RIGHTEOUS SACRIFICE

*The sacrifices of God are a broken spirit; A broken and contrite heart, O God, Thou wilt not despise* (Psalm 51:17).

The Hebrew word *zibhe* means "sacrifice." There was a specific agreement between the tribe of Zebulun and foreigners forged at Mt. Tabor known as the zibhe-tzedek (*tzedek* meaning "righteous"). It was a commerce agreement for trade. What light Zebuluns possess—their own lives reflected their sacrificial willingness to trade with surrounding pagan communities even in business!

Read Hebrews 12:1. Our sacrifices in and of themselves cannot make us righteous. It takes the mercies of God to cause us to relinquish the old nature and truly abide in the dowry of Heaven. Anything outside of this would be carnal striving for His affections, which would leave us devoid of the intimacy for which we were so graciously created.

Zebulun, God designed you to be a people of great sacrifice. God has given you so much and He requires much. A broken and contrite heart gives not out of duty, but selfless love. Yeshua is asking for the exchange of His life for yours. The matrimonial union, whether it is spiritual or earthly, speaks of sacrifices, the giving of one's self. This is a beautiful key to worship. The key to possessing your dominion, Zebulun, is to rely on God to reveal His nature in you as you bring Him the sacrifices of a broken and contrite spirit. Because of your genuine heart to rescue others, take special care not to sacrifice who you truly are when serving others. Never let anyone drain or belittle the glory of God within you, which is your true nature.

## VALIANT WARRIORS OFFERING UP A RIGHTEOUS SACRIFICE

Read Judges 5:18-22. Zebulun, alongside Naphtali, fought valiantly with no regard for their own lives. Zebuluns today possess the same spiritual DNA as their spiritual forefathers: Their own lives are the sacrifice. Be awakened, O Zebulun, to the glorious purpose and destiny within you. Arise, O mighty ones, from the dust and take your place in the kingdom! Live as dead men walking, living martyrs who love not your lives unto death, for such are approved and favored by the King of Glory Himself. Living the daily-crucified life of Yeshua causes you to share both in His sufferings and glory. Read Matthew 16:25 and Revelation 12:11.

## ZEBULUN BECOMING THE "DWELLING" OF GOD

*You will bring them and plant them in the mountain of Your inheritance, The place, O Lord, which You have made for Your dwelling, The sanctuary, O Lord, which Your hands have established* (Exodus 15:17).

It is the workings of the Spirit that brings us to the mountain of our inheritance. What is our mountain of inheritance? Zion is the holy habitation of God, His dwelling place. This promise speaks to us of both the physical and spiritual Mt. Zion. Our quest in life is to ascend to His dwelling. This can only be done through the work of the Spirit in our lives.

Read Hebrews 12:22-23. Zion is a habitation of abiding or the utmost dwelling place of the Most High God. We ascend to the hill of God with clean hands (the work of repentance) and pure hearts (the work of transformation after repentance) through our God-given tools of intimacy. Zebulun ascends to God's "dwelling" through his call to seek first the kingdom by seeking the wisdom of the Father.

Read Deuteronomy 33:27. Zebulun, there is safety when you make God your dwelling by heeding wisdom and seeking after it. Wisdom is a refuge to all who choose to lay hold of her. Our enemies are put at bay when we make God and His wisdom our dwelling place. His counsel alone is the safe place for our souls.

Read Proverbs 1:33, 2:7-8, 4:6 and 14:26. Disobedience births fear. Fear causes one to dwell in torment and out of the dwelling place of the Most High. If we are close to the Father's heartbeat and heed His wisdom, we have nothing to fear. God guards the upright. Those who choose folly choose to walk out of God's protective care. Walk on the path that wisdom leads you into, Zebulun, and you will find refuge and safety. Striving in your own wisdom draws you away from dwelling in God.

> *Then my people will live in a peaceful habitation, and in secure dwellings and in undisturbed resting places...* (Isaiah 32:19).

The tribe of Zebulun, though valiant warriors, were known to be peacemakers. Peace is the atmosphere of the dwelling or habitation of God. The word *Shalom* in Hebrew means "a double portion peace" and "let there be nothing between me and Thee." Our sinful and striving natures can come between that true place of rest we find in the Beloved. In the Hebrew text of the Song of Solomon, Solomon's name (Shlomo) means: "peace is his," and Shulamite means "peace is hers." Yeshua is our Shlomo, for we know Him as the Prince of Peace. Our inheritance is the nature of His rest and delight revealed in us. It is the transforming work of grace coupled with the wisdom of God that births us into the peaceful dwelling of God. Read II Corinthians 5:2.

The dwelling of one's soul is the essence of our matrimonial union with God Himself. In her book, *Song of the Bride*, Jeanne Guyon speaks of the union of souls or dwelling in this way:

> "We can enjoy being united to another person only during certain times, because the other person is external; but the enjoyment of God is permanent and lasting because it is within. Since God is our final goal, the soul can incessantly pour itself into Him as its Goal and Center, to be mingled and transformed there without ever coming out again—that is, unless it should fall away and be rejected by God. It is the same way with a river, which is composed of water derived from the sea, but is quite distinct from it. When it finds itself away from its source, it endeavors in various ways to reach the ocean; and when it has done so, it loses and mixes itself in it—just as it was mixed with the ocean before it left it—and can no longer be distinguished from it. It is to be observed further that God, in creating us, made us participants of His being and fit to be reunited with Him."[2]

Zebulun, in the Garden you belonged to Him, but because of striving according to the flesh, you veered a separate path away from the Father who is your ocean. He is calling you back to Himself to dwell in Him so intimately that your nature cannot be distinguished from His. I encourage you, dear Zebulun, to get lost in His nature, for in doing so you will find yourself! When we choose to gain our lives we lose it, but when we purpose to lose our lives for Yeshua's sake, then and only then can we find true life.

## THE GEMSTONE OF ZEBULUN

Zebulun's gemstone is the aquamarine. It is of the beryl family and of a beautiful pale blue, sea-like color. Aquamarine derives its name from *aqua* meaning "water" and *mare* meaning "sea water." Zebulun's stone emphasizes its call to the sea, the depths of God's nature and humanity. The tribe of Zebulun is known for their sincerely deep heart, wisdom, and peaceful nature.

*He gathers the waters of the sea together as a heap; He lays up the deeps in storehouses*
(Psalm 33:7).

Zebulun, the Father has laid up the storehouses of the deep, the very recesses of His heart for you. In His infinite love for you, He calls you to go deep-sea diving into the mysteries of His very nature. Abba longs to reveal rich insight of who He is and who you are in Him. Seek first His kingdom, explore the depths of it, and you will find all that your heart longs for.

*Surely God will shatter the head of His enemies, the hairy crown of him who goes on in his guilty deeds. God said, "I will bring them back from Bashan. I will bring them back from the depths of the sea"* (Psalm 68:21-22).

Victory is assured to you, my dearest Zebulun, as you dwell in the depths of God's presence. His counsels provide safety from your enemy and afford the intimacy that brings transformation to your soul. When you dwell in the understanding of who God is and who you are in Him, you will not be moved from your dominion. In order to possess true spiritual authority, you must possess the places of the deep within the Father's nature.

*He shall have dominion also from sea to sea, and from the river unto the ends of the earth*
(Psalm 72:8 KJV).

The true defining moment of our dominion comes to fruition when we rest in our true identity in Yeshua. For Zebulun, it occurs when they recognize their heavenly dowry is who they truly are. Our dominion is limitless in the Beloved.

*Thy way is in the sea, and thy path in the great waters, and thy footsteps are not known*
(Psalm 77:19 KJV).

The path God has laid for you, Zebulun, is clear. It is the way of the Cross and Christ's sufferings that causes your faith and character to be built. Yeshua is calling you out of the boat to walk on a substance of faith. Though it may seem ridiculous to defy the natural realm, it is vital in order to possess the dominion for which you were made. He is challenging you to walk in the unseen realms of His Spirit and glory, where He will reveal the depths of His nature and kingdom to you—if you should choose to accept this dare!

## THE SYMBOL OF ZEBULUN

The symbol of Zebulun is a boat, particularly a sailboat. Through this symbol, God chooses to reveal His nature and the strength and frailty of the soul of Zebulun. The boat speaks of their awareness of the human transient nature. Boats were also known as a means of travel and transport. During ancient times it was the primary source of trade.

Read Isaiah 33:21-22. God is longing to establish His nature as a habitation of His peace within you, dear Zebulun. His salvation alone affords a haven of peace in which He longs for you to commune with Him alone. Your transient, humanly frail state only gives affirmation to the heavenly dowry you long to possess. A true Zebulun rests in the knowledge of the transient state of this present life, knowing that his true haven is anchored in the hope and reality of Heaven itself. The boat is also a picture of Zebulun as a carrier of the glory of God. The ocean has often been related to the glory of God and the depths of God's nature.

*For the earth will be filled with the knowledge of the glory of God, as the waters cover the sea* (Habakkuk 2:14).

*Now when Jesus heard that John had been taken into custody, He withdrew into Galilee;*
*and leaving Nazareth, He came and settled in Capernaum, which is by the sea, in the*
*region of Zebulun and Naphtali* (Matthew 4:12).

Zebulun's heartbeat resounds with the cry for souls, specifically missions. Yeshua confirmed this through His ministry within the Galilee region. Zebulun has an earnest yearning to go fishing for the souls of men. They feel the depths of the bleeding heart of the Father. Zebulun may either directly be on the mission field or aid it through finances or prayer. Their passions are tied to the sea of humanity. They deeply identify with the ministry of Yeshua in Galilee, primarily with His works of healing and deliverance and his deep heart of compassion. Zebuluns are very deeply motivated by the gift of mercy.

Read Luke 8:22-24. God is calling you, Zebulun, to discern the spiritual atmosphere around you. It is vital that you seek the counsel of the Father's heart. The spiritual realm, though unseen, is the absolute reality of the kingdom. It can challenge you to look beyond circumstance and call you to a higher realm of abiding in the Master. You are given the innate ability to explore and know the counsels of God. His counsels lie in deep supernatural realms that challenge faith, defy logic, and purify profane agendas. Yeshua is calling you out of the boat, out of yourself, and into unseen realms of glory and faith which charge you to a life of the miraculous! As you dive into the depths of His counsel and understanding, seeking first His kingdom and His righteousness, you can then know the signs of the times (Matthew 16:3).

Step out of the boat, dear Zebulun, and discover the infinite fathoms of miracles, understanding, and love God has for you to explore! Take care not to "lean" on your own understanding. To do so would entail striving and draw you away from your God-given tool of intimacy, which is to seek the depths for the wisdom and counsel of God. When you do step on that water, you are stepping into your dominion. These are keys you need to aide you in your calling to the prophetic, teaching, and your heart for missions.

We perish for a lack of knowledge. Relying on our own knowledge stems from a fear of the unknown. Perfect love calls us to dwell in a daily Spirit-led lifestyle. Fear cripples us to be enslaved to the mundane and become unchallenged, disheartened, and apathetic to the calling of pure love. The Father's chief delight is to bring us into the miraculous and deep spiritual realms of His heart after we first seek His counsels. Yeshua was enabled to live in these realms because He always sought the counsel of the Father first. Yeshua lived a lifestyle of ridiculous faith. That is was why He could walk on the water effortlessly. The natural did not dictate impossibilities to Him, but rather the infinite possibilities He possessed through intimacy with the Father. He could speak to the wind and tell it to be still, because He lived in His dominion. You too can walk in this dominion when you seek first the counsel of the Father. Launch out into the deep, Zebulun! There are many adventures God has for you if you dare take up this challenge of living in ridiculous faith.

## YESHUA: THE ANCHOR FOR ZEBULUN

*...so that by two unchangeable things in which it is impossible for God to lie, we who*
*have taken refuge would have strong encouragement to take hold of the hope set before us.*
*This hope we have as an anchor of the soul, a hope both sure and steadfast and one which*
*enters within the veil, where Jesus has entered as a forerunner for us, having become a*
*high priest forever according to the order of Melchizedek* (Hebrews 6:18-20).

Yeshua is the sole (and soul) anchor for you, Zebulun. He is steadfast in His nature. He never changes. His nature is the only thing we can rely on. We can rest in the fact that His nature is steadfast though His image is often dim and what He is doing seems faint and distant. This is the challenge of perfect love: to abide in ridiculous faith by abiding solely in the anchor of His nature. There are many adventures upon the seas of life. We can rest in Him, knowing that He is the anchor, no matter how tumultuous the seas or storms we may face. His nature is always consistent. God calls you, Zebulun, to abide in Yeshua, the anchor of your soul, for from Him alone will you gain your calling to abide in peace. You carry the mantle and anointing of peace as you abide in Yeshua, your anchor. Yeshua is the peace-speaker. He is the stillness for which your soul longs. Abide in Him, and He will give you rest. No matter what storm rages within, remember in whose arms you're held. In His everlasting, unfailing arms you will find refuge. Seek to know Him as the anchor of your soul.

## JACOB'S PROPHECY

*Zebulun will dwell at the seashore; and he shall be a haven for ships, and his flank shall be toward Sidon* (Genesis 49:13).

### "ZEBULUN WILL DWELL AT THE SEASHORE"

The Father is calling you, Zebulun, to dwell upon His nature, counsel, and promises. It is vital for you to dwell in the Prince of Peace, meditating on His good report for you. There is a wealth of understanding as you dwell at the seashore of Heaven. Treasures of His nature, Word, and love will be revealed to you as you seek first the kingdom of Heaven. His counsel will provide you safety; His promises will give you hope and vision.

*Indeed I will greatly bless you, and I will greatly multiply your seed as the stars of the heavens and as the sand which is on the seashore; and your seed shall possess the gate of their enemies* (Genesis 22:17).

Promises bring purpose for our journey in life. God gave our father Abraham a great promise: That his descendants would be so many they would be like the sand at the seashore. There is no limit to His promise because there is no limit to His nature. When you feel discouraged and weary of waiting for fulfillment of your promises, remember that God keeps His promises. He watches over His Word to perform it, and His nature is always a consistent anchor for your soul.

### "HE SHALL BE A HAVEN FOR SHIPS"

This portion of Jacob's prophecy is directly tied to Zebulun's ministry. Zebulun has a unique ministry to storm-tossed souls. They are both rescuer and refuge. Zebulun has a special gifting from God to bring others into God's rest through the mantle of peace they inwardly possess. As ministers of reconciliation, they provide counsel that brings revelation, discipleship, and transformation. Souls are often drawn to them because of the anointing of peace that rests upon their lives and ministries. Strays seem to always find their way to a Zebulun's door. It is the inner light within each Zebulun that calls the ships (or souls) to dock or rest in their presence. Supernaturally, they are gifted to bring comfort to the most distraught of souls who find themselves within their ports.

Compassion compels the heart of every Zebulun. Take care to use discernment with whom you take in. Do not be moved by guilt or manipulation. Listen carefully to God's counsels for the ships He has given you to care for. Always be Spirit-led so as to avoid burnout or a leeching personality who would try to drain your resources. Not every stray will be sent to you from God. Discernment will help you know a wolf in sheep's clothing and the insincere. Stay grounded in the Word and listen carefully to the Father's instruction. Being the mercy-motivated person you are, it can be a facade when you are moved by anything outside of God's counsel.

## "REPAIRERS OF THE BREACH"

Read Isaiah 58:11-12. The ministry of reconciliation comes from the living waters within Zebulun. Yeshua, the tender Shepherd, will lead beside peaceful waters where He not only calls you to be restored but to bring restoration. There our souls who have become parched and are in desperate need of the Living Water within you.

Read John 7:38-39. Yeshua is the pure Living Water. In Hebrew this verse reads: "from wells of salvation, or Yeshua." Restoration is drawn from the healing nature of Yeshua. Zebulun, when you abide in Yeshua, not only do you partake of the regeneration within Him as the life-giving source, but you can impart it also. The washing of the Word (Yeshua) Himself is restoring the ancient ruins in His proclamation of restoration. He is calling for a stirring in the waters in the earth today, and He longs for you, dear Zebulun, to come join Him at the pool.

Read Luke 4:18-19. Bid others to come to the Living Water in whom they will find complete reconciliation, restoration, and revealing of God's heart and identity in Him. Chasms of restoration lie deep within you and are waiting to be released upon hungry and destitute souls.

## "HIS FLANK SHALL BE TOWARD SIDON"

This portion of the prophecy is a two-edged sword for the tribe of Zebulun. It is both a warning against apathy and a call to stand and oppose darkness. Zebulun was buried in Sidon. His borders did not actually include Sidon in the natural, but it is meant more as a spiritual position. Sidon currently is a city in Lebanon, and in ancient times it was a seafaring city of trade. Though Zebulun's borders were not by the sea, many traders from the sea would use Zebulun's territory as a connection for commerce. They did, however, own and work the fisheries on the Sea of Galilee (which is actually a lake).

Jezebel's father was the king of Sidon. When considering this prophecy, I thought of the ruling principalities in that area of the time. They were not only known for paganism, but for defiant witchcraft and cultic practices. Jacob's prophecy contains a wealth of wisdom for Zebulun. Zebulun, known as a peacemaker, must take care not become apathetic against evil. Pacifying one's enemy is not true peace. It is compromise.

Read Revelation 2:20. It is idolatry that causes one to slumber, but repentance causes one to awaken to the glory of God within. God is calling you, Zebulun, to awaken from slumber. Do not allow apathy to lure you into aborting your destiny. You are called to stand valiantly as a true peacemaker against Jezebel and any other evil that may oppose you and the Body of Christ. Your flank (border) is set in opposition to darkness—against Jezebel, the apostate bride of Satan. Stand and declare the righteousness of God.

## MOSES' PROPHECY

*Of Zebulun he said, "Rejoice, Zebulun, in your going forth, and, Issachar, in your tents. They will call peoples to the mountain; There they will offer righteous sacrifices; for they will draw out the abundance of the seas, and the hidden treasures of the sand"* (Deuteronomy 33:18-19).

I will reiterate some of what I mentioned in Issachar's chapter concerning Zebulun and Issachar because of their shared calling in ministry.

## "AND OF ZEBULUN HE SAID, 'REJOICE, ZEBULUN, IN YOUR GOING FORTH, AND, ISSACHAR, IN YOUR TENTS'"

God is making a distinction between the callings of these two tribes. They were raised together, having been not too far apart in age, and they also camped together in the wilderness. Their bond was made in the Spirit, and therefore it's not surprising that Moses mentions them together in this prophecy. Zebulun was called to go out; it is a call to missions for this tribe. Jacob's prophecy to Sidon is a call to missions also, further confirming this truth.

## "THEY SHALL CALL PEOPLES TO THE MOUNTAIN"

Issachar and Zebulun are linked in their prophetic call. They give expression to their prophetic gifting in different ways: Issachar's stems from his humility and burden-bearing for the kingdom, while Zebulun's call stems from his mission for the lost and the hurting. Issachar would be more of a pastoral/ administrative prophet, while Zebulun would be more of a mercy and teaching-motivated prophet. Unified in the Holy Spirit, together they call God's people to His Mountain, a place to meet and hear the word of God.

## "THERE THEY SHALL DRAW OUT THE ABUNDANCE OF THE SEAS, AND THE HIDDEN TREASURES OF THE SAND"

Issachar and Zebulun are called to the sea of humanity. They both carry a unique prophetic gifting. It is to humanity Issachar hears a kingdom mandate that brings freedom, accomplishing the will of the Father. He is drawn to the deep things of God's kingdom plan for creation through his servanthood. Zebulun hears the call to go out and cast his nets to the souls of man drifting on the sea of life. Prophetically, they both serve a vital connection, both separate and together, for the end-time harvest. Zebulun's ties are clearly to the sea and Issachar's to the land (or earth). In unity, they are called to reveal the heart of the Father in the treasures of the earth.

> *Do not store up for yourselves treasures on earth, where moth and rust destroy, and where thieves break in and steal. But store up for yourselves treasures in heaven, where neither moth nor rust destroys, and where thieves do not break in or steal; for where your treasure is, there your heart will be also* (Matthew 6:19-21).

Zebulun, your heavenly dowry is revealed in the chasms of the Father's deep love for you and humanity. You have a royal appointment and commission to seek out the treasures of Heaven. Do not waste time on earthly burdens and doctrines of man, which serve only to detour you from your high calling. Pursue the Lover of your soul in whom all treasure is found!

## WISDOM AND THE SEA FOR ZEBULUN

> *When He set for the sea its boundary so that the water would not transgress His command, when He marked out the foundations of the earth* (Proverbs 8:29).

Zebulun, you are sea bound in calling and in nature. The foundations of the kingdom of Heaven itself are marked for you to gain the very understanding of God's nature after which you are meant to seek. With the Holy Spirit as your teacher, venture into the deeper depths of the foundations of the Father's heart of love for you. There and only there will you discover your destiny and life's journey fulfilled as you abide in the Creator of life. Seek first His kingdom and righteousness; He longs to reveal the depths of His nature to you!

Read Hebrews 6:7-8. There are many adventures waiting for you as you seek after the treasure of wisdom Himself, Yeshua, your Bridegroom King. Relinquish your apprehensions of self-doubt and carnal understanding and dive into the deep recesses of the King of Love's heart. His wisdom and counsel will aide as a tool of intimacy, which then navigates you to where the treasures truly lie for you.

## THE FACADES OF ZEBULUN
### "DON'T ROCK THE BOAT"

The tribe members of Zebulun are undoubtedly called to be peacemakers. Yeshua said, *Blessed are the peacemakers, for they shall be called the sons of God* (Matthew 5:9). Peace is a vital key to the kingdom; it is a true sign of our inheritance and glorious nature. True peace sometimes requires that we confront. Sometimes the only way to establish a peaceful kingdom is to go to war. Zebulun has the tendency to not want to "rock the boat" and thereby compromise. True peace is achieved only when we seek the counsels of Heaven and refuse to appease man or the flesh. Zebulun, being mercy motivated, will sometimes appease other parties, or worse yet, become apathetic and not deal with the situation at all.

Read Luke 14:31-33. Non-confrontational behaviors not only detour our own destiny but also the destiny of others. When we allow others or our own self-gain to influence our counsels for peace, it can only create warfare. Zebulun, please repent of this if you have engaged in pacifying the enemy. When we don't confront and souls lie in the balance, we then have their blood on our hands. Vain counsels of man oppose Zebulun's call to intimacy. To pacify others is a carnal degradation of destiny.

Read Romans 8:6-8. True peace is life-giving because it is born from the counsels and fear of God, whereas compromise stems from the counsels of and fear of man.

Read Psalm 33:10-11. The fear of man is a snare. When Zebulun steps outside the counsel of God, he is stepping out of his dominion. God will confound the carnal counsels that are vain and profane, but He will exalt those who bow low and seek Him first for His counsel. Never allow the appeasement of others or self to cause you to forego destiny. Seek the plans of His heart, and you will never go wrong!

> *And from the days of John the Baptist until now, the kingdom of heaven suffereth violence, and the violent take it by force* (Matthew 11:2 KJV).

The kingdom of God suffers from violence because we have not confronted our enemies and driven them out. Who are our enemies? Our enemies are our idols of self and the drive to pacify others' needs and our own rather than dwelling in the fear of the Lord. It is necessary to engage in battle and confrontation in laid-down love for the souls who need the counsel of God and His true peace. God is calling you, dear Zebulun, to dwell in the house of wisdom. When dwelling in the house of the foolish woman (the apostate bride, Jezebel), your destiny is in danger of death as you seek after her counsels, cower to her intimidation, and are lured to sleep by her lullabies of apathy.

Read Proverbs 9:1-12 and Proverbs 9:13-18. I urge you, brethren, to take time for introspection and seek God where you have dwelt in the house of foolishness. Foolish counsels bring only death, but the counsels of God bring eternal life!

## NO TOLERATION

Toleration of Jezebel is idolatry. Jezebel sings her lurid lullaby, tantalizing those whose hearts and wills have chosen apathy over intimacy. It is her mission to weave her web of control, intimidation, and apathy over the true prophets of God so that she might cause them to slumber in their dominion. Zebulun, I beseech you to cast down Jezebel and her lying imaginations, apathy, and intimidation that you might come into the fullness of God's nature within you. Continually pacifying the enemy or self, you will become tolerant of Jezebel and apathetic to the call of God upon your life. You are a company of prophets who are called to oppose Jezebel. If you refuse to confront her, you, in essence, become like the prophets of Baal. You will be subjected to what or whom you tolerate.

Zebulun, God desires for you to set your flank toward Sidon. Awaken to the glory of God and glorious destiny within the heart of your Bridegroom King. Led by the Spirit, you must prophesy against her harlotries and call the hardest and coldest of hearts out of slumber from her lullabies of destruction and control. When you engage in battle, remember to first draw near to the Father, seek His counsels, and then carry out His battle plans as the Spirit leads you. Arise, O mighty Zebulun, and thrust your sword (the Word and counsels of God) into the heart of Jezebel and apathy. Refuse compromise and cling to consecration of your will and heart to be bound only to the throne of God itself!

Read Revelation 18:20-24. Walk only in His counsel day and night, for you are valiant warriors set apart for this end time to throw down the kingdoms of the enemy and Jezebel and to build the kingdom of God in the lives the Father has called you to disciple.

## ZEBULUN'S PEN

*Out of Ephraim was there a root of them against Amalek; after thee, Benjamin, among thy people; out of Machir came down governors, and out of Zebulun they that handle the pen of the writer* (Judges 5:14 KJV).

God has placed a mighty pen within the hand of Zebulun. From your golden quill of Heaven, oracles of wisdom and knowledge shall stir the hearts of man to the Creator of love. Seek first the kingdom, for as you do you will be able to inscribe the deliverance and healing of the nations.

*My heart overflows with a good theme; I address my verses to the King; My tongue is the pen of a ready writer* (Psalm 45:1).

It is the prophetic and teaching gifts within you that call you to speak and write the oracles of love and wisdom. Without knowledge the people perish. God has gifted you to inscribe the mysteries of His nature. You will discover the wealth of wisdom within the heart and nature of your King.

## DOMINION RELEASED TO ZEBULUN FROM THE FOUNTAINS OF THE DEEP

*The earth was formless and void, and darkness was over the surface of the deep, and the Spirit of God was moving over the surface of the waters* (Genesis 1:2).

When God created the earth, He was revealing His nature within creation itself. The foundations of the deep contain His endless mysteries that are waiting to be revealed in and to His beloved creation. Zebulun, you are His chosen vessel to reveal the foundations of the deep within the earth. Just as the Spirit of God moved upon the waters, He is hovering over you, moving in you to release the knowledge of His glory in the earth. It is your appointed time, dear Zebulun. It is not mere coincidence that you are reading this now. The Father is longing to release the depths and fathoms of the deep and its storehouses in and through you! Now is your appointed time to go into the depths of the Living God and know Him!

Read Psalm 42:7. There is a sound within the depths of the heart of the Father. He is calling you, dear Zebulun, to explore and resound with this sound. Let the waves of His glory wash over you. He alone will transform you into the haven of souls you truly are. Gifted with the dowry of Heaven, possess your inheritance, O beautiful Zebulun! Return to the nature of God and intimacy you were predestined for!

## PRAYER OF REPENTANCE AND DESTINY
## FOR THE TRIBE OF ZEBULUN

Draw me deeper, Lord, into the depths of Your fathomless nature. Lord, I long to live in the realms of glory and wisdom. I long to go deep-sea diving into the treasuries of Heaven hidden in you, sweet Yeshua! No cost is too great to abide in Your nature. I willingly sacrifice my life. Fashion me into a haven for souls. Draw the weary and storm tossed to my shore. Be the anchor of my soul. Steer me wherever the wind of Your Spirit is blowing. Breathe on my sails, that they might carry me to the nations to which You have called me. Extend my nets to the souls of man; may I be a lighthouse to the world. May your peace take up habitation within me that I might impart it to others. I repent of apathy. Set my flank toward Sidon that I may oppose Jezebel and her cohorts. Forgive me for pacifying men instead of dwelling in Your counsel, which is both my reward and my delight, bringing me life eternal. I purpose my heart and will to dwell within the house of wisdom. I leave all foolishness behind. Yeshua, You alone are my dowry, for You have purchased me with Your blood. Cause me to return to the Garden, that Your nature might be awakened within me. May deep speak unto the deep within me. At the sound of Your waterfalls, Your breakers have washed over me, transforming me to the core of my innermost being. I love you, Lord, and I desire to seek first Your kingdom and Your righteousness. In Yeshua's name, Amen.

---

[1] Edward Bagby Pollard, James, Orr, M.A., D.D. General Editor. "Entry for 'dowry'". "*International Standard Bible Encyclopedia*". 1915 Public Domain.

[2] Jeanne Guyon, *Song Of The Bride* (New Kensington, PA: Whitaker House, 1997) Page 15.

# CHAPTER 12
# MANASSEH: THE FORGIVING ONE

*Instead of your* [former] *shame you shall have a twofold recompense; instead of dishonor and reproach* [your people] *shall rejoice in their portion. Therefore in their land they shall possess double* [what they had forfeited]; *everlasting joy shall be theirs* (Isaiah 61:7 AMP).

Forgiveness is the canceling of debt we could never pay. As believers in Christ, we owe everything to Yeshua, who purchased us from our sin. Forgiveness is the seal of the redemptive work of the Cross. Without the atonement from sin, you and I would be aliens and strangers to eternal life, destiny, and—most importantly—intimacy with the Father.

*For he has rescued us from the dominion of darkness and brought us into the kingdom of the Son He loves, in whom we have redemption, the forgiveness of sins* (Colossians 1:13-14).

Forgiveness calls us to see Yeshua as our rescuer, our knight in shining armor. Surely He has saved us from our enemy, Satan, and brought us into the kingdom of love! When the Father looked down from Heaven and saw the agony and despair of His lost jewels of great price, He sent His only Son to rescue us from the dominion of darkness. The journey of restoration begins with forgiveness. As we travel into destiny, identity, and dominion, our voyage always begins with redemption and forgiveness through the blood of Yeshua. If the kingdom of God is eternal (being that it stems from the very nature of God the Father Himself), then the principles of the kingdom are eternal as well. Read Psalm 103:1-12.

## FORGIVENESS: THE ACCESS TO THE GLORY AND NATURE OF GOD

If redemption by the precious blood of Yeshua is the ransom of our soul, then forgiveness is our reward. The vast wealth afforded to us lays within the nature of forgiveness Himself, our heavenly Father. The Mercy Seat was not a mere part of the Ark of the Covenant; it was always a means of access to the very glory and nature of God, a prerequisite. In Hebrew, the word for "Mercy Seat" is *kaporeth. Kaporeth* stems from the root word *kaphar,* meaning "to cover up, forgive, reconcile, and to atone for offenses."

Read Hebrews 9:4-12. Human flesh cannot touch the glory of God. Our fallen nature is a façade and an enmity to the glory of God (His likeness) within us. It is important for us as believers to know that mercy is the catalyst to entering into not just the "holy place," but more importantly, into the holy nature of God.

*For we do not have a high priest who cannot sympathize with our weakness(es), but One who has been tempted in all things as we are, yet without sin. Therefore let us draw near with confidence to the throne of grace, so that we may receive mercy and find grace to help in time of need* (Hebrews 4:15-16).

Our Bridegroom of blood ransomed us in His mercy and forgiveness to be one with the Father. In a Jewish wedding the engaged couple will draw up a contract for marriage called a *ketubah;* in it lies the terms of what the groom vows to provide for his bride. God's Word is our *ketubah.* Forever sealed upon our hearts, we are bound to the King of Love and His holy matrimonial promise of salvation. Forgiveness and mercy serve as the Groom's signature upon the Bride, thereby giving her access to the Father: the Ark of the Covenant.

*Even when we were dead in sins, hath quickened us together with Christ, (by grace ye are saved;) and hath raised us up together, and made us sit together in heavenly places in Christ Jesus: That in the ages to come he might shew the exceeding riches of his grace in his kindness toward us through Christ Jesus* (Ephesians 2:5-7 KJV).

Our sonship was sealed within the nature of God's forgiveness and mercy. With full assurance of faith we can then boldly stand as heirs to the kingdom. Intimidation and condemnation should never enter into the equation of intimacy with the Father. We can be confident because we have been purchased with the royal blood of Yeshua, therefore we are truly the royalty of Heaven. We are seated in heavenly places. That very seat is the Mercy Seat. Thus, as we are seated and abiding in the mercy nature of God, His glory is revealed to us!

God predestined a great and mighty company of heirs, who, by nature, exude the forgiveness and mercy of His very being. This high calling is bestowed on the tribe of Manasseh. Within Manasseh you will find some of the most beautiful of spirit and purpose. They are naturally mercy motivated. Manasseh is a catalyst of God's forgiveness, calling the Body of Christ to sonship and thereby accessing the glory of God within them. Every fiber of Manessah's being exudes the nature of God's forgiveness to mankind, even unto the meaning of his name.

## THE MEANING OF THE NAME

*Now before the year of famine came, two sons were born to Joseph, whom Asenath, the daughter of Potiphera, priest of On, bore to him. Joseph named the firstborn Manasseh, "For," he said, "God has made me forget all my trouble and all my father's house*hold" (Genesis 41:50-51).

Manasseh means to "forgive and forget." As the oldest son of Joseph, Manasseh learned first-hand the power of forgiveness. Manasseh's earliest school of the Holy Spirit began by watching the Lord's dealings with his father, Joseph. He had a unique inside look at Joseph's pain, anger, redemption, and radical transformation. This training enabled Manasseh as a minister of mercy. It is flesh and façade to remember our debts or others' debts and to make others pay for wrong done—the "eye for an eye" sense of justice. Our human nature, with its striving to be righteous, tries to achieve justice by carnal gains and means. The nature of God, in contrast, calls us to rest in the knowledge of forgiveness, to forget the past, and to dwell on the abiding, redemptive work of the Cross. The Holy Spirit makes it His mission to school every son and daughter of Manasseh in the Father's character of forgiveness.

This is not instantaneous to this tribe by any means, but rather paved with great suffering, hard knocks, the disabling of self-righteousness, rude awakenings of human frailties, and finally, the divine intervention and enabling by the grace of God. The work and life of every Manasseh is the ministry of transformation glory. For a true look into the life of Manasseh, we must look into the life of his father, Joseph. Joseph was acquainted with much suffering, be it from his brothers' selling him to slavery, false accusation, and imprisonment. He endured ridicule and betrayal by those closest to him. God used Joseph's suffering to form His own nature within him. Suffering is the anvil applied to the Father's priceless living stones. As we share in the sufferings of Yeshua, we share in His nature.

*Who comforts us in all our affliction so that we will be able to comfort those who are in any affliction with the comfort with which we ourselves are comforted by the Lord. For just as the sufferings of Christ are ours in abundance, so also our comfort is abundant through Christ. But if we are afflicted, it is for your comfort and salvation; or if we are comforted, it is for your comfort, which is effective in the patient enduring of the same sufferings which we also suffer...* (II Corinthians 1:4-6).

*For I consider that the sufferings of this present time are not worthy to be compared with the glory that is to be revealed to us* (Romans 8:18).

Manasseh's father, Joseph, provided a bountiful inheritance not only physically, but spiritually. Oftentimes when a scripture mentions the name of Joseph (meaning it does not specify either Manasseh or Ephraim), it is speaking of both brothers. The brothers were endowed with the spiritual DNA and blessings of their father. Joseph means "to add." The heart of God is always to add or multiply the things concerning His kingdom within us. Unforgiveness and suffering of the past can subtract and divide us from our destiny and dominion in Christ.

*Thus you shall say to Joseph, "Please forgive, I beg you, the transgression of your brothers and their sin, for they did you wrong. And now, please forgive the transgression of the servants of the God of your father." And Joseph wept when they spoke to him. Then his brothers also came and fell down before him and said, "Behold, we are your servants." But Joseph said to them, "Do not be afraid, for am I in God's place? As for you, you meant evil against me, but God meant it for good in order to bring about this present result, to preserve many people alive. So therefore, do not be afraid; I will provide for you and your little ones." So he comforted them and spoke kindly to them* (Genesis 50:17-21).

Joseph's decision to forgive and forget the suffering of his past brought not only him but his entire family great transformation, healing, and provision. In like manner, this is what God's forgiveness does for us. Forgiveness paves the way to a life of freedom in the Beloved. Joseph knew this truth though he learned it through great suffering. He did not truly inherit God's promises and destiny until he forgave his brothers.

Joseph's Egyptian name, *Zaphnath-paaneah*, means "treasury of the glorious rest." Who is our treasury of rest?[1] Yeshua affords us the wealth of His rest, for it is His very nature we are meant to inherit. Read Hebrews 4:9-16. Manasseh finds his treasury of glorious rest through his God-given tool of intimacy—forgiveness. When God forgives and forgets, He places our sins, our past, and our old wounds at the bottom of the Red Sea: His precious blood. Immerse yourself, Manasseh, in the veins of Immanuel's redemption for you. In doing so, you will find your identity and true spiritual authority! When we forgive and forget, we are abiding in the nature of the Father.

## FORGIVENESS AS PART OF THE FATHER'S CHARACTER

*...or if you forgive others for their transgressions, your heavenly Father will also forgive you. But if you do not forgive others, then your Father will not forgive your transgressions* (Matthew 6:14-15).

Forgiveness is a foundational part of the Father's character. Each attribute of the Father's character is complete, lacking nothing. Indeed, forgiveness is the very essence of His nature. When sin entered into the creation the Father lovingly created, His heart became ravaged by the tearing away of intimacy it caused. His heart continually bleeds for fallen man, who Manasseh is instinctively in tune with—this is the bleeding heart of the Father. Creation began with a perfect union hidden in fellowship with God.

The nature of God's forgiveness and forgetfulness not only calls us back into communion with Him, but also affords us the ability to share in His glory, our inheritance, thereby restoring us as sons and daughters. Forgiving and forgetting are vital keys to unlock chains of bondage and restore the ancient ruins of our lives. I charge you, Manasseh (and the entire Body of Christ), to immerse yourself in the nature of God's character to forgive and forget. You have been handed a powerful set of keys to the kingdom. With them you will unlock many hearts and destinies!

## THE GEMSTONE OF MANASSEH

The gemstone of Manasseh is the onyx, which is shared by his brother Ephraim. The colors of the onyx alternate with light and dark bands, which are colored in brown, red, black, white, and grey or black. The onyx stone for Manasseh and his brother is the black onyx. The stone for Manasseh and Ephraim is primary in Scripture, often referred to it as "Joseph." Joseph's stone spoke of the legacy he left for his sons in his life lessons. Joseph's suffering, triumphs, deep mysteries revealed through dreams, and his innate ability to administrate through divine wisdom all reveal a plan for both tribes. God honored the legacy and life of Joseph through this stone.

## THE ONYX SPEAKS FORGIVENESS

Joseph's suffering speaks to Manasseh the power of forgiveness and releasing those who have held you captive.

*And forgive us our debts, as we also have forgiven our debtors. For if you forgive others for their transgressions, your heavenly Father will also forgive you* (Matthew 6:12, 14).

Read Matthew 18:21-35. The onyx speaks of the darkness of our debt that Yeshua paid with His blood. If He forgave us, how could we not forgive those who wounded us? Joseph released his brothers from the debt after testing their hearts, but his own heart had been tested through years of suffering. No doubt his lessons began in the pit where his brothers threw him, then in the house of Potiphar when he was falsely accused, and once more when he was forgotten by the cupbearer. The inward struggle of his soul molded his God-given identity. No doubt this very thing would mold Manasseh and Ephraim first-hand. Joseph's life speaks volumes to us all to relinquish our debtors and our own debts into God's sea of forgetfulness, the blood of Yeshua!

The onyx stone serves as a reminder of God's vast forgiveness and redemption to Manasseh. Yeshua carries us upon His heart perpetually as the Great High Priest. As He gazes upon the onyx stone (or Manasseh and Ephraim), all He can see is forgiveness. It is important, Manasseh, that you see yourself as forgiven as God sees you. He does not see your past; He sees your destiny. Black is the absence of all color. Many associate black with the idea of sin. I charge you, Manasseh, not to see yourself in the light of your fallen nature and its condemnation, but rather the forgiveness afforded to you by the precious blood of Yeshua and its call to repentance. Forgiveness is the pardon of shame, for it is for freedom that Christ has set us free. Manasseh, see that onyx stone, dear brother and sister, as the absence of your sin, not the presence of it. When the Holy Spirit convicts us of our sin, see it under the blood and come to repentance. There is no guilt in the Father's perfect love. He always provides a way of escape, for forgiveness paves the way to life. Manasseh is a minister of transformation because of his God-given nature of forgiving and forgetting. He can see a soul bound in sin and be moved with compassion because he sees the individual in his predestined state. Manasseh sees with the eyes of the Father and is moved with compassion by what Abba sees. What a powerful ministry and tool this is. I charge you, Manasseh, not only to see others in this way, but to impart this ministry of transformation as you serve and live in a perpetual state of laid-down love.

## THE ONYX SPEAKS OF CHARACTER SHAPING

Onyx is an extremely sensitive and pliable stone that is often used to make cameos. The onyx speaks of Manasseh's character being molded by the Master Creator Himself. Manasseh is a very pliable soul, a trait that serves as both a strength and a facade. They are sensitive not only to the Holy Spirit, but to others as well. People motivated by mercy must guard their gifting with discernment. Manasseh, be aware of who influences or molds you. Unforgiveness, old hurts, and idolatry can mar the beautiful living stone that you are. Repentance and forgiveness will fashion you into a gemstone of the Father's brilliant glory and love. The Holy Spirit is your teacher; beware of any influence that leads you into compromising your righteous inheritance.

## THE ONYX STONE SPEAKS OF MYSTERIES REVEALED IN DREAMS

Read Psalm 78:1 and Psalm 18:11-12. Joseph is known as a great dreamer. He left his sons the heritage of the mysteries of God revealed in dreams. In Genesis 37:19 Joseph's brothers call him "dreamer." The Hebrew word for this is *ba'al*, meaning: "ruler over, leader, to have dominion, owner or possessor." This verse speaks of Joseph as the possessor of dreams; more importantly, that he had dominion in his God-given ability to have dreams and interpret them. Dreams speak of the dark sayings, meaning the depths or mysteries that lie within the heart of God. Psalm 18 tells of how God makes darkness His hiding place. Mysteries of the Father's heart are waiting to be released in this end-time hour. There are mysteries in which God hides Himself. He is calling us to seek Him wholeheartedly, not on the road traveled by many, but in the narrow place, the secret place of the stairs. Read Song of Songs 2:14.

God gives His pearls to chaste hearts who have sought Him in secret places. He can only entrust deep mysteries to those who have been refined by fire and are willing to seek Him in the secret place. Revelation can be tainted or mixed when agenda and pride enters in. God will cause His dreamers to go through a "sifting" process to purge out "mixing." Revelation comes in the secret place void of personal agendas, praise, opinions, and influence of others. We see this take place in the life of Joseph. He gave Joseph the gift as a young boy, but it took years of sifting to mature him before he became the possessor of dreams he is still known as. Divine wisdom and revelation are treasures God wants to release, but He wants them released with purity. If you are called to be God's dreamer of dreams, to interpret and administrate through them, He will chasten you as He did Joseph. Manasseh learned this early on, as his father passed on this innate ability to know the mysteries of God. God conceals in order to reveal meaning. He requires our hearts to remain in the secret place where He thunders great mysteries. Read Proverbs 25:2.

Manasseh, you are a possessor of dreams. Possess your God-given identity and be thrust into the dominion God designed for you. Seek Him in the secret place with your whole heart and you will find Him. Though He has sifted you, know that this process will reveal who God is and who you are designed to be in His glorious image!

## THE ONYX SPEAKS OF THE DARK NIGHT OF THE SOUL

Read Psalm 88:6-18. Have you ever felt abandoned by God? Joseph must have a time or two (maybe even often) in his troubles. Through his legacy Joseph testifies to his sons and to us that God is faithful. We each have a dark night of the soul in our lifetimes. The enemy would love for us to believe we are abandoned. The facade the enemy longs to perpetuate is that God has forsaken us. We can combat this lie with the truth that Yeshua is our Emmanuel, God with us. Yeshua, acquainted with our weakness, experienced the dark night of the soul also. Read Mark 15:34.

David also spoke of this when he wrote, "If I ascend to heaven, You are there; If I make my bed in Sheol, behold, You are there" (Psalm 139:8). He also went on to attest to the Lord's faithfulness as Emmanuel:

*Therefore my heart is glad and my glory rejoices; My flesh also will dwell securely. For You will not abandon my soul to Sheol; Nor will You allow Your Holy One to undergo decay. You will make known to me the path of life; In Your presence is fullness of joy; In Your right hand there are pleasures forever* (Psalm 16:9-11).

As a minister of mercy and transformation glory, Manasseh is called to recount the faithfulness God and the relinquishment of debt and condemnation's guilt. Mercy is the birthing ground of hope, and hope enlightens our path to destiny. Manasseh's character of mercy is formed through great suffering. In suffering, they identify and take on Christ's nature of forgiving and forgetting. Those of this tribe cannot truly have compassion until they themselves have gone through the dark night of soul, been tested, tried, and purified. Every Manasseh goes through this process in order to become a minister of transformation and reconciliation.

## THE SYMBOL OF MANASSEH

*The righteous man will flourish like the palm tree, He will grow like a cedar in Lebanon. Planted in the house of God, they will flourish in the courts of the Lord. They will still yield fruit in old age; they shall be full of sap and very green, to declare that the Lord is upright; He is my rock, and there is no unrighteousness in Him* (Psalm 92:12-15).

The symbol of Manasseh is the palm tree. It carries connotations of righteousness, integrity, beauty, fruitfulness, royalty, rest, and oasis. Each one of these attributes can be found within the noble tribe of Manasseh. Its Hebrew derivative is "Tamar." You may remember Tamar in the story of Judah (Genesis 38:6-26). Though she is not of this tribe, she does exude its spiritual truths within her name. She was known as a beautiful woman, no doubt, but Tamar was most importantly known for her wisdom, discernment, and righteousness. A matriarch of faith, Tamar is a beacon to the tribe of Manasseh, calling them into their heritage of righteousness.

## MANASSEH: THE PLANTING OF THE LORD, DISPLAYING THE FATHER'S NATURE

Manasseh expresses the Father's nature within them as the planting of the Lord in many ways seen in their symbol. The palm tree, with its many metaphors and symbolism, carries a call to every Manasseh. The call is simple to plant your roots deep within the heart of God's nature. The very core of God's forgiving nature to us is seen in the fruit of longsuffering.

## SPIRITUAL ATMOSPHERE

A palm tree endures many elements of the atmosphere around it: rain, wind, and heat. Manassehs have the spiritual grace of being acclimated to the spiritual atmosphere around them. They are, by nature, sensitive yet stoic, upright yet bending and can go through seasons of drought and still remain faithful and upright. Spiritual atmosphere is both a training ground and place of dominion for every Manasseh. In the school of the Holy Spirit, Manassehs learn to be acclimated to the changing patterns around them.

## IN THE HEAT OF THE DESERT

*God is compassionate and merciful: longsuffering and plenteous in mercy* (Psalm 103:8 KJV).

Longsuffering is the cultivation of the Spirit's work of patience, forgiveness, and selflessness in our lives. For the tribe of Manasseh, it is the daily school of the Spirit working God's transformation glory within them. Picture this: a lone palm tree in the desert. Year in and year out it experiences the unrelenting harsh rays of the sun. Despite little to no rain, it flourishes. It endures the abuse of the elements and many passersby, and yet it still provides shelter and oasis to all who rest within its shade.

Think of our Creator and His longsuffering with us, His Creation. His heart is ravaged by our rebellion, lack of trust, and pride, and yet He still bears with us in His infinite grace to redeem us, sustain us, and ultimately transform us. How vast and limitless His nature of longsuffering is for us. He longs for us to mirror this back to creation. Longsuffering is a defining key DNA structure within the spiritual identity of every Manasseh. It is the nature of longsuffering that works with love to bear all things, believe all things, and hope all things. Longsuffering is not a doormat, but bears the fruit of discernment, having been founded upon the nature of God's love, wisdom, and forgiveness. Longsuffering sees the destiny and hope laid before us all: the final prize of Christ-likeness.

The nature of longsuffering is a mirror of Heaven's reflection. It never judges, but bears and champions destiny. Like the palm tree, its strength and reliability provides rest to the weary. Manasseh, like the palm tree, is a quiet strength, withholding against unreliable factors of the atmosphere. God is chastening the longsuffering nature of every Manasseh so that they may in turn bring the ministry of reconciliation.

Longsuffering also speaks of the endurance of our soul and its journey into the transformation we all must go through in life. Longsuffering is a conditioning agent for the race we run.

> *Do you not know that those who run in a race all run, but only one receives the prize? Run in such a way that you may win. Everyone who competes in the games exercises self-control in all things. They then do it to receive a perishable wreath, but we an imperishable. Therefore I run in such a way, as not without aim; I box in such a way, as not beating the air; but I discipline my body and make it my slave, so that, after I have preached to others, I myself will not be disqualified* (I Corinthians 9:24-27).

Living in the state of mercy and forgiveness affords us the grace to live a life abounding in the fruit of longsuffering. When we are fixed on the person of Yeshua, who is mercy, and receive forgiveness for ourselves and others, we can run the race, focused on our prize. Condemnation, unforgiveness, judgment, and rejection are rabbit trails that distract us from Yeshua.

The heat also speaks of the process of refinement within Manasseh. Manasseh goes through often long periods of refinement on the back side of the desert. Manasseh's refinement reaches its maturity when those of this tribe produce fruit in extreme testing by fire. For every Manasseh, inheriting dominion happens only when they forgive themselves. It is then that they reach full maturity as ministers of transformation. The desert is lonely, often not public, a place of soul-wrenching revelation. There, a crisis of belief transforms Manasseh into a stately palm tree that testifies of righteousness. Manasseh's sanctification process frees him of the influence of his past, wounds, compromise, and foolish naïveté. This process affords this tribe discernment with their mercy gifting. The desert is tough, sometimes unrelenting, dear Manasseh, but let patience have its work in you. Manasseh tends to flourish in spite of public opinion and influence, as the spiritual grace of mercy and forgiveness germinates deep beneath the soil of their souls. Read James 1:2-4.

## WINDS OF CHANGE

Winds of change come to all of us. They come from unexpected sources, often taking us by surprise in both supernatural and natural realms. Winds of change bring us transformation. To Manasseh, this holds a wealth of insight. Picture this: winds are beating at the very structure of the palm tree. It's tossed back and forth like a rag doll, but remains unchanged. It is important to note that there are two different winds that will blow in our life—winds of chaos that are brought by the enemy and winds of change brought by the Holy Spirit to transform us. Winds of chaos come to bring idolatry, distraction, and destruction. Winds of change come to bring us a revelation of His glory. Take heed, Manasseh, to which wind is blowing in your life, for God is bringing you to task. He is calling to you at the same time the enemy is bringing his chaos against your identity and dominion. What saves you? Being planted in the work of forgiveness.

Forgiveness comes solely through the incorruptible Cross of Yeshua. There is no stability outside of the work of the Cross. Every mature Manasseh knows this and takes this to heart, for they have learned through times of great shifting to allow the winds of change to fortify their God-given nature. This is how God forms integrity and righteousness within them. Winds of change always come with grace. Winds of chaos always bring striving, self-righteousness, and idolatry.

Turn your spiritual senses on, dear Manasseh. Be mindful of the spiritual atmosphere. It is important that you discern what wind is blowing. Manasseh's have great strength. No matter how far they are bent or stretched, they always maintain a righteous character. When facade(s) have control, they cannot bend, due to idolatry and unforgiveness. Sharing in the sufferings of Yeshua is that stability that brings transformation glory and ultimately the work of reconciliation. Embrace a lifestyle of forgiveness. Let go of all idolatry, for such is the way to life eternal!

Manasseh, know this—the two winds will call you to two different feasts. The winds of chaos will bring you to a feast that your enemy has prepared for you. It is enticing, but once you have digested the malnourishing junk food he has spread for you, you will find yourself still hungry, unsatisfied, and alone. With Satan's feast comes a death to your destiny and identity. You must stay planted in the work of the Cross in order to discern.

## MANASSEH SOUNDS THE MERCY CRY!

Read Isaiah 64:1, Psalm 68:9, and II Chronicles 6:26-28. Manasseh is that mercy cry resounding in the earth. Beloved, the earth is dry, desperately needing an outpouring of the one true God. Floodgates of the deep are waiting to be released. I solemnly urge you, Manasseh, to possess this mercy cry and release it in the earth. Locked within you are deep floodgates of mercy and outpouring. Whether in times of judgment or revival, you must sound this cry: that the King of Glory would rend the heavens and come down. Ultimately it is a call to usher in the King and His millennial reign. His second coming is nigh. Cry out, O mighty Manasseh. Resound your mercy trumpet, for the King is coming from on high!

> *...and yet He did not leave Himself without witness, in that He did good and gave you rains from heaven and fruitful seasons, satisfying your hearts with food and gladness* (Acts 14:17).

> *Therefore be patient, brethren, until the coming of the Lord. The farmer waits for the precious produce of the soil, being patient about it, until it gets the early and late rains.*

*You too be patient; strengthen your hearts, for the coming of the Lord is near* (James 5:7-8).

Through drought and flood, Manasseh is faithful. They have the innate ability to be sustained by grace during extreme seasons of testing and blessing. Perhaps young Manasseh gleaned intently the lessons of his father Joseph during the years of famine and years of drought in Egypt. These extreme seasons of testing brought Israel through a great milestone of identity and destiny. Perhaps you are on the threshold of a season of great testing. Stay faithful—rain will come. Perhaps you are in a season of blessing; stay faithful, apportion the outpouring from heaven's storehouse accordingly as the Father leads you.

Manasseh, the storm clouds of Heaven are pregnant with rain. The fountains of the deep are groaning to be released. You, dear brothers and sisters, hold the key to revival: the mercy cry. Latter and former rains cry out from the throne eternal: My Son is coming soon, and He is bringing His reward with Him!

Read Matthew 24:33-42. Mercy triumphs over judgment. Resound your shofar with a mercy call, Manasseh. Take up your righteous horn and blow! To the four corners of the earth your heavenly gusts you do blow, in His power you will show the world the return of the King, strong and mighty on high!

## JACOB'S PROPHECY OVER JOSEPH

*"Joseph is a fruitful bough, A fruitful bough by a spring; Its branches run over a wall. The archers bitterly attacked him, and shot at him and harassed him; But his bow remained firm, And his arms were agile, from the hands of the Mighty One of Jacob (From there is the Shepherd, the Stone of Israel), from the God of your father who helps you, And by the Almighty who blesses you with blessings of heaven above, Blessings of the deep that lies beneath, Blessings of the breasts and of the womb. The blessings of your father have surpassed the blessings of my ancestors up to the utmost bound of the everlasting hills; may they be on the head of Joseph, and on the crown of the head of the one distinguished among his brother*s" (Genesis 49:22-26 ).

## "JOSEPH IS A FRUITFUL BOUGH"

Joseph's life taught his sons and many generations to come many important lessons. One very key lesson of Joseph is fruitfulness. Both symbols of Manasseh (the palm tree) and Ephraim (the grape vine) emanate the spiritual DNA passed down through their father, Joseph. Abiding is a key lesson for us all. It is the security of life in the secret place that rests solely in the nature of the Father.

Read John 15:1-11. To bear fruit is a kingdom principle. We must reproduce the kingdom in our character, ministry, and in making disciples. Bearing fruit is a key element of intimacy because it is our calling to abide in the nature of God. Yeshua said, "No man come to the Father but by Me" (John 14:6). That way is by abiding. Abiding in the vine is the daily crucified walk to which we are all called. Manasseh walks this walk by abiding in God's forgiveness. Yeshua was the perfect example of abiding in forgiveness. Another part to the equation of abiding and forgiveness is repentance. We must bear fruit in keeping with repentance.

A "fruitful bough" stems from the Hebrew word *ben* or *bane*, literally translating "son, a builder of a family name." It is important to note that this term can also include an adopted son. Manasseh and Ephraim were brought into Jacob's family not as grandsons, but as sons like Reuben and Simeon. There are no grandchildren in God's family, just sons and daughters, direct heirs to the throne. To this day *aliyah* (the act of returning home to Israel) has a law of return based on the fact that if a child has a father who is Jewish but a Gentile mother, he or she is permitted to make *aliyah* under this provision. However, they are not considered directly Jewish. They must convert to Judaism. You and I are heavenly citizens, with full rights to the Father, His kingdom, and inheritance. Both sons carry a ministry of reconciliation. Manasseh specifically carries it through the mercy call.

## "A FRUITFUL BOUGH BY A SPRING"

Manasseh drives his source of life from the living waters of Heaven itself. For Manasseh, these streams are streams of mercy flowing from the Father's heart to lovingly lavish upon His creation. A fruitful bough by a spring reiterates Manasseh's mercy call, a call to abide in the very nature of Mercy Divine. To be sustained in abiding, you must have a constant life source of Heaven's living waters, which are never stagnant. They provide healing, life, transformation, and a continual flow of kingdom reality as we abide in the Vine. Unforgiveness, self-doubt, fear—these things can hinder these living waters from flowing freely.

Manasseh learns this in his journey of transformation; otherwise he would die on the vine. The eternal spring of Heaven encourages Manasseh's branch to grow and to continually regenerate itself. Its fruit must abide in forgiveness and repentance. Manasseh, take care that your waters do not become embittered with the bile of unforgiveness, self-doubt, and fear, for to do so is to cut yourself off from the very life source you so desperately need. Joseph learned this through much suffering, repentance, self-discovery, and forgiveness. God did not add and multiply Joseph until he subtracted and divided those things that caused his streams to become stagnant. Joseph came into dominion when he relinquished his soul wounds into the mercy heart of God. This act of his will allowed the Spirit's work of transformation and the free flow of the eternal spring of Heaven. Bitterness and unforgiveness will shut up living streams. Forgiveness and repentance toward yourself and others will release them.

In 1994 I had an encounter with my own mercy call for Israel. Alone in intercession one day, I began to travail for Israel. During this travail, I received an open vision or encounter. Yeshua was walking the road Golgotha. When I gazed on Him, the crown of thorns became prominent to me. So I asked the Lord, "Why must You wear the crown of thorns?" He answered me and said, "As the thorns pierce My brow, drops of blood obstruct My vision. This is My Father's will, to see with eyes of compassion." At that time I began to weep bitterly. He placed His crown on my head and said, "Now see with new eyes, the eyes of compassion. See the brokenhearted, see the broken, see the lost, see the wounded, and see the captives in their prisons. My daughter, go to them and free them. Be My healing virtue to the lost sheep of Israel."

For about two-and-a-half hours I wept bitterly. I felt the crown of thorns pressing my brow. My vision was obstructed by the blood that ran into my eyes. It stung like salty seawater would. This encounter was one that shook the core of my being. Self-love (the fleshly kind) seemed frivolous compared to the eternal heart of the Father weighing upon me for His precious creation.

Manasseh, your identity and calling is to be immersed in the crown of thorns, for when you see through the eyes of Yeshua, who is Mercy Divine, you will never be the same. Your key to intimacy and to building the kingdom is your mercy call. The streams of mercy are beckoning you to come deeper into the heart of the Father and abide there forevermore.

## "THE ARCHERS BITTERLY ATTACKED HIM, AND SHOT AT HIM AND HARASSED HIM; BUT HIS BOW REMAINED FIRM, AND HIS ARMS WERE AGILE"

Read Matthew 5:10-12. This portion of Jacob's prophecy refers to the story in Genesis 37 where Joseph is persecuted by his own brothers. Whether it is by our own natural families or our spiritual ones, we all have walked through some bitter persecution. Joseph's dark night of the soul began by persecution from his brothers. The Hebrew word *archers* in this text is the same Hebrew word for *husband*, which is *ba'al*.

Read Matthew 10:35-37. Joseph certainly knew persecution in his own household. There are many who come in the name of the Bridegroom who wound their sisters and brothers. Yeshua said, "Blessed are those who are persecuted for righteousness sake, for theirs is the kingdom of Heaven." Suffering is an agent of great transformation. God uses the suffering Joseph endured from his brothers' persecution to develop the nature of forgiveness, compassion, and righteousness within him, thereby building his faith. Manassehs often learn kingdom through suffering and develop their character of mercy because of it.

Read Romans 8:17-19. Suffering is an identifier of the nature of Christ and the work of the Cross within us. Suffering is that refiner's fire that God allows us to go through to bring us to the knowledge of who He is and who we are in His image. Suffering buffets us during the dark night of the soul, testing the intentions of the heart to the very core. No doubt Joseph was tested severely during his dark night of the soul. He was molded by his own journey of transformation. God tore down the facades in Joseph's life of how he saw God and himself and brought Joseph into a place of knowing God and who Joseph was created to be. The Father lovingly purged Joseph's heart intentions of hurt and bitterness to bring healing to him and his family. Read II Corinthians 1:4-6.

Corrie Ten Boom and her sister, Betsy, suffered greatly while imprisoned in Nazi concentration camps for hiding Jews during the Holocaust. During her imprisonment, Betsy made a profound statement that resonates mercy, comfort, and forgiveness to us all when she said, "There is no pit so deep that God's love is not deeper still."[2] Corrie later said, "When we confess ours sins…God casts them into the deepest ocean, gone forever…I believe God places a sign out there that says, NO FISHING ALLOWED." [3]

The Psalmist wrote "in the multitude of anxieties your comforts delight my soul" (Psalm 94:19). Joseph found that very same comfort in his deepest and darkest pit. Yeshua said He would never leave us or forsake us. He also promised us the Holy Spirit would be our Comforter. Allow the suffering in your life to reveal God's glory, even as these great heroes of our faith did. Joseph's bow remained firm during time of testing, meaning he allowed transformation to work through the darkest night of his soul and bring him to the knowledge of glory of God within Him as a priceless living stone. O Manasseh, allow the comfort of His love to heal you and the refiner's fire to change you, for in so doing you too will be revealed!

"FROM THERE IS THE SHEPHERD, THE STONE OF ISRAEL, FROM THE GOD OF YOUR FATHER WHO HELPS YOU, AND BY THE ALMIGHTY WHO BLESSES YOU WITH BLESSINGS OF HEAVEN ABOVE"

Manasseh and Ephraim both are called to leadership, specifically an administrative mantle, which may be expressed in callings such as being a pastor, counselor, advisor, administrator, and apostle. Though both hold this mantle, it is expressed differently, for Manasseh is low-key and laid back in manner. Manasseh's character often shrinks from the limelight, while his brother Ephraim craves the foreground. Manasseh tends to lean toward passive leadership, and Ephraim takes more of an aggressive approach. It is not that Manasseh cannot be aggressive, but it takes a true wind of the Spirit to push him to the foreground. Ephraim, on the other hand, sometimes needs to be pulled back. It is important to have Christ as the head in all things, but especially if you are called to leadership. Yeshua is both the Great Shepherd and the Stone of Israel. Read John 10: 1-15 and I Peter 2:4-10.

God was making a distinction, a seal if you will, for the sons of Joseph. Their mother was a Gentile, so He made it clear they were to be adopted into His family. God revealed

Yeshua, the head, the great Shepherd and Cornerstone of Israel, welcoming Manasseh and Ephraim into sonship! To a people (meaning the Gentiles) who had not received mercy, he grafted into his family to receive mercy. What a confirmation to Manasseh of his sonship and the mercy call!

## "BLESSINGS OF THE DEEP THAT LIES BENEATH…"

This scripture portion has a deep and poignant meaning for all, but especially the sons of Joseph. To understand this, we must understand the depth of what God was saying when Manasseh and Ephraim where brought into the family of God. Read Genesis 47:8-22.

It would seem peculiar that Israel (formerly Jacob) would give the double portion to Ephraim and not Manasseh. Israel had insight into the heart of God. Was Ephraim favored more than Manasseh? Other sons of Israel had foregone the double portion due to various sins (Reuben and his concubine, Simeon and Levi, the sin at Shechem, Judah and Tamar, etc.).

## THE RIGHT AND LEFT HAND OF GOD

The Lord revealed a mystery beginning with a friend and then added to the revelation to me concerning the right and left hand of God. He revealed that the right hand was synonymous with Heaven, the supernatural, and the dominion thereof. The left hand represented the earth, the natural, and the dominion thereof. What the Lord had impressed to me was the union of the heart of the earth, where the knowledge of the glory has been held up, and Heaven's storehouses, where mysteries are held.

> *Let His left hand be under my head and his right hand embrace me* (Song of Songs 8:3).

Yeshua began to speak to me personally about coming into perfect love. Some call it maturity, others the fullness of the kingdom. It is essentially both. The transition and transformation of abiding in perfect love is our journey into becoming or making *aliyah* into the living habitation of the Father.

The Father said, "I am bringing My left hand and my right hand together." The scripture goes on to say in verse 4: "I want you to swear, O daughters of Jerusalem, Do not arouse or awaken my love until she pleases." What He was impressing on me is that there is an appointed time to fully awaken. This awakening is about the fullness, where Heaven meets the earth (Heaven being the right hand and Earth being the left). In verse 5 it says: "beneath the apple tree I awakened you," the apple tree being the Cross.

Beloved, we are at a crucial time, for the fullness of the kingdom has been groaning to be released where Heaven meets earth. Yeshua taught us to pray, "Let your will be done on earth as it is in heaven" (Matthew 6:10). This prayer is a key to knowing that the heart of God is to restore the earth and its union to Heaven. In Genesis 49:25, when Israel blesses Manasseh and Ephraim the second time, he says: "And by the Almighty who blesses you with blessings of heaven above, blessings of the deep that lies beneath, blessings of the womb…" He is blessing them with dominion in Heaven and in earth. The storehouses of heaven, where our treasures lie, and the places of the deep, where the very knowledge of the glory lies, are going to simultaneously be poured upon the earth. The left also can correlate to judgment and the right righteousness. How appropriate that God would have Israel lay His left hand upon Manasseh, who testifies that mercy triumphs over judgment! Do you see the profound depth in what He planned? Manasseh is the intercession for God's mercy upon the earth and Ephraim the intercession of Heaven's destiny. Manasseh, gifted with compassion, cries out for the fulfillment of Heaven meeting earth. What a glorious inheritance you have, brethren.

## MOSES' PROPHECY

*Of Joseph he said, "Blessed of the Lord be his land, with the choice things of heaven, with the dew, And from the deep lying beneath, And with the choice yield of the sun, And with the choice produce of the months. And with the best things of the ancient mountains, And with the choice things of the everlasting hills, And with the choice things of the earth and its fullness, and the favor of Him who dwelt in the bush. Let it come to the head of Joseph, and to the crown of the head of the one distinguished among his brothers. As the firstborn of his ox, majesty is his and his horns are the horns of the wild ox; with them he will push the peoples, All at once, to the ends of the earth, and those are the ten thousands of Ephraim, And those are the thousands of Manasseh"* (Deuteronomy 33:13-17).

### "OF JOSEPH HE SAID, "BLESSED OF THE LORD BE HIS LAND.."

This portion of Moses' prophecy basically reiterates the last portion of Jacob's prophecy. He was also speaking of the fruitfulness and reproduction in verse 14.

### "AS THE FIRSTBORN OF HIS OX…"

The ox is the second symbol for the tribe of Ephraim but is also identified with both sons due to their father, Joseph. The ox, as mentioned before, is a picture of the suffering servant, whom we know is Christ Himself. This is a calling for both sons to lay hold of Christ and His nature as the suffering servant. To Manasseh specifically it is a call to serve in compassion and forgiveness. It says that they will "push the peoples." Jacob said out of Ephraim that many nations would come. Could it be that these two sons have been given a portion to bring in the fullness of the Gentiles? In some way I feel they do play an integral part, even a calling to push, through intercession, apostolic leadership, discipleship, and selfless servant-motivated administration. With the unction of Heaven and the cry resounding for mercy in the earth, they will push creation to return to the Father.

### "AND THOSE ARE THE TEN THOUSANDS OF EPHRAIM, AND THOSE ARE THE THOUSANDS OF MANASSEH."

Manasseh's numbers were not insignificant compared to his younger brother, Ephraim's. What is important to see is that Manasseh is a building block for his brother Ephraim to bring the nations into the knowledge of the glory. Both sons have pivotal callings in the Body of Christ. Ephraim's gifts are multiplied because of Manasseh's intercession and quiet yet powerful leadership. Manasseh's numbers are smaller so that he may be effective where God has called him. He is not "less than," but appropriated a spiritual grace in hidden places, smaller numbers for covert operations of mercy and love within the kingdom of God. Manasseh is called to the narrow place, a journey that will take him down less traveled roads. Manasseh is small but mighty and so very crucial to the kingdom.

### THE FAÇADE OF MANASSEH
### GIDEON: SWAYING YET UPRIGHT

*And what more shall I say? For time will fail me if I tell of Gideon, Barak, Samson, Jephthah, of David and Samuel and the prophets, who by faith conquered kingdoms, performed acts of righteousness, obtained promises, shut the mouths of lions..*(Hebrews 11:32-33).

Read Judges Chapters 6-8. Gideon was a righteous man. His forefather, Abraham, was known for his righteousness. We are righteous through faith, not by our deeds or how good we act, but by our total reliance in God. Gideon embodied the tribe Manasseh in his strength and gifting, and also the facades in his walk with the Lord. He is accounted as a great hero in the faith according to this scripture in Hebrews 11. Gideon is that palm tree tried and tested by the spiritual atmosphere around him, challenged and paralyzed by his own frailties, and propelled to greatness through his rocky faith. He was tossed every which way, yet he remained firmly planted. There is much to learn from him and the inheritance he left for the tribe of Manasseh.

## THE LEAVEN OF IDOLATRY

*Then the sons of Israel did what was evil in the sight of the Lord; and the Lord gave them into the hands of Midian seven years. The power of Midian prevailed against Israel. Because of Midian the sons of Israel made for themselves the dens which were in the mountains and the caves and the strongholds* (Judges 6:1-2).

Israel's spiritual atmosphere during the time of Gideon's conquest was chaotic at best. That atmosphere was a direct result of their idolatry. To better understand this point, it is important to note the history of Midian and Manasseh's tie to its idolatry. In Genesis 25:2 Abraham (after the death of Sarah) marries Keturah, who gives birth to a son named Midian. The sons of Midian become a nomadic tribe from which Joseph is sold into slavery. Moses himself flees to Midian, marries Zipporah, a Midianite woman, and receives counsel from Jethro, the God-fearing priest of Midian. After this, a breakdown comes to the Midianites whereby they fall into idolatry. Moses then orders the destruction of the Midianites because of the sin of Peor in Genesis 25. Yet we find Gideon facing this same stronghold. Why do we find Israel yet again oppressed? The leaven of idolatry was never fully dealt with. In Genesis 31:34 Rachel takes her father's household idols and hides them. Rachel's son, Manasseh's father, marries an Egyptian woman who has a heritage of idolatry. The small leaven kept growing generationally until a son of Manasseh is coming head-to-head with it. Manasseh's part in this would be his tolerance through fear. Tolerance is the breeding ground for idolatry. We cannot simply sweep these things under the rug. They must be purged under the blood!

"BECAUSE OF MIDIAN THE SONS OF ISRAEL MADE FOR THEMSELVES
THE DENS WHICH WERE IN THE MOUNTAINS AND
THE CAVES AND THE STRONGHOLDS."

*…or how can anyone enter the strong man's house and carry off his property, unless he first binds the strong man? And then he will plunder his house* (Matthew 12:29).

The Midianite(s) had the legal right to plunder the Israelites because of the idolatry that was never fully dealt with. Gideon is faced with the generational curses that developed because the strongman was never fully bound. In Judges 6:3 it goes on to say that the Israelites were attacked during a time they had sown their harvest. Their harvest was vulnerable because of the hardness in their own hearts.

Read Matthew 13: 5. Beware, Manasseh, of the erosion of the soil of your own heart. Idolatry will cause the Word of God to fall upon the rocky and unstable places, never finding true root in your soul. Your ground must be tilled before it is planted, watered by the Word. When your rocks of idolatry and fear are plucked out, you can receive the proper radiation of the Son and His glory to illuminate the condition of your heart and soul. Read Jeremiah 17:9.

### "FOR THEY WOULD COME UP WITH THEIR LIVESTOCK ..."

In His mercy, God allowed Israel to be overtaken by their enemies in order that they might return to Him. Israel needed the Father's chastening in order to recognize the gross loss of His presence during their idolatry. They lost sight of communion with Him because their idols had hardened their hearts yet again. In verse 10 the Lord speaks through His prophet that this calamity had befallen them due to their disobedience. The stage is set for God to send a mighty deliverer with the mercy call when judgment is due. It was the righteous judgment of the Lord that brought Israel to this point where He raised up Gideon.

> *Then the angel of the Lord came and sat under the oak that was in Ophrah, which belonged to Joash the Abiezrite as his son Gideon was beating out wheat in the wine press in order to save it from the Midianites. The angel of the Lord appeared to him and said to him, "Adonai is with you, O valiant warrior"* (Judges 6:11-12).

Notice how God addresses Gideon, "O valiant warrior." He is calling him according to his God-given identity and not the façade that answers him back in verse 13.

> *Then Gideon said to him, "O my Lord, if the Lord is with us, why then has all this happened to us? And where are all His miracles which our fathers told us about, saying, 'Did not the Lord bring us up from Egypt?' But now the Lord has abandoned us and given us into the hand of Midian"* (Judges 6:13).

The stronghold of fear reigned over Gideon as doubt and despair; its minions strengthened its resolve over Gideon's soul. This generational curse within him of fear and tolerance was challenged as God called Gideon to awaken to his true identity as a valiant warrior. Gideon literally means "destroyer." God is taking Gideon to task to rise up above his own idol as it overtakes the oppressors of Israel caused by idolatry.

> *The Lord looked at him and said, "Go in this your strength and deliver Israel from the hand of Midian. Have I not sent you?" He said to Him, "O Lord, how shall I deliver Israel? Behold, my family is the least in Manasseh, and I am the youngest in my father's house"* (Judges 6:14-15).

God commands Gideon to *go in this your strength* (meaning to go in the spiritual grace with which He had equipped Gideon). The Father has given us each authority where He has called us to stand. Gideon was in his harvest field at the time the Lord called him to his kingdom moment of destiny.

> *I, therefore, the prisoner of the Lord, entreat you to walk in a manner worthy of your calling with which you have been called.... But to each one of us grace was given according to the measure of Messiah's gift* (Ephesians 4:1,7).

Gideon had a perception problem. He could not see his own greatness. God designed him and his tribe to be small but mighty to confound the wisdom of men. Read I Corinthians 1:26-31.

Gideon continues to be atrophied by fear until he has an encounter with the Lord in verse 22. It takes an encounter to change Gideon's perception. God did not call him to lay the fleece before him. He used it, however, to bring Gideon to an encounter with Himself and a crisis of belief. The crisis Gideon had (and every Manasseh goes through) is the belief in himself. Dear Manasseh, you must see your smallness as your greatness. God chooses you in your weakness to show His greatness. You are a covert operation of God's mercy, forgiveness, and love sent into the narrow place to overthrow kingdoms of darkness.

> *Then Gideon built an altar there to the Lord and named it the Lord is Peace. To this day it is still in Ophrah of the Abiezrites* (Judges 6:24).

Gideon's dark night of the soul brought him to the revelation of who God was. Hounded by fear and insecurities, he was continually challenged by the Lord to surrender his facades. The Lord revealed Himself as his peace to bring Gideon to the task of surrendering his own idolatry. The Hebrew word peace, *Shalom,* in essence means *let there be nothing between me and Thee.* Manasseh, God has an encounter for you where you are confronted with the deficiency of your façade and the glorious image of God within you. Take your perceptions to the altar of the Lord, where He will reveal who He is and who you were fearfully and wonderfully made to be.

## KINGDOM COVERT OPS

Read Judges 6:25-27. Kingdom covert ops are usually not just for those we serve, but serve as an agent of transformation for us as well. God called Gideon to build an altar that would testify against the very stronghold that plagued him and his people. Baal (the idol of his father) and Asherah have a long history as objects of idol worship in the Bible. Baal is known as the husband, prince, or king of Heaven, and Asherah is known as the queen of Heaven, goddess of fertility. Gideon's father was irate when Gideon tore down his family idols. God called Gideon to cut down the Asherah pole and use it as firewood for the altar. He was calling Gideon to rise up and oppose the kingdom of darkness, not only in his own family, but in all areas where the presence of these idols had consistently drawn His people into idolatry.

These two particular gods were the vilest in nature. They claimed to be the gods of Heaven itself. They were the gods Jezebel worshiped. Baal and Asherah wanted dominion over Heaven. These false gods ruled over and trumped all other false gods. Their purpose was to directly defy the deity and authority of God Himself. They were robbing Israel of intimacy with the Father with their demand to be worshipped. Gideon is called upon to defy the enemies of Heaven and make the rightful claim that Elohim was God of Heaven and earth. God continually used this conquest as a covert op in Gideon's own life. He didn't allow Gideon to rely on his resources, but instead forced Gideon to be dependent only on Him. God was out to prove to Gideon that He could use the very thing that Gideon thought disqualified him to qualify him. That is why God cut the size and strength of Gideon's army down. God was looking for fearless men who would be watchful and full of faith.

Gideon was swaying like a palm tree in a hurricane, back-and-forth between fear and faith. God brings us to task to show His glory. He wants our total dependence on Him. To be truly poor in spirit means that our reliance must be on Him, not our abilities or the lack thereof; we become less so He can be greater. Manasseh, God has a pivotal moment of destiny for you where He will call you to task. Be sensitive to His calling. Fear not your own greatness, but possess it!

## DOMINION RELEASED TO MANASSEH, THE OASIS IN THE EARTH

> *The righteous man will flourish like the palm tree, he will grow like a cedar in Lebanon, planted in the house of the Lord, he will flourish in the courts of our God* (Psalm 92:12-13).

Manasseh, you will reach maturity in Christ as you transform by grace into a stately palm tree flourishing in the courts of the Lord. You possess dominion as you become an oasis in the earth through righteousness by faith. Though your faith may have weathered severe atmospheric changes, Christ alone causes you to remain upright. Many a weary soul will find rest beneath your shade. Rest is an important key to the kingdom. It is pivotal to the glory of God. Rest is who Yeshua is, and He has called you to reveal Him as an oasis in the earth. You have been given a unique mantle of the rest of the Lord. You come into the rest of the Lord as you relinquish fear, insecurities, and forgive yourself. Your forefather Joseph left you his mantle, the treasury of rest. Though you learn rest through much testing, Christ has afforded you the rich inheritance of rest and called you to appropriate it in your life and ministry. Souls ravaged by sin find rest in your healing words of forgiveness, mercy, and meekness. Innately you are called to take on Christ's nature to shelter the weary from their striving and toil. You are a beacon of hope in the desert, calling, "come find rest within the Shepherd's care." To the orphans, widows, and the castoffs you radiate forgiveness and mercy. What a stately, glorious resting place you are, that the King of Glory would dwell within you and call many into His glorious nature of rest!

## THE DAUGHTERS OF ZELOPHEHAD

Read Joshua 17:1-6. The daughters of Zelophehad possessed great faith. They were tenacious and unrelenting in pursuit of their inheritance. Defying the fear of man and their facades of insecurity, they righteously went after what was rightfully theirs. What an example to the tribe of Manasseh. This is the heart cry of the Father: Go up, possess your destiny; do not shrink back in fear; go up!

## MEGIDDO AND THE TRIBE OF MANASSEH IN THE END TIMES

Part of the allotment of inheritance in Manasseh was Megiddo. Megiddo is synonymous with the future end-time battle of Armageddon amongst many a bible scholar. Many historic battles have already been fought on that sacred ground. During my first trip to Israel, our tour group went up to Megiddo to intercede. The spiritual atmosphere was intense. In my spirit I could feel the presence of angelic and demonic forces waiting for the battle at the end of the age. In this atmosphere there where many beautiful stately palm trees. I believe prophetically this is Manasseh prophesying mercy during this time of judgment to come. It is a high place which darkness and light engage. How appropriate that Manasseh's inheritance falls where mercy is crying out from the ground!

Biblical archeologists have found remains of a hidden third century church on that very ground.[4] It was hidden due to great persecution at that time. What a beautiful picture of Manasseh as an oasis during times of great suffering. Perhaps there were still a few of the tribe of Manasseh in this hidden church. A time is coming, Manasseh, where you will no longer be hidden. Though small in number, you are mighty, providing oasis in the dark days ahead. With trumpet in hand, be alert and ready to sound the mercy call!

## MANASSEH DISPLAYS ROYALTY AND BEAUTY IN GOD'S HOLY HABITATION

Read Ezekiel 40-41. Ezekiel is taken up in the Spirit of the Lord to see a powerful vision of what I believe is the temple within the New Jerusalem. Gloriously illustrated within the habitation of God is Manasseh upon the furnishings and décor. Manasseh (palm trees) adorns the temple as an ensign of forgiveness, mercy, and righteousness. These attributes of Manasseh are a description and road map into the rest and habitation of the Lord. First we access it through His forgiveness. He cast our sins into the sea of forgetfulness, causing us to become stately palm trees that flourish in His holy habitation where He Himself rests. What a glorious picture, brethren! Manasseh, when you feel insignificant, remember how God has chosen you to adorn His resting place.

> *Your stature is like a palm tree, and your breasts are like its clusters. I said, "I will climb the palm tree, I will take hold of its fruit stalks"* (Song of Songs 7:7-8).

You are His Shulamite: upright, fruitful, and unwavering. Lay hold of your inheritance. Never let fear, unforgiveness, or self-doubt cloud your perception, for you are altogether lovely.

## ADMINISTRATORS OF WEALTH TO THE NATIONS

Just as your forefather Joseph, you are called to administrate wealth to the nations. That wealth is forgiveness and mercy. You are Heaven's financier, reminding the lost that their debt is erased in the payment of Yeshua's blood. You divinely lead creation into the knowledge of the riches of Christ, His wisdom. In the end-time hour, He will call upon you to administrate from the storehouses of Heaven's abundance both spiritually and physically. Be ready, for the time is short. Prepare now, for the greatest harvest of mankind is at hand. Souls are waiting to find rest in your oasis of God's forgiveness.

## PRAYER OF REPENTANCE AND
## DESTINY FOR MANASSEH

Abba, I praise You for You have ransomed me from the dominion of darkness, paid the debt of my sin, and immersed me into the sea of Your forgetfulness, the blood of Yeshua. Yeshua, because You so lavishly redeemed me by grace, I can now enter into the Holy Place. Your precious blood, sprinkled upon the Mercy Seat, gives me access to the Ark of the Covenant, where Mercy Divine abides. In Your great longsuffering, you brought me through the desert place that I might become an oasis for Your glory alone. You are my oasis, sheltering me from the elements that would ravage my identity. Thank You for the anvil of suffering. Though painful it was, Your hand was steadily fashioning me as Your priceless living stone. Help me, Father, to see the onyx as the absence of my sin and to embrace the fullness of Your forgiveness for me and for others. Stake this palm tree in good ground. Though my faith is tested, cause me to flourish in Your courts all the days of my life. I command the stronghold of fear to leave me now; you will no longer erode the soil of my heart. Lord, bring me to the crisis of belief where I am confronted with who You are and who I am in You. I repent of self-doubt. Your gentleness has made me great, O Lord. I am small but mighty in Your mercy and grace alone. May my life beautify Your holy habitation and bring me into the treasury of rest I can only find in You. In Yeshua's name I pray, Amen.

---

[1] Francis Brown, S.R. Driver, *The Brown-Driver-Briggs Hebrew and English lexicon: with an appendix containing the Biblical Aramaic: coded with the numbering system from Strong's Exhaustive concordance of the Bible* (Peabody, Massachusetts: Hendrickson Publishers 1996)

[2] Corrie Ten Boom, *The Hiding Place* (Peabody, Massachusetts: Hendrickson Publishers, 2009) Page 240.

3 Corrie Ten Boom, *Tramp For The Lord* (Fort Washington, Pennsylvania; Christian Literature Crusade, Old Tappan, New Jersey: Fleming H. Revell Company 1974) Page 55.

[4] Scott Wilson, "The Washington Post," *The Washington Post.* November 7, 2005, Accessed May 11, 2011,
http://www.washingtonpost.com/wp-dyn/content/article/2005/11/06/AR2005110600478.html

# CHAPTER 13
# EPHRAIM, THE FRUITFUL VINE

*I am the vine, you are the branches; he who abides in Me and I in him, he bears much fruit, for apart from Me you can do nothing* (John 15:5).

I had often pondered on what it meant to have the mind of Christ. One day during prayer the Lord spoke to me about what it means. He said, "To have My mind is to be consumed by the will of the Father. Whatever the Father is doing, speaking, wherever He is, this is what it means to have the mind of Christ. This is abiding that I spoke of (in John 15) before going to the Cross."

*..I came that they may have life, and have it abundantly* (John 10:10).

The abundant life in Christ comes by abiding in the nature of the Father. Abiding has the sole purpose of positioning us in order to become the habitation of the Living God. Intimacy is the most vital thing in the kingdom. Through the key of abiding comes the source of the fullness of life. Living outside of the Vine (Yeshua) is futile. When we lived in sin we were cut off from life eternal and communion with God.

Abiding calls us to surrender the self-life in order to abide in the will and nature of the Father. Ephraim is a company of sons and daughters who, by nature, call us into abiding in the Father. Every Ephraimite wrestles over the surrender of his or her will in exchange for the Father's will. It takes a lifetime of cultivation to bring any of us into abiding. Abiding is the act of fully embracing the Cross. The tribe of Ephraim serves as a beautiful tapestry depicting the Father's heart of abiding.

Abiding also calls us into the fullness. What is the fullness? It is the knowledge of the glory of God that we might abide in His nature (glory). Abiding will bring us into the fullness, for it is the act of a life that has come through the Cross and come out on the other side in the resurrection living power of Yeshua Himself. Yeshua abides solely within the nature of the Father. He bids us to join Him that we might come into this fullness he has prepared for us. From the foundations of the earth we are made to abide in the Father's nature. The fullness is what we are returning to. Ephraim serves as a picture of the mature Church abiding fully in God's nature, thereby transforming into the habitation of the Living God. Yeshua is our example and leads us into the fullness.

*He is also head of the body, the church; and He is the beginning, the firstborn from the dead, so that He Himself will come to have first place in everything. For it was the Father's good pleasure for all the fullness to dwell in Him, and through Him to reconcile all things to Himself, having made peace through the blood of His cross; through Him, I say, whether things on earth or things in heaven* (Colossians 1:18-20).

The fullness dwells within Christ. Because of His sacrifice on the Cross, we are reconciled to all things in Him, for He abides in the Father's nature, sinless. Christ is the hope of glory, the fullness, that we might be complete in abiding in the Father. Read Colossians 1:24-28.

Yeshua's calling on this earth was to reunite us with the Father. We were not redeemed so we could merely escape eternal damnation. You and I were ransomed in order to become the habitation of the living God, to come into the fullness of the kingdom.

Read Ephesians 1:18-23. Coming into the fullness speaks of maturity, which in essence is fruitfulness. The fullness is where God is calling us that we might become the mature

Church through abiding in Christ. The tribe of Ephraim embodies the calling of the fruitful life in the Vine even to the meaning of the name.

## THE MEANING OF THE NAME

*He named the second Ephraim, "For," he said, "God has made me fruitful in the land of my affliction" (Genesis 41:52).*

Ephraim means, "fruitful, double fruit." Joseph said, "God has made me fruitful in the land of my affliction." Prior to the birth of Manasseh and Ephraim, Egypt had known seven years of plenty. At the time of their births, the seven-year famine had just begun. Their births were truly prophetic. The land was in serious deprivation, void, and needing redemption. It was not only in that state physically, but spiritually as well. Joseph's family was restored through him during the famine. While the earth is in spiritual famine, God is restoring His family. God in His love and mercy births forgiveness (Manasseh) and fruitfulness (Ephraim) during famine. God was adding and multiplying, while Satan was subtracting and dividing.

Ephraim is a testimony of God's abundance and provision in the midst of suffering, drought, and spiritual famine today. Jacob's and Moses' prophecies both speak of Manasseh's and Ephraim's tie to the earth. Theirs is a calling of redemption of the earth; the reunion of the right and left hand of God. God often chooses times of suffering to let us see our own depravity. Suffering, whether it is at the hands of others, caused by our own sin, or a siege upon our lives, is the depravity and famine of the soul. It is a low place that God allows so that we might recognize our need of Him. Ephraim is called to bring the abundance of God's nature to those in spiritual famine. When we come to God and recognize our own spiritual depravity, He then multiples His nature and kingdom within us. He never desires that we fall into spiritual famine, but He will use it to redeem us back to Him.

I see this is as a prophetic picture of what is to come and in some way is already here. The earth is in great spiritual depravity. There has been much time of feasting and abundance, but dark days are coming. While men have been making merry in idolatry, ignorance, and rejecting God, the clock has been ticking closer and closer to the end of days. We are in the last days, brethren! The time of merriment will soon be over and judgment will come. There are souls who are in famine and don't even know they are spiritually famished. There is good news! God has storehouses prepared for the famine that is coming. Ephraim, He is preparing you to be ready to administrate His provision. You are His storehouse! Do you perceive the condition of the earth? We are in dire need of the revelation of His glory. The groaning in the earth increases, as does the depravity of it. It is decaying, for the greater glory shall soon envelop the earth, speaking of when there shall be a new Heaven and a new earth. The solution to this depravity is the knowledge of the glory of God. This is where the storehouses are held solely in Him! Ephraim, you are gifted by God to proclaim His fruitful abundance in the earth's darkest hour. By your very name and nature you are called to bring redemption through the abundance and provision of God's nature.

## GOD'S NATURE OF PROVISION

Read Philippians 4:11-19. The Father's supply is endless because His nature is endless.

*He will be great and will be called the Son of the Most High; and the Lord God will give Him the throne of His father David; and He will reign over the house of Jacob forever, and His kingdom will have no end (Luke 1:32-33).*

Who can fathom the vast nature of God? Provision comes not just from His hand, but it is who He is. He is YHVH Yireh (Jehovah Jireh), meaning "the God who sees and provides." He looks down from Heaven and sees the depravity of the human condition. He has gifted the tribe of Ephraim to see the condition of the human soul and its needs. Ephraim is a watchman who sees the kingdom from Heaven's perspective. If you find yourself amongst this noble tribe, you are moved by the plight of the human soul. The destitute and the poor in body and spirit will call out to you. God has charged you with distributing provisions of His nature to the poor, the orphans, the lost, and hurting. You are an administrator, entrusted to apportion the destiny of Heaven's inheritance to man.

An administrator is not one who "lords over another," but rather a servant of the King. Never lose sight of the call to servanthood. If an agenda of selfish motives or personal gain enters into the equation of administration, you are not only futile in your gifting, but you are abusing your role. Servanthood must come through communion, not striving. If we abide in the will of the Father, then we will faithfully and humbly administrate His provisions. Agendas with selfish motives are snares for which Ephraimite(s) must watch out for. Part of Ephraim's dominion comes from servanthood. Dear Ephraim, immerse yourself in the will of the Father. He is calling you to abide in His nature. His storehouses are bequeathed upon you to administrate provision both spiritually and physically to those in famine. The earth is crying out for Heaven's storehouses. How will you answer His calling?

## THE GEMSTONE OF EPHRAIM

Ephraim shares his stone with his brother Manasseh under the black onyx for Joseph. The brothers share in similar callings but different facets thereof. When you place a gemstone in the light and turn it different ways it will reflect something different though it is the same gemstone. Ephraim has a mercy call (redemption) also. He is given dreams and interpretation, but is called uniquely in his gifting(s) different from his brother Manasseh.

## THE REDEMPTIVE FACET OF EPHRAIM

When Ephraim's onyx facet catches the light of the Son (Yeshua), it radiates a redemptive call through intercession and selfless administration. As watchmen and great deliverers, they are compelled by the plight of the human soul. They carry the burden of man's suffering. Ephraim's call to abide is a call to abide in the redemptive power of the Cross. Their spirits instantly recognize the need to carry man back to the Cross. By their very nature, they carry the Cross in everything they do, for they are abiding in faith for the redemption of lost creation.

## BEARING THE MARK OF THE CROSS

Read Galatians 2:20. Laminin is a cell adhesion protein molecule found within our DNA that holds most cells and organs together. The interesting thing about laminin is what it looks like—the Cross! What holds you and I together is the Cross itself. The Cross bears witness even in our DNA!

*For by Him all things were created, both in the heavens and on earth, visible and invisible, whether thrones or dominions or rulers or authorities—all things have been created through Him and for Him. He is before all things, and in Him all things hold together* (Colossians 1:16-17).

Ephraim, by nature, carries the message of abiding in the Cross. They abide in intercession for creation to come into the abiding work of the Cross, which is its fullness. The onyx is a call to abide for the redemption of creation to come out of darkness into the light and fullness of Christ!

## THE ONYX CALLS EPHRAIM INTO INTERCESSION

Much like the tribe of Levi, Ephraim stands in the gap for humanity. Levi stands in intercession for the matrimony of souls to abide in holiness, whereas Ephraim primarily stands in the gap for the redemptive work of the Cross. Ephraim sees in the onyx the dominion of darkness over creation and persistently intercedes for creation's transformation into God's light. Ephraims are genuinely moved with great compassion at the effects that sin and suffering have on mankind. Often Ephraimites are trained by Levites in their calling of intercession and servanthood. We see this in the lives of Joshua and Samuel. Ephraimite, I urge you to see through Abba's eyes the void of the human condition and His desire to fill it.

## THE ONYX CALLS EPHRAIM INTO APOSTOLIC ADMINISTRATION

As an apostolic administrator, Ephraimites take on the burden of man's depravity. They uniquely build the kingdom through this gifting. The tribe of Ephraim is called to intercede through the gift of intercession against darkness. It is through the gift of administration they meet that need. God often sends them into dark places to proclaim that He alone is the provision of light. Ephraim see lack, which is an absence of light and its provisions, and they faithfully administer YHVH Yireh as provider to the needy. In this gifting you will also see their call to discipleship. Pointing to Yeshua as the head, they build the kingdom by making disciples. Also, you will see them sometimes fulfilling a calling as pastor in this role. It is important to note that when administrating, you are a vessel leading only to Christ Himself. If an agenda of selfish gain enters in, then liberties of spiritual abuse can be taken. Yeshua alone is the Great Shepherd. Ephraim, you must bring others to Him and not to your own kingdom. For this reason there is a process of cultivation that God does within the heart of every Ephraimite.

## THE ONYX CALLS EPHRAIM TO BE A SEER

Read I Samuel 9:15-19. Samuel was a prophet who, through his seer gift, perceived the condition of man's need for God and God's need for man. All three of these giftings work together within this beautiful tribe. The ability to dream and interpret also comes through the seer gift.

## THE SYMBOLS OF EPHRAIM

Ephraim has two symbols that beautifully illustrate God's nature within him: grapes abiding on the vine and the ox. Read Numbers 13:17-33.

### MAKE AN EFFORT TO GET SOME FRUIT FROM THE LAND

The word *effort* in Hebrew is *chazaq*, meaning, "to seize to be strong, courageous, repair, help, lay hold of, to strengthen, mighty, prevail, to overpower or overcome." Moses urges them to be strong, something he said to Joshua in Deuteronomy 31 and something Joshua continually repeated. Joshua, an Ephraimite, and Caleb from Judah were the only two out of the twelve who gave the good report of the Lord. Why? They did not see Canaan and its giants with a façade of fear. Joshua and Caleb were abiding in the vision of the Lord.

Moses was urging the spies to go out and possess fruit from the land of their inheritance. Fruit is the evidence of God's promised inheritance. Grapes are symbolic of the fruit or state of abiding. The only way you and I can possess our full inheritance in Christ is to abide in Him and His promises. If we are snared by facades of fear, we will never fully possess our rightful claim to the fullness of God. The grapes also speak of the fullness of Christ. The grapes found in the valley of Eschol were so enormous they had to be carried by two men on a pole. Eschol in Hebrew means "cluster of grapes." God called the Israelites to go up and possess their inheritance in a place where He was decreeing the fullness of Christ Himself. The way to possess that fullness is in abiding.

Read John 15:1-8. We are called to be fruit producers. The primary fruit we must produce is intimacy: abiding in the nature of the Father. If this primary foundation of bearing fruit for the kingdom is not evident, then the foundation is faulty. Second, we must bear fruit in keeping with repentance. Read Matthew 3:8-10. Repentance is a key fruit to gaining inheritance. Without this fruit, we are cut off from the kingdom. A repentant life is a joyful life lived abiding in the abundance of the kingdom. It is important to have Spirit-led repentance.

The heart is deceitful. Only the Spirit can search the heart of man. Let Him lead you into repentance. Also, the fruit of repentance brings conviction, never condemnation. It is very important to note that when God calls us into repentance, He gives a plan of freedom and hope. Repentance calls us into the restoration with the Vine, Yeshua, and the Vinedresser, the Father. Ephraimites are ministers of reconciliation who call the Body to abide in the fruit of repentance.

## ABIDING IN THE SPIRIT-LED LIFE

*But the fruit of the Spirit is love, joy, peace, patience, kindness, goodness, faithfulness, gentleness, self-control; against such things there is no law. Now those who belong to Christ Jesus have crucified the flesh with its passions and desires. If we live by the Spirit, let us also walk by the Spirit* (Galatians 5:22-25).

Thirdly, we must bear the fruit of the Spirit. Our flesh is constantly at war with the Spirit. The calling of Ephraim is to live a life abiding in Christ, which comes by abiding in the fruit of the Spirit. Each one of those fruits defines the nature of God. Abiding in the fruit of the Spirit allows the cultivation and transformation to come into the fullness of Christ. Each Ephraimite's ministry of transformation begins by allowing the Spirit of God to weed out facades from the vine. Facades choke the fruit of the Spirit from operating in our lives. Ephraimites learn the ministry of transformation by first becoming transformed. Let the Spirit have its way in you, for you have a high calling of bringing the sons and daughters of God into their inheritance through the message of abiding.

## CALLING OF DISCIPLESHIP

*Herein is my Father glorified, that ye bear much fruit; so shall ye be my disciples* (John 15:8).

The last key to bearing fruit is discipleship. In order to make disciples, you must first be one. To become a disciple of Yeshua it takes abiding, repentance, and the fruits of the Spirit. Abiding calls us into knowing who God really is and hearing His voice. Repentance will free us from facades that hinder our walk with the Lord. Cultivating the fruit of the Spirit is activating the nature of God within our day-to-day walk. Intimacy is the core of all of these keys to bearing fruit.

Read Matthew 7:21-23. Discipleship is not based on righteous acts and gifting(s) but rather on relationship alone. A disciple is a lovesick follower of Yeshua.

Read Revelation 14:4. People can do some of the most outlandish things for love. Pure love is when we lay aside our self-nature to serve and give ourselves completely over to the other. True discipleship has gone through the fire where self-love is consumed.

*Those who love their life in this world will lose it. Those who care nothing for their life in this world will keep it for eternity. Anyone who wants to be my disciple must follow me, because my servants must be where I am. And the Father will honor anyone who serves me* (John 12:25-26 NLT)

*Then Jesus said to His disciples, If anyone desires to be My disciple, let him deny himself and take up his cross and follow Me* [cleave steadfastly to Me, conform wholly to My example in living and, if need be, in dying, also]. *For whoever is bent on saving his life shall lose it; and whoever loses his life for My sake shall find it. For what will it profit a man if he gains the whole world and forfeits his life? Or what would man give as an exchange for his life* [in the kingdom of God]? (Matthew 16:24-26 AMP).

## EPHRAIM: GOD'S COMPANY OF KINGDOM REPRODUCERS

We are called to be disciples and to disciple others unto Christ. The tribe of Ephraim, however, is endowed with a unique gifting and desire for discipleship. Ephraim has the gift of multiplication. They have a distinct calling to the nations. There are times in the Bible where Ephraim's name means "nations." Ephraim hears the call that the Father gave to the Jewish people to be "a light to the nations" (Isaiah 49:6).

Read Genesis 49:17-19. Within the heart of every Ephraimite is a call to build the kingdom of God in the nations. Through their gifts they reproduce heirs of the kingdom. It is a burden that constantly calls them to abide for souls to come into the vineyard of Heaven.

## THE OX

The ox serves as the captain tribe symbol for Ephraim. Oxen are synonymous in the Bible with servanthood, strength, harvest, and sacrifice.

## SERVANTHOOD

For Ephraim the ox serves as the embodiment of Christ, the suffering servant that calls him to abide in His nature as such.

Read Isaiah 53:2-12. Yeshua was the symbol of offering, the servant, and strength. He bowed low as a man (though fully God) to become a servant to all. To Ephraim, the Holy Spirit beckons a call to abide in the will of the Father, which is what servanthood entails. In order to abide in and carry out the will of the Father, there must be a complete relinquishment of the human will. Yeshua did not have a selfish bone in his body. He came as one fully identified with the human plight and came to give His life away.

Read John 13:12-15. Yeshua was the perfect example of a true servant. He laid down His own life, in spite of betrayal of others and mockers. He loved everyone from the greatest sinner to the most righteous of men.

Read Matthew 20:25-28. Ephraim's call to servanthood calls them to the daily death of self. True servanthood is not forced labor. Forced labor implies slavery. We are no longer slaves but free men, willing to give away our lives just as Yeshua did for us. Servanthood calls us to abide in the work of the Cross in order to serve others. If our flesh has not been put to death, it can rise up with agendas for selfish gain. I implore you, Ephraim, to allow Christ to lead you as the example of true servanthood in all the Father's will calls you to do.

The symbol of the ox also not only implies servanthood but also the suffering Ephraim goes through. Yeshua called those who are persecuted for righteousness sake "blessed." Ephraim's own name means that he will be fruitful in affliction. Dear Ephraim, as you share in the sufferings of Christ, you are sharing in His glory. This is your great reward. He is your crown of life, bestowed upon you with great honor.

Read Matthew 23:10-12 and James 1:9-12. When we lay down our agendas and our right to be right, healing and deliverance will come to the Body of Christ. Each one of us needs to know our place in the family of God and serve the Lord with all our might. Love is a lifestyle. It's a lifestyle where we relinquish our idols of self. Where, instead of gossiping about the soldier next to you, you exhort him and intercede for him. God's love was unconditional for us. Christ's sacrifice held no boundaries for redemption. Abiding calls Ephraim (and all of us) into laying down their lives and abiding in serving mankind. Read Romans 13:8.

## SERVANTHOOD AND THE CALLING OF THE SAMARITAN

Read Luke 10:30-37. The story of the Samaritan embodies the call of servanthood. The Samaritan people are believed by many to hail from the tribes of Manasseh and Ephraim. Yeshua himself pointed out the calling of mercy and servanthood within these two when he told this parable. This parable calls us to take the blinders of self off and to see the destitute, hear the cries of the poor, the sick, and the unlovely ones. Do not be like the religious man, who ignores the hurting because he has a supposedly more important righteous agenda.

*Pure and undefiled religion in the sight of our God and Father is this: to visit orphans and widows in their distress, and to keep one's self unstained by the world* (James 1:27).

## WILL YOU?

Who will take up My commission of love? Who will go to the hurting, the lost, the betrayed? Who will go in My name and bind up their wounds? Who will show forth My love as a lifestyle? Who will abandon their flesh, hear My voice, calling them to a lifestyle of love? Will you be the spiritual Samaritan? Or the religious man who is too involved in his own flesh, religiosity, and worldly cares to see the spiritually starving, the spiritually wounded, the spiritually dead? Who will speak life in My name to the dead or sleeping spirit man? Who will go forth in My power unto the heathen, unto the oppressed, unto the sick, unto the world? WILL YOU?

## EPHRAIM: THE STRENGTH OF AN OX

*Where there are no oxen, the manager is empty, but from the strength of an ox comes an abundant harvest* (Proverbs 14:4 NIV).

This scripture passage is a true jewel in God's Word. Yeshua came as a lowly servant, born in a manger. A manger is a container that holds grain to feed the oxen, cattle, sheep, etc. The grain itself would have been harvested by a plow led by oxen. What is truly deep and poignant is that without Yeshua (the manger being empty) there would be no sacrifice, strength (grace), or harvest.

What is our strength? The grace of God is the enabling power to carry out the Father's will. The Word teaches us to come boldly before the throne of grace. Without grace we fall on the shortcomings of our own weak strength, the façade of the flesh. When we become self-sufficient, we are relying on the arm of the flesh (façade of striving) and not the arm of the Lord (the truth of abiding). Depending upon the arm of the flesh is profane. It is striving in its truest sense. We are called to abide, not to strive.

Read II Chronicles 32:8, Psalm 44:3, and Jeremiah 17:5. Depending upon the arm of the Lord (His strength) requires that we each relinquish our will and feeble strength. Ephraim, God is challenging you to live upon the arm of His strength. His grace is sufficient for you. Let go of striving and come into abiding. When you depend upon His strength alone, you will not only yield a glorious harvest for the kingdom, but your harvest will be multiplied.

## THE OX: PRESENTING OUR LIVES AS LIVING SACRIFICES

*Therefore, I urge you, brothers, in view of God's mercy, to offer your bodies as living sacrifices, holy and pleasing to God—this is your spiritual act of worship. Do not conform any longer to the pattern of this world, but be transformed by the renewing of your mind. Then you will be able to test and approve what God's will is—his good, pleasing, and perfect will* (Romans 12:1-2 NIV).

Ephraim, your utmost calling is to live a life of sacrifice. As a laid-down lover of Yeshua, the Cross beckons you to live in the power and sacrifice of Yeshua Himself. This is the secret of abiding. It is only from Him and through Him that you abide in the truth of sacrifice. Sacrifice is absolute surrender. We cannot even offer sacrifice without the grace of God. All God asks us to do is surrender our wills and be willing to sacrifice. Full surrender is the relinquishment and right to self. Partial surrender is not surrender. Partial sacrifices are stench to God's nostrils. Cain's sacrifice was not accepted by God because his was a partial, selfish sacrifice. God is a holy God, and He jealously desires sincere worshippers.

Read Psalm 51:16-19. Ephraim, I urge you to live your life on the altar. The moment the flesh and its facades enter in, bring it to the altar. Come boldly before the throne of grace and possess your rightful inheritance. Your harvest of abundance in God's nature is waiting for you to reap as you lay your shoulder to the plow of humility and servanthood. Surrender your self-sufficiency and be empowered by the arm of the Lord. His vast grace empowers you to come into your rightful dominion.

## PROPHECY OVER JOSEPH

For both Jacob's and Moses' prophecies, please return to the prophecies in the previous chapter. It is important to note that the brothers shared in these prophecies under the inheritance of the father, Joseph. Below are a few points that vary regarding the DNA of the tribe of Ephraim. Read Genesis 49:22-26.

Fruit bearing is a kingdom principle. Ephraim is called to abide in the nature of God's redemptive sacrifice and the fruit of the Spirit. Ephraimite(s) take their cue from Yeshua as the lamb, who of His own will was led to slaughter. To abide in a life of sacrifice and live out Yeshua's message of redemption, we too must be lambs led to the slaughter, daily dying to the facades of the flesh. Sacrifice is the fruit of repentance. By God's grace we are enabled to be living sacrifices through abiding in the fruit of the Spirit.

### "OF JOSEPH HE SAID, 'BLESSED OF THE LORD BE HIS LAND'"

This portion of Moses' prophecy basically reiterates the last portion of Jacob's prophecy. He was also speaking of the fruitfulness and reproduction in verse 14. For Ephraim, the call to reproduction is His direct calling of fruitfulness, even to the meaning of His name. Reproduction is the nature of God to multiply the abundance of Himself and His kingdom. Ephraim has the lot of producing heirs with vast multiplication and favor! Kingdom reproduction is a true picture of biblical prosperity.

## THE FAÇADES OF EPHRAIM

*I am the true vine, and my Father is the husbandman. Every branch in me that beareth not fruit he taketh away: and every branch that beareth fruit, he purgeth it, that it may bring forth more fruit. Now ye are clean through the word which I have spoken unto you. Abide in me, and I in you. As the branch cannot bear fruit of itself, except it abide in the vine; no more can ye, except ye abide in me* (John 15:1-4 KJV).

Ephraim's intimacy exists through abiding in the Vine. Grapes that are not fully cultivated are sour, immature, and unable to be eaten. Our Heavenly Father is a gracious Husbandman, tending His vineyard. He takes great care and preparation into bringing forth good fruit. The tribe of Ephraim must be alert to the enemy's deception through the enticements of the spirit of the world.

### THE SPIRIT OF THE WORLD

Read II Timothy 2:1-7. To abide is to disconnect from the spirit of the world and abide in the Spirit of Christ. Ephraim must take special care to disconnect from the world. By nature they are carefree, adventurous souls, but when uncultivated they can easily be seduced by the spirit of the world. Their adventurous spirits can turn into licentiousness. Unchecked, this stronghold can cause them to lose sight of their first love.

Read Matthew 7:13. Licentiousness is the epitome of the spirit of the world. Licentiousness is defined this way: "Lacking moral discipline or ignoring legal restraint, especially in sexual conduct; having no regard for accepted rules or standards."[1] What we give license to is what or who we are abiding in. If we are abiding in Christ and His nature, we will give license to Him; if to the spirit of the world, licentiousness gives way to brazen idolatry. Licentiousness is being drunk with the spirit of the world.

Read Proverbs 20:1. The spirit of the world makes a mockery not only of God but of the priceless creation we are. When abiding in licentiousness, we are abiding in the house of the foolish woman.

*The foolish woman is noisy; she is simple and open to all forms of evil, she knows nothing whatever* [of eternal value]. *For she sits at the door of her house or on a seat in the conspicuous places of the town, calling to those who pass by, who go uprightly on their way: Whoever is simple* [wavering and easily led astray], *let him turn in here! And as for him who lacks understanding, she says to him, Stolen waters* [pleasures) *are sweet* [because they are forbidden]; *and bread eaten in secret is pleasant. But he knows not that the shades of the dead are there* [specters haunting the scene of past transgressions], *and that her invited guests are in the depths of Sheol* [the lower world, Hades, the place of the dead] (Proverbs 9:13-18 AMP).

The Lord is pleading with you, dear Ephraimite, to leave the house of foolishness and embrace wisdom. When you are dwelling in the house of foolishness, you are in danger of giving up your destiny, which is to abide in the fullness of Christ. The Lord is calling you to His banqueting house to drink from His cup (His precious blood), partake of His love feast (His broken body) and of the fruits of the Spirit. How will you answer? Which feast will you dine at? From what cup do you choose to drink from?

### THE CUP OF THE LORD OR THE CUP OF DEMONS

Read I Corinthians 10:20-22. Drinking from the Lord's cup is the epitome of communion, of abiding. Drinking from the cup of demons would be a union with the enemy. Our connection is the will. When our wills become steeped in licentiousness, Satan has a legal right or license to bring all manner of evil. The Lord is a gentleman; He will not cross our will. A will not surrendered ties the Father's hands. The world's intoxication will bring us into a deep degradation of our soul, which, unchecked, results in spiritual death.

> *For you were called to freedom, brethren; only do not turn your freedom into an opportunity for the flesh, but through love serve one another* (Galatians 5:13).

Abiding in Christ requires the surrender of the will, meaning the full surrender of self and its desire to do its own pleasure. Drinking from the cup of demons will be a short-lived pleasure, but do not be deceived, for Satan's scheme is to keep you from the fullness of Christ. If he can lure you away from the banqueting house of the Lord, which is your chief call to abide, then, dear Ephraim, he will keep you from dominion and life eternal. Do not be entertained, for even a moment of small pleasure cannot go unnoticed. Embrace repentance and the fear of the Lord as your lifestyle. Your calling is to abide.

Read I Corinthians 2:12-14 and 11:27. Communion is especially poignant for the tribe of Ephraim. As you abide in His sacrifice, being His broken body and His shed blood, you are abiding in Him. Likewise, Ephraim, you call the Body of Christ into communion.

## EPHRAIM AND THE FACADE OF DIVISION

The tribe of Ephraim possesses fullness of their identity by abiding in fruitfulness or multiplication. Naturally, the façade against multiplication would be division. Satan seeks to divide and conquer the tribe of Ephraim through idolatry. Idols are built by little foxes of sin, who seek to steal from the Vine.

> *Catch the foxes for us, the little foxes that are ruining the vineyards, while our vineyards are in blossom* (Song of Songs 2:15).

In order to catch the little foxes, Ephraim must live a consistent life of repentance. Even small sins, left unchecked, will grow into great facades of idolatry. Foxes are sly, and such is the nature of idols. What does a vineyard produce? Grapes. Grapes make wine. The fruitful vine is the symbol for Ephraim. Wine is a symbol of the joy of the Holy Spirit. Little foxes, or sins, steal our joy. Why do they steal our joy? Disobedience draws us away from communing with the Father. This grows into idolatry when unchecked. Obedience draws us into communing with Him. When do foxes come and steal the fruit? Foxes come to spoil the vine under the cloak of night and darkness. They come when we are asleep. Sin comes when we aren't spiritually alert. We must always be on guard. The Father desires obedience over sacrifice. Our vineyards produce abundant fruit when we are focused, alert, and are selflessly surrendered to worshipping our heavenly Father. This fruit will not only bring joy to us but to others as well. An obedient life is a joyful life.

Read II Corinthians 6:15-17. Ephraim, God is chastening you in His great love and mercy to catch the little foxes that would steal your divine destiny to intimacy and sonship! Drive out the foxes; do not leave any room for even the smallest sin to grow. Foxes will divide you from the kingdom of Heaven, for their deception will lead you into all manner of evil and pain.

## GENERATIONAL IDOLATRY BRINGS DIVISION

As with Ephraim's brother, Manasseh, idolatry entered though a legal right in his generation. Ephraim's mother was an Egyptian, and his grandmother, Rachel, also had a facade of idolatry.

Read Genesis 31:18-42. Idolatry is the severing force that divides us from intimacy with the Lord. Ephraim had an extremely strong thread of idolatry. Generational sins and curses enable facades to keep us from our true destiny, the fullness of Christ.

Read Judges 7:24; 8:1. At a time of chaos and war, pagan enemies were hotly pursuing Israel, the tribe of Ephraim turned on his own brother, Manasseh. The enemy's scheme wrought division within the house of Israel through Ephraim's idolatry of self, dissention, and strife. Gideon was seeking solace and strength from his brethren and found quite the contrary. Ephraim fell into this scheme because he was building his own kingdom and not the Lord's. The tribe lost sight of abiding in obedience, servanthood, and fruitfulness. Sibling rivalry in the Body of Christ must be nipped in the bud. It is not only a poor testimony, but it gives the enemy legal right for wounding, curses, and idols to gain more territory.

Read Romans 16:17-18. An appetite of self-gratification is anti-Christ. Unhealthy spiritual appetites will lead us to repeated sin and idolatry. This grieves our heavenly Father.

> *Now the deeds of the flesh are evident, which are: immorality, impurity, sensuality, idolatry, sorcery, enmities, strife, jealousy, outbursts of anger, disputes, dissensions, factions, envying, drunkenness, carousing, and things like these, of which I forewarn you, just as I have forewarned you, that those who practice such things will not inherit the kingdom of God* (Galatians 5:19-21).

## IDOLATRY BREEDS A CHAOTIC SPIRITUAL ATMOSPHERE

The spiritual atmosphere in Israel drastically changed after the reign of Solomon. A degrading downward spiral began through Solomon's idolatry. Solomon went after other women and their gods so much so that his heart was turned completely against God. God kept His covenant with David, assuring that Solomon's kingdom would be one of peace, but afterwards division was brewing in the atmosphere to make a drastic wreckage of what David fought so hard to build. After the succession of David's grandson, Rehoboam, Israel split into two houses: with Judah taking the southern kingdom and Ephraim having the northern kingdom. Judah's kingdom consisted of all of Judah, Benjamin, and half of Levi, while Ephraim's kingdom consisted of the other tribes.

> *And knowing their thoughts Jesus said to them, "Any kingdom divided against itself is laid waste; and any city or house divided against itself will not stand"* (Matthew 12:25).

Jeroboam was the first king over the North Kingdom (Ephraim). He began with the fear of the Lord, but it wasn't long before the façade of idolatry came to bring division.

Read I Kings 11:26-40. Solomon's disobedience caused him to leave his first love; it called him out of his place of abiding. This brought a curse of division. This resulted in a divided kingdom. The original intention of God was that Judah would rule, and He says in this passage that He would restore the kingdom to Judah. Due to the sin in Judah, God ordained Jeroboam to the throne in Ephraim.

The kingdom was divided due to idolatry. This is not the first time an Ephraimite stepped in to mediate in a role that had been abused. God sent Samuel as both priest and prophet during the time of apostasy of Eli's duty as priest. This is a foreshadowing that Ephraim often embodies through the nature of Christ: prophet, priest, and king. Ephraim was called to foreshadow because God's deepest desire is that we all embody these attributes and because Ephraim's calling to abide is a form of intercession where those roles were lacking in Israel.

## JEROBOAM'S IDOLATRY

Read I Kings 12:25-33. A rampant seduction of division birthed idolatry within the heart of Jeroboam. The sin of Jeroboam began with the idol of self. The first thing to note is when Jeroboam said, "They will kill me." This statement was him seeking his own life. Also, this statement is one of fear, not faith. Jeroboam's forefather, Joshua, made a charge to be bold and courageous. Jeroboam lost sight of this when he chose to abide in fear by saving his own life. Yeshua said, "For whoever wishes to save his life will lose it; but whoever loses his life for My sake will find it" (Matthew 16:25).

The next few actions Jeroboam took snowballed because of this idol of self not dealt with. Jeroboam sought to make a feast day like Judah's (in competition out of envy) and made sacrifices (which God did not call for) and last of all, he called for priests who were not Levites, whom the Lord did not appoint but were rather appointed by Jeroboam. This was a grievous thing to the Lord. Jeroboam lost sight of his call to abide in the Lord, therefore he was disconnected from the Vine. Jeroboam was called by God to speak against Judah's apostasy, and now we find him doing more of the same! The spiritual atmosphere would have been full of familiar spirits that enticed him; instead of standing in the gap, he too fell prey to idolatry. This idolatry eventually grew over time and caused the complete dispersion of the northern kingdom, all while under the rule of Ephraim. Now Judah also had their share of the blame as well, but they kept an essence of communion (as minuscule as it was) with the Lord.

The dispersion of the northern kingdom is what many call the "lost tribes." I do not believe they are truly lost. God often times uses us in spite of our sin. I believe this is true of Ephraim, fulfilling his calling through the *diaspora* as a light in the nations. Jeroboam's idolatry led the northern kingdom in a downward spiral of spiritual obscurity. One man's sin snowballed into a kingdom's demise. I feel that many destinies were aborted. Our sins never just affect us, but impact future generations! How much more could our repentance change the course of history?

Read I Kings 11:26-28. The Word says a curse cannot land without a cause. I feel Jeroboam held much indignation toward the reign of Solomon (the injustice and brazen idolatry) and the suffering he endured at Solomon's wrath. Solomon appointed Jeroboam as an overseer over all forced labor. One would think Jeroboam would learn the lesson of forgiveness his forefather Joseph taught him. Jeroboam, like Joseph, was forced by ill-will and abuse into Egypt. The legal right had a cause due to unforgiveness and possibly some righteous indignation immaturely resolved within Jeroboam's heart.

## THE FAÇADE OF ENVY

Envy is defined by the Miriam's Webster dictionary as: "painful or resentful awareness of an advantage enjoyed by another, joined with a desire to possess the same advantage."[2] Jeroboam's unforgiveness ensnared him and his tribe and his territory till it snowballed into full-blown envy. It is possible this even existed in Ephraim before Jeroboam; the Scripture is not clear. Perhaps Ephraim's appetite for power became unhealthy as it grew with envy and idolatry. Envy is empowered by bitterness or a feeling of lack. The tribe of Ephraim lost sight of God's goodness and abundance toward them and became envious of Judah. It is a dangerous thing to lose sight of your dominion, especially when it is coupled with envy.

> *The envy also of Ephraim shall depart, and the adversaries of Judah shall be cut off:*
> *Ephraim shall not envy Judah, and Judah shall not vex Ephraim* (Isaiah 11:13 KJV).

There is a day coming when God will restore the inheritance within Ephraim. It will come through their repentance of idolatry, envy, and healing of their embittered past. If we lose sight of God's abundance for us and envy another's place of dominion, a deadly demise of destiny is at hand. Sibling rivalry, envy, and idolatry caused the tribe of Ephraim to come out of abiding, fruitfulness, and abundance. The tribe of Ephraim neglected their place of intimacy as fruitful reproducers of the kingdom and instead fell into obscurity. Catch the little foxes as soon as they appear in your vineyard, brethren. God longs to establish you as fruitful reproducers of His kingdom who faithfully administrate from a place of abiding. Read Matthew 3:8-10.

Idols ravaged Jeroboam's heart, causing him to lose sight of his first love. Dear Ephraim, God longs to blow on the flame of your first love. That flame will become a raging inferno by His Spirit that will change the world. All He asks is that you leave your idol lovers and return to Him with your whole heart.

## RETURN TO YOUR FIRST LOVE

Read Hosea 13:1-16. Ephraim, if you do not hearken to the voice of the Lord, your destiny is in grave danger. Instead of being fruitful and bearing sons and daughters for the kingdom, you will be barren, for you neglected the transformation of the Cross. Hearken unto this cry, the cry of wisdom, and flee from the house of the foolish woman. The house of wisdom brings life and will restore you. Wisdom calls you back into fervent and holy love with the Bridegroom. Forsake your idol lovers and live! The Father longs to bring you into fullness. He grieves that your foolishness would leave you prey to the enemy. Do not be deceived that entertaining your flesh is a small thing; it is deadly, and will result in your complete obscurity and loss of dominion! Hear the heart of the Father: Leave all foolishness and its idols behind. Abide in Him, for He alone is your salvation and treasury of rest. Read Philippians 3:13-21.

## EPHRAIM'S ABIDING BEARS THE NATURE OF CHRIST

Abiding in the Vine, Ephraim cultivates into the fullness of Christ. There are no two better examples in the Word than Joshua and Samuel. The fullness of God did not come automatically, but took a lifetime of cultivation. Both men were worthy to foreshadow Christ, and both were fallible men, dependent on God in their weaknesses. Cultivation taught them to abide, to bear the fruit of patience, longsuffering, etc. Joshua and Samuel were pillars of faith and leadership within Israel. Joshua and Samuel both brought Israel into pivotal times of destiny for Israel. As fruit reproducers, they would leave an indelible mark on history while unselfishly abiding as humble servants.

Nothing is automatic when abiding in the Vine. Take to heart, dear Ephraimite that you are on a journey, returning to the fullness of Christ. There are no shortcuts. You must take the narrow way, the highway to holiness. Brethren, there is much pruning, watering, planting, and tender care that goes into your cultivation.

## VISITATION BIRTHS REVEALING AND REVEALING BIRTHS DOMINION

*For to us God revealed them through the Spirit; for the Spirit searches all things, even the depths of God* (I Corinthians 2:10).

Joshua and Samuel were cultivated in similar fashion being that they were mentored by Levites. Levites not only are given oracles and mysteries of God, but they call others into the same. Joshua was trained by Moses, and Samuel by Eli the priest. Joshua and Samuel encountered God, whereby He revealed Himself. This revealing not only brought both men into their destiny, but all Israel as well. Joshua and Samuel walked in dominion because they learned to abide in the nature of God and to seek after the nature of God. In the nature of

God lie mysteries for us; the revealing of these mysteries will cause us to walk in dominion and destiny.

Joshua saw many signs and wonders and unprecedented victory and ultimately brought Israel into their destiny. Why was such an honor bestowed on Joshua? Three reasons: (1) He abided in the nature of God by allowing it to transform him; (2) He had a visitation where he beheld Yeshua, the fullness of the Father's glory; and (3) He got his marching orders from the Adonai T'sveout (Hebrew for Lord of Hosts) and obeyed humbly.

Read Joshua 5:13-15. Joshua met with the Lord of Hosts—Adonai T'sveot—that day. Yeshua revealed himself as a warrior, for he was calling Joshua to lead Israel in one of the greatest conquests: Jericho. Joshua could not have proceeded into Jericho without the revelation of Yeshua Adonai T'sveot. Joshua in Hebrew, *Y'hoshua*, means "God who saves." Joshua came as a servant, abiding in humility, obedience, and holiness. These factors conditioned Joshua and the children of Israel to take the Promised Land. Joshua was a type and shadow of Christ. God raised him up as a mighty deliverer who saved Israel and brought them into their Promised Land. That is what Yeshua did for us!

Samuel also brought Israel into great destiny. He anointed two kings, both of whom made pivotal marks and established the kingdom within Israel. As a priest he stood as a watchmen abiding in intercession for Israel's destiny. All of these are types and shadows of Christ as well. Samuel never could have accomplished any of this if he too had not sought out hidden mysteries. Read I Samuel 3:1-21.

### "AND THE WORD THE LORD WAS RARE IN THOSE DAYS, VISIONS WERE INFREQUENT"

Israel's vision was failing much like that of old Eli's. Desperate times call for desperate measures. Israel needed a watchman who would abide for them to come into kingdom reality. Israel had become weary, despondent, and hopeless. God brought Israel a young boy, Samuel, whose ears and heart were pinned to His chest. Samuel knew how to abide in intimacy. His vision was not failing because his childlike faith and innocence drew him into a revelation of the Most High God! When your vision fails or is prolonged, humble yourself and become like a child. Read Ezekiel 12:21-28.

*My people are destroyed for lack of knowledge…* (Hosea 4:6).

God provided vision for Israel through his servant Samuel. He was to Israel a voice of hope, restoration, salvation, and holiness. Raise your voice, Ephraim, and cry out against the delay, destruction, and divination of Satan's schemes. Abide in the vision of the Lord, for in doing so you (and those you minister to) will come into deliverance and destiny.

### "AND SAMUEL WAS LYING DOWN IN THE TEMPLE OF THE LORD WHERE THE ARK OF GOD WAS, THAT THE LORD CALLED SAMUEL; AND HE SAID, 'HERE I AM.'"

It is important to note the characteristics of young Samuel when the Lord called him.

1.Childlike: Yeshua said we cannot inherit the kingdom unless we become like a child (Matt. 18:3). Samuel was not filled with logic, speculation, the fear of man, or idolatry that would keep him from hearing the Lord call him.

2.Resting: Samuel was lying down; in other words, he was in a state of rest. Samuel was not striving, but resting.

3.Expectant: From the place of rest young Samuel eagerly awaited to meet with God. He put himself in a place to wait upon the Lord.

4.Intimate: Samuel was lying by the Ark of the Covenant in the temple. He was abiding in the Holy of Holies. Samuel was in his God-given authority of abiding; a priest.

5.Administrative: Samuel, though a child, stood in his God-given authority and delivered God's administration.

6.Fearless: He did not bow to the fear of man but the fear of the Lord. Eli carried much more authority in the natural, but Samuel was the only one walking in dominion.

During the time of Samuel's visitation, Eli and his sons let the priesthood become either stale, full of striving works, religious, consumed by duty, or totally carnal. God was birthing the Zadok priesthood through Samuel's abiding, that Israel might come into its priesthood. The Lord's design for Israel's priesthood was that they might draw near to the Lord and minister to Him alone. The Aaronic priesthood had lost sight of this. Samuel was also abiding, waiting for God to establish the government of praise which He brought through King David, whom Samuel years later would anoint.

### "AND THE LORD APPEARED AGAIN AT SHILOH, BECAUSE THE LORD REVEALED HIMSELF TO SAMUEL AT SHILOH BY THE WORD OF THE LORD"

Samuel had a heart-to-heart then face-to-face encounter with the Lord (by His Word—Yeshua, the Word made flesh) at Shiloh. Samuel knew Shiloh was just a place of rest, but he also knew who Shiloh was!

Read Genesis 49:10. You see, Samuel saw the promise through David; "a root shall spring out of Jesse," hallelujah! Amen. Yeshua, the Sabbath rest, revealed His kingdom plan to Samuel.

Read Isaiah 11:1-3. Dear Ephraim, the Lord has an encounter waiting for you. He longs to bring you to Shiloh, your place of rest, Yeshua! Lie close to the Ark, wait expectantly as a child, be ready to obey and administrate the Word of the Lord. Shiloh is Christ in His fullness. The fullness of Christ awaits those who choose to abide in Shiloh! The fullness is coming to help us to "disconnect" from the facade of the flesh, agendas and idolatries, the pain, suffering, sickness, poverty, and shame.

> *For if Joshua had given them rest, He would not have spoken of another day after that. So there remains a Sabbath rest for the people of God. For the one who has entered His rest has himself also rested from his works, as God did from His* (Hebrews 4:8-10).

Joshua and Samuel both were able to abide in the Sabbath rest, and while doing so, to intercede that the whole house of Israel (Jew and Gentile, one in Messiah) might come into the Sabbath rest.

> *For the Son of Man is the Lord of the Sabbath* (Matthew 12:8).

### THE DOUBLE PORTION COMPANY

Read Genesis 47:8-22. When Ephraim was given his inheritance and the firstborn blessing, the Father was prophetically speaking through Ephraim what was to come: the emergence of the Church of the firstborn. In essence this emergence is God releasing the double portion to His Bride.

> *He is also head of the body, the church; and He is the beginning, the firstborn from the dead, so that He Himself will come to have first place in everything* (Colossians 1:8).

## HANNAH: DAUGHTER OF THE DOUBLE PORTION

Read I Samuel Chapters 1-2.

### "TO HANNAH HE WOULD GIVE A DOUBLE PORTION, FOR HE LOVED HANNAH, BUT THE LORD HAD CLOSED HER WOMB"

God was challenging Hannah to come into her double portion despite her barrenness. Hannah was much like the state of Israel, barren, without hope, without a vision, without a son. She was bitterly persecuted and provoked by Peninnah (her husband's other wife). She, like her forefather Joseph, could abide in fruitfulness when division surrounded her. The Lord caused Hannah to bear a son, Samuel. She was repaid double for her trouble! Amen! Dear Ephraim, the Lord has a double portion for you. Abide by the Ark of the Covenant, wait patiently at Shiloh, for He shall surely come, and His reward with Him.

### THE ONE NEW MAN END-TIME ARMY

Read Ezekiel 37:20-22. In this end-time hour the One New Man will arise. That One new Man is Messiah Himself. As we abide in the One New Man, we are being transformed into this army of which Ezekiel speaks. God is declaring that the division of His kingdom is over! No more shall His temple of Living Stones be divided, but they shall be multiplied in Christ, the One New Man! Hallelujah! What once was dead shall come forth in resurrection power—the church of the firstborn—from the dead. As we lay our lives down, abiding in the death of the flesh and all its facades, we will then come forth in militant cadence as the One New Man army of God! Can you hear the sound? It's the four winds calling you to assemble, Ephraim. Call the sons and daughters of God back to life. Call them into resurrection life in Christ, the One New Man!

> *For I will bend Judah as My bow, I will fill the bow with Ephraim. And I will stir up your sons, O Zion, against your sons, O Greece; And I will make you like a warrior's sword* (Zechariah 9:13).

God is reuniting Judah (Jew) with Ephraim (Gentile) in this end time. Both are mighty but not as useful on their own. Together Judah and Ephraim are unstoppable! They usher in the King of Kings. Hallelujah!

## PRAYER OF REPENTANCE AND
## DESTINY FOR EPHRAIM

Yeshua, draw me into Your banqueting house. Call me to Your love feast. You are a tender husbandmen tending to the vineyard of my soul. Catch the foxes that spoil the vines. (Pause and let the Holy Spirit reveal the "little foxes" in your life). I repent, Lord, for becoming intoxicated with the spirit of the world and licentiousness. I repent of envy and let go of all idolatry. I choose to drink from the cup of the Lord. Call me deeper to abide in Your nature, Yeshua. You are the Vine. I am a mere small branch, yet You call me a fruitful bough. Cause me to bear fruit in keeping with repentance. Yeshua, it's Your kindness that will lead me to repentance. I let go of facades of striving and my attempts to build my own kingdom. Teach me, Abba, how to build Your kingdom. May the mind of Christ cause me to administrate faithfully from a place of abiding. I let go of the bitterness of my past. Heal the wounds of archers' arrows left deep within me. (Take time and see what the Lord will heal here). Yeshua, You are the treasury of rest to me. You alone are my Shiloh. Call me to rest in Your Holy Temple. May I live my life prostrate at the Ark of the Covenant. Cause me to be a fruit producer who brings great multiplication to Your kingdom. Let Your kingdom come, Your will be done on earth as it is in Heaven. In your precious name I pray, Lord Yeshua, Amen.

---

[1] "Licentious." *Merriam-Webster.com.* Merriam-Webster, n.d. Web. 2 September 2011. <http://www.merriam-webster.com/dictionary/licentious>.

[2] "Envy." *Merriam-Webster.com.* Merriam-Webster, n.d. Web. 12 September 2011. <http://www.merriam-webster.com/dictionary/licentious>

# CHAPTER 14
# BENJAMIN: THE BELOVED

**W**hat do you think of when you hear the word *child*? I think of words like: pure, innocent, untainted, dependent, unassuming, expectant, and full of faith. We all enter this world as children, dependent on the nurture of the family God has given us. Some of us find it in great measure; others of us find it, but it is dysfunctional; some of us are left as orphans. Abba Daddy has no orphans. There are no stepchildren or grandchildren either. God's family is made up of blood-bought heirs. Yeshua gave an important key to inheritance in Matthew 18:

> *At that time the disciples came to Jesus and said, "Who then is greatest in the kingdom of heaven?" And He called a child to Himself and set him before them, and said, "Truly I say to you, unless you are converted and become like children, you will not enter the kingdom of heaven. Whoever then humbles himself as this child, he is the greatest in the kingdom of heaven"* (Matthew 18:1-4).

As heirs we inherit the kingdom. We must become dependent children. Children have no pretense or guile. God calls His sons and daughters to be innocent of sin through the shed blood of Yeshua. He longs to dote on us, to lavish us with His nature and His many gifts, but most of all He longs for fellowship with us. Our Father's heart beams with radiant joy for we are His favorite ones! Did you know that when He thinks of you, His heart dances! Join Him, beloved, join Him in the dance. Dance in the rain with your Father God, dance in fields of grace, dance in His lavish love bequeathed to you! He is dancing over you even now! Every heir of the kingdom of Heaven is uniquely celebrated, loved, and treasured. No cost is too great to redeem Abba's creation, for He sent His only begotten Son that we might enter into His eternal kingdom of love!

> *For God so loved the world, that He gave His only begotten Son, that whoever believes in Him shall not perish, but have eternal life* (John 3:16).

You and I were bought with the most lavish gift God could give us: salvation. Salvation affords us not only the entrance into the kingdom of Heaven, but it is the continual process of making *aliyah* (to ascend or return) to the Father. Read I John 3:1-11.

## "SEE HOW GREAT A LOVE THE FATHER HAS BESTOWED ON US"

The Father has taken special care and design with His creation. It is His delight to have fellowship with us as His children. We are His chief joy. Within the tribe of Benjamin, you will find blissful lovers of the Father whose childlike nature is unparalleled. Benjaminites radiate the glory of the Father in that they embody the persona of a child Bride preserved for the King![1]

> *My beloved is mine, and I am his…* (Song of Songs 2:16).

---

[1] Author's note: I chose the term "child bride" to paint a prophetic picture of how the tribe of Benjamin possesses identity through intimacy. A child bride speaks of an innocent child-like bride, whose faith and purity draws her Bridegroom. Historically speaking, child brides married from the ages of 10-18 and often would consummate the marriage years later. Melisende d'Outremer, "Women Of History," *Women of History Blogspot*, August 29, 2007. Accessed July 22,2015 http://womenofhistory.blogspot.com/2007/08/medieval-marriage-childbirth.html .

This beautiful, beloved tribe possesses an instinctual awareness that they are truly treasured and loved by God. Like the Shulamite, they begin their journey with ecstatic, contagious love. A Benjaminite's love goes through a metamorphosis of maturity. In the beginning of the Song of Songs the Shulamite says, "My beloved is mine, and I am his." Her view of love is faulty, ridden with fear and self-doubt. In this verse the Shulamite has not yet become grounded in perfect love. The perfection of Yeshua's love for all of us is a journey, a metamorphosis into maturity.

Our faulty human nature can so easily lead us into lies of rejection, foolishness, and self-love. Toward the end of the Song of Songs the Shulamite grows in maturity and states, "My Beloved is mine and His desire is toward me." It is the bearing of the Cross that causes us to be perfected in love. A believer who has matured into the habitation of perfect love is one for whom no one could tell the difference where Yeshua begins and they end. They are indeed one, or in Hebrew, *echad* (pronounced ekh-awd). Yeshua explains it best this way:

> *The glory which You have given Me I have given to them, that they may be one, just as We are one; I in them and You in Me, that they may be perfected in unity, so that the world may know that You sent Me, and loved them, even as You have loved Me* (John 17:22-23).

To mature in Perfect Love (Yeshua), one must take on the hidden life found only within the Cross.

> *For you have died and your life is hidden with Christ in God* (Colossians 3:3).

## BENJAMIN'S BIRTH A BIRTHING OF RADICAL DOMINION

Read Genesis 35:1-21. The events surrounding Benjamin's birth have a profound significance on his life and also on his tribe. His birthing is a picture of radical dominion and sonship. Prior to Benjamin's birth, Jacob underwent a radical transformation.

> *Then Jacob was left alone, and a man wrestled with him until daybreak. When he saw that he had not prevailed against him, he touched the socket of his thigh; so the socket of Jacob's thigh was dislocated while he wrestled with him. Then he said, "Let me go, for the dawn is breaking." But he said, "I will not let you go unless you bless me." So he said to him, "What is your name?" And he said, "Jacob." He said, "Your name shall no longer be Jacob, but Israel; for you have striven with God and with men and have prevailed"* (Genesis 32:24-28).

Jacob's radical transformation essentially was a change in his nature. Jacob means "deceiver, supplanter," and Israel means "one who wrestles with God" and "prince of God." The name of Jacob reflected the facades in his life, whereas Israel reflected his destiny. The Lord revealed to me an important mystery. Upon studying many scriptures, often (though not every time) when the Lord prophesies the name Jacob (in the prophets) he is speaking to the facades and idolatry and sin. When He calls out the name Israel, He is most often times speaking of destiny or promise. Jacob stepped into destiny when He wrestled with God. What was Jacob wrestling for? I believe he was wrestling for the nature of God to be revealed to him. Taking that into account, Benjamin was the only son born after this wrestling. In essence Benjamin was born into destiny—a breaker anointing.

Benjaminites carry a special favor from the Lord. Things seem to be handed to them on a silver platter. What is the key to such favor? The Lord has a cup of favor for the Bride of Christ. Instinctively, Benjaminites know this and even carry a mantle of favor. Why? Because

Benjamin was born after Jacob/Israel's breakthrough. His father's identity changed, and therefore his own nature changed also. Israel stepped over into the beginning of his dominion, not just for himself but also for his people. God gave me a beautiful revelation that I feel has much insight for the Bride of Christ. I believe it also speaks of the tenacity within the heart of every Benjamin.

## "I WON'T LET GO!"

I had been in an intensive time of seeking the Lord for a long time. He called me to do a watch between the hours of 5-7 in the morning. Specifically, this watch was for breakthrough, to cry out for the fullness of the glory to cover the earth, and to petition God to release the poor (the desperate in soul, spirit, and body) from oppression. In fact, Holy Spirit called this "the breakthrough watch" and said to call out to the Father as the Lord of breakthrough(s), in Hebrew *Baal Perazim*. There were no exact formulas to achieve this, but the Lord did charge me to seek out of a place of desperation for myself. The Lord said, "You must cry out with all that is in you; you must abide in that place of being poor in spirit to cry out for the poor." To gain this place of intercession, it's about intimacy with our Beloved High Priest, not works, anointing, and gifts to manipulate a desired outcome. In other words, it was heart-to-heart, face-to-face, gut-wrenching intercession with all of my might. With this charge I proceeded to passionately pursue the Lord during this "breakthrough watch."

The final watch (Yeshua interceded in the Garden of Gethsemane during this time) is between the hours of 3-6 A.M., or daybreak. I have heard it said that between these hours is when Satan's schemes are in full fury and activation (the most heinous of crimes occur most often during this time). What is important to note is that between 5-6 A.M. breakthrough happens, spilling over into the first hour of the first watch till 7 A.M. At the break of dawn Jacob was blessed and received his identity, dominion, blessing, and most importantly, the fulfillment of God's promise of supernatural inheritance for him and the Jewish people. Jacob, while wrestling with the Lord, said, "I will not let you go unless you bless me."

The Hebrew word for *man* in verse 24 is *'iysh*, meaning not just "man" but "a dutiful and protective husband." Jacob wasn't wrestling from a place of duty (Martha mindset), but intimacy (a Mary heart). The Bride of Christ is at the end of her wrestling. The dawn is breaking! She has fought hard and long through the night, persevering for the fullness of His glory and her right to dominion within the earth. I saw the Bride of Christ bowed low, yet wrestling with the Lord Himself in a vast harvest field of wheat and barley while the sun was dawning. She would not let Him go until she received the fullness of His glory. Mind you, the time of this all happening was just a day before or maybe even the first day of Shavuot, the barley harvest (Gentiles know it as Pentecost). Jews traditionally read the book of Ruth during this feast. This story depicts the promise of the One New Man; Jew and Gentile, one in Yeshua, our Boaz. Benjamin's birth occurring after this breakthrough is profoundly significant in that they carry an anointing for breakthrough, also referred to as a "breaker anointing."

## BETWEEN BETHEL AND BETHLEHEM

*So Rachel died and was buried on the way to Ephrath* (that is, Bethlehem) (Genesis 35:19).

A beautiful mystery is revealed in this portion of scripture for not only the tribe of Benjamin but for the entire body of Christ. Now it was between Bethel and Bethlehem that Benjamin was born. Bethel comes from two Hebrew words: *bet*, meaning "house," and *El*, meaning "God," therefore Bethel means "house of Elohim (God)." Bethlehem is comprised of the two Hebrew words *bet* (house) and *lechem* (bread), therefore Bethlehem means "House of Bread." As believers we're all born into the house of God which is the house of Israel (restored). Our journey in life is found between these two prophetically significant cities. The ultimate destination is habitation.

The beautiful type and shadow in the Word is this: Abba Father is calling us not just to remain in Bethel but to journey into Bethlehem, the house or habitation of Bread; Yeshua, the Bread of Life! What a glorious revelation of the Father and our Bridegroom bestowed to us! It's not enough to just come into His house. He longs for us to become one (*echad*) in His habitation—Bethlehem, where our Savior chose to reveal Himself! For Benjamin this is a special promise, abiding in the Bread of Life, Yeshua, you come into the fullness of your eternal brilliance as Abba's costly living stone. It's a call of restoration of God's house, journeying from visitation and thus being transformed into habitation, the very fullness of Abba's destiny!

Read Matthew 2:1-6, Matthew 1:23, and John 1:14. Benjamin, as you come into (assimilate, are grafted) into Yeshua, you become a habitation of the Living Word. Benjaminites are sons and daughters of the Word. They have a deep hunger to devour the Word. Benjaminites, because they possess a zeal for deep knowledge, the Word, and truth, can often be scribes, teachers, and scholars.

## THE MEANING OF THE NAME

Benjamin, or *Benyamin* in Hebrew, means "son of my right hand." We know from Scripture that Yeshua sits at the right hand of the Father.

> *So then, when the Lord Jesus had spoken to them, He was received up into heaven and sat down at the right hand of God* (Mark 16:19).

The right not only signifies the supernatural and Heaven, but dominion and authority as well. The Creator carved out of His own nature a son who would embody dominion, as would his lineage. Dominion, in essence, is the fullness of kingdom reality kissed with destiny. Ephraim holds the promise of fullness whereas Benjamin's calling is a seal upon the family of God: dominion. By nature and calling they are appointed by God to come into dominion and bid creation to do the same.

The only way to enter into the kingdom is by coming to Abba as a desperate child. We must come needy and dependent, knowing He is a rewarder of those who diligently seek Him. What does a child do when they want something? They persistently ask until they receive. They also recognize that only the parent can provide for them. If we are self-sufficient and prideful, we do not see our need for Him. Narrow is the gate and few are those who find it. Those who find it are laid-down lovers who come to Abba as children! Do you want to obtain your keys? Become a radical, laid-down, childlike lover of Yeshua!

## THE WARFARE AGAINST BENJAMIN'S BIRTH

Benjamin's birth was bittersweet for Israel. Within Rachel's womb was a militant fighter who fought to be born. There is heinous warfare in the birthing of every Benjamin. Sometimes it is literal in their actual birth, while at other times it's their birthing into the kingdom (salvation and also maturity), and both could be true. Satan sought to set himself against this seed. Rachel's womb was torn (most likely due to severe hemorrhaging), where she bled to death from birthing young Benjamin.

Read Mark 2:18. Benjamin's birth was violent and full of sorrow. His mother named him *Ben-oni*, which means "son of my sorrow." Rachel's soul was travailing for the loss of children. There is travail within the heart of our heavenly Father for the tribe of Benjamin. In a beautiful type and shadow of Benjamin's two Hebrew names, we see Yeshua revealed.

Yeshua became *benoni*, a man of sorrows. We see this in His journey from the Garden of Gethsemane to Calvary.

Read Isaiah 53:3-4. Upon ascending to Heaven, Yeshua became Benyamin, son at the right hand of the Father. How precious it is that Yeshua has been revealed to and through Benjamin; that you should carry both His suffering and His great glory of dominion; that you should be seated in heavenly places in Him!

Satan knows when radical deliverers, history makers, and fearless warriors are about to be birthed. At the time of Yeshua's birth, Herod was killing children right and left. Likewise, at the time of Moses' birth, Satan was aborting the children of God. Other instances are the Holocaust, the Crusades, genocides in Africa, and abortion, which was legalized in 1973. Satan's desire is to kill the righteous seed. No birth is insignificant in the kingdom of God, either spiritual or physical. Life is precious to God. Israel, having discernment, named his son Benjamin, son of my right hand. He was prophetically declaring that Benjamin would come into kingdom authority. Dominion is a journey. For Benjamin, it involves much warfare and travail. In times of warfare Benjaminites are known for their tenacity. There is a fight of survival. There is a high price to be paid, dear Benjamin, for your life, and it can only be paid through the Cross and your surrender to it. When you cling to the Cross, its power will be the prevailing force that will bring you into absolute victory.

Benjamin was the only son born after Jacob wrestled with God and God changed His name. Benjamin was born into a time when Israel was coming into his dominion. Israel himself was coming into full maturity. The nation of Israel itself has had to wrestle for its identity and dominion. There is a continual travail in Heaven for the Jewish people. As believers, we must stand in the gap and travail for dominion for Israel and the Jewish people.

Read Isaiah 66:6-8. The groanings and travail for God's people and His land are a continual cry from His heart. Creation groans for the revealing of a kingdom of laid-down lovers, and the Father longs to use you, dear Benjamin, to travail for Him. He has caused your very life and existence to be a living intercession for creation to come into the fullness of Christ. What glory shall be revealed to us, what manner of love of Daddy God is waiting to be seen in and through us, dear brethren? Does your heart not rejoice at such news? Lift up your voice and declare the revealing of Zion, for from there does our existence lie: Jew and Gentile, one in Messiah! Yeshua is coming and His reward with Him. The reward is dominion! He is coming from where? The right hand of the Father. Messiah is coming in the dominion of our heavenly Father! Hallelujah! Join in Heaven's travail that the Lord may birth many sons and daughters within the noble tribe of Benjamin.

## BENJAMIN REVEALS GOD'S LOVE

During prayer the Lord spoke something profound to me over Benjamin. He said, "What I birthed in Reuben, I consummated in Benjamin." The travail for Benjamin gives birth to the revealed dominion in the earth. God began to reveal the nature of His love within Reuben, but He consummated the work of perfect love in the birthing of Benjamin (a prophetic foreshadow of Christ), meaning "son of my right hand." The name of Reuben, meaning "see a son," calls us to catch the revelation of God's love revealed in sonship. The Lord is saying, "See a son, a company of sons. See My Son revealed (Reuben) and see yourself as an heir to My kingdom (Benjamin)." In Benjamin He consummates His Bride by saying, "You are My Beloved, the son of my right hand; see yourself consummated in your authority!" For through Benjamin God calls us to reign as sons and daughters! Reuben speaks of the beginning of our walk with Yeshua, beginning with the Cross, the work of salvation. Through Benjamin the Beloved speaks of us at the Marriage Supper of the Lamb, the consummation of the ages! The right hand of God brings the consummation of the left hand of God. Do you see the plan of God through Manasseh (left hand) and Ephraim (right hand), who travailed for Benjamin, who is seated in Christ at the right hand? Beloved, that's where we are seated in Christ alone, in order that we might possess kingdom authority. The keys to the kingdom are released through repentance, obedience, intimacy, and child-likeness.

## THE GEMSTONE OF BENJAMIN

*...and the fourth rows a beryl and an onyx and a jasper; they shall be set in gold filigree* (Exodus 28:20).

Benjamin's particular stone is transparent green jasper (a deep green/blue color) with splatters or striations of red. Those red markings are the testament of Messiah's blood. The degree of sonship is written all over Benjamin's stone! The blood of Christ testifies to your inheritance of salvation, freedom, healing, and great favor. What a family legacy! It is believed by some that when Christ died, His shed blood fell upon the rocks that were of jasper.[1] Whether or not this is true, it holds beautiful imagery for this tribe. The green color testifies of eternal life hat Benjaminites possess. God uses their stone to testify against hell in the fight for their dominion. The war may be great concerning your very existence, but you, dear Benjaminite, shall declare with great boldness, "Death, where is your sting? I shall live and not die and declare the works of the Lord!"

I feel it's appropriate to reiterate what was said in the chapter of Reuben referring to Benjamin.

Read Revelation 4:3. Benjamin's stone is the jasper and Reuben's, the sardius. This scripture is referring to Yeshua. It says that His appearance was like that of jasper and sardius. Interestingly, Benjamin, the youngest of the twelve, is mentioned first and the firstborn, Reuben, last.

Read Matthew 19:30. We are the expressed image of Yeshua. Our identity is found in Him. Reuben is the passionate lover, and Benjamin is the beloved. That's how we come to Him: as His passionate lover and His Beloved. Hear God declaring your sonship before His throne, see yourself at His right hand, endowed with power and great favor, for this your destiny!

## JASPER: THE DECREE OF ADOPTION

There is an age-old façade against creation, and its ruler is the orphan spirit. The orphan spirit's main objective is to deceive mankind and rob them of their destiny, which is sonship. An orphan spirit is a continual driving of the spirit of slavery, keeping one in the dark, feeling rejected, abandoned, unloved, and hopeless. Here's the facade buster:

Read Romans 8:14-19. Benjamin, your jasper stone is a decree of sonship sealed within the nature of God given to you. It is not only *to* you but *through* your own life that this holy decree resounds in the earth and spiritual realms. Your decree of sonship not only resounds in heaven above, but on earth and in hell. The tenacious boldness you have comes from knowing who you belong to—Abba Father! This is why you have the ability to boldly defy darkness and come before the throne of grace. You know the covenant of life in the shed blood of Yeshua. If anyone needs a decree of life and sonship, it's you, brother and sister Benjamin!

## TRANSPARENCY EQUALS THE FEAR OF THE LORD

Read Revelation 2:17. The jasper stone can change into a clear transparent stone. God is calling you, dear Benjamin, to undergo a spiritual metamorphosis like the jasper to a clear white stone. This speaks of transparency, which comes from the fear of the Lord. So how do you become transparent to have the fear of the Lord in your life? "He, who has an ear, let him hear what the Spirit says to the churches." Hearing comes by obedience—not a reluctant obedience, but self-sacrificial obedience, stemming from a pure heart that longs to obey out of intimacy and love.

Read James 1:22-24. Our mirror is the Word of God, whereby we can see what disobedience may be hindering us from our communion with the Father. Sin is a blockade, and repentance removes all hindrances from our communion with God. Hearing is a vital step in our obedience, and communion brings us into the fear of the Lord. No one knew this more than the apostle Paul, a Benjaminite.

Read Romans 7:14-25. It takes God's grace and the Holy Spirit to be made aware of our sin, and it takes the fear of the Lord to be transformed into a transparent living stone. Transparency comes from being rid of self, which entails bowing low. As a Benjaminite, the Apostle Paul learned this lesson after much chastening of the Lord, fiery trials, and the relinquishment of self.

## THE SYMBOL OF BENJAMIN

The symbol of Benjamin is the wolf. This symbol is so rich in meaning and identity and is best explained within the prophecies of Jacob and Moses as well as other scripture references. I will fully explain this beautiful tribe's symbol better in the next portion of the book.

## JACOB'S PROPHECY

*"Benjamin is a ravenous wolf; In the morning he devours the prey, and in the evening he divides the spoil"* (Genesis 49:27).

Life's journey fashions us into who we are. It not only fashions us, but it fashions the generations to come as well. This is true of the identity of the tribe of Benjamin. Benjamin's life not only left a mark in history; more importantly, it impacted eternity. It is important to note when we are building in the kingdom of God, joint with Him in Christ, that we are not building temporal man-made agendas of Christianity, TV programs, and massive churches. All such things are temporal. When we build with God, we build an eternal kingdom that does not know decay. Trusting in temporal means of building in the kingdom would be like building sandcastles in Heaven. Sure it's fun, but the waves will come and wash them away. What legacy do we leave if we build with temporal means and intentions? Jacob was not just building his family legacy through his sons. Israel was building a spiritual kingdom whose architect and maker was Almighty God Himself. Israel said at the beginning of the prophecy to his sons: "Gather yourselves together, that I may tell you [that] what shall befall you in the last days," (Genesis 49:1-2).

Just as his grandfather and our great forefather Abraham did, Israel (Jacob) foresaw an eternal family of God. He knew God was building an eternal family that would reach far beyond his or his son's lifetime. Israel was not just speaking of his present and past generations but also of the many sons and daughters yet to be birthed who would be preserved for the last days (end times). Beloved, you and I are whom he was speaking of.

Read Hebrews 11:8-12. When Israel began to prophesy to Benjamin, he was impartial even though Benjamin, along with Joseph, was truly one of Israel's favorites. In fact he's known as the *beloved*. Israel's physical sight may have waned, but his spiritual sight was very keen, for he discerned both the destiny and facades that would befall young Benjamin and his generations.

## "BENJAMIN IS A RAVENOUS WOLF"

This portion of the prophecy is like a two-sided coin for the tribe of Benjamin. It speaks both of their strengths and destiny, as well as their weaknesses and facades that hold them captive. The tribe of Benjamin's appetite can either be a propelled by a desperate hunger for God or they can crave the wanton desires of self. *Ravenous* is defined as: "very eager or greedy for food, satisfaction, or gratification;" a *ravenous appetite*, meaning: "excessively grasping or covetous" or "living on prey."[2]

Yeshua further reiterates this truth when he says, "You cannot serve both God and mammon."

> *No man can serve two masters: for either he will hate the one, and love the other; or else he will hold to the one, and despise the other. Ye cannot serve God and mammon* (Matthew 6:24 KJV).

Mammon comes from the word *mammonas* (Chaldee in origin), meaning "riches and wealth." Mammon is an appetite for the world and worldly things, for the temporal fleshy things that will never satisfy us. Also when He says:

> *But he answered and said, "It is written, Man shall not live by bread alone, but by every word that proceedeth out of the mouth of God"* (Matthew 4:4 KJV).

So what can make our appetites holy or profane? Our hearts. The temperature of our hearts determines the bread we feast upon in our souls. When feasting upon the fear of the Lord, Abba bestows fresh, piping hot bread from the ovens of Heaven. However, if we are foolish, we will become like dogs scraping by for stale breadcrumbs. Wisdom and the fear of the Lord is the leaven indicator of hearts; it determines whether we have feast or famine. Take care, Benjamin, that you are not like a mere dog scraping by for moldy stale bread morsels. God is calling out for you to forsake folly and live! Heed wisdom, for in doing so you shall be satisfied.

Read Philippians 4:11, I Timothy 6:8, and Hebrews 13:5. Jacob, upon prophesying to his son Benjamin, saw into the spirit and soul of young Benjamin and his generations to come. You see, Jacob had never forgotten a valuable lesson. In his wisdom, he remembered his own appetite as well as his brother Esau's.

Read Genesis 25:22-34. Appetites of both Jacob and Esau determined their inheritances. Though Jacob (Israel) obtained his inheritance through his fallen nature, that of being a deceiver and supplanter, he was still given the portion God meant for him to have. What would have happened if Jacob would have obtained it without deceitful scheming and trickery? Perhaps there would have been less heartache and warfare in the family. I feel Esau still would have begrudged his brother and enmity would still have remained between the two. Nevertheless, Esau committed the greater of the two evils, for he gave up his birthright for a temporary bowl of lentils. Esau's heart temperature already had made his bread that he feasted upon his whole life long—a stale bread of compromise, sin, and idolatry—all because he fed a profane hunger. Read Hebrews 12:16.

Jacob allowed this situation to transform him from his old nature of being a supplanter to coming into his destiny as Israel, a forefather of Israel. So in hindsight, Jacob warns his son Benjamin, in whom he sees a profane appetite, and tells him to curb his appetite. Read Proverbs 13:25.

*Nephesh* (pronounced: neh'-fesh) is a very interesting Hebrew word. Strong's defines *Nephesh* as: "soul, self, life, creature, person, appetite, mind, living being, desire, emotion, passion, seat of emotions, passions, and appetites, living being."

> *The spirit of man is the candle of the Lord, searching all the inward parts of the belly* (Proverbs 20:27).

The Hebrew is literally: "One who eats to the satisfying of his appetite." The verb in this word is the Hebrew word *'akal*. It covers "devour" and "consume." We see the heightened and profane, ravenous appetite of the wolf of which Jacob forewarns in his prophecy to Benjamin (previous to this instance in scripture) in the following scriptures.

Read Judges 19:17-30. This, by far, is likely the most deplorable sin of the tribe of Benjamin. Verse 22 speaks of the certain sons of Belial. *Belial* in Hebrew (יעלבל‎ pronounced: *bel-e-yah'-al*) means: "without profit, worthlessness; by extension destruction, wickedness, evil, naughty, ungodly (men), wicked." These wicked men first tried to overcome and rape the Levite by having their way with him, and when the old man refused to allow this, they raped the Levite's concubine. *Qedeshim*, the Hebrew word meaning, "Those practicing sodomy and prostitution in religious rituals," refers to these sons of Belial. Their sin was as vile as the sin of Sodom. Profane hunger was driving the sons of Belial. The tribe of Benjamin should have been leading the charge against the sons of Belial, but to the contrary, they defended them, warring against and viciously attacking their brethren. Apostasy grew into full-blown abomination.

Read Ephesians 4:19-24. In this time of Israel's history, the tribe of Benjamin was not living up to the name their forefather Israel gave them, i.e., *Benyamin; son of my right hand*, but rather *Benoni, son of my sorrow*, which their mother, Rachel, had named her son. What a prophetic foretelling of a façade that could possibly hold them prisoner. Sin brings much sorrow, devastation, trouble, and warfare. The tribe of Benjamin gravely stepped out of their place of dominion and God-given identity during this time.

## "IN THE MORNING HE DEVOURS THE PREY"

Judges 19:25-27. Strong's Hebrew/Greek Dictionary defines *ravenous* as the Hebrew word טרף‎ *ṭâraph* (pronounced taw-raf), meaning: "to pluck off or pull to pieces; causatively to supply with food (as in morsels); to catch, feed, rend in pieces, tear (in pieces)." The sons of Belial, like a ravenous wolf, tore the Levite's concubine to pieces when they violently raped her till morning. Take heed, tribe of Benjamin, to the cautionary tale of the sons of Belial. Evil possessed these sons of Benjamin and, in their wantonness, they forfeited their place of dominion. Their profane hunger condemned their souls before God and all of Israel. The sons of Belial's bloodthirsty deeds cost them dearly. Read II Corinthians 6:14-18.

## DON'T TOUCH THE BRIDE!

Read Judges 20:3-48. The Levite in this scripture leaves a sobering picture: Don't touch the Bride! The wicked sons of Belial abused and raped the Levite's wife until she died. This scripture is a warning to all tribes not to abuse the Bride. A few years ago I was miraculously delivered and healed of being in a very abusive church. The weekend that the Lord freed me I was driving back home when I had a profound open vision encounter. It was night and the heavens (skies) pulled back, and I saw Yeshua riding straight toward me, eyes ablaze with flames of fire, upon a white stallion. In his hand was a brilliant flaming sword, and He most vehemently said, "The abuse of My Bride has gone on long enough!" He then cut the soul tie and bondage off of me. Instinctively I knew the abuse I had suffered (and allowed) was spiritual rape. I let out the most deep, gut-wrenching wail, and was free—I have never looked back since. The Lord has done a beautiful work of restoration in me. There is one thing I know: God does not tolerate abuse in any form of His Bride. The Levite in this scripture may have reacted severely to some, but he was declaring prophetically and most vehemently by the Spirit of the Lord: Do not touch My Bride! Take care that you, young Benjamites, do not give way to selfish, ravenous pleasures that will lead you to wickedness like the worthless sons of Belial. Not only will you jeopardize your destiny, but you could abuse the Bride. A ravenous appetite gone unchecked will result in spiritual death like the sons of Belial and nearly the whole tribe of Benjamin.

*Meats for the belly, and the belly for meats: but God shall destroy both it and them. Now the body is not for fornication, but for the Lord; and the Lord for the body* (II Corinthians 6:13 KJV).

## ISRAEL PURGES THE TRIBE OF BENJAMIN ONLY TO RESTORE THEM

Read Genesis 20:7-48: "But they saw that evil had come upon them…." How terrible that it was not until an atrocious battle that the rebellion of Benjamin was revealed to them. It took them literally being wiped out to the point of extinction in order to repent. The other tribes of Israel did not confront their brethren in the flesh but rather in resurrection power; they "went up against the children of Benjamin on the third day." The other tribes had bowed low by seeking the Lord and his counsel to confront their brethren, the Benjaminites. Prophetically, we see a picture where they were dwelling in the third day, the fullness of identity rooted in the victory of the Cross. This could have been avoided if Benjamin had not fed the profane hunger that led to this heinous debauchery.

## HOW BENJAMIN LOSES DOMINION

Read Judges 20:15-17. The tribe of Benjamin is a valiant and tenacious tribe, a true force to reckon with. Other than Judah, they are most likely the fiercest warriors. Twenty-six thousand Benjaminites arrogantly waged a vile and profane war against 400,000 men and, for a time, overtook them! Sin will never go overlooked. The tribe of Benjamin learned a hard lesson; their sin did find them out. They lost a grave possession of their dominion during this time.

As mentioned earlier, Benjamin is known as the son of my right hand; but they also possess the left hand: the fullness of dominion. In essence, they possess the right hand and left hand of God. Their brethren Ephraim (the right hand) and Manasseh (the left hand) went before them, preparing the way so that Benjamin (and all of us, prophetically speaking; an intercession, if you will) might possess the right and left hand of God. Where things went devastatingly awry for the tribe of Benjamin is when they disconnected from the right hand of God. They were not seated in heavenly places, abiding in the nature of Christ, but rather engaged in a catastrophic abomination borne of profane self-will. Their left hand, when unbalanced (not in unity with the right hand), carnal, and unchecked, can be desperately wicked.

Notice the humility of the other tribes. Each day they sought the Lord how to handle this grave offense from the Benjaminites. The children of Israel were so grieved, not only at the atrocity of the sin of the sons of Belial and the pride and ruthlessness of the tribe as a whole, but were even grieved to have to punish them. The Lord had to deeply purge the ravenous nature of Benjamin. A Benjamin's selfish nature, unchecked, will snowball into a full-blown rebellious and ravenous nature. The apostle Paul knew this well (as he was also a Benjaminite) when he said, "a little leaven, leavens the whole lump." We can wound many through our own selfishness and profane agendas.

The Lord used this Levite man, in essence, to prophesy to and judge the sons of Belial, and rightly so. It may seem harsh for him to cut his own concubine into twelve pieces, but he was making a declaration of holiness and judgment. God's Word is the standard, and as we step outside His will, He will bring His Word to align us into a state of sincere repentance. However, if we do not take heed at the Holy Spirit's drawing to repent, we then give legal right to the enemy and incur harsh judgment. Do not allow your appetite to take control over you, young Benjamin, for it can cause you to forego dominion and, when unchecked, strip your inheritance from you.

When Jacob spoke of this first portion of prophecy to Benjamin, he was speaking of the tribe in its immature state saying, "Benjamin is a ravenous wolf, in the morning he devours his prey." The morning in this instance refers to the early part of a Benjamin's walk. Grave mistakes can be both avoided and/or repented of when we are aligned with the Cross and the Word.

Read I Peter 2:2. Discipleship is vital to all of us. For Benjamin, their growth is stunted without the sincere milk of the Word. Far too many a Benjamin has spent a lifetime in immaturity because the proper time of growth and discipleship was never fully realized. How sad. Truth without action (unheeded) is sour milk. Nobody likes sour milk. In order to gain full maturity, do not bypass the essential time of discipleship within your walk, young Benjamin. Too many a believer, whether a Benjamin or other tribe, has been left circling the same mountain over and over again because they did not grasp the sincere milk of the Word.

## "AND IN THE EVENING HE DIVIDES THE SPOIL"

Read I Corinthians 4:20. Evening pertains to the latter portion or maturity of a Benjaminites walk with the Lord. The heart cry of Abba Father is for His beloved Benjamin to come into maturity, which is Christ, the head. A wolf comes into maturity—moreover true dominion—only through age. We walk out our salvation with fear and trembling. The wolf must separate from the pack, becoming a lone wolf. When a Benjamin comes into his lone wolf stage, he is truly being put through the fire, walking his or her own Golgotha.

Read Lamentations 3:11-33 and Mark 15:34. A true Benjaminite comes into maturity when separated from all familiar things or people, whether they be good or bad. It is when God takes out His measuring stick and says, "It's time to grow."

Read I Corinthians 13:11. When we put away childish things, we are coming more into being the true Church, refined by fire, without spot or wrinkle. During this time, you will be purged deep and wide to become the Lord's Bride. This stage, though seemingly decimating and lonely, can be the most beautiful and treasured time of your life if you let the Spirit have His way with you. Stripping of self always brings renewal to the soul, for as we are chastened, we begin to abide in perfect love. During the time a lone wolf is on his journey, he or she must seek out food, shelter, protection from predators, and eventually find a mate and begin forming another pack. As believers, this metaphor can be taken as a life application through the Word of God.

Read Song of Songs 5:5-8. Benjamin begins his lone wolf stage with the relinquishment of self, a crisis of belief. Like the Shulamite, immature and selfish Benjaminites will hesitate when the Bridegroom calls because they are caught up in themselves. The crisis of belief comes as they realize who their selfishness has separated them from: Love Himself. Sometimes the Lord will hide His face from us (though we are not forsaken) because we have distanced Him with our own sin, selfishness, or apathy. Mark, dear Benjamin, the season of separation, for the Lord is calling you higher into the depths of love, that you may be perfected in love.

## SEEK OUT FOOD

Read John 4:32-34. Yeshua made a statement to the disciples that cuts deep to the soul. The soul, the *nephesh* (appetite) of our being, must seek after the kingdom. Therefore the *nephesh* must be chastened to desire the things of God and thereby be transformed to fully inherit them. Carnal methods birth a carnal end, but spiritual methods such as repentance, prayer, feeding on the Word of God, being chaste unto the Lord, and fleeing from idolatry are essential to finding not merely an adequate food supply but a wholesome abundance in the nature of God. These spiritual disciplines help us obtain a supernatural life of victory (empowered by the Cross and the Holy Spirit) and eternity with the Bridegroom! God has called us to His love feast. Obedience is the only way to wine and dine at the Bridegroom's table. For obedience is feasting upon the Father's will. Yeshua Himself was tested, that His *nephesh* would be chaste also.

Read Matthew 4:1-4. Yeshua, tempted in every as we have been, was faced with the challenge of keeping His appetite pure. When we seek out other methods and means of filling our hunger, we forego dominion. Yeshua came into the wilderness to be tested, just as Adam and Eve were.

Read Genesis 3:1-6. What the first Adam failed to do (because he was in the flesh), Yeshua did. Yeshua, alone in the wilderness, like a lone wolf tried and tested, found His food at His Father's table. He did not allow his own *nephesh* to overcome him, but rather he overcame His own *nephesh* and wrought dominion for us!

Dear brother and sister Benjaminite, when you enter your wilderness, know that there is *One* who has gone before you. He is the Living Bread from the house of Bet-lechem. Abiding in His father's will, Yeshua became the bread of life, purchasing your (and all humanity's) way back to the Garden of the Lord. An hour comes to every believer where he or she is tested only to inherit dominion. When the Lord places you, dear Benjaminite, in the wilderness, know that your soul (*nephesh*) is being chastened by the Lord. Seek only after Him and His Living Bread. You must lay aside immaturity, clinging to men, selfish means, rebellion, and zealousness not tried by fire. In doing so, you will come into the fullness Christ has for you!

## SHELTER

Read Song of Songs 2:14. The secret hidden life is a life of becoming chaste through much refinement where one finds not only maturity but the fullness of identity and destiny. It is as a lone wolf that Benjamin really comes into who he or she is as the Bride of Christ. Any co-dependent tendencies will be stripped, faith stretched, and self-survival skills crucified. For every Benjaminite must come into the shelter of the Almighty by first being hidden in Christ, in the secret place of the stairs.

Read Psalm 61:3 and Psalm 119:114. A wolf will often find shelter by whatever means possible. The elements and pursuit of an enemy often times will drive a wolf to use their instincts and find cover. The same is true spiritually for all Benjaminites. Benjaminites are always being moved by the spiritual atmosphere around them, good or bad. Wolves often find shelter in caves. We find our shelter in the Rock of our salvation, Yeshua, the only true hiding place. Trust your God-given instincts of sight and hearing, which are extremely keen like a wolf.

## PROTECTION FROM PREY

Read James 4:7. Worship is vital in order to resist and engage in successful warfare, without which we'd be striving and leaning upon the arm of the flesh. Many a person becomes susceptible to the enemy by negating this vital truth. True protection comes from worship coupled with obedience. This can be summed up into one word: abiding.

Read John 14:30. Why did Satan (the prince of this world) have nothing in Yeshua? Yeshua lived continually abiding in the Father. In order to remain under Abba's protection and give no place to the devil, we must come into abiding in Christ. The curse cannot alight without a cause. If the enemy has no place in you, curses and facades cannot remain!

> *Like a sparrow in its flitting, like a swallow in its flying, So a curse without cause does not alight* (Proverbs 26:2).

## FINDING A MATE AND BEGINNING YOUR PACK

A lone wolf comes into full maturity when they have found their mate and begin a pack (or family) of their own. It is only when you lose yourself through the Cross that you gain the fullness of being in *echad* (unity) with your Bridegroom, Yeshua.

Read Luke 9:23-24. Endure, brethren, until the end, for the Lord is chastening you to be His Bride without spot or wrinkle. His grace is sufficient for you. As you abide in the resurrected Lord, you will be found faithful as His Bride. I urge you to be found as one of the five virgins, chaste, ready, with adequate supply of oil, watching and waiting for His return. For Benjamin, the lone wolf in full maturity is likened unto the church of Philadelphia, a pillar in the house of God.

Read Revelation 3:12. Maturity for any believer is obtainable. Deepest maturity can be found in a transformed bride who decreases so that the Bridegroom may increase. It is only then that an unadulterated selfless gospel can be preached. A mature Bride is a co-laborer with her husband working alongside Him in her Father's fields.

Read Song of Songs 7:10-12. For a Benjaminite to come into ministry is when he begins to develop his or her pack. United with the Bridegroom, they begin to build the family (pack) of God.

## MOSES' PROPHECY

*Of Benjamin he said, "May the beloved of the Lord dwell in security by Him, who shields him all the day, and he dwells between His shoulders"* (Deuteronomy 33:12).

## MAY THE BELOVED OF THE LORD

Read Song of Songs 8:5. Endowed with an eternal assurance, a true Benjaminite rests in the knowledge of *who they belong* to and in full maturity of *who they are*. Amongst this gleefully childlike company you will find the true spirit of the Bride. The only way to truly enter the kingdom is to become like a child. A true Benjaminite knows how to possess a security rooted in true childlike faith.

Read Matthew 18:2-4. The tribe of Benjamin possesses a unique gifting of childlike faith. Because of this faith, they go on to do many mighty exploits for the kingdom of God. Benjaminites walk in this authority because they are resting in their Father and the Bridegroom.

Late 2007 I was accepted into an internship for Succat Hallel, a 24/7 house of prayer in Jerusalem. I had eleven days' notice to go. At that time the Lord placed a message by missionary Heidi Baker in my hands. Its message became my anthem for my miraculous appointment in Jerusalem. Heidi spoke about a time when she was beginning her mission in Mozambique, Africa. She was alone with no place to stay or food to eat and so she called on the Lord. It was then a little old missionary came up to her and handed her a set of keys, saying, "I have a house. I need you to live in it…and I have food, eat it or the rats will eat it," and then the little old missionary lady left without telling Heidi the address. Heidi reiterated a valuable point. We've all been given the keys, but we don't know how to get there. What's the address, the way into the kingdom?

Heidi explained, "You must first become like a little child." She then proceeded to walk over to a little girl and ask her, "Do you think God can make bread?"

And the little girl sweetly nodded her head *yes*.

Heidi again asked, "What about spaghetti? Do you think He can make spaghetti?"

The little girl again resounded a blissfully innocent and unwavering *yes*.

So, back to my time expecting to go to Israel, with no money or means to go but believing in full faith it was my appointed time to go. My prayer became, "Abba, You can make spaghetti." And in no time I went. Mind you, Abba provided a first-class ticket to Israel thirty minutes before going to the airport! Upon landing for Israel, I got my bags and proceeded to the *sherut* (combination of a van and a bus), where I sat with eight ultra-orthodox Jewish men. We were about to drive out of the airport, and one of the men was discussing one of his daughters, beaming from ear to ear. He told of his daughter's last request before he left for Israel (in these exact words), "Abba, can you make me spaghetti?" And so began my miraculously supernatural appointed time in Israel. I tell this little story to say that if we come as expectant children, there is nothing our Daddy won't do!

Childlike faith is natural for Benjamites. They know who they are and who their Daddy is. Under the apple tree (Christ Himself), you were born, Benjamin, and raised by Holy Spirit. It was there you were awakened to come into the nature of God as an innocent blissful bride, leaning upon her Beloved. Your strength and security lies in this truth.

## "DWELL IN SECURITY BY HIM, WHO SHIELDS HIM ALL THE DAY AND HE DWELLS BETWEEN HIS SHOULDERS"

Read Matthew 8:5-10. The story of the centurion is not only a beautiful picture of faith but one of possessing dominion. The centurion walked in his God-given authority because he never wavered in his faith. Doubt is the thief who tries to steal dominion from the children of God, for it is by faith we inherit the promises of God. To doubt is to strive, and to believe is to enter into the rest of the Lord.

Read Hebrews 6:12. The centurion was not slothful in his faith but believed wholeheartedly. His faith amazed even Yeshua! Benjaminites likewise are a tremendous people of authority and thus inherit dominion through uninhibited faith. How do they possess such rare, untainted faith? They live in kingdom reality, inheriting promises in tenacious childlike faith; they refuse to accept the facade of doubt. A Benjamite's faith is a key to his dominion, for he lives his life as Abba's favorite one. They are secure in the love of God.

Read Isaiah 9:6-7. Yeshua carries, as both king and high priest, the government upon His shoulders. Shoulders in Scripture carry the connotation of government or authority. Levites likewise carried authority as they carried the Ark of the Covenant upon their shoulders. Benjaminites carry dominion, the dominion of childlike faith and favor upon their shoulders. The tribe of Benjamin is endowed with fearless faith because they know Who is carrying them! Yeshua, who is the epitome of the government of praise, carries the Beloved, *Benyamin, son of my right hand*. Benjamites stand in unwavering faith because they are confident of the dominion of heavenly places they stand and walk in! In times of testing, a Benjamin only need rest upon shoulders of his Bridegroom King, who carries him from victory to victory, faith to faith, and glory to glory!

## THE FAÇADES OF BENJAMIN
### THE ORPHAN SPIRIT ROBS DOMINION FROM BENJAMIN

The orphan spirit is a separation from both the love and image of Abba Father. One of the greatest travesties in the earth today is the ravaging devastation the orphan spirit has wrought. Satan's greatest conquest is to use the orphan spirit to deceive us into believing that we are separated from the love of God. This is the resolution of the orphan spirit.

*A voice was heard in Ramah, weeping and great mourning, Rachel weeping for her children; and she refused to be comforted, because they were no more* (Matthew 2:18).

Rachel prophetically was interceding for the revealing of the sons and daughters of God. Her own heart was ravaged as she lay hemorrhaging and dying, knowing she would never raise young Benjamin. Rachel had a life-long struggle with infertility until she bore Joseph, and then she died at Benjamin's birth. Her loss echoes into eternity, for I believe in the spirit she saw many aborted and or orphaned children and was inconsolable. Her travail is still resounding today in the earth and heavenly realms and beckons all of us, but especially her beautiful Benjamin (the tribe as a whole), to come into the fullness.

One of the greatest snares for this tribe is immaturity, a failure to come into the fullness of sonship. They also can allow the facade of the orphan spirit to deceive them by staying in bondage to the past and its suffering. Benjamites struggle coming into the fullness of sonship when they allow the orphan spirit to deceive them into believing that they are abandoned by God. When a Benjamin cannot see that he is made in the likeness of God as *Benyamin, son of my right hand*, he is enslaved to the lie of the orphan spirit that he is *Benoni, son of sorrows*. With the orphan spirit come strongholds of rejection, shame, poverty, anger, disillusionment, and self-doubt. These very snares likewise keep the Bride of Christ as a whole captive from coming into the fullness of the glory of God. It's façade-busting time, Church, for the revealing of the sons and daughters of God is here! Hallelujah!

Read Psalm 10:18. The Lord has inclined His ear to you today, O Benjamin. He alone will deliver and vindicate you from the oppression of the orphan spirit. Immerse yourself in Abba's love. He is carrying you from glory to glory.

## CHARACTERISTICS OF THE ORPHAN SPIRIT

*Lie of abandonment*: The lie of abandonment is the hook used by Satan to keep you from sonship and ultimately dominion. True kingdom reality is that your heavenly Father is omnipresent, walking with you. He has gone before you; He is your glory and rear guard. Love never fails. You are in the palm of His hand, and your walls are ever before Him! He that keeps Israel never slumbers nor sleeps! Stand upon the following verses to renounce the lie of abandonment. Read Deuteronomy 4:31, Deuteronomy 31:8, and Psalm 94:14.

*Shame*: Shame is not a garment any child of God is called to wear. Shame is no more than a residue of unjust condemnation. It must be cast off, for we are King's kids. As heirs of righteousness, we must disengage from the lie of shame in order to fully inherit the promises of God. More importantly, we must burn the filthy rags of shame, for as children of the Most High God, our portion is to rejoice that we are endowed with the glory, clothed with His very nature. Rest in the work of forgiveness and acceptance of your Father God.

> *Instead of your* [former] *shame, you shall have a two-fold recompense, instead of dishonor and reproach* (your people) *shall rejoice in their portion. Therefore in their land they shall possess double* [of what they had forfeited]; *everlasting joy shall be theirs* (Isaiah 61:7 AMP).

*Doubt:* The lie of doubt causes us to question our own sonship and Abba's ability as our faithful Father. For the tribe of Benjamin, doubt is most deadly. When doubt reigns, dominion waxes dim. Doubt is the open door that robs a believer of possessing the kingdom. Brother and sister Benjamin, do not allow doubt at the table with you. Your kingdom authority, your vial of preciousness is that you, blissful Bride of the King of Kings, captivate your Bridegroom King, move the heart of Almighty God your Father, walk in supernatural favor, miracles, signs and wonders, and dislodge hordes of hell with your simple childlike faith. Refuse to doubt; refuse to fear. Perfect love will cast out the root of doubt in your life. Seek Him whose love divine will remove the scales of doubt from your eyes to demonstrate how secure you are in His love. Possess the dominion that is rightfully yours! Read Mark 11:23.

*Alienation*: Alienation is a displacement of authority and identity. In and of itself, it is a type of replacement theology (the lie that the Church has replaced Israel is replacement theology, for it deceives us that Abba no longer has a plan or purpose for Israel, but also as Gentiles we are removed from our brethren Israel). It is a vapid lie that seeks to deceive us into believing that we do not belong in our Father's house. It also seeks to keep us from kingdom connections. Sometimes this lie grows through abuse that either our natural families or the hirelings in the Church have placed on us. It must be seen as a lie and shaken off. Alienation will cause the believer to always feel like an outsider, always looking in but never entering in. It is a grave deception, brethren. Do not allow this facade to remain in your life. Ask Abba to reveal how to fit into His building, what place you possess in His heart. Ask Him how to see yourself as joint-to-joint with your brothers and sisters in Christ. You are no longer an alien or a foreigner to the covenants of promise! The revelation of the tribes is a picture of how you fit in! Renounce the lie of alienation and receive Abba's love and your place in His heart!

Read Ephesians 2:10-13, 19. As fellow citizens, we as the Church are grafted into Israel, not a replacement for Israel.

*Hopelessness*: Hopelessness robs us of our ability to dream with God, for without hope we lose our vision, our pursuit of the joys of life in His kingdom. Many a heart goes astray because they have lost hope. Hope is the enlightenment of the eyes of our heart, causing us to endure with joy and finish our race. People perish for a lack of vision, and hope is the promise of the vision fulfilled. Read Jeremiah 29:11, Colossians 1:27, and Isaiah 42:4.

*Stigma through speculation*: Read James 2:1-9. Stigma through speculation is an ignorant assumption, a perception based on someone's status. What is absolutely inexcusable about this is that many believers perceive their brothers and sisters in Christ this way. Take the picture of an orphan: Imagine a mother passes by saying to her children, "Have nothing to do with that child, he's a dirty little orphan." Stigmas are false judgments that can cause painful persecution. Yeshua himself bore the stigma of being a bastard child of Mary. Clearly He was no bastard child, for He is the only begotten Son of the Father. He knew what it felt like to be an orphan, for when he took the sin and shame of the world, the Father momentarily turned His face from Him. Sin has made us all orphans; that is why we are separated from God, fatherless until we come to the Cross, the façade buster of the orphan spirit!

The apostle Paul, a Benjamite, knew far too well of stigmas also. As an apostle he faced great persecution, stigmas from his sinful past and the suffering of hunger, imprisonment, and adversity. But Paul was no orphan; he was a fool for Christ. A fool for Christ challenges the ignorant mindsets of religious and learned men. He even suffered stigma in the midst of his peers of apostles and those he ministered to. Why was Paul not a victim to an orphan spirit? He knew who he was and who carried him! He was a true son of Benjamin, resting upon the shoulders of His Bridegroom and possessing the fullness of his dominion!

Read I Corinthians 4:3-13. To be free of stigmas, know who your Father is and who you are. Walk in your God-given authority, or someone will take it and use it against you! Do not allow stigmas to keep you in a pit of pity and rejection. Daddy wants to carry you, dear Benjamin; come rest upon His shoulders. Forgive those who have held stigmas about you.

Repent of stigmas you yourself have had of bitterness, stemming from negative beliefs others held against you.

*Poverty*: Poverty is the absence of inheritance. When a child is orphaned, he or she is left without parents and without a legacy of love, provision, wisdom, guidance, nurturing, and comfort. This can be seen in both physical and spiritual loss. Poverty itself alienates, brings shame, causes stigma through speculation, and brings feelings of abandonment. Poverty is a sneaky thief that steals from the children of God. For Benjaminites, poverty can directly oppose their dominion, destiny, and identity. Poverty is a destructive facade within the tribe of Benjamin.

Read John 10:1-18, 25-29. The lie of the orphan spirit perpetuates the cycle of poverty. The spirit of poverty is actually greedy in nature. It seeks to devour, kill, and destroy those in its path. Poverty allows the orphan spirit to keep us on that never-ending hamster wheel: the lie that Abba has abandoned us. Faithful fathers provide for their children (within their power). We, the children of God, are most certainly not beggars, for we are heirs of righteousness and the glory of God.

Read Psalm 37:25. Upon praying for this tribe and this façade (as well as the orphan spirit), the Lord gave me a clear picture using the classic children's book, *A Little Princess* by Frances Hodgson Burnett.[3] I believe it is a prophetic picture for those who have wrestled against spirits of poverty and the orphan spirit. Sara Crewe, the little princess, goes from being an affluent and pampered rich girl to a pauper overnight through the reported death of her father. In the end she discovers that her father was not dead, thus Sara was never orphaned or poor and all is restored. Many of you deal with the facade of poverty. Here's the facade buster: If you are in Christ, you are not a pauper, nor are you an orphan. The Lord wants to take us from peasant rags to the palace, for that is our rightful place. There are times of testing and maybe even brief seasons when He may hide His face from us, but He is always there. He is Emmanuel, God with us, and YHVH Yireh (Jehovah Jireh; our provider). Abide in childlike faith and obedience, and He will give you a strategy to overcome poverty.

Read II Corinthians 8:9-15 and Philippians 4:19. Poverty can come through two ways. Both rob dominion from the children of God. The first way poverty comes is through an oppression of the enemy, be it through birth (generational curse), sickness (leaving one unable to work and medical bills), a fallen economy, or greed by another afflicting you. All are circumstances no one willingly chooses. The second way poverty comes is through laziness and or greed (living beyond your means). Both plague the tribe of Benjamin. It is urgent, brethren, to rightly discern between the two. I have seen and heard believers misjudge that all poverty is laziness (a false doctrine) and immediately attach a stigma to that person by their ignorance and or prideful assumption. Both means of poverty require an antidote of wisdom, truth, and unconditional love.

When poverty comes by means of oppression, the spirit of poverty is activated by the enemy's greed to steal a person's inheritance. Poverty through laziness and greed will cause a person to forego dominion (this is based in the facade of selfishness, which we will cover next). Whichever way poverty comes in, whether oppression or laziness, both these afflictions can be overcome, for Christ died and conquered both. If you have been misjudged or have misjudged the poor, take into account how Yeshua felt about the poor. He loved the poor; in fact, he spent most of His time ministering to them. There are many instances in Scripture where God rebukes those who oppress the poor. At times, neither Yeshua nor the disciples or early apostles had a place to even lay their heads. God does not despise the poor, but most vehemently opposes the thief who robs His children of their inheritance.

Read Deuteronomy 15:4-15. God made provision and instruction in the Torah (the first five books of Moses) for the poor. If we kept Torah alone, the poor, widows, and orphans would be well taken care of. Yeshua taught and lived according to Torah, as did the early church. The façade of poverty has robbed mankind for ages. Poverty comes to oppose and defy the sonship of every Benjamin. Poverty, though often connected with natural provision, is not exclusive to it. We can have a poverty of soul. The wealthy can be enslaved to poverty, for if their *nephesh* (spiritual appetite) is greedy, the enemy is already at work to steal from them. Paul said it well: In whatever state he was, he had learned to be content. The state of being content is that of being childlike. Young Benjamin himself faced the façade of poverty and overcame.

Read Genesis 42:1-3. Famine was in the land. Jacob attempted to shield young Benjamin from poverty and adversity, but God would soon take young Benjamin to task.

Read Genesis 42:15-38 and Genesis 44:10-12. Once Benjamin was summoned, Joseph tested him. I believe what the Lord was using Joseph to test was the *nephesh* (soul's appetite) of young Benjamin. Would a profane hunger of greed control him, or would he bow low when the silver cup was placed in his sack? A profane *nephesh* (referring to the ravenous wolf) will lead us into poverty, but a holy one will deliver us from it.

> *Not that I speak in respect of want: for I have learned, in whatsoever state I am to be content* (Philippians 4:11).

It was through Joseph's younger brother, Benjamin, that a lifelong family separation and persecution was ended, for when Joseph saw his only brother (full-blooded from his mother), he could no longer hold on to the bitterness of all that his other brethren had done to him. It took seeing Benjamin for the Lord to open the eyes of Joseph and to break the poverty of soul and famine that had befallen the family. God used Benjamin to restore dominion and obedience! Through Benjamin, poverty was eliminated. Joseph blessed young Benjamin five times the amount of his brethren in silver and in raiment. Five is the number of grace. The raiment (or clothing) was a symbol of Benjamin's authority and identity, of being endowed with grace. He had the breaker anointing, which testified against the spirit of poverty.

A reversal of fortune is coming to the tribe of Benjamin. Your inheritance is the favor of God! Yeshua paid the price that you might walk free of the oppression of poverty. If you have engaged in poverty through your own greed (selfish wants and desires, living beyond your means) or laziness, repent and God will restore you. Give no place to the enemy. If you put your hand to the plow, unlimited favor will be restored, but more importantly, dominion will be restored. Read Proverbs 12:24, Matthew 25:26, Romans 12:11, and Hebrews 6:12.

## THE FAÇADE OF REBELLION AND WITCHCRAFT

Read I Samuel 8:4-22. The *nephesh* (spiritual appetite) of King Saul was indicative of the nation of Israel prior to (and during) his reign. The nation of Israel did not hunger and thirst after righteousness. They wanted a man-made system to rule them. Israel wanted to do it their way and not God's way. Read Deuteronomy 7:6-11.

The story of King Saul is a cautionary tale to the tribe of Benjamin. For in King Saul we see a Benjamite, anointed but never maturing into his calling. It was Saul's own *nephesh*, which was full of rebellion that caused him to forego dominion. Warning signs of King Saul's immaturity, which would lead to his rebellion, were evident early on in his reign. He engaged in the orphan spirit.

Read I Samuel 9:21. Saul clearly engaged in the lies of the orphan spirit. He was riddled with self-doubt. He did not know who he was as a son of God. He felt shame for being smallest in the smallest of tribes and insignificant, instead of seeing that God uses the weak things of the world to confound the wise. He alienated himself. He was giving excuses why he couldn't reign. Have you ever done that with God?

*Immaturity:* Read I Samuel 10:16. Saul, after being questioned by his uncle, is unable to recount all that the Lord spoke through the prophet Samuel; the most important fact being that he was to be anointed king of Israel. Whether it was because he was insecure and intimidated or for another reason Scripture doesn't say, but the erratic behavior that would plague his reign began to surface here.

Read I Samuel 10:21-23. Here we find a newly anointed king running from his place of dominion and destiny like a young boy hiding behind the skirts of his mother. He would have an on-again, off-again obedience track record with the Lord. When the Spirit of the Lord was upon him, he excelled, but he could not hold onto his place or position of authority. As soon as the Spirit of the Lord would lift from King Saul, he resorted back to the erratic and immature behavior, which, un-dealt with, led to his rebellious demise. He was green at best and could not handle the anointing placed upon him. King Saul did not heed the instruction and warning given by Samuel.

Read I Samuel 12:20-25. A downward spiral is clearly evident in Saul's reign as king, but even more in his walk with the Lord. From the beginning, the end is seen in Saul's life. Like many who abort their callings, he failed to embrace a lifestyle of obedience and suffered dearly for it.

Read I Samuel 13:3-4. Saul boasted and glorified himself in accomplishments he should have admonished his son Jonathan for. His self-seeking, boastful agenda knew no bounds, even to his own family. Conceited, far from humble, the devil was already knocking at his door, and the thief was primed to steal his inheritance.

## THE LEAVEN OF REBELLION GROWS IN KING SAUL

Read I Samuel 13:7-14. It was at this point King Saul should have done some sincere repentance, motive checking, and relinquishment of self, but as we will soon see in the next portion of scripture, he deceptively engaged in his own agenda and was in blatant rebellion toward God. King Saul's failure to seek the Lord brought confusion to his mind until he was eventually depraved of mind. Rebellion kills. Disobedience always brings confusion.

Read I Samuel 14:20, 24-30. Saul calls for the Ark without inquiring of the Lord to do so. His own people were in great fear and confusion because Saul walked in the counsel of his own selfish desires and rebellion. Contention within his own household was evident, as Jonathan was a stark difference from his father Saul and thereby challenged his own father's foolish oath. This would lead not only to division but to the abortion of King Saul's destiny. Saul was a self-indulgent tyrant who abused his authority to accomplish his own agenda.

*And Saul asked counsel of God, Shall I go down after the Philistines? Wilt thou deliver them into the hand of Israel? But he answered him not that day* (I Samuel 14:37 KJV).

## REBELLION KILLS

Read I Samuel 15. Rebellion is like a welcome mat to the door of our heart that tells Satan, "Come on in and make yourself at home." Entertaining it will always call us out of intimacy with the Father, for it is sin that separates us from God. Light cannot fellowship with darkness, and if we are children of the light, we will emanate the light of our Father God. King Saul not only rebelled against God, but he was deceptive when confronted with his sin. Our sins will find us out. Whether or not we walk in dominion is dependent on whether we embrace the chastening of the Lord, followed by a sincere repentance. Sin will deny the Cross, bringing death. Obedience embraces the Cross and brings life.

Read Deuteronomy 30:19 and Romans 6:23. King Saul's rebellion was the open door to every evil spirit. Rebellion is as the sin of witchcraft. Take heed, dear Benjamin, to the cautionary tale of King Saul, and do not make rebellion your bedfellow, for in doing so you will open the door to witchcraft.

Read I Samuel 16:14-15. Saul's ravenous appetite for rebellion caused him to be overcome by evil spirits. Driving spirits, madness, insomnia, confusion, depression all came through entertaining a profane *nephesh* in Saul. Rebellion gives a legal right to destruction. I believe that there were many legions of demons that were unleashed upon Saul because of his rebellion. Saul willingly relinquished his destiny, identity, and dominion when he made the decision to live in blatant rebellion.

Read I Samuel 18:6-29. Saul's ravenous appetite of sin overtook him. Madness, fear, suspicion, and jealousy consumed him like a pack of angry wolves upon helpless prey. Saul became prey through his own rebellion.

## THE DEADLY DEMISE OF WITCHCRAFT

Read I Samuel 28:3-20. Witchcraft is an abomination to the Lord in any form. King Saul called up the spirit of Samuel through a sorcerer. It is this very act that sealed his final fate, for the leaven of rebellion grew into full-blown witchcraft and sorcery to such a degree that the Lord required the life of Saul for his rebellion. Rebellion, no matter how small, if not repented of will grow into a deadly demise of dominion. Witchcraft is a great travesty to you, dear Benjamite. Do not entertain it for a moment. King Saul dies at the hand of his enemies, the Philistines, all because he fed the *nephesh* of rebellion within him. His head and body were dismembered and made a mockery of amongst the Philistines. Take heed, lest rebellion make a mockery of the destiny and dominion you are called to walk in. Embrace the Cross, repent of rebellion, and live.

## THE IDOL OF SELF DENIES THE POWER OF THE CROSS

*Then said Jesus unto his disciples, If any man will come after me, let him deny himself, and take up his cross, and follow me* (Matthew 16:24 KJV).

The idol of self is the true root of rebellion, witchcraft, and immaturity. Self denies the power and the authority of the Cross. To deny the Cross is to deny intimacy, identity, destiny, and dominion. Moreover, indulging in the idol of self, which is sin at its core, is to deny sonship. When we engage in sin, we are slaves of sin, but if we surrender to the Cross, denying self, we inherit eternal life. The choice that befell Adam and Eve is no different from yours or mine. Will we entertain the profane *nephesh* of sin and indulge in self (doing things our way), or will we hunger and thirst after righteousness? Clearly, King Saul engaged in the idol of self, vehemently denying his right to sonship as he entertained his own flesh. The apple didn't fall far from the tree, for when his daughter, Michal, saw David dancing before the Lord, she foolishly engaged in a selfish rampage against her own husband. For this she was left barren. The idol of self leaves many a destiny barren in its wake. Do not be deceived, brother and sister Benjamin, for selfishness is contrary to building the Father's kingdom. Selfishness is when we build our own kingdom, denying sonship and the price of freedom that Christ paid for us.

## THE JASPER TRANSFORMATION OF PAUL

Read Acts 7:58, 8:1-3, 9:1-2. Prior to Saul's (the apostle Paul's) encounter with the Lord that led to his conversion, he clearly displayed that he was a Benjamite in his immature state. Saul, a learned man, studied the law of God with great zeal. The tribe of Benjamin has a great zeal and appetite for knowledge. Saul had an outward form of godliness (religious works) but denied the power thereof, which is the Cross of Christ and the law fulfilled (II Timothy 3:5). In his self-righteous mission, he devoured the Church. Saul's *nephesh* was clearly wicked; he was among those who persecuted and killed Stephen (Acts 7:54). Like a ravenous wolf, he was all too ready to kill in the name of God. He most likely justified himself in rationalizing that this was even the will of God to persecute the church. Saul, however, had a rude awakening with the Truth.

Read Acts 22:3-8. Saul is confronted face-to-face with the facade of his own selfishness, rebellion, and wickedness. Yeshua appeared so greatly in His glory that it blinded Saul. What Yeshua was revealing unto Saul was the blindness in his own heart. Yeshua, the Living Word, divided the profane *nephesh* of Saul, revealing his true intentions, which were indeed wicked and sinful.

> *And he said, "Who are You, Lord?" And He said, "I am Jesus whom you are persecuting"* (Acts 9:5).

Saul was transformed by the Cross and would go on to become the great forefather of the Church whom we know as the apostle Paul. His green jasper stone changed into a clear jasper stone when Abba Father gave him not only eternal salvation but also a new heart, restoring him in sonship, identity, and dominion. Paul became a pillar in the house of God that day, leading not only generations of his time but millions throughout history to sonship in Christ through his selfless ministry of the gospel. His life was a drink offering poured out that you and I might inherit a gospel unadulterated.

Paul's conversion is one of the most radical in Scripture and maybe even perhaps in history, for he allowed the anvil of the Cross and its suffering to transform him into becoming a true Benjamin, a son of the right hand of God, ruling and reigning with Him! What a testimony, what an encouragement to you, dear Benjamin! For you, too, have been confronted with the Truth and allowed Yeshua, the Living Word, to bring you into the kingdom of God! Rejoice, for you are no longer an orphan, a slave of sin, hopeless, and without purpose, but an heir of righteousness, a true son and daughter of God's right hand! Dominion is yours. Will you take hold of it this day in childlike faith, humility, and purity? Possess the kingdom, for it is your inheritance as a child of God!

A faithful band of selfless deliverers and heroes within the tribe of Benjamin beckon you, dear Benjaminite, to arise and come forth in the fullness of your destiny. The apostle Paul certainly was one of them. Flawed yet fiercely loyal, they provide a legacy that will encourage, strengthen, and propel you into destiny. Each endured by faith and prevailed to inherit dominion as they relinquished the idols of self, rebellion, and immaturity. When the battle raged, they raged harder. They defied odds, overcame stigmas, and possessed the fullness of sonship.

## JONATHAN

Jonathan defied a faulty rebellious protocol of his father, his own rights to the throne, to stand unapologetically and bravely with God's anointed, David. Jonathan counted his true father to be God Himself. He denied the fear of a tyrannical father, whom the Spirit of the Lord had left, and chose rather the fear of the Lord. Jonathan possessed a wisdom and maturity beyond his years. He selflessly laid down his life for the true kingdom call and for David, his spiritual brother.

Read I Samuel 18:1-5. Jonathan and David's relationship is a beautiful picture of unity in the Spirit. Jonathan was a prince and in succession to the throne. He was very discerning of his father (a profane *nephesh* of self and rebellion) and of David (a holy nephesh of obedience and worship). Jonathan saw his father's selfish agenda, rebellion, and jealousy. He saw in David the makings of an anointed leader. His spirit witnessed the gifts and calling on David's life. What is so beautiful is that he gave David his princely robe, his armor, and his sword. In doing so, he acknowledged David's authority, conferred on him by the Lord. David received great fame from his victories in war. Jonathan could have very easily become spiteful and jealous like his father, Saul. Instead, he became David's dearest friend, servant, and comrade in battle. If the Body of Christ would come into this kind of selfless humility and serve one another in pure love, what freedom and victory we would have!

## ABNER

Read II Samuel 3:17-21. Flawed yet faithful, Abner stayed loyal to Saul until Saul's death. He continued to serve the kingdom of the house of Saul until he foresaw the Spirit beckoning him into the kingdom shift of King David's rightful reign. He was humble enough to surrender a life-long battle, stigmas, pride, selfish desires, differences, and preconceived ideas in order to unite Benjamin and the other tribes under David's reign. Until Abner had made a pact with David, only Judah was under David's leadership. What is most fascinating is that after David's reign and the northern and southern kingdoms split, the tribe of Benjamin stayed faithful to Judah. None of that would have been possible if Abner had not been faithful to surrender to the Lord and His leading. To this very day Benjamin, as part of the southern kingdom comprised of Judah, Levi, and Benjamin, is now part of the two-and-a-half tribes who make up the Jewish people. Little Benjamin has become part of a great nation, for which we have Abner to thank because of his selfless surrender and faithfulness. Read Psalm 68:27.

## SAINT FRANCIS OF ASSISI

Though this next man is not in Scripture, he is most worthy of mentioning as a valid example to the tribe of Benjamin. Saint Francis of Assisi was a monk during the late 11th and early 12th centuries. Myth and legend surround him from the Catholic faith, but no matter what you may or may not believe about him, the truth is that he was a selfless lover of Yeshua and mankind. Born to privilege, Francis was the son of a wealthy textile merchant. He was practically nobility, born with a silver spoon in his mouth. In my opinion, he was a true Benjamite, a Gentile grafted into Israel. He was a spoiled, rich young man, favored with everything, lacking nothing…women, money, prestige, etc. Francis seemingly had it all. Francis went to Jerusalem to fight in the Crusades in 1204, when he fell ill. Upon his sickbed, he had a radical encounter with the Lord, who commissioned him to "build His church."[4]

Upon returning home to Italy, Francis's radical conversion was not well received. His family deemed him a madman. A fool for Christ's sake (sounds similar to the apostle Paul's conversion), Francis went to the city square, stripped himself of all noble attire, and declared that he had no father and mother, that God in Heaven was his Father. He then selflessly spent his life ministering to the poor, embracing celibacy, modeling humility, and building the Church. What really earmarked him as a radical of his day (and even by today's standards) was his embrace of the Cross. Saint Francis of Assisi was known for having stigmata as he shared in the sufferings of Christ. I believe these "signs" are a form of deep travail and mark of the glory of God. The Bible talks about how those who share in Messiah's sufferings also share in His glory.

Read I Peter 4:12-13. A revelation of His glory awaits all those who share in the sufferings of Christ. When we allow the daily bearing of the marks of the Cross to truly produce a lasting revelation of the Kingdom, we are revealed as the true sons and daughters of Abba's glory! The works or hype of religion and flesh bring only self-exaltation, which is fleeting and profane. Instead, consider your Bridegroom, who identified with and bore your suffering to reveal His glory and your identity as an eternal heir to His kingdom. What glory lies within the Cross, O Benjamin! Possess your true authority by laying down your life unto death, for an irrevocable, incorruptible glory lies within your Bridegroom King!

## MORDECAI

At the time of Esther, the Jewish people had fallen into Babylonian captivity. Living in a time of unrest and anarchy, they were displaced from their homeland in a pagan country. Deliverers and heroes were sorely needed, when two unlikely candidates arose to bring salvation to the Jewish people. Mordecai, a Benjamite, was a scribe for King Ahasuerus. He was a zealous, learned man who greatly feared the Lord. He had taken the charge to raise his young orphaned niece, Hadassah, in the fear and nature of the Lord. Mordecai is a picture of the mature Benjamite, who embodies a spiritual father, intercessor, and selfless deliverer. He possessed great discernment, wisdom, and humility. As anarchy grew in the kingdom, King Ahasuerus called a lavish feast and bid his wife Queen Vashti to come before him. She defiantly refused, and therefore was banished. Fiercely loyal, Mordecai alerted Queen Esther of the king's servants' plan to murder King Ahasuerus. Haman, a type and shadow of antichrist, arose with plans to completely annihilate the Jewish people. In his blatant pride, Haman demanded worship, but Mordecai refused to bow. Here's where the story turns fascinating. Haman was a descendant of King Agag, whom King Saul in his rebellion did not kill. An entire nation's very existence and destiny lay in the balance, all from one man's rebellion. Mordecai and Esther are both direct descendants of King Saul. Enter Esther, one of the mightiest heroines of the Bible.

## ESTHER: THE EMERGENCE OF THE MATURE CHURCH

*But let the brother of humble circumstances glory in his high position* (James 1:9 AMP).

In life, the anvil of suffering, past mistakes, and everyday cares can bring us to humble places. It is our surrender and obedience that determines whether or not we will come into true greatness and inherit dominion. Read Matthew 5:10.

Esther enters into her destiny through a multifaceted paradox in which God primes her to display His glory. She is an orphan, yet she has risen above an orphan mentality; a God-fearing Jew in the midst of pagan culture; a young woman sent to contradict a male-dominated system and protocol; a humble servant sent to oppose and overthrow an anti-Christ named Haman. She lived in a lavish palace, yet she and her people faced a deadly peril. Esther is derived from the Hebrew word *hester*, meaning *hidden.* Her Hebrew name, *Hadassah* means myrtle and a picture of righteousness. There is an opportune time to reveal one's identity to an enemy. Her Persian name, Esther, means, "star." Her own nature and purpose was represented by two great contrasting extremes, but doesn't the Lord choose the weak things of the world to confound the wise?

Read II Corinthians 4:6-12 and Esther 4:16. Pressed in on every side, Esther, her Gentile maidens (a type and shadow of handmaiden intercessors for Israel), Mordecai, and the Jewish people fasted for three days. She bowed low and sought the Lord. In fact, she fasted and denied more than her appetite for food, but as a mature Benjamite, she refrained and denied the profane *nephesh* of selfishness and rebellion.

Read Esther 4:14. I see Queen Vashti, who came before Esther, as a cautionary tale to the tribe of Benjamin: Satan will always present an abortion of destiny. Will you be selfish and rebellious like Queen Vashti? Or will you make a mark in the kingdom of God and lay down your life, embracing the Cross, like Queen Esther? Read Revelation 12:11.

## THE REVERSAL OF FORTUNE FOR BENJAMIN AND THE BRIDE

I write this next portion for Benjamin but also for the entire Bride of Christ so that you may be strengthened, ready for your appointment of revealing, for it is indeed here:

*For your shame ye shall have double; and for confusion they shall rejoice in their portion:*
*therefore in their land they shall possess the double: everlasting joy shall be unto them*
(Isaiah 61:7).

A reversal of fortune is coming for the Bride. Long-awaited victories will soon emerge in the areas of healing, finances, ministry, relationships, and family salvation. Unlimited favor will soon be released as the Bride comes into her destiny. Like Esther when she approached King Ahasuerus, destiny will collide with eternity, as you are granted favor with the King. Benjamin, *the son of my right hand*, is a picture of the revealing of the sons and daughters of God, as mentioned in Romans 8, and the triumphant Church without spot or wrinkle as described in the Book of Revelation.

Read Revelation 14:4-5. Dominion is ultimately about the reversal of fortune. When I say, "the reversal of fortune," I am not just talking about material wealth, but the fullness of the glory of God that we are meant to possess before our Bridegroom returns. Wounding from the past will grow dim in the light of His love. Wholeness of body, mind, and spirit will suddenly change every dimension of our lives. The waste places, no longer desolate, will become too small for us. There won't be room enough because the favor and goodness of God will overwhelm us. Where there was defeat, discouragement, and confusion, we will see absolute victory, hope, and peace. Rejoice, oh Benjamin, bride at God's right hand, for in you we see the revealing, the consummation of sonship, and the bride reigning with Yeshua, our Bridegroom King!

## PRAYER OF REPENTANCE AND DESTINY
## FOR THE TRIBE OF BENJAMIN

Abba Father! I cry out to You: Reveal Yourself to me and likewise bring the revealing of who You foreordained I truly am! I am your blissful Bride, Yeshua, needy and dependent upon Your grace. Deliver me from the lies of the orphan spirit. Help me to shed the orphan rags of shame, alienation, doubt, stigma, and poverty. Holy Spirit, teach me how to live in abandoned childlike mentality and faith. I repent of entertaining a profane *nephesh*. Deliver me of hunger after self-indulgent ways. Reveal to me where the idol of self has led me away from living a life empowered by the Cross. Expose the leaven of rebellion. Strip away any rebellion in me that has exalted itself against your authority. Seal me, O Lord, to inherit the fullness of my destiny. I want to possess the dominion You have endowed me with. I am your Hadassah, hidden to be revealed. Purge me deep of everything that would keep me from possessing the fullness of the kingdom. Call me to the battle, the Cross before me and the world behind me. I vow to love not my life even unto death. Transform me to become a clear jasper stone. Chasten me to perfect love, that I might come into full maturity and see myself seated with You in heavenly places. In Yeshua's name I pray, Amen.

---

[1] Denise Freeman, "Gemstone Dictionary", *Gemstone Dictionary.com*, 2007-2013. Accessed July 28, 2013, http://gemstone dictionary.com/bloodstone-meaning.php

[2] "Ravenous." Merriam-Webster.com. Accessed July 15, 2013. http://www.merriam-webster.com/dictionary/ravenous.

[3] Frances Hodgson Burnett, *The Little Princess* (New York, NY: Charles Scribner's Sons, 1905).

[4] Paschal Robinson, "St. Francis of Assisi." The Catholic Encyclopedia. Vol. 6.( New York: Robert Appleton Company, 1909.) July 26, 2015, http://www.newadvent.org/cathen/06221a.htm .

# CHAPTER 15
# THE NEW JERUSALEM:
# THE HABITATION OF THE LIVING GOD

*How lovely are Thy dwelling places, O LORD of hosts!* (Psalm 84:1).

In our current fragile human state, we are but mere tabernacles whose tent pegs are affixed to this earth. Within us abides the hope of our glorious redemption. Oh what greater glory awaits us, brethren: habitation! You and I who are left wandering this earth are seeking a resting place because of the Fall. We find rest in the habitation of the Lord as He builds us as His priceless Living Stones! What we pine for is who we truly are in Christ: the New Jerusalem. Creation since the Fall has been on a journey of identity. When identity is truly revealed, we find a call from the Spirit of God to ascend, to make *aliyah* to the Holy City, to be transformed into the Bride, the New Jerusalem.

Read John 4:19-26. Worship (intimacy) reveals identity. One does not come face-to-face with someone and remain unaltered. As we encounter the Father with unveiled face, we become like Him. Our utmost destiny is that we might take on His reflection found in the embodiment of habitation. Facades that the tribes warred with are likened unto funhouse mirrors, distortions of truth that birth mistaken identity. The glory reveals us to our core, stripping away the mistaken identities and enlightening us to inherit true sonship, who we are as the reflection of Christ. It is no small thing that the Lord has laid this revelation before you. You see, beloved, He is pursuing you, all of you, to be revealed in His image as the Bride you truly are. Let us revisit the story we began in the beginning of this book and see what glorious climax awaits us!

## THE BRIDE MADE READY

Down through the epochs of time and eternity hung a destiny of the Father YHVH, His Son, Yeshua, the Bridegroom, and the Bridegroom's betrothed, Yerushalyim. Cataclysmic wars were fought in seen and unseen realms where true identity was travailing to emerge. At times the fulfillment of restoration of YHVH's and Yeshua's mountain seemed like an impossible dream. Forever the unwavering optimists, the Father and Son, hung their hopes that Love Divine would win, for Love Divine believes all things and hopes all things. Love Divine never fails.

Then Reckoning Day finally arrived. The Bridegroom decked Himself in His finest wedding array. Donning His high priestly breastplate, He was reminded of how much He truly loved Yerushalyim. As His Father's light was catching every stone, an indescribable brilliance exploded from His breastplate. Yeshua began carefully taking His bloody *tallit* (Jewish prayer shawl) and deliberately began to wrap Himself in it. This Vesture had been dipped in the Precious Blood and was proof that He and He alone had paid the full portion of Yerushalyim's dowry. With a swift hand and vehement purpose, He began wielding His sword, while summoning His armies, eagerly awaiting His Father's final word.

Overlooking the vast expanse, the Bridegroom was at a loss for words. There in all her majesty, stood Yerushalyim, a bride whose beauty was indescribable. The moment had finally come for the Bridegroom and His Father to make habitation with Yerushalyim. The blushing Bridegroom was more like a giddy schoolboy than anything. He was finally going to be reunited with His Beloved for eternity! A wealth of emotions overcame Him. Reminiscing upon the journey He had made with His Father, He began relishing every joy, heartache, and war that He had fought for her. Yerushalyim was both beautiful and terrifying as Tirzah (Song of Songs 6:4), for the fullness of the Father's glory dwelt within her.

"She displays You well, Father," Yeshua thought. "She is truly all glorious within."

Step by step, as Yeshua walked closer to His Bride, He found His heart beating more and more wildly! The Bridegroom's passion and anticipation were about to get the better of Him. The Father spoke words of wisdom to His Son saying, "Linger and relish every moment of this, Son. After all, you have an eternity to enjoy her as I do." Tears began to soak His luminous raiment; this moment was the fulfillment of His and His Father's joy! The Father took His Son into His arms and passionately embraced Him for the longest time, and then He said, "Let's go get Your Bride, Son."

## PERSONAL ENCOUNTERS IN THE NEW JERUSALEM

*Great is the Lord, and greatly to be praised, in the city of our God, His holy mountain. Beautiful in elevation, the joy of the whole earth is Mount Zion in the far north, the city of the great King. God, in her palaces, has made Himself known as a stronghold (Psalm 48:1-3).*

The following two accounts are encounters I experienced in the New Jerusalem. God is timeless. The only explanation I can feebly give to such a strange and wonderful thing is this: The apostle John experientially saw things thousands of years ahead of his time, a foretelling, when he was given the oracle of the book of Revelation. I am by no means calling these two encounters I have had the infallible Word of God, but merely stating that God can grace us into such intimate encounters of which we cannot fully fathom, yet can receive by faith because He is worthy! We all see and know in part, this just happens to be what was allotted to me by His lavish grace and mercy.

The first encounter occurred in 1994 and was experienced from a panoramic perspective. The second encounter took place twelve years later in 2006, of which I experienced a far more "up close and personal" revelation of the New Jerusalem. Neither were dreams or open visions, but rather translations from what I believe was through Abba's heart and nature. Both encounters I feel appropriately set the stage of how we as believers will enter into the habitation after the Marriage Supper of the Lamb. It is my earnest prayer as you read these accounts that your heart is provoked, your spirit made fully alive, and your identity and destiny revealed in Abba's *maon kadosh*— Yerushalyim, the New Jerusalem. This is just a mere fractional glimpse of what awaits us!

## THE GOVERNMENT OF PRAISE, 1994 ENCOUNTER

In a small group home meeting, a psalmist was playing melodies of Heaven. Many times when the psalmist would play before the Lord, an open Heaven would occur. I even had one previous encounter during a time he had led worship. This night, however, was different. I remember trembling from the Presence before I even got to the front door. The worship began to swell as the psalmist played on Abba's heartstrings; I could hear a distinct call to ascend. As I bowed low in worship, the glory permeated all around in a golden fog. I found myself unable to function in my natural body, lying limp on the floor and unable to speak. I could feel atmospheres drastically begin to shift.

Awareness came over me that I was no longer in the living room as I had been just moments before. Then two large angels, who would serve as my escorts, appeared by my side. We were just outside the city, yet in a completely different realm. I saw an eternal canyon-like abyss filled with a lake of fire, or as Scripture would note it, Hades.

Read Revelation 20:12-14. The sounds, smells, sights, and feeling of this realm was the epitome of death. Death with its minions of fear, pride, perversion, hatred, and every other vile thing one could imagine was there. The souls that were sentenced to this horrific eternal hell were expelling blood-curdling screams, consumed with loneliness and utter despair. Alongside the outer banks of this pit were people who I dare say did not even resemble the beautiful creation they once were on this earth. Their bodies piled up on the edge of the pit trying to escape, but no escape was available. Their eyes were rotted into their sockets and their flesh-like, thin tissue was decaying rapidly. Their insides were rotting from the inside out, with myriads of maggots consuming them moment-by-moment. Each one was panting for water, living water. Living Water only existed within the New Jerusalem. No thirst would ever be quenched except there. Read Isaiah 66:22-24.

The saddest thing Yeshua will have to say to some of His creation is, *"I never knew you; DEPART FROM ME, YOU WHO PRACTICE LAWLESSNESS"* (Matthew 7:23).

*Now this will be the plague with which the Lord will strike all the peoples who have gone to war against Jerusalem; their flesh will rot while they stand on their feet, and their eyes will rot in their sockets, and their tongue will rot in their mouth (Zechariah 14:12).*

The angel standing to my right said, "These are those who have rejected the Son; they have chosen to live outside of inheritance." Then the angel on my left spoke saying, "Look not on them anymore, let us carry on. Your inheritance awaits you."

Let me pause a moment in telling this encounter. Here I was outside the New Jerusalem, and I saw Hell. The most excruciating travesty of creation is that souls who were created to inherit eternal life, identity, sonship, destiny, and dominion were in close proximity to their ultimate destiny, which they each rejected—habitation. Each one had chosen to deliberately reject Yeshua by engaging in facades. This may seem like a harsh picture, but I pray it serves two sobering points: (1) There is NO LIFE outside of Yeshua; no hope, no promise, NO LOVE; (2) being that this is an absolute reality, let us be sober and diligent to snatch as many souls from the fire before Messiah's return! The true "hell" for these poor souls is that they will see from not too far off the destiny and inheritance they forfeited by rejecting Yeshua.

## ENTERING INTO THE CITY

I felt in my mind what Lot must have felt, leaving behind precious people who willfully choose disobedience. I dared not turn back, so with single eye and heart I started walking forward with the angels. Moving forward felt much like the peeling of an onion. Death and all its foreboding darkness, putrid smells, despair, and fear fell off as a magnetic force of Love Divine and His light summoned us to the City. Between these realms at first was silence, then distant sounds, becoming clearer as we came to the edge of the City.

Approaching the final realm came with great impact. I could feel the chords of my heart pulling toward the King. The brilliance of the light exceeded that of millions of stars. Stepping into the New Jerusalem, I heard a sonic boom powerfully erupt, ripping through the final realm. I feel my feeble words are an injustice to what I saw next. The beauty of the New Jerusalem is beyond human comprehension to grasp. There before me was a vast sea of worshippers. Teeming with life, it went as far as the eye could see. Each worshipper possessed a fragrance, color, sound, movement, and ensign of his or her own. Strangely, I could distinctly decipher each one. A worshipper's fragrance had specific notes exclusive to each nature. Their fragrance was developed over a lifetime of tears, brokenness, joys, and victories won; it was the essence of their intimacy. The music is both collective and individual. There was no chaos, but rather the epitome of harmony.

I have heard a lot of heavenly music, but this worship was beyond what I had ever heard in Heaven prior to or since this encounter. Saints were worshipping from the core of their beings. No one was holding anything back. It was like each person's God-given nature was fully restored to what it was designed before the Fall. Each was then fervently pouring it out to the Father and Yeshua, who then would echo back a return of the same! It was an explosion for the senses. This vast sea sparkled like every precious gem, cumulatively catching the radiance of the Father and Yeshua. It's like the sea would roll toward the *maon kadosh*, the habitation of the Lord (a mountain, yet temple-like in appearance) and then roll out from it. It was one tumultuous wave upon another, rolling in and out in praise and worship.

The City is literally governed by praise. Adoration and thanksgiving were its bylaws. The atmosphere was worship. Its essence was endowed with majestic beauty that could be felt upon the skin, much like the mist in the Garden of Eden. It was an absolutely blissful state of being. Everyone was mature, developed fully into what the Father created each person to be. We were gleeful children whose innocence had been completely restored. Around me was an effervescent feeling of peace and communion all wrapped up in Abba's embrace.

Unity was unparalleled. Everyone was fully functioning in his or her dominion, according to each particular tribe. Joint supplying joint, the City was built because of the importance of family. Cultivated community was the core of why there was absolute unity. It was community without agenda, offense, pride, or competition. There was no hierarchy. All were equal and loved for who they fully were. Each person according to the tribe performed functions and services and supplied what was needed in the Father's kingdom. No one was alone. All were intimately known and honored both as a family unit and as individuals.

While I saw the gates and the temple (being the Father and Yeshua; of which we had habitation within), its importance wasn't magnified, for it would be saved for the second encounter I would have some twelve years later. The main focus for the first encounter was millennial praise and worship. To this day there are times during praise and worship that I feel a slight glimpse of what I encountered that day, and my spirit soars in the glorious hope of what we will soon all inherit.

## RETURNING TO THE NEW JERUSALEM, 2006 ENCOUNTER

During this second encounter there was no meeting or psalmist playing on the keys. I wasn't even in a time of concentrated prayer and worship. In fact, I was minding my own business, going about my everyday routine. I remember stepping outside to get some fresh air. Then it happened. There were no glory clouds or angels preceding this encounter to draw me in. I was suddenly apprehended by the Spirit of God and taken back to the New Jerusalem.

There she was in all her glory, the most magnificent specimen. She was indeed a Bride, as ancient as she was young, timeless like her Father. Radiant, she exuded her Father's pleasure toward her. *Utopia* some might say, but she was far more than that. Yerushalyim was indeed the essence of beauty, for she was far more than just Heaven come to earth. She was more than the Garden of Eden restored. Yerushalyim had become the habitation of the Living God. At the Marriage Supper of the Lamb, Yeshua and Yerushalyim wed, their marriage consummated. It was the restoration of all things. Heaven and the new earth were married just as Yeshua and Yerushalyim were! I have had many encounters in Heaven. When I encountered the New Jerusalem, I have to say it actually far exceeded everything in Heaven I had previously encountered before or since, for in it, the earth and Heaven's destiny was fulfilled. All was new, for Love Divine consumed everything and everyone!

The golden city itself went in an upward, spiraling pattern, which wrapped around the mountain of the Lord, much like the layers of a bridal gown. Living waters were sourced from Abba's *maon kadosh*, which would then vein out into a river. On that river, I saw the ship of Zebulun. The water was so pure and pristine. It even made music, as does everything within the New Jerusalem. It sparkled like millions of tiny diamonds, and the water was calm, yet it danced. I saw many animals in the City, both on water and on land. Every kind of fruit tree, vine, flower, and shrub flourished so beautifully. They themselves were like multi-faceted jewels. The gates were pristine jasper; the gold streets were so reflective they seemed like mirrors. The tribes' foundational stones were just as they are mentioned in Revelation 21, and they would sing praises to the Lamb night and day! The New Jerusalem was a living, breathing entity. No matter where I went, I could feel, hear, and beat as one with the New Jerusalem. I was a part of her, and so are you!

One thing and one thing alone arrested both my gaze and my heart. Central to everything within the City was the habitation of the Lord. It was a mountain, yet it was a temple-like structure. This holy habitation was the highest elevation within the City. It was Abba and Yeshua who embodied this extraordinary structure. The Cornerstone, Yeshua, was the largest, most brilliant emerald, located on the right-hand side of the temple. He was the stone, yet He was fully God and man seen clearly through it. It is a difficult thing to describe; it was both terrible and awesome! He was wearing His tallit, and it was stretched over the Temple. The Living Stones within the Temple all reflected the Head. No matter which way you turned it, you could clearly see Christ. At the same time, I clearly saw every saint. The saints were according to the tribes; however, no stone was the same. Each was perfectly cut as though parts of a master puzzle and fit in a specific place in Abba's *maon kadosh*! The Temple was so striking, it left me dumbfounded that there could be anything more beautiful and glorious than this magnificent habitation. Immediately after this encounter, I began to write this book. In my heart I feel this encounter served as a commissioning to write Living Stones.

## WHAT WILL MILLENNIAL LIFE BE LIKE?

What role do the tribes play in the millennial kingdom? Who am I in the New Jerusalem? To answer, we must look to what I feel is the most accurate representation of both what habitation is in Scripture in Isaiah 66. Read Isaiah 66.

Isaiah was specifically referring to habitation and the millennial kingdom in this prophecy. In verses 1-2, God is posing the question of what is habitation: "Where then is the house you will build for Me? Where is the place that I may rest?" Scripture tells us that His Temple, the place where He has chosen to have *maon kadosh* with us, is inside us. The fullness of intimacy, identity, destiny, and dominion lie with us possessing *maon kadosh* with Him. Isaiah 66 is a call to and revelation of the One New Man Body in Christ. To the Gentile, it is a call to carry the Jewish people in a lifestyle of laid-down love, humility, servanthood, and intercession. To the Jew, it is a call to unite with the Gentile that they might fulfill their (the Jewish people's) utmost calling to be a light to the nations (to the Gentiles).

It is the birthing of a nation that will reveal habitation. Israel, the land and the people (Jews), is one of the most vital keys to the end-time move of God. Ultimately for both, it is a call of habitation and holiness, streaming from the Living Word of the Lord, resounding from the holy shofar in Zion. It calls us to forsake idolatries that restrain our destiny of becoming the habitation of the Lord, His holy temple from within. For the priests of the Lord, this is the call to cry out against the abominations within the glorious temple of the Most High God. It is a comfort to those persecuted for righteousness sake and a promise of vindication and joy to those waiting to be rewarded. Isaiah 66 calls us to the mountain of the Lord, Jerusalem, to make *aliyah* to the heart of God Himself. It is a message of restoration, hope, and destiny.

I encourage you to embrace this living love letter from Abba, our Papa. The destiny of Jew and Gentile are revealed as we ascend to the habitation, Mt. Zion, and become the Bride of Christ, the New Jerusalem. Amen! Bless His Holy Name! It is important to be aligned, even now, as this will play a pivotal role in His return. The gifts do not stop operating in the New Jerusalem, but rather they reach their fullness. There will be schools of worship, the prophets, etc. Why is this needed if everyone has salvation? The nature of God is infinite. The gifts and callings of God are thereby useful throughout eternity to know Him and work alongside Him in His kingdom reign. All these things are pertinent to the New Jerusalem and possessing *maon kadosh* with the Father. In verses 18-23, Isaiah is prophesying about what millennial worship will look like. It is important to note that he mentions the Sabbath, the new moon(s), and the Feasts of the Lord. These things are an essential part of millennial life, for they are connected to worship.

There are roles each person will have in the kingdom, just as on earth. When people pass from this earth, they go on to develop, grow in, and fulfill their destinies, with each one found in their tribe in Heaven. In the New Jerusalem, each one will be entering into the fullness of identity, intimacy, gifts, and callings found through the tribes. It is important to be aligned even now, as this will play a pivotal role in His return.

The tribes are like families: cumulatively we are one big, happy family. Each one of the tribes is a like an immediate family, within which you and I have vital functions to fulfill. Each one is valued and different, yet all are celebrated. In Isaiah 66 the tribes are coming up to Jerusalem to present their offerings to the Lord. The Feasts are appointed times God chooses to meet with us corporately. It's like a big family gathering. It especially mentions, "I will take some of them as Levites and priests." Who is "them" to whom Isaiah makes reference? Isaiah is speaking of Gentiles who are grafted into the tribe of Levi, many of whom will play an integral part in the Temple and the feasts of the Lord just as they did thousands of years ago. Cumulatively, it also speaks of us as a kingdom of priests.

We will be ruling and reigning with Melchizedek (Yeshua). In John 7:37 Yeshua makes one of the most vital declarations of who He is during the Feast of Tabernacles. James begins his greeting "to the twelve tribes abroad." These references to the tribes, Feasts of the Lord, Sabbath, and the new moon festivals in Scripture are absolutely intentional. Moreover, they are invitations from the Father, a summons of appointment. The millennial reign of Christ is the ultimate appointment: It is the honeymoon of Bride and Groom. Every living stone has an appointment individually and corporately with the Father and the Bridegroom.

*He chooses our inheritance for us, the glory of Jacob whom He loves. Selah* (Psalm 47:4).

Before the foundations of the world, Abba chose our inheritance for us within a particular tribe. The glory of Jacob is the identity we have found within the Father's DNA through one of Jacob's sons. This is how God fulfills His Word to Abraham: "Indeed I will greatly bless you, and I will greatly multiply your seed as the stars of the heavens and as the sand which is on the seashore; and your seed shall possess the gate of their enemies" (Genesis 22:17). God is all about family. The tribes are the infrastructure of His family and how we function as a family unit!

*His foundation is in the holy mountains. The Lord loves the gates of Zion more than all the other dwelling places of Jacob. Glorious things are spoken of you, O city of God. Selah* (Psalm 87:1-3, 5-6).

## THE INHERITANCE:
## THE EZEKIEL 48 GATES IN THE NEW JERUSALEM

It is important to note the context of Ezekiel's prophecy. Chapters 40-48 serve as an important foundational picture of the New Jerusalem. As mentioned before, the order of tribes, being the breastplate, the encampment around the Tabernacle of Moses, serves as pivotal types and shadows of what God is saying. Ezekiel 48 reveals inheritance.

Read Exodus 15:17. If the habitation of the Lord is not built by human hands, then our inheritance is not either. Both the habitation of the Lord and the inheritance within (being the gates and the city) are incorruptible. Abba's inheritance for us all is born solely of His nature. The possession of our inheritance is fully found in the New Jerusalem. The wealth and renown of our heavenly Father's legacy will be bequeathed to us. The amazing thing is it was given to us by His lavish grace to us, paid in full by our Bridegroom, Yeshua. We do not strive for our inheritance; we *abide* for inheritance. Inheritance, when fully received, is the fullness of salvation. It is our utmost destiny to come into inheritance found within the gates of the New Jerusalem. Our lot is sure, predestined to inherit all of Abba's Kingdom and His *maon kadosh*! It is the Spirit within us that bears the hope of this glorious promise.

## SPIRIT FLOOD: THE HABITATION OF THE HOLY SPIRIT

In Chapter 47 Ezekiel prophesies about the river that multiplies from "ankle deep" to "enough to swim in." This directly ties to throne room worship and the role of the Holy Spirit in the millennial kingdom. The connection of worship and the Holy Spirit speaks of the fullness of God inhabiting the New Jerusalem with the fullness of the glory. The river is the Spirit Flood. The Spirit Flood is the role the Holy Spirit plays in the New Jerusalem. The Spirit Flood in Chapter 47 is the fulfillment of Habakkuk 2:14: "For the earth will be filled with the knowledge of the glory of the Lord, as the waters cover the sea."

The term "Spirit Flood" is coined by author Jennifer A. Miskov Ph.D., an authority on revival history, who in her book *Spirit Flood* states,

> "Regardless of whether we have already had an intense experience with the Holy Spirit or if we already speak in tongues, what if we prayed more regularly for God to 'overflow' and 'submerge' us; or even to 'destroy' or 'ruin' us in His Spirit? Rather than desire to receive a 'touch' of the Holy Spirit, or to be 'filled' a little with the Spirit, why not pray to be overwhelmed, overshadowed as Mary was (Luke 1:35), flooded, baptized again and again in the Spirit so much that one is swimming in the Spirit? Why not move beyond asking for, 'tiny streams' and instead ask for 'rivers of living water' to overwhelm us?"[1]

We are born of the Spirit, so therefore the Spirit Flood, i.e., Holy Spirit, has a direct correlation to our identity as sons and daughters and our corresponding inheritance within the New Jerusalem. The Holy Spirit is like our mother with the pivotal role of birthing sonship as mentioned in Romans 8.

> *Or do you think that the Scripture speaks to no purpose: "He jealously desires the Spirit which He has made to dwell in us"?* (James 4:5).

It is the vehement jealousy of the Bridegroom that allows the Spirit to inhabit us, for when we are born of the Spirit, we know (having a witness and seal) that we are the sons and daughters of God.

> *Jesus answered, "Truly, truly, I say to you, unless one is born of water and the Spirit, he cannot enter into the kingdom of God"* (John 3:5).

The Holy Spirit is the identifier of identity. Its crucial role in the millennium will be to bring sons and daughters into their fullness as God's children so that we may be equipped to rule and reign for an eternity. The Spirit Flood plays a vital role of connecting a life source of anointing, outpouring, and life from its streams. Holy Spirit's role then, as the Spirit Flood, takes His rightful place in the Godhead within the Temple. It will come from the Temple and supply the entire city! Amen!

Ezekiel's Temple and gates do not contradict the New Jerusalem mentioned in Revelation 21; rather, they make up a clear blueprint that sets the stage for Revelation 21. Ezekiel's gates are a picture of inheritance within the city whereby the King of glory enters into habitation with His Bride.

Read Psalm 24:7. The "heads" speak of our position within our own gate and within our own tribe, as in the Tabernacle of Moses, where the tribes were assigned to a particular directional order. However, in Ezekiel's order there are no caption tribes and the order is drastically shifted. This intentional shift of order speaks not only of a radical transformation to the Bride, but of her dominion as well. Read Ezekiel 48:31-35.

## THE NORTH GATES

Within the North Gates we find the tribes of Reuben, Levi, and Judah. Here we see a company of lavish, laid-down lovers. Reuben, the passionate lover, is restored to his place of dominion and sonship as he rightfully takes his place in Abba's *maon kadosh*. The firstborn son will then truly carry the renown of Christ in the millennial kingdom. The North Gates specifically carry the message of the Church of the firstborn. We see it through Reuben the eldest, Levi, the company of first fruits, and through Judah, who carries Christ Himself, the firstborn among many brethren. Within the North Gates we can see God proclaiming the mandate of Revelation 1:5-6, "and from Jesus Christ, the faithful witness, the firstborn of the dead, and the ruler of the kings of the earth. To Him who loves us and released us from our sins by His blood—and He has made us to be a kingdom, priests to His God and Father—to Him be the glory and the dominion forever and ever. Amen."

Within the North Gates we also see a vital union that has always repeated itself: Levi and Judah. Why is this so vital? Levi and Judah both cumulatively carry two essential things now and in the millennial kingdom: (1) Consummation (Judah) and habitation (Levi), and (2) The spearheading of the Melchizedek reign of Yeshua. Yeshua, who is Melchizedek, will reign from the Temple. The tribes of Levi and Judah will spearhead all manner and forms of worship and govern through praise. The Levites will go on to minister in the courts of the Lord and teaching. Harp-and-bowl worship will be a way of life. They will be working hand-in-hand with King David for this and also Moses. Levi and Judah together will bring all the tribes into their identity as a kingdom of kings and priests under Melchizedek.

## THE SOUTH GATES

Simeon, Issachar, and Zebulun possess their inheritance within the South Gates. The heartbeat of the South Gates is souls, revival, and the harvest. In it we see a passionate hearer called to fan the flames of revival fire, the humble burden-bearer who has co-labored for the harvest, and the haven for souls who has received them and taught them. In the New Jerusalem the tribes of Simeon, Issachar, and Zebulun will reap the reward of the harvest sown on this earth. Each one will be intimately acquainted with the souls for which they have labored with blood, sweat, and tears. It will be a reunion that lives in the satisfaction of those who received inheritance. They will then prophetically contribute to cultivate an atmosphere of continual revival through their prophetic giftings.

There are some things sown on this earth that will take an eternity to harvest. The South Gates will be reaping the harvest of this earth during this time. Revival will continue to emerge as we transcend from one realm of glory to another. Zebulun will still act as a haven for souls providing rest, comfort, and teaching to those needing a respite from this earth. Issachar and Zebulun, I believe, will continue to work together in schools of the prophets. Zebulun will continue to scribe new revelation. Simeon will be carrying a fresh word from the throne, functioning as the ears of the body. The call of the prophetic is very vital to the South Gates; in fact, it empowers it.

## THE EAST GATES

A true administrative thrust is apparent in the Eastern Gates of the city, where we find the tribes of Dan, Manasseh, Ephraim, and Benjamin. God's sovereignty is clearly displayed within these tribes. A voice of justice (Dan) has been restored, full forgiveness has been birthed (Manasseh), the fruitful vine abiding solely in the True Vine (Ephraim), and a Bride has reached her maturity and possessed dominion (Benjamin). These tribes combine administrative and apostolic giftings, serve the millennial kingdom in building, overseeing storehouses, and vindicating justice of things past. Together, Manasseh and Ephraim will be the storehouse under their father Joseph, supplying the New Jerusalem, administering wealth, wisdom, and discipleship to babes in Christ. Benjamin will continue in a very apostolic rule under the tutelage of the apostle Paul. Dan will be both celebrating the righteous judgments and declaring them in the millennium and in eternity.

## THE WEST GATES

Gad, Asher, and Naphtali find their glorious habitation within the West Gates. The West Gates truly embody the heartbeat of Joel 2. They have birthed sons and daughters to glory (Naphtali), cultivated ancient wells of revival and revelation (Asher), and served as prophets in Elijah's stead, restoring hearts of the Fathers to the children (Gad). They are true repairers of the breach who will continue this work in the New Jerusalem. They will be cultivating identity, dispensing fortunes lost, and celebrating the joy of Abba's love. Asher will be directly tied to the work of the Spirit Flood. I see the tribe of Asher throwing parties all over the city. The tribe of Naphtali will be nurturing young babes in the Kingdom. While Gad, no longer a wanderer, will be resting in the work of habitation. Gad will be a vital prophetic voice under the guidance of Elijah as well.

## THE FAMILY REUNION OF ALL REUNIONS

Read Psalm 68:5-6. There are no orphans in the Kingdom. No one will be lonely. The millennial reign of Christ will be one big family reunion. It will be the wildest, most joyful, and lavish party that ever was. Inheritances and fortunes will be fully restored, and the fatted calf is a staple on the family table.

Read Psalm 68:24-29. Family processionals will be going up to the Temple and all around the city declaring the majesty of the King!

Read Genesis 28:14. Abraham will finally see what his heart has longed for: his family. His destiny will be fulfilled in the New Jerusalem. You and I are a part of this glorious promise. Whether Jew or Gentile, all will have an equal place in habitation and in the family, for there is no separation of the two. The Temple is the Father's vision by which His Son, Yeshua, will habitat with His Bride. It is the house both He and Yeshua will govern from. The city, the inheritance, is the allotment given to us.

Read Acts 3:25. I believe that Abraham will be allotting inheritance and individually welcoming every family member. As any father, he will get to dote on his children and instruct them. Abraham is only a mirror of how we will ultimately be reunited with the heavenly Father.

Our heavenly Father's role will be the sweetest portion of our inheritance and reunion, for in His *maon kadosh* we will be possessed, fully inhabited in His nature. We will return to our state before the Fall and know Him intimately as Adam and Eve did. Nothing will separate us from the Father, for the presence of sin and its facades will be no more. The kingdom restored will like be a perpetual Sabbath Day. Everything will return to His design and embody the fullness of His nature.

## THE MILLENNIUM: THE THOUSAND-YEAR HONEYMOON!

As the Marriage Supper of the Lamb commences, a thousand-year honeymoon we know as the "millennium" will begin. Consummation will give way to habitation as we enter into wedded bliss with the Bridegroom King. The whole purpose of the millennium is that the fullness of intimacy might be restored to a Bride and her Groom. We will be learning how to habitate as the Lamb's wife.

As any good wife, we will be attending to His every need, making a home with Him, and living in adoration of our Groom.

## LIVING STONES: THE MATURE CHURCH FITTING TO HIS BUILDING

Read I Peter 2:4-10. As Living Stones we are being built up as a spiritual house for the sole purpose of becoming God's *maon kadosh*. Christ is the head of His Church, as Paul refers to this in Ephesians 5:22-32. As the Church, each one us must come into maturity as we pursue intimacy, repentance, and the relinquishment of facades. It is our ultimate destiny to enter into habitation as one of His priceless Living Stones. In the New Jerusalem we are also foundational stones of the city, seen in Revelation 21.

> *The foundation stones of the city wall were adorned with every kind of precious stone. The first foundation stone was jasper (**Benjamin**); the second, sapphire (**Dan**); the third, chalcedony (**Levi**); the fourth, emerald (**Judah**); the fifth, sardonyx (**Joseph, Manasseh, and Ephraim**); the sixth, sardius (**Reuben**); the seventh, chrysolite (**Zebulun**); the eighth, beryl (**Naphtali**); the ninth, topaz (**Simeon**); the tenth, chrysoprase (**Asher**); the eleventh, jacinth (**Gad**); the twelfth, amethyst (**Issachar**) [emphasis mine] (Revelation 21:19-20).*

The stones have long been shrouded in mystery and debate in regard to their order. There are at least 32 different interpretations of which stone belongs to which tribe. Much of this has to do with loss of translation, culture, and other unknown factors weighing in on the matter. The mystery especially clouds the Revelation 21 allotment of stones. After spending time in prayer and research I stumbled upon Pliny's explanation of the stones, which I, for the most part, agree with.[2] The foundational stones are not in any particular order as in one above another, but rather a sequence. Again, there are no captain tribes and no directional order given. I believe it is actually a circular pattern around a city or mountain. This is important, as we are born into one of these foundational stones.

> *Nevertheless, the firm foundation of God stands, having this seal, "The Lord knows those who are His," and, "Everyone who names the name of the Lord is to abstain from wickedness" (II Timothy 2:19).*

Here is a purposed meaning I hope will speak volumes to you:

(1) Benjamin: the jasper stone; the last shall be first, just as in the throne room.
The favored child has a crucial place.

> *...having been built on the foundation of the apostles and prophets, Christ Jesus Himself being the corner stone (Ephesians 2:20).*

(2) Dan: the sapphire; having a justifiable place in the sequence between Benjamin and Levi. The number two means *witness*. Dan carries an inner witness of justice and mercy!

(3) Levi: chalcedony; Pliny derived that it was indeed of a carbuncle (garnet), a glittering red stone most likely an oriental ruby, which appears like a garnet. It is the third stone, which is also Levi's birth order stone and beside Judah in this order as well. The number three deals with completion, perfection, and the Godhead.

(4) Judah: emerald, the fourth stone alongside Levi, further confirming the Melchizedek calling and all that they share with Levi. Four is the number of earth, directly tied to praise and consummation.

(5) Joseph or Manasseh and Ephraim: sardonyx (onyx). Five is the number of
grace and appropriately fits these two tribes.

(6) Reuben: sardius (ruby). Six is the number of man and appropriately deemed for Reuben, the firstborn, a redemption of man. The blood red stone says that the blood speaks a better word: sonship!

(7) Zebulun: a light sea-green stone, which could be interpreted as the aquamarine stone. Seven, of course, speaking of God's perfection in Zebulun and the Sabbath rest. Zebulun finds security in Yeshua as his anchor.

(8) Naphtali: beryl, translated from a Hebrew word that most likely is the diamond. Pliny describes that the term *diamond* most likely did not exist among the ancients, which is why it refers back to the Hebrew word form of beryl. The eighth stone represents new beginnings. For the tribe of Naphtali, this speaks of birthing and the embodiment of their very identity.

(9) Simeon: yellow topaz; nine being the fullness of blessing. There are nine fruits of the Spirit, and Simeon is very connected to the work of Holy Spirit and revival.

(10) Asher: chrysoprase; Pliny describes this as an agate. Ten speaks of God's law. Asher becomes balanced in God's Word and delights to keep God's commandments.

(11) Gad: jacinth, or blue topaz. The 11th hour speaks of a prophetic calling of Elijah to prepare the way of the Lord!

(12) Issachar: amethyst. Twelve speaks of government: the twelve apostles, the twelve disciples, and the twelve tribes—a place of great honor!

The order is profound for the tribes, but what is more important to note is that because they are all foundational stones, the tribes are all on the same level! There is no hierarchy in the kingdom, for there is only One lifted high, and His Name is Yeshua, the chief cornerstone!

## THE MAN CHILD: THE FRUIT OF CONSUMMATION AND HABITATION

*And she was delivered of a son, a man child, who is to rule all the nations with a rod of iron: and her child was caught up unto God, and unto his throne* (Revelation 12:5 ESV).

The man child is what the Bridegroom and His Bride will produce from consummation and habitation. What is the man child? The man child is a product of the Church (the One New Man Church, Jew and Gentile) coming into maturity. In Biblical eschatology the man child is synonymous with the book of Revelation (12:5)—the mature Church. The man child is the fruit of a mature Church who has forsaken all other lovers, been sanctified by the Word, and thereby producing the work of the Father's kingdom. I am by no means speaking of something sexual in nature, but rather a prophetic type and shadow of what happens with the exchange of the Bridegroom, Yeshua, and His Bride, the Church, co-labor in their Father's kingdom as husband and wife. The man child is a cumulative picture of the Church partnering with Yeshua in ages past, present, and future to produce the fruit of sonship in the earth!

What a promise to take hold of, brethren. It is in the New Jerusalem that we will begin to mature and grow as the Bride. The birth pangs, travail, and sacrifice will pale in comparison to the glory of raising up this man child. The man child, when born, is ready to run, not crawl, into the kingdom of God. It has taken ages of self-sacrifice, relinquishment of sin, and the passionate pursuit of intimacy to bring forth an heir to the kingdom: the fruit of salvation.

My last thoughts, beloved Bride, are these: Know that you are a splendid display of Abba Father, preserved for your Bridegroom, King Yeshua, and empowered by His Holy Spirit. As His Bride, be ready for His coming, for it is hastening at great speed and even greater glory. Do not let facades dictate your destiny. Cast off idolatries and lovers and pursue true intimate holiness. You were born for great things! You were born for habitation. May His glory shine upon the revealing of who you truly are in Abba's *maon kadosh*: a Living Stone of great beauty and worth. Allow this book to prepare you for your Groom. This book is a great tool of transformation that I believe can prepare you to be who you truly are: the habitation of the Living God!

As both a Levite and priest I bless you:

Y'var-ekh'cha Adonai v'yeesh'm'recha: Ya-eir Adonai pa-nav ei-ley-cha vee-chu-nei-cha: Yee-s Adonai pa-nav ei-lay-cha v'ya-sem l'cha shalom, amen.

May the Lord bless you and keep you: May the light of God [His face] shine upon you, and may the Lord be gracious to you: May the presence of the Lord be with you and give you peace, amen.

## PRAYER OF DESTINY

Abba Father, thank You for the privilege of being allowed to take this journey of identity with my brothers and sisters. Abba, I ask that each one who has read this book will know who You are first and foremost and who they are in Your holy habitation. I pray that each living stone, for whom You sent Your only begotten Son to pay the price, will come into the fullness of his or her destiny. I thank You, Father, for their lives. I champion Your DNA, which is so uniquely displayed in each one of them. I relish the joy that one day we will all know You as You are and will know each other. Thank you for this revelation of the tribes and my own journey of habitation while penning this love letter. Yeshua, turn the light on and remove every façade that hinders Your Bride from becoming who she truly is. I command every snare hindering their identity, destiny, and dominion to be loosed from them now in Yeshua's mighty name. I speak to every dormant identity, gifting, calling, and dream, and I command you to come forth. Arise and shine, for your light has come, and the glory of the Lord has risen upon you. Awake, oh sleeping Bride, and come to your hour of destiny. Awake, O sleeper, and let the light of Christ shine upon you, His precious Living Stone. In Yeshua's name I pray, Amen!

[1] Jennifer A, Miskov, *Spirit Flood* (Birmingham, England: Silver to Gold Publishers, 2010), Page 38.

[2] Charles George Herbermann, Edward Aloysius Pace, Condé Bénoist Pallen, John Joseph Wynne, Thomas Joseph Shahan *The Catholic Encyclopedia: An International Work of Reference on the Constitution, Doctrine, Discipline, and History of the Catholic Church, Volume 14* (New York, NY, The Encyclopedia Inc., 1913), 1913, Pages 306-307.

# BIBLIOGRAPHY

Bevere, John. *Breaking Intimidation.* Lake Mary, FL: Charisma House, 1995.

Brown, Francis, and Driver, S.R. *The Brown-Driver-Briggs Hebrew and English lexicon: with an appendix containing the Biblical Aramaic: coded with the numbering system from Strong's Exhaustive concordance of the Bible.* Peabody, Massachusetts: Hendrickson Publishers 1996.

DeShazo, Lynn. *Be Magnified.* Colorado Springs, CO: Integrity's Hosanna! Music 1992. https://www.weareworship.com/us/songs/song-library/showsong/2423

Dictionaries, Oxford. "Oxford Dictionaries" *Oxford University Press.* http://www.oxforddictionaries.com/us/definition/american_english/pomegranate (accessed July 08, 2015).

d'Outremer, Melisende. "Women in History." *Women in History Blogspot.* August 29, 2007, Accessed July 22, 2015, http://womenofhistory.blogspot.com/2007/08/medieval-marriage-childbirth.html

Einai, Gal. "Gal Einai." *www.inner.org.* March 13, 2014, http://www.inner.org/category/parshah/numbers-bamidbar/chukat/feed

Elan, Yoav. "Beis Hamikdash Topics." *Beis Hamikdash Topics Blogspot,* February 17. 2014, Accessed March 19, 2015. http://beishamikdashtopics.blogspot.com/2014/02/preparation-of-incense-and-view- of.html

Grubb, Norman. *Rees Howells Intercessor.* Fort Washington, Pennsylvania: Christian Literature Crusade/Lutterworth Press, 1952.

Guyon, Jeanne. *Song Of The Bride* New Kensington, PA: Whitaker House, 1997.

Freeman, Denise. , "Gemstone Dictionary", *Gemstone Dictionary.com,* 2007-2013. Accessed July 28, 2013. http://gemstone dictionary.com/bloodstone-meaning.php

Hargis, Dr. Ariel. "Preparation for Praise and Worship: Series I." Ephraim and Judah International home group study;  Rabbi Hargis referenced the Midrash Tanchuma, Pikudei 9 about bronze mirrors, Lakeland, FL September 8, 1995.

Hargis, Dr. Ariel. "Shavuot Conference." Ephraim and Judah International Messianic Congregation, Dallas, Texas, June 2, 1995.

Herbermann, Charles George, Pace, Edward Aloysius, Pallen, Condé Bénoist, Wynne, John Joseph, Shahan, Thomas Joseph. *The Catholic Encyclopedia: An International Work of Reference on the Constitution, Doctrine, Discipline, and History of the Catholic Church, Volume 14.* New York, NY; The Encyclopedia Inc., 1913.

Hodges-Burnett, Frances. *The Little Princess.* New York, NY. : Charles Scribner' Sons, 1905.

Hurnard, Hannah Rose. *Hind's Feet On High Places*. London; Christian Literature Crusade, 1955.

Institute, The Temple. "The Temple Institute." *International Department of the Temple* Institute, March 19, 2015. https://www.templeinstitute.org/incense.htm

John, Elton. Rice, Tim. Zimmer, Hans. Twillie, Carmen. Weaver, Jason. Irons, Jeremy
Lane, Nathan. Sabella, Ernie. Williams, Joseph and Dworsky, Sally. *I Just Can't Wait To Be King, The Lion King Original Motion Picture Soundtrack*. Los Angeles, CA: Buena  Vista Pictures Distribution, Inc., 1994. Track 11.

"Justice". *Merriam-Webster.com*. Accessed April 10, 2008.
http://www.merriam-webster.com/dictionary/justice

"Licentious." *Merriam-Webster.com*. Merriam-Webster. Accessed September 2, 2011.
http://www.merriam-webster.com/dictionary/licentious

MacDonald, David. *The Encyclopedia of Mammals*. New York, NY:
Facts On File, 1984.

Miskov, Jennifer A. *Spirit Flood*. Birmingham, England: Silver to Gold Publishers, 2010.

Pollard, Edward Bagby; James, Orr, M.A., D.D. General Editor. "Entry for 'dowry'".
"*International Standard Bible Encyclopedia*". 1915 Public Domain.

"Ravenous." *Merriam-Webster.com*. Accessed July 15, 2013.
http://www.merriam-webster.com/dictionary/ravenous

Richardson, Benjamin W. *Ten Lectures On Alcohol*. New York, N.Y.:
National Temperance Society and Publication House, Public Domain 1881.

Robinson, Paschal. "St. Francis of Assisi." The Catholic Encyclopedia. Vol.
6. New York: Robert Appleton Company, 1909. Accessed July 26,2015.
http://www.newadvent.org/cathen/06221a.htm

Platt, Rutherford H. *The Forgotten Books Of Eden*. New York, N.Y.: Alpha House, 1926.

Signh, Sundar S., *I Have Decided To Follow Jesus*, Public Domain.

Smith, William, *Smith's Bible Dictionary*. London, England, 1863. Public Domain.

Ten Boom, Corrie. *The Hiding Place*. Peabody Massachusetts Hendrickson Publishers, 2009

Ten Boom, Corrie. *Tramp For The Lord*. Fort Washington, Pennsylvania: Christian Literature
Crusade Tappan, New Jersey: Fleming H. Revell Company1974

*The Babylonian Talmud, Sukkah 53a-b*. Public Domain.

Tinney, Chris V. and Thomas M. Sr. ."The Book (stick) of Levi." Accessed March 19, 2015.
http://www.academic-genealogy.com/ancientgenealogylevi.htm

Uittenbogaard, Arie. "Abarim Publications Biblical Name Vault," *Abarim Publications*.
    April
        30,2015.http://www.abarimpublications.com/Meaning/Reuben.html#.VZzo6_lVikq

Wilson, Scott, "The Washington Post," *The Washington Post*. November 7, 2005, Accessed
May
        11,2011,http://www.washingtonpost.com/wpdyn/content/article/2005/11/06/AR2
        005110 600478.html

Zodhiates, Spiros. *The Hebrew-Greek Key Word Study Bible New American Standard
Bible Revised Edition*. Chattanooga, TN: AMG Publishers, ©1984, 1990, 2008.

# RESOURCES

The author recommends the following resources.

Author website: www.allgloriouswithin.com

All Glorious Within Ministries- "Calling creation to awaken to the glory of God within". After Marie Fowler was marked with transformational encounters the Lord began to pose this question:

> Thus says the LORD, "Heaven is My throne and the earth is My footstool Where then is a house you could build for Me? And where is a place that I may rest? (Isaiah 66:1).

It was this very question that began Marie's search for intimacy and identity with God. This ultimately led to the revelation of habitation and the 12 Tribes of Israel. Marie Fowler is an Ambassador of Identity whose passion is to build God's house within the context of family. All Glorious Within Ministries offers a unique discipleship program within the context of the revelation found in *Living Stones*. This program is offered both online and in thriving worship community houses.

If you are interested in our discipleship program, speaking engagements, or book distribution please contact us at mariefowlerlivingstones@gmail.com .

Marie Fowler also serves on the board and leadership team of Heart for Zion Ministries in North Florida and is commissioned by Destiny House in Redding, CA.

Heart for Zion Ministries- Founders Michael and Sherry Major

The Glory- Its Nature and End-Time Purpose by Michael Major

Michael Major has written a book, five years in the making, which sheds new and revelatory light on the glory of God, examining scripture and actual experiences of believers today. This book delves deeply into God's ultimate purpose for releasing His glory in these end times. Topics discussed include Glory vs. Anointing, distinguishing the Holy Spirit from the Spirit of Christ, the glory's attraction to death and suffering, Israel's preeminence in understanding the glory, its role in Christian unity, and the unique phenomenon of destiny acceleration -- God's process of transforming the Bride of Christ for the coming of the LORD. Readers will enjoy a thorough and in-depth study of this increasingly relevant and often-misunderstood topic -- a must read for Christian leaders with a heart for revival.

Author and ministry website: www.thechabod.com

Spencer Williams- Christian Artist- Fine Art and worship silks
*New Jerusalem Canopy* is featured on *Living Stones* front cover. www.jesuspaintings.com

Made in United States
North Haven, CT
06 February 2023

32127199R00135